OREGON'S DOCTOR TO THE WORLD

OREGON'S DOCTOR TO THE WORLD

ESTHER POHL LOVEJOY AND A LIFE IN ACTIVISM

Kimberly Jensen

UNIVERSITY OF WASHINGTON PRESS
Seattle and London

© 2012 by the University of Washington Press
Printed and bound in the United States of America
Design by Thomas Eykemans
Composed in Chaparral, typeface designed by Carol Twombly
17 16 15 14 13 12   5 4 3 2 1

University of Washington Press
PO Box 50096, Seattle, WA 98145, USA
www.washington.edu/uwpress

Library of Congress Cataloging-in-Publication Data
Jensen, Kimberly, 1958–
Oregon's doctor to the world : Esther Pohl Lovejoy and a life in activism / Kimberly Jensen.
    p. ; cm.
Includes bibliographical references and index.
ISBN 978-0-295-99224-2 (pbk. : alk. paper)
I. Title.
[DNLM: 1. Lovejoy, Esther Pohl, 1870–1967. 2. Physicians, Women—Oregon—Biography.
3. Physicians, Women—United States—Biography. 4. History, 19th Century—Oregon.
5. History, 19th Century—United States. 6. History, 20th Century—Oregon.
7. History, 20th Century—United States. 8. Women's Rights—Oregon—Biography.
9. Women's Rights—United States—Biography. 10. Women's Rights—history—Oregon.
11. Women's Rights—history—United States. WZ 100]
610.92—dc23   [B]   2012026726

For Todd, with gratitude

CONTENTS

ACKNOWLEDGMENTS

This book exists because conscientious and committed librarians, archivists, and organizational staff maintained and preserved records. It exists because granting agencies and others provided funding and time to do this work. It exists because colleagues' work and assistance inspires and challenges me, and because supportive friends and family believe in me and understand the importance of women's history and of telling Esther Lovejoy's story. To all of these people I am most grateful.

Amy Khedouri and Maxine Fraade, daughters of American Women's Hospitals executive secretary Estelle Fraade, donated Esther Lovejoy's papers to the Historical Collections & Archives at Oregon Health & Science University in Portland. That act ensures that Dr. Lovejoy's work will never be forgotten. I am grateful to Ms. Khedouri for her generosity in sharing additional materials with me as she continues to develop her own interpretations of Lovejoy's life. Anyone who studies the life of Esther Lovejoy and the history of the American Women's Hospitals understands the vital role that Estelle Fraade played in that important work, and I honor her work and memory.

The generous Frankovic family of Spokane and Seattle provided time, information and materials about Esther Lovejoy. My thanks also go to Dr. Shelley Ross of the Medical Women's International Association and to Dr. Eliza Chin and Sarah Hegy of the American Medical Women's Association. This project benefitted greatly from the assistance of Chuck Kraining and the staff of the Seabeck Conference Center, Seabeck, Washington. Mr. Kraining was so generous with materials from Seabeck history, and my stay of several days to write at the conference center made all the difference. I thank them for their support and for their important work in preserving Seabeck history.

It is impossible to articulate my thanks to Sara Piasecki, former head of the Historical Archives & Collections at Oregon Health & Science University, and to Karen Peterson, Historical Archives & Collections archivist. Their enthusiasm for the project and their joy in my discoveries have been a historian's dream realized. Maija Anderson, who now fills the responsibility of head of Historical Archives & Collections, has proved a strong supporter. My thanks also to Joanne Murray, director, archivists Margaret Graham and Matthew Herbison, and to Karen Ernst and the supportive staff at the Legacy Center, Archives and Special Collections on Women and Medicine and Homeopathy at the Drexel University College of Medicine in Philadelphia, Pennsylvania, for their incredible support across many archival visits. Thanks to the staff members at the Sophia Smith Collection, Smith College, Northampton, Massachusetts; the Arthur and Elizabeth Schlesinger Library at Radcliffe; the Wellcome Library in London; the National Library of Medicine in Washington, DC; and the National Archives II in College Park, Maryland.

My thanks also to the archivists and librarians at the Oregon Historical Society Research Library, including Geoff Wexler, Scott Daniels, and Shawna Gandy; to Diana Banning at the City of Portland Archives and Records Center; to Austin Schultz, Mary Beth Herkert, and Layne Sawyer at the Oregon State Archives in Salem; to Linda Long and James Fox at the University of Oregon Knight Library Special Collections in Eugene, and to Tamara Vidos and her staff, whose work to keep Oregon newspapers preserved and accessible at the Knight Library at the University of Oregon is so vital; to Larry Landis and staff at the Valley Library at Oregon State University in Corvallis; and to Jim Scheppke and staff at the Oregon State Library in Salem and to the staff at the Lewis and Clark College Special Collections in Portland.

My appreciation also goes to Mary McKay and Rose Marie Walter of the Willamette University Archives, Salem, Oregon, for their assistance with Willamette Medical Department materials on early women physicians, even though much of that material will have to wait for another book. Sincere thanks to Wilma Pope, Linfield College alumni coordinator, Good Samaritan School of Nursing Archives, and Mary Margaret Benson, Linfield-Good Samaritan School of Nursing Archives, for their kind assistance with Emily Loveridge's manuscript "As I Remember." Thanks to Debbie Davidson, City of Roseburg, staff of the Douglas County Clerk's Office, Roseburg; Renee Edwards, Circuit Court of Oregon, Eighth Judicial District, Baker City, Oregon; Jim Mullen, Oregon University System Records manager at Oregon State University; Erin Maudsley, Auditor's

Office, Kitsap County, Washington; and the staff of the Kitsap County Historical Society.

I was very fortunate to have financial support from a variety of organizations for this project. I received an Oregon Council for the Humanities Research Grant in 2005–6 for this project and benefitted not only from financial support but from audience questions at presentations I made as part of the grant. I also received a Foundation for the History of Women in Medicine Fellowship from the Francis C. Wood Institute for the History of Medicine, College of Physicians, Philadelphia, Pennsylvania, in 2005–6 that enabled me to conduct crucial research, and a Herbert Hoover Presidential Library Association travel grant in 2005–6. At the Hoover Library, Pat Hand and her staff were helpful from the first email contact to my Saturday morning departure. Lynn Smith provided sound and helpful advice, and Matt Schaefer and Spencer Howard gave truly exceptional support to me each hour of each research day. Tim Walch offered sound advice about the collections.

Western Oregon University has been a generous supporter of this project. I received a major project grant and numerous conference travel grants, and a sabbatical leave to write. I received a Mario and Alma Pastega Award for Excellence in Scholarship in 2011, which provided important support. The staff of the Hamersly Library at Western Oregon University smoothed the way for my acquisition of materials and interlibrary loans, and host my precious microfilm reader. To them I give highest praise. Sue Payton at the Technology Resource Center provided invaluable assistance with images. My colleagues in the History Department and in the Social Science Division, as well as faculty supporters across campus, have been unstinting in their support. My particular thanks to David Doellinger for advice about Soviet women's history, and to Maureen Dolan and Mary Pettenger for feminist theory and perspectives. My students have helped me hone my ideas in discussions about women's history in general and Esther Lovejoy in particular, and I am grateful to have the chance to work with them. Thanks to Toni Kelley for her research assistance.

Linda Kerber has been my mentor in women's history from graduate student days, and my debt to her can never be repaid. And I am enriched by continuing University of Iowa connections with former graduate school colleagues and new generations of Iowa students. I treasure the support and insights of my colleague and collaborator Erika Kuhlman in our shared interest in transnational history. G. Thomas Edwards, Rebecca Mead, Karen Blair, Sue Armitage, Judith Zinsser, Sheri Bartlett Browne, Jean Ward, Shanna Stevenson, Ingrid Sharp, Alison Fell, and the contributors to *Women and Transnational Activism in Historical Perspective* all influenced my scholarship for the better. Michael Helquist is a generous scholar and biographer of Marie Equi, who has shared citations, ideas, and insights with me. Thanks also to Virginia Metaxas for sharing her insights about Esther Lovejoy and the American Women's Hospitals. The members of the Portland Women's History Writing Group have made thoughtful comments about my work and created an intellectual sounding board, for which I am most grateful. My thanks also to Cynthia Culver Prescott for her comments on a chapter draft. Eliza E. Canty-Jones and Jan Dilg have been staunch supporters and conspirators in Oregon women's history. Thanks to all of my colleagues working with the Oregon Women's History Consortium and Century of Action: Oregon Women Vote 1912–2012; to those on the editorial board of the *Oregon Historical Quarterly*, which Eliza Canty-Jones facilitates with such skill; to colleagues at the Oregon Encyclopedia Project; and to colleagues on the Oregon Heritage Commission. I am particularly appreciative of David Lewis's help with Chinuk Wawa.

I am grateful to chairs, commentators, roundtable colleagues, and audience members at conferences and annual meetings of the American Historical Association, the Berkshire Conference of Women Historians (and to Judith Zinsser and the thoughtful biographers in our seminar), the Western Historical Association, the Western Association of Women Historians, the Pacific Northwest History Conference, the American Association for the History of Medicine, the Society for Historians of American Foreign Relations, the Pacific Coast Branch of the American Historical Association, organizers and participants in the Gentler Sex conference in London, and the Gender and War Symposium at Idaho State University.

My sincere thanks to the editors and staff of the Oregon Encyclopedia Project, in association with partners at McMenamin's and Sisters of the Holy Names in Portland, who all provided invaluable opportunities for me to address audiences across these several years of my project. Thanks to the Portland Humanists, local branches of the American Association of University Women, the Mary Leonard Law Society, the Willamette Heritage Center, the Oregon State Library, the staff of the Multnomah

County Central Library and Historical Collections & Archives at Oregon Health & Science University, the Oregon Health & Science University Alumni Office, and the Oregon Civics Conference, for inviting me to present my research and to gain vital feedback.

Marianne Keddington-Lang was there at the beginning of this project with early support for my work on Esther Lovejoy and woman suffrage in Oregon. Her assistance with the manuscript at the University of Washington Press, and the support of other press staff members, including Mary Ribesky, Tim Zimmerman, Rachael Levay, Alice Herbig, Phoebe Daniels, and Kerrie Maynes, has been invaluable.

I am most grateful to my parents, Mary and Forrest Jensen, for their support of my work, and to Karen Jensen for her tireless advocacy and good cheer. My thanks to friends and supporters Jeanne Deane, Jean Bottcher, Cindy Massaro, Debbie Evans, Pat Dixon, Erin Marr and Janice Hoida. To Todd Jarvis my absolute thanks for his understanding, interest, creative ideas, and cartographic skills—and for making life so sweet.

My grandmother Mary Alice Powell Lindsay ignited my early interest in women's history and activism. Her legacy informs my work, and I honor her memory.

OREGON'S DOCTOR TO THE WORLD

Introduction

OREGON'S DOCTOR TO THE WORLD

ON a warm and clear August 17, I left my research work in the early afternoon and headed down from the archives at the Oregon Health & Science University on Portland's Marquam Hill and across the Willamette River to Lone Fir Cemetery. This was the anniversary of Esther Clayson Pohl Lovejoy's death and I wanted to commemorate it with a visit to her grave site as I became more involved in researching her life in activism. The marker of Esther's first husband, Emil, dating from 1911, guided me to the plot. Her son Freddie's 1908 gravestone lay beside his father's. Their markers are identical, except that the father's bears the emblem of the Woodmen of the World, one of the fraternal organizations to which he belonged, a membership forever out of reach for his young boy, who died so young. Frederick Clayson, Esther's favorite brother and Freddie's namesake, murdered in the Klondike on Christmas Day 1899 and the first buried in the plot, lay at the center. The marker of Esther's sister Annie Clayson Blanchard was to his left, and the next belonged to Annie Clayson, Esther's mother. Far away, in the back corner of the plot and in purposeful isolation, was the grave of Edward Clayson, the infamous "Patriarch" who caused so much pain to Esther, her mother, and the family. George Lovejoy, Esther's second husband, whom she married in 1912 and divorced in 1920 in challenging circumstances, was understandably not included here. I felt that I was coming to know them all as I analyzed the long life of this activist who did so much to shape the woman suffrage and public health movements and transnational medical relief in almost a century of life from 1869 to 1967.

But where was Esther Lovejoy's marker? I had seen photos of it and knew that a ceremony interring her ashes had taken place in 1967. But on this summer day the holly trees that Annie Clayson planted to commemorate the Christmas Day slaying of her son Frederick towered above the plot, and the previous autumn's leaves made a prickly protective blanket over everything. As I cleared the area in front of Emil's and Freddie's headstones, Esther's small granite marker began to reveal itself.

I was struck by the power that nature had across the stretch of years to completely obscure a marker placed with care to commemorate a life. Or perhaps I had it wrong and it was nothing more than a temporary wash of dirt and leaves from Portland's spring rains. But the invisibility of her marker seemed an apt symbol of the contrast between Esther Lovejoy's consequential life and activism and her less than realized place in our collective historical memory. Clearing the leaves, dirt, and debris from her grave at the cemetery that day became a metaphor for my ongoing research into her life: opening the many archival boxes and microfilm containers, searching for the materials that would reveal her history, and bringing together the many strands of her activism to uncover and interpret her legacy.

Lovejoy shaped an influential and substantial life of progressive activism as an Oregon physician, public health policy maker, suffragist, congressional candidate, and historian, and as an organizer and director of transnational networks of women physicians providing global medical relief. She called for social justice with programs for city, state, and international health and for an end to war. Yet because most of her papers have not been available to scholars until very recently, her work and contributions could not be analyzed in depth. A decade ago Amy Khedouri and Maxine Fraade, the daughters of Esther Lovejoy's longtime colleague Estelle Fraade, the executive secretary of the American Women's Hospitals and Lovejoy's executor, donated the bulk of Lovejoy's papers to the Historical Collections & Archives at Oregon Health & Science University in Portland. Khedouri holds additional materials, and her generosity in sharing these has enriched my study immensely. Lovejoy's personal and institutional letters, reports, and other documents are available in many other archival holdings, such as the Legacy Center, Drexel University College of Medicine, in Philadelphia. Lovejoy's published books and articles have also been vital to this analysis, as has the extensive newspaper coverage of her career. These sources provide a rich foundation for an analysis of Lovejoy's life and activism.

Lovejoy's early life and career in the Pacific Northwest gave her experience with, and strategies to implement, what she termed "constructive resistance," the ability to take effective action against unjust power.[1] Constructive resistance shaped her subsequent work in public health, in the votes for women movement, and in transnational medical relief. Lovejoy's biography offers the possibility of studying, from the perspective of one long and eventful life, strands of feminist activism from the local to the regional, national, and transnational. Many historians of medicine know Esther Lovejoy as the long-serving director of the medical humanitarian relief organization the American Women's Hospitals and as the historian of women physicians whose *Women Doctors of the World*, published in 1957, continues to stand as a comparative and transnational history of women in the field. Some historians and historically conscious residents of Oregon and the Pacific Northwest and beyond know of Lovejoy's city health work. And, as we commemorate the centennial of woman suffrage in Oregon in 2012, and in the nation in 2020, others are coming to know about Lovejoy's leadership in the movement. But to understand the complexity and impact of Lovejoy's developing theories about women and the state, and about the concept of international health achieved through social justice, it is essential to consider her long life of activism as a feminism developed as a "life-process."[2] By analyzing the whole, the events and processes along the way take on new meaning.

Lessons from Lovejoy's Pacific Northwest childhood in the logging community of Seabeck, Washington Territory, the urban world of Portland, and a Clackamas County, Oregon, farm engendered Lovejoy's strong views about the intersections of women's citizenship, women's labor, and women's control over their financial and reproductive lives. Her father Edward's unjust control over her mother's life, labor, and citizenship, and his power over Esther and her siblings provided her first experience of the abuse of power and the remedy of constructive resistance to that unjust authority. Hers was a working-class upbringing with a childhood spent in useful work for her family's financial survival. Work was vital to her life, but she vowed to build a career with work that she loved and work that had meaning. She was also determined to control her wages and the fruits of her labor. Lovejoy's struggle to achieve a medical education as a working-class woman involved wage work behind department store counters. She achieved her goal of a medical degree with award-winning honors, but her professors refused to grant her the internship that was her due because she was a woman. She established a medical practice with her own shrewd determination and with the support of an organized women's medical community in Portland and beyond. All of these experiences led her to support a broad program for women's rights and what Alice Kessler-Harris has termed "economic citizenship,"[3] and led to the development of Lovejoy's social justice theory of civic, national, and international health as a remedy to the systematic social diseases of discrimination and inequality.

Esther Lovejoy lived and worked in Portland, Oregon, during the Progressive Era, and an understanding of her work to build coalitions among women's organizations as Portland city health officer from 1907 to 1909 and her work for women's civic power through the vote and beyond reveals much about Portland's progressive activist matrix. Lovejoy shared the Progressive Era critique of "the interests"—corporate and banking powers that oppressed citizens—and advocated the progressive remedy of expert and government problem solving. Yet Lovejoy gendered "the interests" as male, and based her solutions on the civic empowerment of women. She also viewed motherhood as a life philosophy. The personal became powerfully political for her when her son Freddie died from what appeared to be tainted milk in 1908. For the rest of her life she fought for healthy communities through legislation and action by empowered women citizens. Her Portland-era work and ideas were the foundation of a consequential career of reform, and her experiences fostered her lifelong commitment to women's organizing for women.

An analysis of Lovejoy's challenges and choices also provides a prelude to what women outside the western suffrage states would face after achieving the vote in 1920 and suggests parallel stories in other woman suffrage states prior to the passage of the federal amendment. Moreover, Lovejoy's story demonstrates that western women voters and activists influenced the course of national suffrage politics in key ways; they were not simply objects of the organizational policy of groups such as the National American Woman Suffrage Association and the Congressional Union. Restoring Lovejoy and Oregon women to the history of woman suffrage in the United States suggests the dynamic relationship between the local and the national and the importance of understanding regional differences in the shaping of this and other social movements. Lovejoy's service in appointed office at the municipal level and her campaign for US Congress in 1920 provide valuable information about women who sought this additional step of full civic credentials and service via office holding, and about the history of women and their struggle for complete citizenship.[4]

Nancy Cott has noted that "striking continuities tend to be over-looked" if the achievement of the Nineteenth Amendment and votes for women nationwide in 1920 "is supposed to be the great divide and only electoral politics is its sequel." Esther Lovejoy's activist career provides a vital example of someone who bridged this great divide.[5] Lovejoy's life in activism moved from the local to the national to the transnational as she chaired the American Women's Hospitals medical humanitarian relief organization from 1919 to 1967, served as the first president of the Medical Women's International Association from 1919 to 1924, and thereafter combined the work of the two groups. Lovejoy's activism did not just bridge the "great divide" in women's political activism. Her work with the American Women's Hospitals after the First World War places her story within the growing historical scholarship that emphasizes the artificial boundaries between war and peacetime, focusing instead on the "Long War" of the twentieth century and beyond.[6]

Scholars such as Alan Dawley and Leila Rupp have emphasized the internationalist turn taken by progressives in the United States during and after the First World War. For Dawley, Jane Addams's concept of "world consciousness" and the interdependence of peoples and nations stands as the "key to progressive internationalism."[7] Esther Lovejoy was certainly world conscious and believed in interdependence. But an examination of her life suggests that her idea of interdependence embraced a transnational identity and an expanded vision of the possibilities of transnational activism. Transnationalism "takes the interconnectivity of people around the globe and the flow of people and ideas across national boundaries as its starting point." Lovejoy and other transnationalists reexamined "ties that continue to bind humans to citizenship and to the nation" in favor of a global perspective.[8] Lovejoy came to believe that international health, social justice, and an end to war could come only from the work of women engaged in constructive resistance above and across national boundaries. It was not only their interdependence that would bring full civic equality and social justice to women, but also a new way of viewing the world transnationally and acting together from that view. This transnational identity enabled Lovejoy to cross some boundaries of race and ethnicity, moving beyond white privilege, to embrace gender solidarity in her reform agenda. Lovejoy and her colleagues forged a "without borders" philosophy of medical humanitarian action that was similar to the ideologies of later medical relief organizations such as Doctors Without Borders but part of a larger feminist vision.

As an activist and feminist theorist, Lovejoy had what Cyntha Enloe has called a feminist curiosity about the lives of the women around her, including her own.[9] This made Lovejoy a vital subject and actor in the movement for woman suffrage, public health, and transnational feminist organizing. She addressed women's health and medical concerns, but her feminist curiosity also stimulated her to ask questions and seek answers about their economic, cultural, and social lives and to contest inequalities based on gender. Lovejoy approached city health, national health, and eventually international health through a positive social justice platform that involved empowering women with full civic rights (including economic rights) to shape their communities and promote health and well-being. An initial supporter of the First World War as a progressive conflict to end future wars, Lovejoy came to identify the particular elements of violence against women in wartime and in the unending political and humanitarian crises that followed, and called for an end to war as a key ingredient of international health. This was, she said, "Woman's Big Job."[10]

The chapters that follow examine the evolution of Esther Clayson Pohl Lovejoy from her earliest lessons in constructive resistance during her childhood in Seabeck, Washington Territory, and in Oregon, to her developing theories and her activism for women's civic rights and economic citizenship in medicine, public health, and suffrage in Portland, and then to her transnational feminist work for international health during the First World War and beyond. The book traces how one activist challenged continuing barriers to medical education and practice and confronted state policies that limited the rights of female citizens. Lovejoy also navigated the shifting tide of possibility for and backlash against women's civic equality in global affairs, including finding transnational connections in the First World War and addressing what historian Erika Kuhlman has identified as the "reconstruction of patriarchy" in the war's aftermath by helping to found and then direct transnational organizations.[11] Lovejoy's life also underscores the work of many historians who urge us to understand that the attainment of woman suffrage was not an end to activism but a gateway to other fields of feminist work.[12] Esther Lovejoy labored in the fertile field of transnational feminism in between what historians have often termed the "first wave" of feminism that led to suffrage and the "second wave" of the 1960s. Her activism calls for new historical categories and analysis.

As we commemorate centennials of the achievement of woman suffrage in Oregon, the West, and the nation, Lovejoy's leadership and theoretical contributions encourage us to rethink what we know about the broad movement for women's rights and underscore how important the state and the region were to that movement. And, as we continue to face global challenges to social justice and peace, Lovejoy's strategies and vision continue to offer a path toward international health and human rights.

Esther Clayson Pohl Lovejoy went by different names at different periods in her life. I have tried to maintain fidelity to her history by referring to her by the name she carried at each stage of her life. From birth to her marriage to Emil Pohl in April 1894, just after her graduation from medical school, she was Esther Clayson. She was Esther Pohl during her early medical practice, her service as a member of Portland's city health board and as city health officer from 1907 to 1909, at Emil Pohl's death in 1911, and for part of the Oregon suffrage campaign of 1912. She married George A. Lovejoy in August 1912 and took on his last name, sometimes hyphenating Pohl-Lovejoy and sometimes using Pohl Lovejoy. After their divorce in 1920, she retained the name Lovejoy until her death in 1967.

CHAPTER 1

Lessons in Constructive Resistance

O N a rainy day at the end of November 1882, thirteen-year-old Esther Clayson held her baby sister as her mother helped them board the *Gem*, the steamer that was taking them away from the logging town of Seabeck, Washington Territory, and from Esther's father, Edward. With money saved in secret, they left the house as if they were going shopping in town. Then they kept going, first by ship and then by train to Portland, Oregon. This "getaway" became the climax of Esther Clayson Pohl Lovejoy's unpublished autobiography of her childhood, an account that traces her experiences in two intersecting worlds. One world was the verdant garden of Washington Territory, where Clayson explored life with her three brothers, scampering about on wrecked ships and making games of adventure last into the dark hours of the summer nights. In the midst of stunning mountains and Puget Sound, and in the luxuriant growth of the woods near Seabeck, the natural world opened to Clayson's young senses and mind. But another, overlapping childhood world involved abuse and loss, painful power struggles and work for survival, hard lessons in what she would later call constructive resistance.[1]

Esther Clayson traced her family origins in the rhythms of work, family, migration, and the politics of social class. Her mother, Annie Quinton Clayson, was born August 9, 1845, in Portsmouth, England, to John Quinton and Polly Woodruff.[2] The Quintons were a working family of tailors and seamstresses in this vital British navy port town. Annie was "born with a tailor's thimble on her finger," Esther recalled later. "It was no shining silver tip, but a strong practical instrument with a hole in the end, like her father used to support his large family." As the oldest of eleven children, Annie began helping her father in his Portsmouth shop at the age of five and was soon assisting her aunt, a Paris-trained dressmaker. By the age of fifteen Annie was skilled in tailoring, dressmaking, and other arts of the needle.[3]

Esther's father, Edward Clayson, was born on July 10, 1837, in the village of Bridge, southeast of Canterbury in the county of Kent, England, one of sixteen children of Charles and Esther Hughes Clayson. Charles worked as a gardener on a local estate, and the family maintained a kitchen garden and livestock at home. The large number of children increasingly taxed family resources. When one of his sons picked a "rare blossom" from the estate and offered it to the landlord, Charles lost his job. "Cold and hunger finally forced the family into the poorhouse," Esther recalled, "where they developed an undying hatred for overseers and a lasting sympathy for inmates." Edward and two of his brothers absorbed these lessons and decided to join the Royal Navy as a way out. Edward started service as a cabin boy, then achieved the rank of able seaman and served in the Crimean War.[4]

Annie Quinton met Edward Clayson when he came to Portsmouth to sail for duty in British Columbia. "It was love at first sight with both of them," Esther claimed, "and trouble from the start." They married in 1864 and rented a small house across town from Annie's family in Portsmouth. Three weeks later Edward left for duty at sea, bound around Cape Horn for the Pacific Northwest coast. Annie contracted with a neighborhood tailor for piecework, and Edward Jr., called Ted, was born in 1865. Annie then received word that her benefits allotment was at an end because Edward had left the Royal Navy. But soon "one enthusiastic letter after another" began to arrive from Port Gamble, Washington Territory, a place Edward considered "the richest and loveliest corner of the world." He was working for the Puget Mill Company on Hood Canal, and his descriptions of a land of abundance were enticing. Ten years of hard work in the fruitful Pacific Northwest, he told Annie, would allow them to return to England with a comfortable nest egg.[5] With this dream in mind, Annie and two-year-old Ted made the voyage to Washington Territory in 1867. Annie understood this to be a temporary sojourn before her return to Portsmouth, where she could provide a comfortable home for her extended family.[6]

Edward won the contract to carry the mail between Port Gamble and Seabeck and soon moved the family to property he purchased across the inlet from Seabeck's Washington Mill Company.[7] He delivered the mail by sailing sloop or rowboat and lost the contract in 1870 when men with faster and more efficient steamboats outbid him.[8] Esther's wealthy uncle, William H. Clayson, a captain in the Royal Navy serving with the coast guard in China, staked a new business venture by shipping tea to his brother Edward, who then sold it at ports along Puget Sound.[9] But the tea venture was precarious at best and lasted only a short time. Whether delivering mail or tea, Edward drank along the way and ended the day at the bar with friends. Knowing that Edward was spending the family savings, and hearing rumors of gambling debts, Annie wrote to her brother-in-law, telling him to stop sending tea.[10]

Edward's shifting employment was unsteady, but Annie's industry was the family bedrock. In Port Gamble she went from sewing by hand to using the latest hand-cranked Singer sewing machine, and when the family moved to Seabeck, Annie took her business with her.[11] The machine was both a companion during Edward's frequent absences and the tangible symbol of her earning power that would take them back to England.[12] Annie could make almost any garment, from layettes to dresses, suits, and burial shrouds. Esther recalled that she made skirts and petticoats "with tiers of ruffles or rows of pleating, and uncounted lengths of such frills and flounces passed over the plate of her machine." The real moneymakers were shirts for loggers sewn from big bolts of red, blue, and gray flannel brought in from Victoria, British Columbia. Annie Clayson's shirts had distinctive trademarks: high-quality work with a particular "finish of the buttonholes, a herringbone stitch on the collar, or an embroidered design in a contrasting color on the breast pocket." High demand for her work caused sales of the mass-produced "shoddy shirts" at the Washington Mill Company store in Seabeck to plummet.[13]

Annie's work and earnings were particularly important because the Clayson family grew by four additional children in these years. "Morning-sickness was the beginning, and homesickness the end of many of her days on Hood's Canal," Esther recalled.[14] William, the second child, was born in Port Gamble.[15] Esther was the first to be born in Seabeck, on November 16, 1869, then Fred, his mother's favorite and Esther's shadow in work and play, and then came Annie May, who, Esther noted, "belonged to our family but not to our gang" in the Seabeck years.[16]

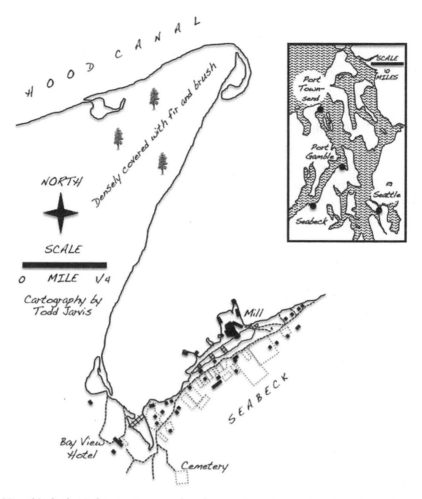

Map of Seabeck, Washington Territory, based on Geodetic Map T-1558-1 of Hoods Canal, 1883, Washington Territory. Courtesy of Charles Kraining, executive director, Seabeck Conference Center. Map by Todd Jarvis.

The Washington Mill Company at Seabeck was part of the extensive Puget Sound extractive lumber industry established in the 1850s. Brokered and administered in San Francisco, it was big business and expanded steadily in the second half of the nineteenth century. By the 1880s, according to historian William G. Robbins, the lumber industry "underwent a technological revolution . . . that vastly increased production and provided manufacturers with readier access to markets." Railroads provided transportation and land grants. These developments paved the way for the "capitalist transformation" of the region.[17] San

Francisco investors established the Washington Mill Company in 1857, and the mill fed a global appetite for lumber products and also engaged in shipbuilding for the carrying trade until it burned completely in 1886 and was abandoned.[18] Seabeck was part of a cluster of "little kingdoms" such as Port Gamble and Port Madison in Kitsap County, "where the lumber companies managed affairs as they saw fit" and workers lacked power. In this exploitative lumber economy, mill managers such as Seabeck's Richard Holyoke were "the representatives of colonial powers," according to historian Robert E. Ficken, "administering economic decisions made in distant San Francisco."[19]

With some 250 residents in 1880, most of whom were Euro American (native born and first-generation immigrants) and male, Seabeck was a company town.[20] In 1870, 93 percent of Kitsap County residents were either directly employed by the Washington Mill Company, were directly related to someone who worked there, or labored in industries that supported the mill. Ten years later, over 86 percent of residents were still tied to the company. The mill administrators controlled county politics and elections with a heavy hand and influenced county commissioners whose fortunes depended on the mill's success.[21] The company store sold up to $10,000 worth of merchandise per month in the 1870s, with well over half of the items sold on credit. The store reported over $20,000 in profits in 1877.[22] The workers did not stay long. From 1868 to 1876 some 83 percent of mill employees left within a year or less.[23]

Edward Clayson had started his new life in Washington Territory working in the Port Gamble sawmill. He left the mill hoping to gain independence and make a solid living by carrying the mail and then selling tea.[24] After both failed, in the early 1870s he established a logging camp on his acreage across the small bay from Seabeck to sell lumber directly to the Washington Mill Company. Between eight and fourteen such camps operated along Hood Canal, and the mill owners had a monopoly on most of the lumber they cut.[25] As men came to work for the Clayson logging enterprise, Annie opened a boardinghouse to shelter and feed them. "The pretty little house with two dormer windows projecting from the roof and looking eagerly over the bay had not been designed for a logging-camp," Esther recalled, "but with father as architect it developed sprawling wings to serve this new purpose." One wing became a dining and living room, and the loft above was fitted out with sleeping bunks furnished with straw tick mattresses.[26]

The Clayson logging camp was to be the primary family business, but Annie's camp boardinghouse grew steadily by its side. Annie learned how to feed a large group by observing the cooks she employed. Her own baking was legendary, and soon there were often more guests than loggers. The family added another wing and outbuildings, and Annie supervised the kitchen, purchased supplies, and kept the books for the "hotel that was developing spontaneously."[27] Edward's attempt to manage logging camp affairs fared no better than his mail or tea businesses. His next step was to expand Annie's boardinghouse into the family-run Bay View Hotel.[28] Kitsap County commissioners granted his petition for a saloon and a liquor license, and Edward later added ninepins and billiards as attractions.[29]

As saloonkeeper and proprietor of the Bay View, Edward Clayson fought with mill administrators and with the commissioners. He described Seabeck as a "penal colony" and cast himself as the "only free man" living in "free territory" across the inlet from the mill.[30] He was embroiled in a conflict about a bridge that connected his property with the town, and ultimately the mill company, which owned the land, had the bridge destroyed.[31] The first mill officials and many early residents were from Maine and supported the prohibition of alcohol; they controlled town policies until 1869, when public pressure from workers and proprietors to grant liquor licenses won the day. Even though prohibition in Seabeck ended before Edward Clayson began the Bay View enterprise, elements of the alcohol conflict peppered his relationship with the town and mill thereafter.[32] Clayson also worked to prove that the Washington Mill Company and other Kitsap County firms had cut timber illegally on lands in the public domain, and to expose the graft that went along with the practice. All of this fostered what Esther later characterized as a "man against monopoly" political philosophy that led Clayson to embrace the Populist Party, Dennis Kearney's Workingmen's Party, Henry George's "single tax," and eventually Theodore Roosevelt's Progressive Party. "Petty personal immorality, like petty larceny, didn't matter much" to him, Esther recalled later. "But grand immorality, corporate transgression, the circumvention of the law, and the exploitation of the Public Domain and of working men should be put down with a strong hand."[33]

Edward viewed his short-lived newspaper, the *Rebel Battery*, published in 1878, as another weapon in his war with the mill. He shot rhetorical barrages at mill administrators and represented the virtues of the

Bay View Hotel as a thorn in their side. "The hotel is located just outside of the borders of the Kingdom," he wrote. "It is the first respectable hotel ever built in Seabeck," and "the money you spend in this hotel does not help, either directly or indirectly, to swell the funds of the . . . powerful monopoly [of the mill.]" The Clayson family was "numerous enough to run the whole concern from the concert room to the hotel buildings to digging out stumps on the farm." He advertised good food, convivial surroundings, a flowing bar, music, and a "splendid Base Ball Ground."[34]

In the pages of the *Rebel Battery* Edward Clayson invited mill workers to "find aid and comfort at the Bay View Hotel," meaning "free meals, drinks, and cigars." Annie called them "guests of honor" with great irony, and was angry and frustrated as they siphoned off any profits the Bay View might make. Esther and her brothers considered them "bilks" who "didn't care a hang about injustice to labor or the devastation of the national forest. For want of a better hearing, Father read his writings to them, and they had to listen and applaud or go hungry." Mill administrators branded the Claysons "outsiders, trouble makers, disturbers of the peace," and mill workers risked their jobs if they patronized the Claysons' establishment. Annie tried to be a peacemaker and broker between her husband and their neighbors, the mill administrators, and the legitimate patrons of the Bay View. Given the circumstances, it was a challenge at best, and the Clayson children negotiated their way through childhood in the middle of it all.[35]

As a young girl, Esther considered her family's Seabeck logging camp "a glorious playground" beyond compare. She later remembered a parade of "bullwhackers, fallers, buckers, barkers . . . greasers to grease the skids of the road, and hook-tenders to tend the iron hooks and chains used in getting the logs out of the woods." Bullwhackers were the "mighty men who thought nothing of giving a boy or a tomboy two bits, and sometimes four bits, on pay days," she recalled. "These small coins were called 'chicken feed' by the best men in our crew, and as little chickens we never lacked for pocket money while the loggers had any to give."[36] Esther, tagged "Daredevil Dick" by her father, won the right to follow along with her older brothers on fishing expeditions by catching the bait; they all explored the woods and shipwrecks and invented games of adventure. Sometimes, to the great scandal of Seabeck, they danced naked in the shallow water separating their home and camp from the town. It was bad enough for her brothers, Esther remembered, "but for a little girl to act that way was just too terrible" for the "ladies," who could see her "plainly with strong glasses" across the bay. The "call of the woods, streams, and flowing tides was always in our ears, and off we would go whenever we got the chance. . . . For if we heard Mother calling we were in duty bound to answer, but if we were so far away that we couldn't hear her, how could we help it?"[37]

In spite of the call of the woods, Esther and her siblings, like other children in the late nineteenth-century West, were also vital laborers in the family economy. Steven Mintz has identified two "divergent conceptions of childhood" that emerged in this period as a result of the Industrial Revolution, westward expansion, and immigration: "useful childhood" and "protected childhood." The idea of a "useful childhood" rested with parents' need for the labor of "working class, farming, and immigrant children" and was "based on the premise that all family members, including children, should contribute to a family's support." And a "protected childhood" was valued by the emerging middle class in cities and aspired to by many upwardly mobile working-class and farm families.[38] Esther's upbringing fit the model of a "useful childhood" exactly. "On the frontier," as historian Elliott West notes, "the child's working sphere was expanding, not contracting," even as "protected childhood" became a more prominent model of childhood in the Midwest and the East. And division of chores by sex was often impractical in the Pacific Northwestern setting in which the Claysons lived and worked.[39]

"From the time we could walk we were taught to do our part of the day's work," Esther wrote. This included gardening; caring for chickens, pigs, and cows; washing dishes, preparing food, and keeping the kitchen fire burning and supplied with wood; and "the daily job of making the beds and waiting on the tables as soon as we were old enough to carry dishes, about nine years."[40] Just steps away, the ocean was brimming with salmon and clams, and the streams with trout. Fertile soil gave wild blueberries, blackberries, raspberries, and hazelnuts for the asking, and, with cultivation, yielded fruits and vegetables that loaded the harvest basket and table. Timber stands met saltwater estuaries and shorelines, and birds and other animals completed the chain of plenty—but all of this had to be harvested. Esther's experiences reinforce Elliott West's point that gathering, fishing, and hunting were vital to the family subsistence economy in the region and that these "burdens rested heavily upon shoulders of women and children, the latter in particular."[41] And in the case of the Claysons, gathering and fishing blended with the family's cash economy. "Wild berries and fish, including clams and crabs, were among the natural resources of the country, and at an early age we supplied the table with a good part of these commodities. The world at large has never known such clam chowder, baked salmon, wild blackberry and blueberry pie as Mother served with regularity at the Bayview Hotel," Esther wrote.[42]

For Esther, this labor "took a good deal of the joy out of living for us youngsters, but we looked forward hopefully to the time when we might get real jobs doing work we liked and getting paid for it, instead of doing all kinds of work we didn't like for nothing."[43] There were a few ways to make money outside the family economy. Coins came from the bull-whackers on payday. Esther and her brothers procured "skunk livers with the gall-bladders intact and full of bile" for half a dollar each for Chinese American workers in Seabeck who "knew about the curative value of bile before the medical profession at large found it out."[44]

Education, formal and informal, also played a part in Esther's useful childhood. When she revisited Seabeck in 1953, Esther Lovejoy returned a worn copy of the *Complete Works of Robert Burns* that her father had borrowed from the Seabeck Public Library in about 1875, a volume that had survived over seventy-five years of her life and travels.[45] Libraries, books, and family reading were a common part of a child's education in the Pacific Northwest and in other western settlements in this period.[46] Edward Clayson was a reader, writer, publisher, and political analyst, so books, newspapers, and ideas were a fundamental part of Esther's childhood education. Annie Clayson used singing to instruct her children; Edward taught them to play a variety of musical instruments and led them in a band.[47]

Esther started attending school in Seabeck in 1873 when she was four years of age. "The early admission was a great advantage to our family," she recalled. "We were not much help at the Bayview Hotel before we were eight or nine years of age, and after that our time was too valuable to waste" at school.[48] Seabeck was embedded in a territorial public education system that boasted many schools and high student attendance rates but suffered from poor pay for teachers and low financial investment in students. Washington Territory had the largest number of public schools per school-age resident of any western state in 1870 and 1880, and tied for the second-highest school attendance in the region in 1870. But in 1880 the territory was second from the bottom in the region in expenditures per school and ranked tenth of fourteen in average monthly teacher salaries.[49] It is not surprising that Edward Clayson reported frequent turnover of teachers at the Seabeck school.[50]

Territorial legislation passed in 1873 required school districts to provide and maintain a school "with necessary fuel and appendages, and such privies and outhouses as decency requires."[51] By 1877 legislation mandated that classes be taught in English only, with required instruction in reading, writing, grammar and spelling, arithmetic, physiology, geography, and US history, in step with other regional classrooms. Teachers could be suspended for espousing partisan politics or religion. It was their duty "to endeavor to impress on the minds of their pupils the principles of morality, truth, justice, and patriotism; to teach them to avoid idleness, profanity, and falsehood." In keeping with the vision of public schools as a vehicle for civic assimilation, teachers were to instruct students "in the principles of a free government, and to train them up in a true comprehension of the rights, duties, and dignity of American citizenship."[52] Within the school building, students were divided into several grades for the eight-year grammar school curriculum, but there were no high schools in Kitsap County in this period.[53] During Esther's student days, district taxes opened the school doors in Seabeck for six to eight months of the year, and in 1881 there were thirty-four students in Seabeck's school.[54]

In her autobiography Esther emphasized that she could compete successfully with other children for academic honors in the face of fierce class differences. "In addition to coming from 'free territory' and being the daughter of 'that dirty rebel,' I was a tomboy in my own right and a little smarty in a class of older children," she noted. "The big boys were tolerant of my small presence, but most of the big girls were less charitable"; they told her to "stay on her side of the bridge." To some of the girls she was "a strange bird in the flock—a little shitepoke. Naturally there was a good deal of pecking, but life with three brothers had taught me endurance, and I was not without a spirit of retaliation." She gloried in the chance to lead the spelling match. "With malice aforethought" she selected the word "ornithorhynchus" (the scientific name for a duck-billed platypus) for one of her chief tormentors, the privileged daughter of "a ship captain in the Company's service." Not surprisingly, the girl failed to spell the word correctly. "Down she went toward the foot of the class with all her airs and frills on that duck-billed animal from the wilds of Australia," Esther recalled in triumph.[55]

If Esther was an outsider to the Washington Mill Company families of Seabeck because of her father's challenges to the company and her family's constant economic struggle to make ends meet, she possessed power and status as a result of her Euro American heritage. Being white, as historian Peggy Pascoe has demonstrated, was a form of property and propriety in the Pacific Northwest during these years, and white residents had legal privileges in terms of marriage, property, and inheritance.[56] Esther's years in Seabeck coincided with the intense changes in westward migration and the growth of the extractive lumber economy that placed what Alexandra Harmon has described as "unprecedented pressure" on native Coast Salish residents of Puget Sound to "accept American terms for relations." In 1860, seven years before Annie Clayson's arrival, Native Americans made up half of the population of the Puget Sound area; by 1890, seven years after the Clayson family departed, whites outnumbered native residents by twenty to one. Harmon traces the "tug of war" among whites who wished to segregate and supervise Native Americans on reservations, others who wanted to hire them for labor outside of reservation boundaries, and native peoples who worked to find the best strategies possible within these changing circumstances.[57] In Seabeck during the 1870s, as in other mill towns, native residents worked for wages in the lumber mills, and there were some fifteen to twenty Native American workers on the Washington Mill Company payroll each year.[58] The wife of a local tribal elder was the "head washerwoman" at the Clayson's boardinghouse.[59]

In Seabeck, the Clayson children grew up speaking Chinuk Wawa, historically referred to as Chinook Jargon, a language of exchange between native and Euro American communities.[60] But white privilege was encoded in their experience. In her autobiography, Esther wrote about "Old Sam, the Indian chief, who lived with the tag-end of his tribe" and who watched the construction of the ship *Cassandra Adams* each day with wonder, disapproving of any more timber cutting and not trusting that such a large ship could be built.[61] Esther's mother Annie hired two native men, one woman, and their canoe at a desperate time, and they saved the Clayson family from foreclosure by getting them to Port Gamble when the mill owners had plotted to prevent them. Reportedly they were spurred on by the promise of alcohol.[62]

The hierarchies of ethnicity and gender in Seabeck were particularly clear. In the early days, Esther wrote, "Hunters, trappers, scouts . . . made no bones about" being with native women, and neither did "settlers proving up on claims and hoping for wives of their own color at a later date. Some of the soldiers stationed for a time upon the frontier" had such relationships, "openly or on the sly." The mixed-heritage daughters of these couples were "proud of their fathers although they had never met. Such girls were very attractive but unattainable to men like [white trapper] Buckskin Charley, and pure white women were akin to angels, remote and colorless, to be worshipped at a distance."[63]

Because Esther Lovejoy wrote her autobiography many years and many experiences after Seabeck, it is difficult to analyze what she wrote about the Chinese cook, Cloey, and his role in her story. The mill employed some Chinese American workers at the lowest pay and created separate housing for them in town.[64] "Some of our white cooks were weak sisters where liquor was concerned," Esther recalled, but in these years before the Chinese Exclusion Act of 1882, many Chinese men were looking for work in the region and many native-born workers resented them. Esther's mother was willing to hire a Chinese man as cook, particularly because "sober and reliable white cooks were hard to find." Esther characterized Cloey as someone strange and different but also as "a pillar of patience, ready at all times to take the blame and stretch or shrink the truth to save us from the just reward of misconduct." In addition, the family's "popularity with the children of Seabeck depended largely" on him, because he took the time to make "wonderful cookies in the shape of elephants and other animals which we distributed liberally." The cook's skill made some of the anti-Chinese loggers who were customers at the Bay View "tolerant" because "they knew what a hard time Mother had with white cooks . . . and principles regarding the nationality of cooks weaken in an atmosphere of genuine wild-blackberry pie."[65]

Cloey was skilled at dissembling when Edward Clayson was concerned. "The head of the house and the business should be recognized in all of its branches," Esther wrote. To maintain his authority, her father came to the kitchen on occasion to give a few orders. "During these inspections Cloey's manner was perfect. His inscrutable mask of deep respect and attention contrasted so pleasantly with the offensive you-be-damned attitude of some of the loggers." But the "instant the door was closed his ingratiating smile was replaced by a vindictive frown . . . and there was nothing less than murder in his imprecations."[66]

Contradictions were at the heart of Esther's useful childhood. Her father and mother needed the work of their children to sustain the family economy, yet her father squandered what they produced. Edward critiqued the power of the Washington Mill Company over workers and community members but tried to exercise complete control over his family. His actions made Esther and her siblings outcasts and his excesses robbed them of subsistence. Nonwhites had little power in Seabeck, giving Esther and her family status as a result of their whiteness. But Cloey's protective mask of respect and attention, and Sam's suspicions of the logging enterprise offered strategic lessons for Esther's own developing critique of power and authority.

Esther's future critique of unjust power was also nourished by her observations of systematic, institutional authority that supported and strengthened her father's control and violence. Anglo-American common law granted stark and capacious power to husbands and fathers, including the right to decide where his wife and family would live (the *domicil* in legal parlance), the power to discipline and punish his wife and children, and the "right to the wife's marital companionship and personal services," including sexual intercourse, household work, child raising, and any earnings from wage work. Wealthy women could seek legal protection, and in some community-property states (which Washington would become after statehood in 1889) a woman had a right to half of the marital property upon the death of her husband. But husbands were in charge of the "community" during marriage.[67] During the years that Annie Clayson lived with her husband Edward in Port Gamble and Seabeck, Washington Territorial legislators and jurists supported (1871), denied (1873), and then reinstated (1879 and 1881) protections enabling married women to control their separate property and earnings, but women continued to be liable for their husbands' debts.[68] And within the power relations of a marriage and the isolation of a Seabeck residence, Edward Clayson's authority as a husband and father had other systems of support. Annie had few protections against her husband's use of the family's assets, and the gendered inequality of property and marriage was one of the key lessons of Esther's childhood.

Seabeck had no banks, so Edward Clayson required that all the silver coin earned by the family be concealed in a cigar box under his mattress. Esther remembered that he had a "special hiding-place for gold behind the rafter near the eaves in the unfinished attic of the house."[69] Annie deposited the earnings from her sewing enterprises into the cigar box, and Edward considered them his to use as he saw fit; in this he was backed by tradition and law. Moreover, he made the big economic decisions for the family. After Edward failed to retain the mail contract, and as the tea business fizzled, Annie's plan was to clear a portion of their Seabeck land, plant fruit trees on part of it and leave the timber stands on the rest, and then sell it to the Washington Mill Company for a profit. The family, she believed, could then return to England with a nest egg and a new start.[70]

Annie Quinton Clayson. Reproduced by permission of Oregon Health & Science University Historical Collections & Archives, Portland, Oregon.

Edward had a different view. He wanted to make his fortune in the logging business by using the family funds as seed money and selling the timber on their property to the Washington Mill Company. Annie protested that it was "her money" and that he "had lost more than he had made." Loggers who boarded with them had urged her to keep out of the logging business. The Washington Mill Company wanted the Claysons' property because it stood strategically at the head of the bay, where workers could place a log boom to contain and collect floating logs. A sale of that property to the mill would bring the family a strong return on their investment. "But if he went into the logging business with no sale for the logs save to the mill," Esther remembered, "he would surely become entangled and that powerful company would swallow them whole"—which it eventually did.[71]

Edward "roared" a storm of words and abuse at Annie for "meddling in matters beyond her sphere" and for challenging his authority as head of the household. He invoked God, the Old Testament Solomon who warned against contentious women, and the New Testament Paul who insisted that women should be silent. Esther recalled that she and her brothers stood "beside Mother with tears in our eyes and fear and fury in our souls." During such confrontations, Esther wrote, "we children were a unit on Mother's side, but Solomon and Saint Paul were always against her." And then "there was a calm after the storm—there always was. Purged of ill-feeling by an emotional outburst, Father was always happy, smiling, and forgiving, and he expected his family to share his change of mood."[72]

There were many such cycles of anger and abuse, fear and fury, and calms after the storm. "When he was in a good humor, we could disregard general orders and do almost anything without fear of reprimand," Esther recalled. "But when the weather was bad, we had to beware of squalls, and woe betide the one caught in an act of disobedience at a time when he was brooding over trouble with the loggers or the mill company."[73] Esther's description recounts the cycle known to those familiar with domestic violence. Edward expressed his anger in a powerful matrix of emotional, economic, and physical abuse, with a period of good feelings to follow.

Esther recorded other instances of physical and emotional violence by her father. Edward believed that corporal punishment was good for growing boys, and he used it on his sons. Esther's gender protected her to some extent. But when she and Will defied their father and played on floating logs in the harbor, "Will got his ducking first, and then my turn came. . . . Father was able to give his entire attention to my case, and for once I got the worst of it." Edward pushed Esther down into the water, holding her by the back of the neck, brought her up for air, and pushed her down again. Each time she surfaced he asked, "Now, you little daredevil, will you stay off of those logs?"[74]

Esther's father also had the legal power to control her mother's choice of residence and even her citizenship and nationality. When Edward's debts mounted in the logging business, Annie wanted to return to England. She had been contributing to the "home money" fund through her own sewing work and managing the kitchen, but Edward wanted to "make a fresh beginning in the hotel business." He informed Annie that "she might as well know the truth: he had already taken out his papers, and she was a citizen of the United States whether she liked it or not."[75] From 1855 until 1922 federal legislation provided that "any woman who is now or who may hereafter be married to a citizen of the United States and who might herself be lawfully naturalized, shall be deemed a citizen." This meant that women who were not US citizens and who married American citizen husbands or those whose husbands became citizens through the naturalization process were "the first and only group of adults to receive United States citizenship derivatively." Their civic identity resulted not from their own actions or intentions but from their husbands' relationship to the nation state. While many women certainly welcomed US citizenship, the law did not give women the right to choose. And for women like Annie Clayson, US citizenship was, as Candice Bredbenner notes, a "conscripted allegiance."[76]

In the 1860s and 1870s many immigrants, like Edward, took out their "first papers" to declare their intention of becoming citizens,[77] and many became citizens after the required five years of residency. Others did not, and it appears that Edward was among them.[78] Still, his "first papers" status allowed him to vote, serve on regular and grand juries in Seabeck, and run for public office.[79] We can't know what Annie understood about their citizenship status, but Esther's account gives the strong impression that Edward believed that he was a citizen and acted accordingly, with all of the implications for Annie's own status and her dependency on him. It appears that after his announcement, both Edward and Annie considered the question of their return to England closed.

Edward decided to celebrate his intention to live permanently in the United States as a "free man" by inviting the town to a grand opening of the family's Bay View Hotel. But Edward's independence was based on Annie's dependence. "Ten years of hard work had been wasted," Esther remembered, "and one failure after another was nothing to boast about. Her frowning, perspiring face was an open book to us children, but nothing could dampen Father's enthusiasm." The food they served symbolized the inequities in the family. "Those chickens belonged to Mother and she had sacrificed them unwillingly. With our help she had hatched, raised, killed, plucked, dressed, cooked and served them. After the chicken was all gone, the mashed potatoes and gravy cleaned up, and the last sections of wild-blackberry pie engorged," her father made his official declaration of independence. "He was denouncing monopolies—grasping lumber corporations, particularly the Washington Mill Company and everybody

Panoramic image of the Washington Mill Company at Seabeck, Washington Territory, in the 1860s. Courtesy of Charles Kraining, executive director, Seabeck Conference Center, Seabeck, Washington, and also of Fredi Perry Pargeter.

connected with its management." But "Mother's expressive face and the discordant clatter of dishes, knives, forks and spoons were not in tune with his mood, so he went out on the front stoop to smoke a cigar and commune with understanding souls who live in literature." Annie and the children "cleaned up the wreck and dined on the leavings of the previous day."[80]

Three sections of Esther's Seabeck autobiography focus on her development of ways to resist Edward's unjust power and, in turn, the larger institutions and systems that supported it. In each section—her discussion of systems of health care, including midwives and contraception; her version of the christening of the ship the *State of Sonora*; and the "getaway" of the Clayson women—Esther explored the possibilities of constructive resistance.

Various systems of healing and health care available in Seabeck provided early lessons about gendered practices of medicine and empowerment. Seabeck residents had access to some of the most advanced university-trained physicians in the nation, thanks to their proximity to the Marine Hospital Service just thirty miles away, in Port Townsend. The service was part of a federal public health plan for sailors that attracted male physicians trained in the latest medical and surgical theory and practice in the world's leading universities. Legislation passed by the US Congress in 1798 developed by the 1870s into a system by which any sailor seeking medical or surgical care would make a direct visit to a marine hospital physician stationed at or near a customs house and receive either outpatient care or a stay in the hospital. This system created a legacy of federal responsibility for the medical treatment of some workers, and Congress transformed and expanded the institution into the Public Health and Marine Hospital service in 1902 and the Public Health Service in 1912.[81]

After Annie Clayson contracted inflammatory rheumatism and suffered for months, she went to Port Townsend as a private patient of Dr. George Calhoun.[82] From 1865 to 1883, Calhoun and Thomas Taylor Minor held the contract with the US government to provide care for sailors.[83] Calhoun had studied with surgeon and bacteriologist Joseph Lister at the University of Glasgow and had served as a contract surgeon with the Union Army in the American Civil War. He had implemented new techniques, including progressive quarantine regulations a decade in advance of the National Quarantine Act of 1878.[84] Minor, a Yale University–trained doctor and former Civil War surgeon, had joined Calhoun as a partner in 1868. The Marine Hospital Service purchased their hospital in 1883, the year the Clayson family left Washington Territory.[85] The hospital had space for private patients such as Annie in a hundred-bed-capacity general ward, and private rooms for those who could pay more.[86] Other male physicians about whom we have little information also engaged in private practice in the area during the Clayson family's residence.[87] The Sisters of Charity of Providence Hospital in Seattle sold an insurance plan for hospital care to loggers in the area for fifty cents per month.[88]

The midwives of Seabeck represented a separate women's world of healing that included vital contraceptive information that was kept inside their circle to protect women in the community. Annie Clayson came to Washington Territory with an infant son, had six other pregnancies that went to term during the years of her marriage, and had many miscarriages.[89] Esther recalled that "child-bearing women on Hoods Canal during the sixties and seventies depended mostly upon the mercy of God, and God was not always merciful." When one child died in infancy and Annie herself was close to death, she feared another pregnancy. "When she learned from a midwife who had recently arrived in Seabeck that those blessings could be regulated," Esther wrote, "the family birth-rate dropped suddenly." Esther remembered this midwife, Annie Craig, with gratitude. "She saved Mother and other women on Hoods Canal incalculable suffering and undoubtedly reduced the death rate among them." Craig used both mechanical and chemical contraceptives, suggesting acidic douches and sponges or other barrier methods in use at the time, including early diaphragms.[90]

Sarah Rounds also worked as a midwife in the community in the late 1870s and 1880s, assisted by other women who came together around a birthing mother in what Judith Walzer Leavitt has termed "social childbirth." Rounds, in her mid-thirties in 1880, charged ten dollars a week for work that included prenatal visits, labor and delivery, and postpartum care, a pattern similar to the work of other midwives in other communities of the time.[91] She cared for Annie during a difficult stillbirth delivery and remained with her after the local physician, Dr. Kendrick, was called to the case.[92] At times Annie Clayson and other women in the community assisted Craig and Rounds in providing for women's health.[93]

Edward Clayson referred to Annie Craig as a "low hag" and a "criminal."[94] "Father resented that midwife, who, he said, was putting loose ideas into the silly heads of the women of Seabeck," Esther wrote. "In his openly expressed opinions, she was a pest, a blight upon human life, destroying the seed of mankind with her mechanical and chemical abominations." Edward was not alone in his condemnation of women's control of their reproductive lives. Some policy makers and commentators, joined by Social Darwinists, feared low birthrates and worried that the white race would diminish and the "darker races" multiply. "The concept of race suicide," Esther continued, "did not originate with Theodore Roosevelt. Father thought of it first . . . the future of the country depended upon the reproduction of the right kind of people—his own kind."[95] Religious and legal systems also worked against the use of contraceptives. But midwives made them available and taught women how to use them, giving women like Annie Clayson a measure of control over their bodies and their fertility, a vital lesson in constructive resistance.

Esther's account of her christening of the *State of Sonora* in 1880 reflected similar themes of resistance.[96] The ship was built by contract at the Seabeck mill through an independent firm in San Francisco for a Mexican company. The shipwrights boarded at the Clayson's Bay View Hotel, as did the contractor when he was in town, and the community began to speculate about which young girl would receive the "coveted honor" of christening the steamer. "At previous launchings," Esther recalled, "this distinction had been a mark of favor with the Company." But, with the independent contract, "it was a free-for-all and the contractor from San Francisco was cultivated and recommendations made for his guidance." In the weeks leading up to completion of the steamer, Washington Mill Company families put their daughters on display and

Esther Clayson, age eleven, on the day she christened the *State of Sonora* in Seabeck in 1880. Courtesy of Amy Khedouri.

even took their Sunday dinners at the Bay View Hotel in full view of the contractor.[97]

When Esther was chosen, Edward Clayson boasted that the contractor had recognized a superior man who should be rewarded by having his daughter christen the ship.[98] But Esther cast herself in the role of Cinderella. She had turned to her advantage her work waiting tables at the Bay View, serving the contractor with all her skill and attention while other girls and their parents courted him. And the fact that some of those company girls had been her tormentors at school made the victory all the more sweet. Working at the Bay View, she not only knew what a bottle of champagne looked like but was certain that she could break one "on the bow of the ship better than any of them." For her the steamship was a "wonderful outsider," and so was she. Her mother, the proud seamstress, made a beautiful dress for Esther, with all the trimmings, but had to stay home from the christening launch to prepare the dinner to follow. Esther and her father crossed into the "enemy territory" of the Washington Mill Company, where she "broke the bottle of champagne with ribbons on its neck over the bow."[99]

Back at the Bay View, Esther recalled, she was the "star of the evening. With an apron over my gala dress I waited on the tables, and saw to it that my friend, the contractor, got the breast of chicken." Her father accompanied her on the violin as she sang the "Star-Spangled Banner." When Esther faltered at the high note, her mother, "with her hands full of dirty dishes," came in and picked up the song where her daughter had left off, bringing it to a successful conclusion. After the anthem, the contractor "told her that a fine voice was a great gift and should not be wasted in a place like Seabeck."[100] In her story of the event, Esther emphasized her intellectual accomplishments and success in school and her ability to do the job without a hitch. She also knew that a wider world awaited her. "Women who could not adapt themselves to frontier conditions in Washington Territory had to find a way out, die, or break into the insane asylum at Steilacoom," she noted.[101] In time Esther and her mother would make their escape.

Annie sympathized with the unfair treatment of the mill employees but told Edward that they needed to leave Seabeck to provide a better future for their children. "The family had been enslaved for years by his conflict with the Company, and she was sick of it all," Esther recalled. Edward's battles meant that the family was destitute and could not purchase anything from the company store, and that Annie had to depend on sympathy and kindness from other residents to survive.[102] She began to organize the escape, but it took time and careful planning to keep Edward unaware. Esther wrote with great irony that her mother "had to earn the money for our fares in her dining-room, and then steal it from herself little by little." Business was dropping off at the Bay View because of Edward's campaign against the mill, and Annie saved "week after week" to have enough to depart safely. "This was a nest-egg if ever there was one," Esther insisted, because Annie deposited the money "in the hen-house under the straw nest of one setting hen after another" in order not to risk having Edward find the whole sum in one place. The plan included its own security system. "Those hens could be depended upon to make an awful squawk if the nest was disturbed."[103] Annie Clayson chose the quintessentially female space of the hen house, where the "egg money" now held a new meaning of empowerment.

In November 1882 Annie had saved enough money for the getaway. She took Esther and one-year-old Annie May to Portland, where her brother Harry Quinton lived. "She hated to leave the boys behind, but running away with five children was more than she could manage, and she had to take me to carry the baby," Esther remembered. "For just that once I was glad to be a big sister."[104]

Jacob Hauptly, Seabeck's butcher and justice of the peace, who befriended and supported Annie Clayson, offered some additional information in his diary about the escape and its aftermath. Hauptley was aware of trouble far in advance of Annie's departure. He had traded with Edward Clayson for meat and cattle, and when the family credit was used up, he let the Clayson boys come to help out at his butcher shop in exchange for meat he could not sell.[105] In April 1881 he wrote in his diary, "Clayson is in a fix—about Klootch" ("wife" in Chinuk Wawa).[106] On November 30, 1882, Hauptly reported, "It is rumored on the Spit to day that Mrs. Clayson has left her Husband. She went on the [Steamer] Gem Tuesday and Rumor has it that she is gone to Portland, Oregon." The next day, "Clayson put up Notice giving any body or Every Body Hell that Started the Rumor about his wife leaving him. The Notice was so vulgar that I tore it down."[107]

From the beginning, Portland seemed like home to Annie and was a safe and comfortable place for Esther. The name of the city "was English, and the woman who ran the little boarding house where our young uncle lived dropped her *h*'s all over the parlour as she enumerated the attractions of the city. It was very much like 'ome, she said, but a lot better for poor folks." Work was available, and there were horse cars, theaters, and department stores. "Meanwhile Father was fussing and fuming and burning his fingers in the kitchen of the Bayview Hotel," as Esther's brothers later told it. Her father's "enemies would dance the Highland fling barefoot if they ever learned the shameful truth, and against his principles he was obliged to pretend that he knew about the whole damnable escapade."[108]

Throughout the next several months, into the spring of 1883, Annie and Edward engaged in negotiations. Edward wanted her back, as Esther remembered it, and Annie refused to live in Seabeck. "Father stamped and stormed and called Saint Paul to witness the rightness of his position. At the altar of God this woman had promised obedience, and this was the way she was keeping her vow. The enormity of her offence, and the magnanimity of his forgiveness, was stressed repeatedly, but it was a no go." Eventually they agreed to live in Portland, purchase a hotel there, and try again.[109] Edward leased the Bay View, but when an 1886 fire destroyed most of Seabeck and the mill and the hotel burned to the ground, he lost his remaining equity and assets.[110]

Portland offered new promise, but life at the family's Golden Rule Hotel on the east side of the Willamette River recreated tension and conflict between Edward and the rest of his family as he entertained those he called "guests of honor" in the hotel bar.[111] Charlotte, the youngest child, was born during this temporary period of reconciliation in 1884. Esther continued her useful childhood by working in the hotel and caring now for two younger sisters. Portland had a high school, but demands for Esther's labor at the hotel meant that she did not attend.[112] She did receive additional instruction from "homeless men-of-letters who were in arrears for their board at our hotel" in both Seabeck and Portland. Later in life, when filling out *Who's Who* questionnaires and requests for biographical information, Esther would smile at "the suggestion of social exclusiveness in the truthful statement that our early education was under private tutors."[113]

When the Golden Rule Hotel failed in 1886, the family moved to a farm near Jennings Lodge, in Clackamas County, Oregon, to try again. Edward's brother William, who had staked him in the short-lived tea business, purchased the land.[114] But Edward was no farmer. Annie and her children did the work, and, "frustrated by the circumstances of life, including a family that could not be bent to his moods, he was violently temperamental," Esther recalled. But the dynamics of power were changing in the family. The Clayson sons were becoming strong young men, hard workers who learned from the neighbors how to farm successfully. Edward expected obedience and approval from his family but did not have the power he once had to force them to comply. When they did not respond or follow his instructions, he became enraged and told them to leave. Finally, Esther recalled, "the family, acting together, took him at his word and he never got over his surprise and indignation."[115]

In 1888 the family left Edward and the farm and returned to Portland "with hardly enough money to keep us a week. But life without Father was easy. We soon found work, and some of us sent ourselves to college, and none of us ever ran into debt or failed in business."[116] Esther's next steps would take her from the world of her childhood and into the world of wage work. Work was central to her life, and to train for, take part in, and enjoy meaningful work that paid well and over which she had control was one way to constructively resist her father and the systems that supported his undeserved power.

CHAPTER 2

Becoming a Woman Physician

THE Clayson's Golden Rule Hotel was just off the east side landing of the Stark Street Ferry, the main transportation link across the Willamette River between Portland and East Portland. A city's worth of daily traffic, with all its sights, sounds, and possibilities, passed in front of fifteen-year-old Esther's doorstep. It was "there at an early age I was first attracted to the medical profession," she later wrote, "not because I felt the traditional urge to relieve suffering, but because of a beautiful young lady who used to pass every morning." The woman was Belle Schmeer, who was on her way to her classes at the Willamette University Medical Department in Portland. Observing her, Esther concluded that "if that's what women doctors looked like after they grew up, I wanted to be one."[1]

Dr. Callie Brown Charlton provided Esther with a model of financial success and independence. Charlton attended Esther's mother, Annie, at the birth of her youngest daughter, Charlotte, in East Portland in June 1884.[2] Esther, who had observed midwives at work in Seabeck, was impressed as she studied Charlton's skill with her mother and new sister, and noted with interest that "she got fifteen dollars for her services without even washing the baby."[3] Such wages were a strong recommendation for the profession. For the daughter of a vulnerable working family defined by struggle, women medical students and doctors were dazzling. Esther's adolescent vision of Schmeer inspired in her a sense of elegance and style, while Charlton suggested the possibility of financial stability and self-reliance.

Callie Brown Charlton, MD. From H. K. Hines, *An Illustrated History of the State of Oregon* (Chicago: Lewis Publishing, 1893), facing p. 973.

When Esther Clayson returned to Portland with her mother, sisters, and brothers without her father Edward in 1888, she brought with her the lessons learned about work, gender and power from the failed experiment on the Clackamas farm. "Women on farms had to work as well as weep," she noted, and she resolved never to be the "'helpmate' of an Oregon farmer or a pioneer hotel keeper" like her father. At eighteen she got a job working behind the counter at Lipman and Company dry goods store, a less-than-satisfying position. "Medicine as a career was steadily becoming more desirable," she noted, but at the same time less attainable, for financial reasons. When illness came, Annie Clayson invited Callie Charlton to dinner and asked her to bring along her medical bag.[4] Charlton was a single woman, widowed and with a daughter, who had made her way in medicine and business against financial and social odds. She and the Clayson women, who had also weathered many family and financial storms, likely felt they had much in common.[5]

Esther asked Charlton for career advice, and the doctor told her that medicine "was the best vocation possible for a woman." She loved the work and sometimes made $2,000 a year. That "settled the question" for Esther: "Two thousand dollars a year and an independent life and work you loved instead of $300 a year for work you hated" at a department store.[6] Charlton recommended that Esther enroll at the recently established University of Oregon Medical Department (UOMD) in Portland. Esther followed her advice and began her medical coursework in the fall term of 1890.[7]

Medical education for women in the United States in the nineteenth and early twentieth centuries was shaped in powerful ways by region, the interplay of advocates and opponents, the creation of separate female medical colleges and the push for coeducation, and the establishment of alternative medical schools in homeopathic and eclectic theory and practice, and attracted many women students and practitioners.[8] Elizabeth Blackwell was the first woman in the nation to receive a medical degree, but after her 1849 graduation from Geneva Medical College in New York, the faculty and administration banned women from attending. Frustrated by opposition to women in established schools in eastern and midwestern states, supporters founded seventeen female medical schools, both "regular" and homeopathic, between 1848 and 1895. But by the first years of the twentieth century, just two "regular" women's schools, the Female Medical College of Pennsylvania and the Woman's Medical College of Baltimore, and one homeopathic institution, the New York Women's Medical College, remained open. Coeducation, a particular feature of western and midwestern medical schools, including those in Oregon, was the trend, but women faced many barriers as well as segregation in these mixed settings.[9] In addition, women's struggle to gain a place in medical education and practice occurred simultaneously with what Robert Nye has identified as a pervasive masculinization of professional culture in nineteenth-century medicine in the United States.[10]

Homeopathy and other alternative medical systems appealed to many women students who saw both increased opportunity in fledgling institutions and a more engaging medical theory and practice. In the decade from 1890 to 1900, as Esther Clayson attended and graduated from a "regular" medical school at the UOMD, seven hundred women matriculated at homeopathic medical schools across the nation and made up eighteen percent of homeopathic medical graduates for those same years.[11] In 1893–1894, the year Clayson completed her medical degree, she was among 1,349 women medical students in all medical institutions, some 7 percent of the 20,192 students enrolled in medical programs in the nation.[12]

Oregon was the first western state to admit a woman to medical school; Mary Sawtelle attended Willamette University Medical Department in Salem from 1869 to 1871.[13] The first women in Oregon to receive medical degrees were sisters Ella J. Ford and Angela Ford, who graduated from Willamette in 1877.[14] When Esther Clayson graduated in 1894, after taking a year off to work full-time at department store counters, she became the second female graduate of the University of Oregon Medical Department.[15] As part of a second generation of women physicians trained in the state, and as a resident of the West, where attitudes were somewhat more favorable to women doctors, Esther had some advantages. But she also encountered many gendered barriers, obstacles that she tried to meet with constructive resistance.

Esther Clayson dreamed of a medical education but was a member of a working-class family. When Esther and her family returned to Portland in the summer of 1888, Annie Clayson was forty-three years old. She did not list herself as a dressmaker in the *Portland City Directory* during this period, but she may have gained clients by reputation rather than advertising. The work required by her large household probably consumed most of her time, and the wages earned by Esther and her three brothers—Ted was twenty-three, Will twenty, and Fred sixteen—would have been important contributions. Ted was a driver for the Union Carriage and Baggage Transfer Company; Will, Esther, and Fred worked as clerks in various retail stores. They lived together in a rented residence at 247 6th Street for the first years. After Ted moved out on his own in 1891, the family moved two doors down the street, to 241 6th.[16]

When Esther decided to apply for medical studies, her family opposed the idea. They "had little confidence in the outcome and thought I had undertaken too big a job."[17] Admission to the UOMD for the three-year course of study required the equivalent of a high school education, a one-time matriculation fee of $5, $120 in tuition for one full-year term, and $10 for a demonstrator's ticket proving attendance for each course.[18] Esther's young lifetime of reading, years at Seabeck's grammar school, and tutoring by the "guests of honor" at her family's hotels enabled her to pass the entrance examination. After paying sixty dollars, half the tuition for her first year, she matriculated.[19] But her money ran out after the first year, and in April 1891 she returned to department store work. It was a frustrating interruption, and the loss of her connection to her class was "heart-breaking." But, as she later remembered, "there was no

Lipman, Wolfe, and Company, Portland, 1892. From *The Oregonian Souvenir, 1850–1892: Portland, Oregon, October 1st, 1892* (Portland: Lewis & Dryden, 1892), 57.

THE DEKUM BLOCK.

help for it. There were no scholarships to be won, and eighteen months behind hosiery and underwear counters was the price of my last two terms at the Oregon Medical School." Esther returned to department store work at Lipman, Wolfe, and Company and eventually headed the women's hosiery department at Portland's Olds and King before returning to full-time studies in October 1892. The year away meant surrendering the honor of being the first woman to graduate from the UOMD to her classmate Helena Scammon.[20]

Clayson was part of a growing corps of some 60,000 women working in department stores in cities across the nation in the early 1890s. Department store managers created an environment of spectacle, convenience, and, above all, plentiful goods for patrons, especially for women, who shopped with their friends and lingered in elegant lounges, lavatories, and tea rooms. By 1890 department stores encompassed three intertwined worlds: for store managers, a world of large profits but administrative woes; for customers, a world of elegance but also the "trials of dealing with clerks"; and for saleswomen, a world of work, in which routines were "spiced by a few dazzling possibilities for advancement" and "low wages, overwork, and persistent class-based conflict with customers" often had to be endured.[21] Departments were generally segregated by sex, and women workers often joined forces against the male "floorwalkers" who were their direct supervisors.[22]

Lipman and Wolfe and Olds and King were in a period of expansion in Portland at the time that Esther was working. Olds and King moved and expanded three times from 1878 to 1891.[23] Esther's starting wage at Lipman and Wolfe was twenty dollars per month, plus premiums or P.M.s—bonuses from five to fifty cents earned for selling "tag ends of old stock and undesirable goods." Esther was good at moving this stale merchandise. Any "taint of commercialism which may have appeared in my long professional life," she suggested sardonically, "should be attributed to the demoralizing influence of those P.M.'s." Her wages plus premiums amounted to some $300 per year when she started work and rose to $400 in her final months before returning to medical school. This compared to average annual earnings of $486 for all workers in US industries in 1890, excluding farming. Clerical workers (usually male) averaged $848 per year, and public school teachers (usually female) averaged $256.[24]

When medical school was not in session, students often studied with a physician preceptor. During her eighteen months away from the classroom, Esther studied with Dr. Frank Blaney Eaton, an eye, ear, nose, and throat specialist on the faculty at UOMD.[25] She originally consulted Eaton because she was experiencing eye strain and then persuaded him to take her on as a student so that she could build a stronger foundation in chemistry, physiology, and anatomy. Each day she left her hosiery counter at eleven, took fifteen minutes for a quick lunch in the women's restroom, and then hurried to Eaton's office for her lessons, returning to work within her hour lunch break. Eaton was no feminist but agreed to be her preceptor. Perhaps, Esther later mused, it was because he saw promise in the "girl born in the backwoods who emerged from behind a drygoods counter every day with a compend of *Gray's Anatomy* and a few dry bones of the human skeleton concealed about her person." She was a Pygmalion who "blossomed as the rose," and as she succeeded, she became a "sharp instrument to prod" the young male students at UOMD who had "all sorts of educational advantages."[26]

Throughout her life, Esther Lovejoy told the story of her department store days as a way to emphasize her working-class roots and her early credentials in the battle between workers and those who had power over them. She also underscored her ongoing constructive resistance to unjust and arbitrary authority. Her experience also symbolized the rite of passage from adolescence to adulthood and from the nonmedical world into her chosen profession.

The villain of the drama was the "hateful" floorwalker, Esther's immediate supervisor, who represented all the naysayers about women's potential for success in education and the professional world. Esther's supervisor told her to give up on her dream of becoming a doctor, warning that she would "never get through" medical school, and that even if she did, she "would be no good as a doctor." Trapped at a counter while her medical school classmates were getting a year ahead of her, Esther vowed that she would "get out from under his thumb." When she became a doctor, she declared, "all floorwalkers would bow politely when I came in" and "no saleslady or salesgentleman would ever be able to sell me a P.M."[27]

When work was slow Esther brought out her *Gray's Anatomy* and the box of bone specimens she kept under the counter to prepare for her sessions with Eaton. Her staunch ally at the store was an Irish immigrant who had belonged to the Fenian Brotherhood and now worked in the men's department. He praised her for her "spunk," and gave a "warning cough" whenever the floorwalker loomed nearby. At once Esther would heed his call, hide her book, and get "busy dusting and arranging the stock."[28]

The "showdown" came "one quiet morning." Esther was "standing behind a screen of lingerie studying the scapula with a genuine specimen lying beside my open book," when she "became aware of a sinister presence. Somebody must have tattled, for the [floorwalker] had slipped in behind the counter on the opposite side of the central row of shelves and rounding the rear end, was standing beside me." He was "shocked" to find "a dead man's bones in the Ladies' Underwear!" He had suspected for some time that she had been "stealing time" from management by studying at work, but "this—this, pointing to my precious casket, was conduct unbecoming a saleslady." He told her that she had a week to "choose between a profession for which women were totally unfitted," meaning medicine, and her job at the department store. Instead, with the help of her Fenian supporter, Esther secured a new position at the Olds and King hosiery department for higher pay, working until her return to medical studies in the fall of 1892.[29]

With her hard-won earnings deposited at the Portland Savings Bank, Esther returned to her studies, confident that she could make ends meet for the next two years, until graduation. But in the spring of 1893 the nation fell into a severe economic depression; a crash of the stock market that May was followed by bank failures, businesses collapsing, and rising unemployment. Farm prices fell, and some 8,000 businesses, including major railroads such as the Northern Pacific and the Union Pacific, went bankrupt. Seven banks in the city closed, including Esther's Portland Savings Bank, as over 600 financial institutions failed nationwide.[30]

The far-reaching depression and the bank closure threatened to destroy Esther's dream of a medical degree, and "it looked as though I was doomed to be a saleslady for life." But she was able to get eighty cents on the dollar for her Portland Savings Bank certificates, and so "cashed in immediately and hid my school money under my bed, where it was comparatively safe." The experience contributed to her continuing concerns about finances and the misuse of power, and her skepticism about those in charge. "Those who believed in the management of the Portland Savings Bank and its securities paid in full for their faith," she asserted. Later, when she was city health officer in Portland, she learned that a stoker in the city crematory found the "last remains of a wicked capitalist partly responsible for wrecking the Portland Savings Bank" in front of him. The stoker had lost money with the bank failure, and "instead of placing the ashes of this bank wrecker reverently in the golden urn . . . the long-suffering stoker threw them down the sewer." The incident "supports the theory that justice will be done and virtue triumph in the end," Esther insisted.[31]

As a working-class woman, how did Esther Clayson compare to other female medical students of her day? Most female medical students in the United States, like their male counterparts of this period, were from middle- and upper-middle-class families. Many also had a father, a brother, or an uncle who was a physician, or were part of reform-minded, activist families or families of some education.[32] This was certainly true for most of the women physicians with whom Esther would work in the Medical Women's National Association and in other groups during and after the First World War. Bertha Van Hoosen (University of Michigan 1888), Rosalie Slaughter Morton (Woman's Medical College of Pennsylvania 1897), Emily Dunning Barringer (Cornell 1897), Mary Elizabeth Bates (Woman's Hospital Medical College Chicago 1881), and Marion

Craig Potter (University of Michigan 1884) were all from financially well-off families, although Van Hoosen's parents would not finance her medical school education after her undergraduate degree.[33] These leading women physicians had very different backgrounds and foundations from Esther's.

Yet Mary Putnam Jacobi (Female [later Woman's] Medical College of Pennsylvania 1864), daughter of publisher George Putnam and part of an educated and middle-class family, wrote for publication and taught school to help support her family "during a rocky period in the publishing business" before pursuing her own medical education. Writing in 1891 as one of the most eminent women physicians of her time, Jacobi saw many women for whom medical school was a struggle. "To work their way through the prescribed term of studies, they have resorted to innumerable devices—taught school, edited newspapers, nursed sick people, given massage, worked till they could scrape a few dollars together, expended that in study—then stepped aside to earn more."[34] Add department store work, and Jacobi was describing Esther Clayson precisely. In her analysis of women medical students in late-nineteenth-century Washington, DC, Gloria Moldow found that many women combined medical school with full-time employment. In 1894, National University Medical College administrators estimated that half of their female students were employed, and "the majority as clerks or teachers." The District of Columbia's Columbian Medical School's statistics were similar.[35]

Esther Clayson's female colleagues at Oregon's two medical schools also came to their studies from varied economic circumstances. Belle Schmeer (Willamette University Medical Department 1886), who passed by the fifteen-year-old Esther's East Portland hotel on the way to her classes at Willamette, was the wife of a confectioner.[36] Callie Brown Charlton (Willamette University Medical Department 1879), widowed in 1872 at twenty-two with a sixteen-month-old daughter, taught school in the Holladay Addition in East Portland to save for tuition and to support her small daughter.[37] Helena Scammon (UOMD 1893) grew up on a farm in Chehalis County, Washington Territory. She attended the UOMD for two years, from 1889 to 1891, and took a year off and returned in 1892–1893 to graduate.[38] Sarah Marquam (UOMD 1890) was the daughter of Philip and Emma Marquam; Philip was a wealthy investor, Portland landowner, and Oregon legislator.[39] Inez DeLashmutt, the daughter of Portland mayor and business magnate Van B. DeLashmutt, attended

UOMD for one term in 1892–1893. That year she "came to school every morning in a carriage with a coachman driving a fine pair of prancing horses," the kind of "turnout," Esther recalled, "used on ceremonial occasions by the mayors of large cities in England." Van DeLashmutt lost a fortune in the 1893 crash, and his daughter did not return to medical studies. "Down came our amiable schoolmate and her proud horses in the crash, and, medically speaking, she never rose again."[40]

As Esther made her difficult way through the economic challenges of medical school, she was also being initiated into the life of a female medical student. She was entering a specific male world that a first generation of women students had passed through and influenced but that continued to be an arena of masculinity that many male physicians wished to defend against women competitors. From 1890 to 1894 at the University of Oregon Medical Department, women made up 15 to 17 percent of the student body.[41] The institution was growing and becoming better equipped for advanced instruction. When Esther returned to the UOMD in the fall 1892 term, the school was just moving to its new location at 23rd and Lovejoy Streets. The *Annual Announcement* noted that the three-story building "is a model of convenience, being furnished with all the aids to medical education which modern advancement requires. Laboratories for chemical, bacteriological, and other work are provided, and arrangements made for special attention to these important practical departments." The new building was "heated by hot water, and provision made for excellent ventilation." There were lecture rooms on the first and second floors to accommodate more students. And the school was strategically located. The 23rd Street electric car passed "every few minutes," the Good Samaritan Hospital was across the street, and St. Vincent's Hospital was nearby, with its new building under construction on nearby Hoyt Street, even closer to the school.[42]

Esther Clayson's medical education was a combination of theory, classroom observation and dissection, and practical experience with patients. During these years, the UOMD offered a wide range of course work in surgery, chemistry and toxicology, the theory and practice of medicine, anatomy, *materia medica* (the study of medicines) and therapeutics, bacteriology, histology, obstetrics, gynecology, physiology, psychological medicine ("diseases of the mind"), ophthalmology, genitourinary diseases, diseases of children, dermatology and hygiene, medical jurisprudence, pathology, and diseases of the ear, throat, and nose. Department faculty

University of Oregon Medical Department at 23rd and Lovejoy Streets, Portland. Reproduced by permission of Oregon Health & Science University Historical Collections & Archives, Portland, Oregon.

members were on the staff of the Good Samaritan and St. Vincent's Hospitals and held clinics at each location three days a week during the term. Hospital clinics provided practical experience for students to assist with the diagnosis and treatment of disease. Students also observed various surgical operations, and a photograph of Clayson in an operating room at St. Vincent's during her student years establishes her presence at just such a teaching event. There was also an outpatient dispensary located at Good Samaritan that gave students "ample opportunity for the study of diseases usually met with in office practice." Emily Loveridge, superintendent of nursing at the Good Samaritan, recalled that the hospital beds of that time "were of straw, whose ticks were washed and filled in between occupants." The maternity ward "had only three beds and a tall hard bed we used for a labor bed, also four cribs and a stove in which we burned wood and heated water on its flat top. Building up a good fire in it when we bathed the babies, we nearly roasted out the mothers."[43]

Esther Clayson (at far right) observing an operation at St. Vincent's Hospital, Portland, as a student, ca. 1890–94. Reproduced by permission of Oregon Health & Science University Historical Collections & Archives, Portland, Oregon.

Medical students took a three-year course, with four accompanying years of study under a medical preceptor. To graduate they had to be "of good moral character" and be at least twenty-one years old. They had to "attend at least two courses of Practical Anatomy and Clinical Instruction" and pass examinations in anatomy, surgery, physiology, chemistry, *materia medica* and therapeutics, obstetrics, practice of medicine, and gynecology, with additional coursework assigned by faculty members. Students had to present their demonstrator's tickets used to gain admittance to lectures or other evidence of attendance.[44]

Candidates for UOMD graduation also had to present "satisfactory evidence of having dissected the entire cadaver."[45] Esther Clayson joined thousands of medical students for whom the anatomy course and dissecting table were boundaries that separated medical professionals from the rest of the community, a rite of passage that meant more than just memorizing the names and locations of bones, organs, and tissues (whether behind a department store counter or in a classroom). Across the cadaver, medical students had to confront death, disease, and the philosophical and ethical issues with which they would wrestle as physicians. As John Warner and James Edmonson note, this "privileged access to the body marked a social, moral, and emotional boundary crossing" that was part of the "larger, shared story of becoming a doctor."[46] The entire third floor of the new UOMD building was devoted to dissection. Unlike previous women students in Oregon and the nation, who were segregated in this area of study, Esther Clayson experienced dissection and anatomy instruction side by side with her male classmates.

In fictional and in nonfictional accounts, Esther left some record of her own experience with this medical rite of passage. In an undated work of fiction, she recreated the dramatic sights and smells of the dissecting room and underscored the depersonalization of the female body being studied by the male medical students. Here the cadaver of an indigent "Jane Doe" who had died giving birth in the county hospital came before them on the table:

> The "good material" of the obstetrical ward had become the "good material" of the dissecting-room—a rich mine of physiology, anatomy, and pathology to be carefully and patiently worked out. The room was low and ill-ventilated, but the strong fumes of tobacco smoke somewhat mitigated the odor of decomposition. Some of the subjects had been there for weeks and were still being worked upon. . . . The floor was covered with filthy, maggoty saw dust and the walls and ceiling daubed and dotted with pustules of dissected tissue thrown there in a forced spirit of levity. A demonstration was in process and the students were crowded around the subject and teacher. Several members of the class, who had temporarily left their personal work at the different tables, still wore their dissecting robes, while others were perched on high stools with their hats pushed back on their heads and their quiescent pipes or cigarettes in their hands. Every man was absorbed in the work and oblivious to his surroundings.[47]

Years after her own dissecting room days, Esther observed, "Medical students are proverbially prankish. This may be a matter of compensation—an unconscious effort to maintain a normal balance in an abnormal atmosphere." Scholars also suggest that such pranks were often attempts to preserve male solidarity.[48] "Whenever a peddler came around," she recalled, "the students would send him upstairs, where he would suddenly find himself in that ghastly attic with two or three partly dissected cadavers and a group of young ghouls who would stop work and begin sharpening their scalpels." At other times "the boys used to send the peddlers upstairs to me—the lady in the dissecting room. The peddlers would come up and be horrified."[49]

Esther recalled another occasion when an indigent man visited the dissecting room in disguise and challenged the ethics of the medical students. During this man's recent jail sentence, a friend of his had died at the Multnomah County Hospital, alone and in poverty. The newspapers had reported the friend's burial in the public area reserved for the poor, the "potter's field." But this man had heard a rumor that his friend's body had been given to the medical school for dissection. He posed as a broom seller to gain entrance to the dissecting room, and saw that his friend was now a cadaver on the table. He told the medical students who he was and complained about the deception, asking them pointed questions about the use of his friend's body and the false newspaper report. He told them that his friend had entrusted his watch to him before going to the county hospital because he feared one of the doctors might make off with it while he was ill. "And if you'd steal his body, wouldn't you manage to steal his watch if you got the chance?" their visitor asked. The male students were up in arms about the accusation. Esther found the man's questions "hard to answer" but very important. The indigent man brought a "new angle on medical ethics" and social class to the medical students in the dissecting room.[50]

The study of anatomy claimed another prominent part in Esther Clayson's life. The UOMD, she recalled, "produced the best anatomist it was ever my good fortune to meet," her future husband, Emil Pohl. The two started out as classmates, but Pohl graduated in 1893, a year ahead of Clayson. As a senior student, he served as "unofficial demonstrator of anatomy," and the faculty then offered him the official position for the 1893–1894 year. Esther Clayson and Pohl married three weeks after her graduation.[51]

Gender played a significant role in faculty opinions of students and in the options students had for specialization. In the senior year, each student had the chance to "attend and conduct, under proper supervision," one case of childbirth at the hospital clinic at St. Vincent's or at the Good Samaritan. The faculty acknowledged that such "practical knowledge of midwifery" would "prove of great value in their future professional work."[52] Esther understood this well. "Midwifery was the key to family practice, and family practice was my immediate objective."[53] She concentrated on obstetrics and gynecology, while her male colleagues competed for surgical experience. "The boys had the best of it in general surgery because they were usually chosen by the operators to assist in one way or another and the patients were anesthetized." But in obstetrics and gynecology, "the women students found themselves in a preferred position." In these specialties the "patients were wide awake, and with the modesty of the early nineties they resisted the exposure of their persons above the ankles and protested against being 'gaped at and pawed over' by strange young men."[54]

Dean Simeon Josephi lectured on obstetrics, and in keeping with the practice of the day used a leather manikin to simulate a woman in pregnancy and childbirth for students beginning their practical study. Obstetrical manikins had been in use since the eighteenth century, and it appears that Josephi was using a full-body model at UOMD "to demonstrate all kinds of cases." Clayson believed that "only a leather mother and child could have survived the instrumental deliveries of the athletes in our class."[55] As a text, Josephi assigned the 1892 (fourth) edition of William Thompson Lusk's *The Science and Art of Midwifery*, a 712-page compendium exposing students to every possible situation of pregnancy, birth, and early child care, in addition to any and all possible complications, with a host of illustrations and specific therapeutics. Rusk taught his student readers that pregnancy, labor, delivery, and after care were medical and sometimes pathological events that required having a knowledgeable physician in attendance.[56]

Yet Esther saw other possibilities in providing care, beyond merely managing a case, and related them specifically to gendered ideas and roles. Dr. Curtis Strong was professor of gynecology and clinical obstetrics. He and most of the UOMD faculty members were in general practice, and this included obstetrics. In Portland in the 1890s, labor and delivery routinely took place in the patient's home. "Attending physicians were expected to remain on their jobs from the beginning of labor until the mothers were out of danger" and their babies were stable. "Throughout the long hours of a tedious labor, the doctor usually dozed within hearing of the patient's bedroom and judged the progress of the case by the tone and tempo of her screams for help," Esther recalled. But "a woman medical student was a godsend under such circumstances." Staying by the patient as labor progressed, "she hush-hushed the sufferer, assuaging her agony and keeping her quiet by sympathetic attentions and encouraging suggestions until the doctor's services were actually needed." Here was "sympathy" along with the "science," an advantage that Esther believed was hers in this all-important field.[57] Her male teachers found her assistance irreplaceable and gave her many opportunities to assist; this, combined with patient preference for a woman practitioner, was a boost to her plans to engage in family practice. "I wouldn't have exchanged my opportunities in gynecology and obstetrics under the guidance of Dr. Strong for all of the privileges my classmates enjoyed in general surgery and in certain other subjects that were academic to me," she asserted.[58] Esther seems to have found a pragmatic resolution to the gendered nature of medical school training that she encountered.

At the conclusion of her studies on April 2, 1894, Esther Clayson graduated from medical school along with six male classmates. W. L. Buckley was valedictorian and won the Saylor Gold Medal for the highest scores in both "primary and final branches"; he had also served a year as house surgeon at Good Samaritan Hospital, a position not open to women. W. W. Stockwell and A. D. MacKenzie had served as senior students at Good Samaritan and St. Vincent's Hospitals, again an opportunity apparently available to male students only. Of the six male classmates, MacKenzie reported that he was staying in Portland for a year of graduate work as house surgeon at St. Vincent's, Stockwell was headed East for graduate training, and three were returning home to establish private practice: A. S. Cassidy in Australia; Edwin Ross in St. Helens, Oregon; and Buckley in Stockton, California (but perhaps, he said, Portland would call him back). The report did not mention Calvin White's plans, but he remained in Portland to practice. Esther received the Wall Medal, awarded that year for the "best standing in the primary branches" of anatomy, physiology, *materia medica,* and chemistry, demonstrating that she backed up her practical clinical experience with sound classroom accomplishments in science. Yet, the *Medical Sentinel* reported, "Dr. Clayson does not know, as yet, just what she will do."[59]

Esther's uncertainty was most probably due to the fact that the faculty had just refused to appoint her to the internship for which she was qualified. "I worked my own way and graduated from the Medical Department of the University of Oregon with medalic decorations," she later recalled. "The possibility of a woman winning an internship had never occurred to anybody until that awful thing actually happened and then the faculty sat in solemn conclave and decided that women were ineligible for these positions. I received the usual assurances of personal regard—but the internship went to a man." The faculty then changed the wording in the catalogue to read: "Internes would be appointed from the 'eligible' candidates having the highest standing," and "eligible" referred to men only.[60] Esther's Wall Medal and class standing at graduation would certainly have won her an internship if she had been a man.

At the end of the nineteenth and into the twentieth century and beyond, internships and access to hospital training became more and more important for all physicians as medical education and practice increasingly focused on new hospital technologies and processes. Women had gained some acceptance as medical students, but now the male gatekeepers of institutions raised the gendered bar to a new level as women sought these important next steps to professional acceptance.[61] Esther's experience mirrored that of many women as she confronted this next milepost of professional inclusion. Some women followed the nineteenth-century pattern of separate medical education by forming separate hospitals and infirmaries that would give women the opportunity for internship experience. Women physicians and their supporters in San Francisco created the Pacific Hospital for Women and Children in 1875 (later the Women's and Children's Home) to provide internship and staff positions for women physicians. For most of the nineteenth century, this hospital provided the only internship opportunity for women medical students in Western states.[62] During Esther's medical school decade in the 1890s, the San Francisco hospital was one of only eight US hospitals that accepted women for internships on a regular basis. A 1901 nationwide survey found just thirty-one women in medical internships, forty in residencies, and two serving as house surgeons.[63]

Denied the internship for which she qualified, the newly married Esther Pohl took a different approach. She had identified obstetrics as the key to family practice and her ability to make a living as a doctor. Getting one's foot in the door of a household for a delivery could open the way to treating the entire family. Pohl targeted the Volga German community known as Little Russia or Little St. Petersburg in the Albina neighborhood along Union Avenue in East Portland.[64] "Patients do not flock quickly to a young woman starting the practice of medicine in a big city," she later mused, and she was "no exception to the rule." But she had a friend who managed the telephone office in the area, and "to keep awake in the dead of night she used to listen in on the party lines." Late one night the operator overheard a man on the telephone line trying to find a doctor for his wife after two days of labor, and she telephoned Pohl with the information and an address. When Pohl arrived, "The older women in the house, including the midwife, had no confidence" in her as a young, female doctor. But she moved past them and went to the patient, who was too exhausted to continue. Pohl "sterilized her forceps in the kettle on the stove and delivered the baby," a happy conclusion to a difficult labor. Her notoriety spread, and her practice became established in the district.[65]

Pohl used her feminist curiosity to look beyond childbirth and medical issues, and into the lives of the women she treated. In an undated short story she wrote titled "The Luck of Some Women," a "woman doctor in a western city" is called to a household where a young woman is suffering a difficult labor. It is the house of her husband's domineering uncle, Peter Wolfe, the most prominent man in the Russian German immigrant community. The young woman and her husband are devoted to one another but struggling financially. When the woman doctor delivers the baby safely, the midwife refers to the young mother, so obviously loved by her husband: "The luck of some women!" Two years later the doctor is called to assist with a delivery. She finds the "same fair girl she had attended on that stormy night two years before, and instead of her handsome young husband, Peter Wolfe is trying to comfort her." Wolfe's first wife and his nephew have died in circumstances that suggest that he murdered them both and is now married to his nephew's wife. Now Wolfe wants his new bride to have the best money can buy and has built a new house for her. The woman doctor notes that her patient recoils from Wolfe, "When his hand touched her hair she squirmed away in more than physical pain." As she delivers the woman's second child, the doctor realizes that violence has created this situation and that the young woman is now living in a prison. The story concludes with the ironic comments of the midwife washing the baby: "'What is this for a strong boy!' she exclaimed enthusiastically and complicitly. And, in a lower tone: 'Such a fine house! Such a good man with money! The luck of some women.'"[66]

In the lean years of her early career, Pohl used a bicycle to get to her house calls and equipped it specially "for carrying an obstetrical case." Her friend Nan Strandborg recalled that Pohl was among many women doctors who cycled. "I have retold, many times, how in the early days you and the other women doctors carried on their obstetric profession riding bicycles to and from" cases, "and how you used to stop for rest and coffee at the little shop that kept open nights, on your way home from ushering another little pilgrim into the world in the 'wee small hours.'"[67]

Pohl worked to establish her practice in the context of a lively and competitive medical marketplace in Portland. By training at the UOMD, she had entered the "regular" medical establishment. Other Portland and Oregon physicians were practitioners of alternative systems, including homeopathy, eclectic medicine, and physiomedical medicine. Homeopathy "came into considerable favor, especially in Portland," in the late nineteenth century.[68] There were no medical schools in the state that represented these alternative systems, but Oregon homeopaths organized a state society in 1876 that represented an active group of men and women practitioners in the 1890s and beyond. Eclectics formed an Oregon state society in 1890.[69] Of the 641 licensed Oregon physicians in 1898, 7 percent were homeopathic, 6 percent eclectic, and 87 percent regulars.[70] Chinese American physicians provided still another medical system in the city; six had offices in Portland's Chinatown from 1890 to 1895.[71] In 1890 the 4,539 Chinese American residents in Portland made up almost 10 percent of the city's population.[72] And Portlanders outside the Chinese American community may have selected a Chinese American doctor because they offered less-invasive treatments for many conditions, including sexually transmitted diseases, and because they provided abortifacients.[73] Pohl was also in direct competition with midwives. Eleven women listed their services in midwifery in the *Portland City Directory* in 1894, and more were undoubtedly in local practice. By 1900 over half of the babies born in the United States were still delivered by a midwife.[74] And an array of products and practitioners available in the popular medical marketplace comprised still another medical system of patent and self-help medicine. Many of these products or regimens targeted venereal disease, impotence in men, and the early stages of unwanted pregnancy or gynecological problems in women.[75]

Historian Regina Morantz-Sanchez has explored the power of patient choice in the late-nineteenth-century medical marketplace and discovered what she terms "female patient agency." Her analysis of Brooklyn, New York, in that time period reveals that the city's middle-class women did not depend on doctors alone for information about their health. They "kept carefully abreast of developments in gynecology . . . [and] sought the advice of numerous practitioners." Morantz-Sanchez concludes, "If they deemed treatment ineffective, they readily moved on, demonstrating no enduring loyalty to a specific doctor or a particular mode of therapy."[76] Portland, with its many varieties of systems and therapeutics, offered a similar medical marketplace. And because Esther Pohl began her practice in the middle of a severe economic depression, she may have faced particularly strong competition from other practitioners, including midwives, who were more affordable to potential clients.

To get experience and enhance her standing in this marketplace, in 1897 Pohl enrolled at the West Chicago Post-Graduate School and Polyclinic and at the Chicago Clinical School for postgraduate training.[77] She also traveled to Vienna in 1904 and again in 1910 for graduate clinical work, joining some ten thousand other US physicians who trained there from 1870 to 1914, before extensive postgraduate residencies were available in the United States.[78] During her 1904 studies Pohl made a pilgrimage to visit Elizabeth Blackwell, the first woman medical school graduate in the United States, who was then living in Hastings, East Sussex, England. She also traveled to Jerusalem, Anatolia, and Egypt, and wrote about her travels for the *Oregon Journal* newspaper, increasing her notoriety back home.[79] With the additional professional gloss of clinical study in Vienna, Pohl noted that after 1904, "People in better circumstances in town came to me."[80] She purchased a red Cadillac for her professional use, and believed that she was "the only woman in Portland driving a car regularly on her daily work" at the time. The Cadillac "had the habit of breaking down on the street car tracks, to the delight of the men in the trolley, who would then get out with the conductor to inspect the auto." Then "they would push the car over the bridge in a nice, friendly way."[81] Not surprisingly, other physicians traveling to cases at all hours were also prominent among the early automobile owners in the city.[82]

Esther Pohl developed her early medical practice in the context of the Progressive Era flowering of city-level reform.[83] And in these years between 1890 and the First World War, women physicians across the nation were active "far out of proportion to their actual numbers" in what Regina Morantz-Sanchez characterizes as "social medicine."[84]

Women physicians such as Pohl worked to establish public health programs, industrial medicine, settlement houses, and other Progressive Era structural and legislative reforms associated with healthy cities, schools, and communities in the industrializing nation. This was part of the broader social activism, in which many women were engaged, to organize labor unions and improve communities through club work and civic voluntarism, to sponsor civil rights and antiviolence measures, and to campaign for woman suffrage.[85]

Women physicians in Portland joined other reformers to create what Daphne Spain has characterized as "redemptive places" in the city.[86] In the fall of 1896, two Portland physicians, Eliza Ingalls and Mary Leonard, established a free medical dispensary in association with the "noon rest" facility for working women sponsored by the Multnomah County Woman's Christian Temperance Union.[87] Female physicians and nurses assisted other Portland women with the work of charitable organizations such as the People's Institute settlement house, established in 1904; the Neighborhood House, established by the Portland branch of the Council of Jewish Women in 1905; and the Women's Union.[88] The Sisters of Mercy administered the Mercy Home, "founded in 1896 as a home for young ladies clerking in stores or offices," and for those working as nurses and in other occupations in Portland. The nurses of the Sisters of Mercy also managed the St. Joseph's Home for the Aged, a charity that had eighty residents in 1907. By 1907 the city also had a baby home, the Boys' and Girls' Aid Society, the children's home administered by the Ladies' Relief Society of Portland, the Flower Mission and Day Nursery, the Salvation Army Rescue Home, and the Patton Home for the Aged.[89] African American women engaged in nursing on a voluntary basis within the network of Portland's separate African American fraternal organizations, including the Masons and the Oddfellows.[90]

Pohl and other women physicians volunteered as medical staff at the Portland branch of the Florence Crittenton Refuge Home, an institution for unwed mothers. In December 1903 Pohl and her colleagues Mae H. Whitney Cardwell and Emma J. Welty were chosen as staff physicians by the Crittenton board of managers, with Pohl as chair.[91] Within the month the three physicians had plans for a maternity room for labor and delivery so that the young women could give birth at the home rather than at the hospital.[92] Two years later, Pohl continued to direct an enlarged medical staff.[93] Katherine Aiken has noted that the preference for women physicians in the Crittenton network, an official policy in the Portland home, stemmed from the belief among administrators and staff that "women physicians were more sympathetic to unmarried mothers than their male counterparts" and that "women patients maintained greater control over their own health care when women physicians attended them." This maternalist view cast the woman physician in the "role of both mother and doctor" for young women away from home.[94]

As an active member of the Portland Woman's Club from her induction in 1899, Pohl contributed her medical expertise to the club's activist and educational programs. She presented lectures such as "The Advancement of Surgery in the Nineteenth Century" and "The Indigent Child." And she chaired the club's committee on public health and served on that committee for a number of years.[95]

Pohl was also a leader of the Portland Medical Club, an all-female professional and social association that promoted Progressive Era social medicine in Portland. Four women doctors, Helena J. Price, Florence King, Viola M. Coe, and Mae H. Whitney (later Cardwell), organized the club in 1891. It was the first all-female medical society in the West, the third in the nation for "regular" women practitioners, and the first in a wave of all-female medical associations in the 1890s.[96] Portland Medical Club members presented papers and cases for discussion to help them develop skills and confidence in framing and presenting their own work. They also gained confidence by posing questions as members of the audience. The women shared valuable information and gained the kind of practice and support necessary to be ready to participate on equal terms with men in other medical society meetings.[97] Their separatism was a strategy with a dual purpose: to create an all-female group to provide support and networking, and to gain the skills necessary to compete with male colleagues and succeed in established medical societies.[98] As Morantz-Sanchez notes, women's medical associations gave a "sought-after fellowship, while simultaneously training their members in the unwritten 'rules' of professionalism."[99]

Portland Medical Club membership waned in the mid-1890s, but the group was reactivated in July 1900. Esther Pohl participated in this revived organization after 1900 and became its president in 1905. That year fifty-four women physicians comprised 8 percent of Oregon's licensed physicians. Two-thirds of them, including Pohl, were in Portland.[100] The society offered strong support and professional training for the city's women physicians and became a vehicle for members to partici-pate in Progressive Era social medicine. Over the years, Pohl presented papers on smallpox, abortion, difficult labor cases, spinal meningitis, and a variety of unspecified clinical cases, and she participated in dis-cussions of the papers and cases of her colleagues. Club members took action in various fields of social medicine. Pohl became part of a commit-tee to investigate school health and hygiene, and promoted successful club resolutions supporting meat inspection and opposing "expectora-tion in the streets" as a means of controlling tuberculosis.[101] Pohl and the group were using their all-female society to gain important professional experience and to begin to wield political clout in community and public health affairs.

As she worked to become a woman physician, Esther Pohl also prac-ticed constructive resistance. Well-paying and enjoyable work and wages that she controlled were key goals formed during her Seabeck and Clack-amas farm years, and she found ways to build a pragmatic career given the gendered constraints she encountered. She also insisted on keeping her career after her marriage. And, with her colleagues, she built sepa-rate women's institutions to provide a platform for professional develop-ment while developing Progressive Era social medicine in the Portland community.

CHAPTER 3

Golden Hopes for Family and Career

AT her graduation ceremony on April 2, 1894, Esther later recalled, "The six young men had new suits, and I was arrayed in my wedding dress. A few weeks later I was married, and that dress served for both occasions."[1] The dress is a particularly apt symbol of that juncture in Esther Pohl's life. It underscored the difference between the path-breaking woman medical student and her six male colleagues that presented themselves in their new suits at graduation. The dress also reminds us that she was not then someone who had the financial resources to afford different ensembles for her graduation and for her wedding. And the proximity of the two events and the use of the same dress for both suggest the ways that career, medicine, marriage, and family were intertwined in the next steps in her life.

Medical school brought Esther Clayson and Emil Pohl together. Emil was born in Kewaunee, Wisconsin, on December 31, 1870, the third son of Annie Hubacek, born in Prague, and Wenzel Rudolph Pohl of Vienna. In Kewaunee, Wenzel worked as a saloonkeeper, Annie kept house, and Emil and his brothers Rudolph and Albert attended local schools.[2] Like Esther, Emil had a wealthy uncle, and the family looked westward to Portland, Oregon, where Wenzel's brother Albert had a successful medical practice and extensive real estate holdings. Dr. Albert Pohl was an early leader in homeopathic medicine in Oregon. He established his practice in 1848 and was one of the founders of the Oregon State Homeopathic Medical Society in 1876.[3] His work and investments made him wealthy and influential:

Esther Clayson at graduation from the University of Oregon Medical Department, April 1894. Reproduced by permission of Oregon Health & Science University Historical Collections & Archives, Portland, Oregon.

by the 1880s he owned more than an entire block in the Caruthers' Addition of Portland, with an estate worth $35,000, and in 1887 stockholders elected him as a director of the Portland National Bank.[4]

Emil and his family migrated to Portland in stages in 1886 and 1887. After about a year, Emil's father returned to Kewaunee, while Emil, his mother, and his brother Rudolph remained, the young Emil clerking for Edward Dekum and Company, a firm that sold books and stationery in the city.[5] In September 1889 Albert Pohl died, leaving his considerable estate to be shared by his brother Wenzel and sister Johanna, with generous legacies for his two Portland nephews. Nineteen-year-old Emil received $3,000, and Rudolph, thirty-two, received $5,000.[6]

Albert Pohl's financial legacy and example as a successful physician were probably both key factors in Emil's choice to enter the University

Esther Pohl, MD. Repro-
duced by permission of
Oregon Health & Science
University Historical Collec-
tions & Archives, Portland,
Oregon.

of Oregon Medical Department in the fall of 1890. The family had deep
medical roots. Emil's family, Esther later wrote, "had been connected
with the history of medicine in Central Europe for generations," and
the *Oregon Journal* reported that Emil was "descended from a family of
distinguished physicians."[7] As a medical student Emil excelled, particularly in the study of anatomy and in clinical work. In April 1893 he was
one of six UOMD graduates (including the first woman graduate, Helena
Scammon), and he received the Wall Medal for the "best report in clinics"
among the students that year.[8] Esther later described him as "a natural
scientist . . . a fine-fingered technician with patient and uncompromis-
ing fidelity to the job." In his final year as a student, he was the school's
unofficial demonstrator of anatomy, and after his graduation the faculty appointed him to the official position, which involved facilitating
the acquisition of bodies, preparing them for dissection, and supervis-
ing students in the dissection room.[9] That year Emil also entered a brief
medical partnership in East Portland with DeWitt M. LaMoree, MD, a

Emil Pohl, MD. Reproduced by permission of Oregon Health & Science University Historical Collections & Archives, Portland, Oregon.

physician who may have been an associate of his uncle Albert in homeopathic practice.[10]

Emil and Esther both entered the University of Oregon Medical Department in 1890, yet because Esther took a year off to work, postponing her own graduation by a year, their relationship changed from that of classmates to that of staff member and student. Esther later humorously characterized the formation of their relationship in terms of the "extracurricular opportunities" in a coeducational medical school. It is not clear when Emil and Esther began to plan for marriage, but they were engaged before her graduation on April 2, 1894. They married on April 25, 1894, at Esther's home at 241 6th Avenue in Portland, with family and friends in attendance.[11]

Esther and Emil were not alone; doctors often married other doctors at this time, both in Oregon and in the nation. Sarah Marquam married her Willamette University Medical Department classmate Charles E. Hill soon after their 1890 graduation; Marie Miller married Octave Goffin after their UOMD graduation in 1901, and together they practiced in Sherman, Oregon. Belle Schmeer divorced her first husband and later married her 1886 WUMD classmate Henry McDonald, and the two practiced in New York.[12] Mary Putnam married pediatrician Abraham Jacobi in 1873. Emily Dunning married Dr. Benjamin Barringer the day after she completed her residency at the Gouverneur Hospital in New York in 1904.[13]

There were many women physicians in this period who embraced same-sex relationships, and others who were single, but Regina Morantz-Sanchez notes that "the marriage rate for women physicians was disproportionately high in the nineteenth and twentieth centuries, until other professions caught up in the 1940s." Her research demonstrates that "between one-fifth and one-third of women physicians married in the nineteenth century," with a marriage rate "twice that of all employed women and four times the rate among professional women" by 1900, just at the time that Esther and Emil wed. Moreover, "a significant number of them married men who were themselves doctors." Morantz-Sanchez suggests that this was due in part to the ability of women physicians to work from their homes and be self-employed, "perhaps combining practice with a physician-husband," and that there were "neither social nor legal proscriptions against the married woman physician as there were, for example, for teachers." Women physicians were also "much less likely to abandon their work once they married."[14] Esther was entering a partnership that offered the possibility of continuing her own work and maintaining her independence, a vital goal formed in her Seabeck and Clackamas farm years.

During Emil's final months of medical school, his father Wenzel died in Wisconsin. He left his estate, some of which was prime Portland property recently inherited from his wealthy brother Albert, to be divided among his wife Anna, sons Emil and Rudolph, and daughter Anna Jordan.[15] Emil sold some of these Portland lots, and in stable financial times this inheritance, added to the recent bequest from his Uncle Albert, would have provided him with a strong foundation to begin his practice and married life with Esther.[16] But in the mid-1890s the nation entered one of the worst economic depressions in its history. As Esther later recalled, the couple was young, and after their marriage believed that "life was perfect. [Emil] had inherited a small fortune, and [we] could afford to wait for practice, but in the cleanup following the Great Depression, this was wiped out."[17] For the rest of their marriage, even after the return of financial security, the two would try to reconcile love, hope, economic opportunity, professional dreams, and reality in a complex relationship.

Emil was restless in these difficult financial times as he tried to find a secure path forward. He left his medical partnership with DeWitt LaMoree and he and Esther established a joint practice with an office in their East Portland home, perhaps as a way to economize. He attended postgraduate clinics in surgery, gynecology, and dermatology at the Chicago Polyclinic in the spring of 1896. That fall he took a position as house surgeon at the Slocan Hospital in New Denver, British Columbia, and became licensed to practice there. The hospital was funded by subscriptions from surrounding mines, and physicians also worked in outlying camp dispensaries treating simpler cases and preparing the more serious cases for transport to New Denver.[18] By the spring of 1897 Emil was back in Portland.[19]

That summer Emil joined Portland's rush into "gold fever" and departed for Skagway, Alaska. The discovery of gold in the Klondike country in 1897 was a magnet for many seeking their fortunes, a new chance for those whom the depression of the 1890s had battered down, and an irresistible lure for adventure and opportunity. With some combination of these motivations, Emil Pohl joined Esther's brother Fred Clayson to head for the gold fields. They were passengers on Portland's first ship to the Klondike region, on the initial voyage of the Oregon Railroad and Navigation Company steamship *George W. Elder* to Skagway, Alaska, on July 30, 1897. They were in company with some 400 other "eager gold-smitten souls," including six women, and some 130 horses, dozens of dogs, and 450 tons of freight. Many hopeful adventurers rounded up 2,000 pounds of supplies each to take with them. Esther was probably among the hundreds assembled at the dock to see them off. "No such crowd ever gathered before at a Portland dock to Godspeed voyagers," the excited *Oregonian* reporter observed, "and there was cause, for surely no such cargo of golden hopes ever sailed from this port."[20]

The Klondike gold rush shifted the center of gravity of Esther's family from Portland to Skagway and beyond for many years. Esther's brother Will was a passenger on the third voyage of the *George W. Elder* and arrived in Skagway in September 1897, bringing "a huge cargo of merchandise, including all of the shoes that could be bought in Portland" with him. He joined his brother Fred in business in the F. H. Clayson and

Esther (left) and her sisters Charlotte (center) and Annie May (right) in an undated photograph. Courtesy of Frankovic Family.

Company store.[21] Esther's mother Annie joined them in October 1897, and Esther's two sisters, Annie May, fifteen, and Charlotte, thirteen, arrived that December. Over the next several years, Annie May taught school, and Charlotte attended school there.[22] Fred built the first new house in the settlement and, after the arrival of other family members, left them "holding the fort at Skaguay while he went over the top on the snow trail by way of the Chilkoot Pass" to the gold fields to trade.[23] The family arrived at a time when other women and families were also beginning to join men, signaling what Catherine Holder Spude has called "the transition from ephemeral camp to established community." By 1900, 23 percent of Euro Americans in Skagway were women over twenty-one, and dependent children made up 16 percent of the population.[24]

As retailers, the Claysons participated in a transnational exchange of food and supplies that, as Kathryn Morse demonstrates, linked the industrializing world with the resources of Alaska and the Yukon, transforming them forever.[25] From the time of her brother's arrival, Esther later recalled, "Fred Clayson was a trader as well as a miner and a visionary."[26] He was the first merchant to come from Skagway to Dawson in the Yukon in the early spring, and eager men paid him top prices for food and supplies. He was also the last trader to leave Dawson in the fall, allowing him to accurately assess what would be needed the next spring. F. H. Clayson and Company became part of the trading networks linking Alaska and the Yukon with Seattle and Portland.[27] By the fall of 1899, Esther estimated that Fred had accumulated over $40,000, a substantial and quickly won fortune.[28]

Esther joined Emil and her family in Skagway in the spring of 1898 following her postgraduate clinical work in Chicago. She recalled, "A few log houses and frame buildings had been hastily constructed at Skagway, where the temperature was low and the wind cold and penetrating." In addition to mining and business offices, "there were saloons with dance halls, gambling, and other sex service, offset by one church with a big Yukon stove which radiated warmth and kept the place full of men weekdays as well as Sundays." But that spring, Esther, her mother, and her sisters were still in a minority in the district. "The families of some of the businessmen at Skagway were arriving on every boat from the South, but there were very few women among the thousands of men camped in tents along the trail."[29]

Whatever Emil's intentions for business and mining in this transnational region that spanned Alaska, British Columbia, and the Yukon, he was also prepared to practice medicine. In addition to his Oregon and British Columbia credentials, Emil also obtained a medical license in the Northwest Territories in February 1898. Alaska had no licensing requirements, but passing these other examinations meant that he could practice in the locations where physicians who were only licensed in the United States could not.[30] There is no evidence that Esther had similar credentials, and the fact that she kept all of her other licenses and diplomas suggests that she did not seek them. It would appear that she was not yet certain about her professional medical future outside of Portland.

A cerebrospinal meningitis epidemic enveloped Skagway that spring, with cases spreading to nearby Dyea and "all along the trail to Lake Bennett, a distance of forty miles from Skagway."[31] Esther recalled that the first cases of those who contracted the disease died within days. "At that time and place there was no serum or specific drug to treat this disease," she noted, "and no trained nurses to care for the patients." The only course of action was isolation and intensive care. Presbyterian minister Robert McCahon Dickey took the lead in the emergency. "Funds were raised and a log-stable built for mules was converted into a hospital for meningitis cases." The community provided solid support. "Even the notorious character Jefferson (Soapy) Smith," Esther recalled, "who was afterward killed by the leader of a vigilance committee appointed to clean up the town contributed to the support of that hospital." Esther and Emil provided medical care until the epidemic passed.[32] "At first we lost every case," she remembered, "but soon we were saving about half of them."[33] In their accounts of the epidemic, neither Esther nor Emil mention Native Alaskans specifically, but disease epidemics took a devastating toll on indigenous peoples during and after the gold rush. Yukon and Alaskan tribal communities had been severely affected by diseases to which they had no historical immunity that were brought by Europeans and Americans during the period of the fur trade. Now Native Alaskans and Yukon peoples worked as packers and provided food and provisions, placing them in direct danger as eager gold seekers brought new diseases in their wake.[34]

Esther returned to Portland in June of 1898 with the expectation that she and Emil would live and practice together again in the city "as soon as it was financially possible." She opened an office in the Alisky Building at 3rd and Morrison in downtown Portland, and the next year moved several doors down to share an office with Amelia Ziegler, MD, who came to Portland after her 1898 graduation from the Woman's Medical College in Kansas City, Missouri.[35] Portland birth records indicate that Esther's practice was expanding; she was the physician in charge of twenty Portland births from October 1898 to October 1899.[36]

Meanwhile, Emil was on the move again. He left Skagway for Atlin, British Columbia, in 1899, and then followed a new gold strike in Nome, Alaska, through 1901. He also spent time in Dawson, Yukon, and in Portland. In Nome he became involved directly in medical, political, and community life. In the fall of 1899 there were eleven physicians in that new boom town of several thousand, and by 1901 Emil was one of twenty doctors, including one woman, Dr. Sarah Allen, in a city that had grown to a population of 12,486.[37] Emil advertised his services as a physician in the local newspaper and was a member of the American Medical Society of Nome. In 1899 he helped to battle a typhoid epidemic in the sanitation-challenged town.[38] He served in the Nome senate that year and worked on the ways and means committee of that legislative body, and was a founding member of Nome's Arctic Brotherhood, the male fraternal organization established in many gold rush towns.[39] Esther visited him there in the summer of 1900, surveying the scene from his second-floor office on the main street of the city with "stores, banks, hotels, saloons, gambling dives, and dance halls on the main street with elevated sidewalks on each side and mud knee-deep in the middle."[40] Nome was another boomtown, with women comprising just 10 percent of the city's population.[41]

Esther's brothers, mother, and sisters remained in Skagway, and F. H. Clayson and Company thrived.[42] Fred served a term on the city council, expanding his reputation and influence. The younger brother who had tagged along during their childhood was now a successful adult, and Esther felt a new connection with Fred. She later described him as "a big man at twenty six," dignified, courageous, and resourceful, with "a great ability to do things with his head and his hand." One of her most pleasant memories of him in Skagway, she recalled, "was at the wash-tub washing clothes in full view of people passing and joking him about it." But "he had so much dignity of soul that a little thing like that did not phase him in the slightest."[43]

Fred was murdered for the considerable gold dust and cash he was carrying while on his way by bicycle from Dawson to Skagway on Christmas Day 1899, and his death crushed Esther and her family. It may certainly have contributed to Esther's decision to focus her life and work in Portland rather than in the gold fields. Fred's disappearance that December, along with his traveling companions Lynn Relfe, a Dawson bookkeeper, and Lawrence Olsen, a lineman for the Dominion Telegraph Company, became transnational news in the Yukon, Alaska, Seattle, and Portland. Will Clayson participated in the search for his brother Fred's body and for his killer, and the family hired private detective Philip Maguire to work with the Royal Canadian Mounted Police on the case. Fred's body washed up on a sandbar on May 30, and the bodies of his two companions were found in June, all with gun-shot wounds. Using forensic evidence, including blood, buttons, teeth, trajectory estimates, and Fred's keys, investigators made a compelling case that George O'Brien had robbed and murdered the three in an ambush along the frozen trail. After a twelve-day trial in Dawson in June 1901, a Yukon jury found O'Brien guilty of murder and he was hanged on August 23, 1901.[44]

Fred's death created a family transition and dispersion, and for Esther it seems to have symbolized a sobering line between her youth and her adulthood. In May 1900 the members of the Arctic Brotherhood arranged "one of the largest [funerals] ever held in Skagway." Then Annie Clayson took her son's body back to Portland. Esther noted that "she selected a family plot in Lone Fir Cemetery in the heart of the city with the sweet sounds of life around it. There she planted holly trees (as well as roses), and at Christmas Time [commemorating the day of his murder] the berries are flaming red and warm above them like the jacket she wore when he was a babe at her breast."[45]

Esther's hope that she and her husband would practice together in Portland when finances stabilized continued to be tempered by Emil's Alaskan interests. By 1901 the couple had a Portland residence at 393 Williams Avenue, just east of the Willamette River, across from the center city. Their son Frederick Clayson Pohl, namesake of Esther's beloved brother, was born on December 26, 1901, attended by George F. Wilson, MD, a professor of surgery at the UOMD. Esther worked until the last months of her pregnancy, delivering her last baby of 1901 on Halloween to a couple that lived down the block, at 503 Williams Avenue. She returned to work after Freddie's birth, delivering another baby in June 1902.[46]

After Freddie's arrival, Emil continued to divide his time between Alaska and Portland. He attended patients with cases of cerebrospinal meningitis in Portland in January 1901 and April 1902, but spent the summer of 1902 in Alaska.[47] And for much of 1903 he was in New York City for additional postgraduate work, winning praise for his surgical skills and his knowledge of anatomy.[48]

Esther's mother and sisters returned to Portland from Alaska during this period, a time when Esther would undoubtedly have welcomed assistance with her son in Emil's absence. Esther helped to anchor them as they returned to the city for school and for work. Annie May attended the University of Oregon Medical Department for one term in 1900–1901.[49] Charlotte, the youngest, enrolled at the Portland Business College in 1901.[50] The sisters married Skagway men in a double wedding ceremony on January 27, 1903, in Portland. Annie married William Blanchard, and they soon returned to Skagway, where he resumed his work as a clerk. Charlotte married John Snook, a deputy US marshal in Alaska, and the next year they moved to his home in Salmon, Idaho. By the time of the 1903 wedding, Esther's mother was living with her at the 393 Williams address.[51] With this support system in place, in 1904 Esther made her own personal and professional sojourn in Europe and Palestine to travel and do clinical study in Vienna. Emil was in Portland for at least part of the time Esther was away, and her mother and other family members provided childcare for Freddie.

Writing about these years later in life, Esther noted that motherhood gave her both "a deep satisfaction" and also a "philosophy."[52] With

Esther Pohl and her son, Freddie. Reproduced by permission of Oregon Health & Science University Historical Collections & Archives, Portland, Oregon.

her mother Annie's assistance, Esther combined motherhood with her work and her activism; her philosophy that motherhood was a civic role that should be supported by the community also gave her a particular perspective on her work as physician, suffragist, and public health advocate. The arrangements at 393 Williams Avenue made it possible for her to maintain the work that was so important to her and to raise her son. Esther recalled that when she came home from work, Freddie loved to sit in her lap and help to steer her car to its parking place.[53] When she was appointed Portland city health officer in 1907, Freddie, at five, was a frequent visitor to her city hall office and became a "great favorite" among the staff.[54]

In 1906 Emil moved his Alaska interests to Fairbanks. Esther later recalled that by this time she had "lost faith in gold strikes and stuck to her practice in Portland." To this she added, "Work is a panacea for disappointment and other evils."[55] These comments indicate that she realized that Emil was not likely to live and work full-time in Portland. Her words also suggest that her work and career, built so carefully with the shadow of Seabeck and the Clackamas farm on her mind, helped define who she was and enabled her to move forward in spite of her disappointment about Emil's "golden hopes."

At the close of the summer vacation in early September 1908, Freddie Pohl was at the Oregon coast with his grandmother, Annie Clayson, and with his aunt Charlotte and cousin John Snook, who were visiting from Idaho. Freddie became ill, and the family returned to Portland on Wednesday, September 9. The next day, "his condition became so alarming" that Esther took him to St. Vincent's Hospital. George F. Wilson, the doctor who had delivered Freddie, diagnosed peritonitis and performed surgery to try to relieve the affected area. Freddie died on the morning of September 11. Emil was in Fairbanks and received word by telegram. Esther's "bright chap . . . died as if he had been struck with an ax, in spite of all that could be done for him." She had city bacteriologist Ralph Matson conduct a post mortem, and he found perforation of the bowels, something both he and Esther attributed to "bad milk." Two days later Esther sent a telegram to let Emil know that their son would be "buried today by side his uncle Fred [at Lone Fir Cemetery] god bless you and Comfort."[56] Family and friends were with Esther in Emil's absence. The *Oregon Journal* reported, "A large number of the city employees who knew the little fellow, and of the friends of his parents, attended the funeral."[57] On the day of Freddie's burial, Esther told Emil by telegram, "Am strong shall go to work immediately," another example of the value of work to her in tragic and difficult times.[58]

After Freddie's death, Emil continued to pursue mining and medicine in Alaska, and came to live for part of the year in Portland, where he shared an office with Esther in the Failing Building.[59] By this time he had taken over the practice of a Fairbanks colleague, W. G. Cassels, who had decided to leave Alaska. By 1910 he held varied mining interests, including a copper mine near the Kennecott Bonanza Mine east of Fairbanks, and gold mines on Cleary Creek near Fairbanks and on the Democratic Pup, a tributary of Tenderfoot Creek near Richardson, Alaska.[60]

Esther made at least one trip to Alaska to be with Emil in 1910. Then that summer she traveled to Vienna for additional postgraduate medical study and on her return stopped on the East Coast. She made an extended stay from November 1910 through May 1911 with her sister

Charlotte in Boise, where Charlotte's husband John Snook was the warden and Charlotte the matron of the Idaho State Penitentiary. Esther's woman suffrage colleague and friend Anna Howard Shaw wrote to her there, expressing her hope that she could rest in Boise and heal from the loss of Freddie. "You did go at a very rapid pace here in New York and I thought seemed for you, whom I always considered as a calm and judicious person, rather nervous." "Notwithstanding the fact that time is a wonderful healer," Shaw continued, "there are always scars which never can be healed."[61]

The only surviving correspondence between Esther and Emil are two letters he wrote to her during this period. They reveal Emil at a professional and personal crossroads as well as a relationship complicated by distance, desire, and loss. In the first letter, penned June 20, 1910, Emil noted that he had sent $500 by wire for Esther's trip to Vienna. "I am sorry I will not be with you for I need you more than ever and hope when we meet again we will always be together no matter where I happen to be. For myself I never seem to earn very much." He wrote of his hopes for the copper property and of a brief business trip to Seattle. Esther had apparently asked him to join her in Vienna or at other points in Europe. "About the trip abroad I would far rather go into some new & wild region," he told her. But they did plan to meet in New York. He asked her to leave contact information so that he could find her and wire her about his own situation. "Fairbanks," he told her, "is very dull and this fall it will be absolutely dead." He closed "with a longing hope of seeing you before long" and "much love."[62]

Emil's second letter, written at the end of November 1910, reached Esther in Boise. He was responding to two letters Esther had written expressing her anger that he had not come to New York. "I hardly know how to write you," he began. "You have been looking forward to this trip of yours for years and when I encourage you in taking it, thinking it will please you, you give me the dickings [sic]. I am sure I don't see through it but I guess I am dense." He had wired and written from Seattle, but she said she had not received his communications. "I did not have enough money to travel with you," he wrote. His colleague Dr. Cassels had been considering a return to the Fairbanks practice but had changed his mind, and Emil "felt that the only thing to do after finding out" was to return to Fairbanks, which he did in October. "I would rather be with you, Het, than anything I know of in the world." He would have "settled in some other place" to make a living, he told her, "if it was not for the fact that I don't want to be called a quitter. That's the real reason I have denied myself your company & wanted [for] money."[63]

Emil turned to talk of the future and the challenges to their relationship. Weariness, worry, financial questions, and possibilities all strode through his thick sentences. The copper mine was a "disappointment," but "people that know more than I do about those affairs still think it is good." "Fairbanks is a thing of the past as far as practice goes I am making a living & that's all." Emil wanted to draw his affairs together in the spring or summer and then "go out for good unless some new camp should open up." He discussed finances and timing for Esther's next trip to Fairbanks. If she came in the summer and stayed a month, they could both return to Portland together. "On the other hand, I could send you a little money from time to time and you can have a good time. I don't want you to practice just take it easy." "There is nothing in Fairbanks that you will like, except that we will be together. . . . I will come out this summer and we can go to N.Y. for the winter when I can take up some official line & then settle either in Portland or elsewhere for good." He assured her, "I want to be with you and don't want to be separated from you any more . . . I am as tired of this business as you are and feel like giving up & locating somewhere permanently for I know this is only for a time."[64]

In a postscript Emil wrote, "I had finished your letter several days ago but was called away suddenly." It was "one of the hardest trips I ever had left here at noon one day traveled all night and got back to Fairbanks ten o'clock p.m. next day without any rest. Covering 110 miles with dogs and horses." It was just over a month before his fortieth birthday. "I feel that I am getting old and time to settle down to something that is permanent. I am anxious to get this off by today['s] mail so must close as I still feel all in after my trip. With much love, Your affect. Husband Emil."[65]

Five months later, in April 1911, Emil contracted spinal meningitis and after a three-week illness died at St. Matthew's Hospital in Fairbanks on May 11.[66] Esther was still in Boise and left for Portland as soon as the telegram reached her with the news.[67] The *Fairbanks News-Miner* reported his death in a long obituary, praising Emil as "a skillful physician and surgeon, an upright citizen, a polished gentleman and a generous and sympathetic friend." The Eagles, "of which order the dead was a beloved and esteemed member," held a memorial service. "On that day his friends who are scattered in a score of camps the territory over, will pause for a moment to pay their tribute of respect to this ardent lover of the Northland who is gone beyond."[68] Esther came to Alaska to retrieve Emil's body and began the return journey to Portland with his coffin on July 6. Friends and family joined her to bury him next to Fred and Freddie in the Clayson plot at Lone Fir Cemetery.[69]

As Esther completed medical school, established a practice and a family, lost her son and husband, and began her public health and suffrage activism, her father Edward Clayson located in Seattle and set up shop as publisher of a weekly newspaper he named the *Patriarch*. After Annie and her children had left him on the Clackamas farm in 1888 and returned to Portland, Annie had sued Edward and obtained a divorce.[70] It is not clear where he spent the next several years, but there was considerable conflict among his siblings in the wake of his brother William Clayson's death, including the division of the Clackamas property, with an estimated value of $20,000.[71] Edward Clayson appeared in the *Seattle City Directory* in 1893 selling cigars on 325 Pike Street and continued there until 1899, when he became a "newspaper man," and then in 1901 established the *Patriarch*.[72]

Fred Clayson's murder on the Dawson Trail in 1899 had introduced additional conflict into the family. In his will, Fred left his estate to his brother Will as executor, with the expectation that Will would divide the estate among the immediate family except for his father. Fred's attorney told the *Daily Alaskan,* "The will was executed for the sole purpose of depriving" Edward Clayson of any of his son's property. Fred had informed his attorney that his father had "forced my mother and the children to earn a living ever since I can remember, squandered it, giving them nothing in return but abuse and brutality."[73] Edward Clayson contested the will that put his son's Skagway fortune out of reach, and he appealed the case through to the Washington State Supreme Court, where Will Clayson and Fred's wishes prevailed.[74] In 1902 Esther's mother Annie agreed to relinquish some of her claims to Fred's property to her son Will in exchange for payments of sixty dollars a month from him for the rest of her life. In the coming years she would bring half a dozen suits against Will for nonpayment.[75]

In Seattle, Edward Clayson used his newspaper, the *Patriarch,* to rail against his many enemies, including prohibitionists, woman suffragists, "effeminate" men, same-sex partners, and Chinese Americans, and voiced his violent opposition to divorce and birth control. He called for a "Husbands and Fathers Convention" to establish "the Patriarchal Republic." Clayson supported local tavern owners, the single tax, the Populist Party, and Theodore Roosevelt (until Roosevelt endorsed woman suffrage). He entered Populist Party politics at the local and national level, and was a candidate for the Washington State senate in 1910, and a candidate for the Seattle City Council in 1913.[76] In the pages of the *Patriarch*, he weighed in on local politics and personalities with either no-holds-barred invective or effusive adulation. Clayson went to court for libel several times, including proceedings initiated by women barbers in the city, whom he had accused of prostitution.[77] Esther later called the *Patriarch* "a periodical of personal opinion supported by the liquor interests." Within its pages, she noted, her father "carried on a losing fight against Prohibition, Woman's Suffrage, and other movements which he believed meant harm to the country."[78]

Annie Clayson was a primary target of Edward's journalistic wrath. Many pages of the *Patriarch* condemn wives who divorce their husbands, and he published a graphic "Divorce Compass" with deceit and wickedness at its center.[79] In January 1903 Edward pled guilty to federal charges of "having sent libelous, scurrilous, and defamatory matter through the mails." *Seattle Republican* editor Horace Cayton, Sr., noted, "Mr. Clayson seriously differed with his wife in matrimonial affairs years ago and since that time they have lived apart." And "since that time he seems to have been very bitter against her and the libelous material" in the federal case "was intended for her personally." Clayson was "sore at women who seek divorces from their husbands." Cayton suggested that if "Mr. Clayson . . . would give up fighting with his wife and other women [with] whom he differs and confine himself solely to literary productions, he would cover himself with much fame and glory in his old age."[80]

It was impossible for Edward Clayson to follow Cayton's advice. Clayson also used the *Patriarch* to make accusations against Esther at major events in her life. His description of Esther's speech on behalf of medical women at the 1905 National American Woman Suffrage Association convention at the Lewis and Clark Exposition in Portland identified "a young woman, thirty-six years of age, whose maiden name was Esther Clayson, occupying the rostrum." The group had to "take their medicine," he wrote, from "this insolent young wench." Elsewhere he referred to Esther as a "criminal limit hen" (the term he used to describe supporters of contraception) and a "married woman without a husband whose insolence is mistaken for dignity by educated and depraved people" (evidently a reference to the fact that Esther and Emil were often apart).[81] He called Esther and her mother Annie "the biggest pair of liars that ever set foot in Portland."[82] When Freddie Pohl died in 1908, Clayson accused Esther of causing her son's death through "criminal neglect" and even of poisoning the child.[83] He frequently reprinted his parody of the Oregon suffrage movement that featured Dr. Esther C. (Clayson) Knowall.[84]

The invective continued until, in 1914, at age seventy-seven, Edward Clayson ceased publication of the *Patriarch* during an illness in his final months of life. Esther visited him before his death on January 3, 1915. "At the time of his last illness . . . he remembered me chiefly as a little girl, and in a faltering voice he tried to sing a song he had taught me before I was six years old: 'The spring had come, the flowers in bloom, the birds sung out their lay, Down by a little running brook, I first saw Maggie May. She had a roguish bright blue eye, was singing all the day. And how I loved her none can tell, my witching Maggie May.'"[85] The family arranged to have Edward Clayson's body shipped from Seattle to Portland. They buried him in the family plot at Lone Fir Cemetery on January 4, 1915, but at the far left corner, separate and alone.

The Clayson women remained close to one another. Esther's mother Annie was an "especially active" member of the Portland Woman's Club and worked for woman suffrage.[86] She lived in the Williams Street house until she died, in her eightieth year, attended by Esther's friend and colleague Amelia Ziegler, just after celebrating Thanksgiving with her daughter Annie May on November 28, 1924.[87] Esther and her sisters continued their close relationships until the end of their lives. A rich, gossipy, three-page letter Esther wrote to Charlotte sometime in the 1920s while traveling home to New York suggests a particular closeness between the two.[88] After moving to New York, Esther made frequent visits to Charlotte and her family (the Snooks) in Salmon, Idaho, and Annie May and her family (the Blanchards) in Ashland, in southern Oregon. Annie May died in 1963, and Charlotte in 1970.[89]

The closeness among the women of the Clayson family does not appear to have extended to their surviving brothers, Ted and Will. Certainly the legal conflicts between Annie and her son Will over Annie's support were a factor. Will stayed in Alaska after Fred's murder and operated stores in the mining communities of Seward, Cordova, and Anchorage. He served on the Anchorage city council for many years and was mayor in the early 1920s. Will and his family relocated to Portland in 1929, but Will returned to Alaska frequently to manage his businesses until his death in 1950.[90] Ted worked as a millwright in Portland and died in 1944.[91]

CHAPTER 4

City Health and the Business of Women

FROM 1907 to 1909 it was a rare week that Esther Pohl found no coverage in the Portland newspapers about her work as the city's health officer. Most of what she read was favorable. Her tactics for battling rats carrying bubonic plague may have differed slightly from those for dealing with city council members who blocked her reform plans, but her goals were the same. Pohl believed that a city's health was a political issue and a matter of social justice demanding strong leadership and citizens empowered to create change—particularly women citizens. Holding appointed office before women in Oregon could vote in statewide elections, Pohl learned essential lessons about the process of politics and formulated a political identity as a progressive Democrat. And she found that city health was predominantly the business of women, women who needed the civic power of the vote to make their voices heard.

Pohl's political mentor was the charismatic and principled Democratic mayor Harry Lane, MD, who named her to the city health board and then to the post of city health officer. Pohl came into appointed office in Lane's city administration at this particularly progressive moment in local, regional, and national politics. Lane, who was Portland's mayor for two terms, from 1905 to 1909, was at the heart of the local reform impulse. He took on the Republican machine and the powerful business interests that he believed had corrupted the city and robbed the people. "I will take the office of mayor, if elected, with clean hands," he vowed, "and then return it clean to the people."[1] On the people's behalf,

Lane battled special interests in business, graft in city government, and fraudulent contractors. He believed that city government should implement and oversee policies for public health, manage and regulate public utilities, and initiate effective city planning and services. In 1905 every other elected position in the city was held by a Republican, and only one council position went Democratic in 1907. The city council was protective of the old system and of business interests, and most often viewed Lane and the appointees in his administration as interlopers to be thwarted. Lane and the city council had "the most adversarial relationship" of any mayor and city council in the history of Portland. Lane vetoed 169 bills during his four years in office, and the city council overrode over half of them; strong words in documents and in city council meetings were the norm.[2] With the Democratic *Oregon Journal* defending the reform goals of the Lane administration, and the Republican *Oregonian* and the *Portland Evening Telegram* in opposition, Pohl's schooling in appointed office often seemed like street brawling.[3]

Lane was born in Marysville (now Corvallis), Oregon, in 1855, the son of Eliza Jane and Nathaniel Lane, and grandson of Joseph Lane, Oregon's first territorial governor and US senator. Like Pohl, Lane worked to save money to attend medical school and graduated from the Willamette University Medical Department in 1876. His anticorruption activism came early: as director of the Oregon State Hospital for the Insane from 1887 to 1891, his investigations of corruption put him up against contractors, administrators, and politicians who were profiting from the fraudulent sale of state goods. Lane garnered great loyalty from friends and colleagues, and devotion from patients, including those in need whom he treated without charge. A man with an unwavering dedication to ending corruption, Lane could, with characteristic good humor, tell the assembled members of the Oregon State Medical Society at a 1908 Portland convention, "Generally speaking this is a closed town, and you will have to conduct yourself with moderation, but if you have some little badge for identification, I will fix it with the Chief of Police when you get caught out at night."[4] Lane greeted the National American Woman Suffrage Association convention in Portland in July 1905 and supported votes for women throughout his career. He appointed three women to city offices: Esther Pohl as health board member and city health officer, Sarah A. Evans as market inspector, and Lola Baldwin as a police officer. In a 1908 veto, Lane refused to authorize the sale of "one old horse" who had "passed the most of its life in active and faithful daily service to the City . . . for the little gain to be wrung for the feeble life left within him." The city, he said, must either continue to care for the horse or "deprive it of its life in some less calculating and more humane way."[5]

Later in life, Esther listed "Dr. Lane's effect on my health work" as one of the building blocks of her career.[6] Lane's progressive vision of and support for social medicine, his insistence on scrupulous accounting in the people's business, and his willingness to take on opponents with facts, humor, enthusiasm, and a savvy sense of publicity all set him apart as a mentor. As with other progressives, he favored the use of experts, the new technology of medical science, and legislation to enable the government to protect citizens. Harry Lane's political ideas and actions resonated with Pohl's own commitment to constructive resistance and activism. She became a partisan, politically, in her years of city health service as a progressive Harry Lane Democrat.

Portland's first board of health, composed of the mayor, the chair of the city council committee on health, and the chief of police, began work on July 1, 1873, just seven years after the establishment of New York City's Metropolitan Board of Health. In 1903 the city charter was amended so that the board of health would include three physicians.[7] Dr. Mae H. Cardwell was the first woman to serve on an Oregon city health board after this new and more robust structure was created.[8] The year 1903 also marked the establishment of a state board of health, and Harry Lane served on this first Oregon state board from 1903 to 1906.[9] On August 9, 1905, the newly elected Mayor Lane appointed Esther Pohl to the Portland Board of Health, along with two of her former medical school professors, doctors A. J. Giesy and George F. Wilson.[10]

Pohl, Wilson, and Giesy came to the board of health after Harry Lane fired their predecessors. Lane had come into office on an anticorruption platform, and the health board had run up bills of over $1,100, primarily for construction work on the city garbage crematory, without getting requisitions from the city to cover them.[11] Pohl and her colleagues also came to the board at a time of strenuous conflict over the low pay of the city health officer and physician.[12] After much wrangling, the Republican city council brokered a deal with Lane: if he would accept their candidate for city health officer, Cortes H. Wheeler, MD, they would authorize a salary for that office at the substantial sum of $3,000 per year. After weighing the matter, the health board accepted the arrangement on February 1,

1906.[13] Harry Lane won reelection as Portland mayor on June 3, 1907, and just over a month later Wheeler resigned as city health officer. The stated cause was a dispute with Lane over Wheeler's accounting and the back dating of a requisition for health department expenditures.[14] In Lane's view, Wheeler had violated the law and the public trust in a way that threatened Lane's entire philosophy of civic authority and anticorruption.[15]

At a special July 11, 1907, meeting of the city health board, Lane announced that three male physicians, Theo Fessler, Edward Kane, and Walter Spencer, had applied for the position of city health officer; board member George Wilson "stated to the Board that the name of Dr. Pohl had been suggested." Then, "following an informal discussion, the following vote by ballot was taken, resulting in three votes for Dr. Pohl and one blank, whereupon Dr. Pohl was unanimously elected Health Officer." Pohl's colleagues Lane, Giesy, and Wilson all voted for Pohl; the blank meant that Pohl did not vote for herself but did not vote for anyone else.[16] Wheeler was removed from office, but, to the immense chagrin of the city council, his high salary was in place for his female successor. Pohl's appointment and salary made local, regional, and national news.[17]

Throughout her life, Pohl was proud of her appointment to this important position but careful to qualify her attainment. She was in the vanguard of women in public health office, and, if not the first female city health officer, the first in a major US city, and many followed her. This seems to be an accurate representation of her achievement. According to reports in the *Woman's Medical Journal,* at the time of Pohl's service, several women had gained appointments as city and county physicians.[18] Kate P. Van Orden, MD, was chosen to be a member of the Alameda, California, health board in 1904, a year after Portland's appointment of Mae H. Cardwell, and Minnie C. T. Love, MD, served on the Colorado State Board of Health beginning in 1905.[19] Before Pohl's appointment, there were several women who worked as city health officers in Peoria, Illinois; Le Mars, Iowa; and Madera, California.[20] And in 1907 S. Josephine Baker, who had been a medical inspector for the New York City board, was appointed assistant commissioner of health for the city.[21] By 1912, three years after Pohl left her position, Dr. Rosalie Slaughter Morton counted 225 women who worked in some capacity with a board of health in the United States. Morton gave Portland and Pohl top billing, along with Baker, now director of the child hygiene division of the New York City board of health.[22]

Esther Pohl (seated at left) at Portland City Health Office, ca. 1907. Reproduced by permission of Oregon Health & Science University Historical Collections & Archives, Portland, Oregon.

Pohl came to the city health office as she had to medical school and medical practice—a woman in a largely male world. Her contemporary S. Josephine Baker wrote of her need to wear "shirtwaists and tailored suits" because, as the "only woman executive in the New York City Department of Health," she "badly needed protective coloring."[23] Pohl seems not to have worried. A photograph taken of her with her staff in the city health office in 1907 shows her dressed in a white shirtwaist and skirt, with a hat that may have been more for the camera than for everyday wear. The other women in the office wore standard shirtwaists with dark skirts. It is not possible to judge Pohl's tenure by one day's clothing, but it appears that she chose stylish, feminine dress to define herself as city health officer on that very public occasion.

Gender mattered in many other ways, as a story Harry Lane told his daughter Nina illustrates. Lane had forgotten his twenty-fifth wedding anniversary on September 5, 1907, until friends delivered some gifts to city hall, one of which was a silver mayonnaise serving set. Realizing the importance of the day but due at an executive board meeting, "as a favor I asked Mrs. Dr. Pohl who was there, to rush out and get something suitable and nice for me to give to Momma." At the conclusion of his meeting, Lane "grabbed the package" from his office and hurried home without unwrapping it. When Lola Lane opened the box, a silver mayonnaise server lay inside, larger but almost identical to the one that their friends had given them. "I never intended to let on but what I selected it myself and I was up against it," Lane confessed to his daughter. "So I told her how I had to get some one to get something for me and she wanted to know who it was and I had to tell her the truth so I told her that I sent a policeman after it and she got sore and said it was some fool and jackass of a woman that got it for me." They fought, made up, and had a happy anniversary. But, as Lane confided to his daughter, "I haven't had time to exchange it so still have it on hand and will have to keep it over I guess. You must not give me away as to who bought it, for me I always stood by you, and it won't be more than fair, for you to stand by me in this matter."[24] Lane characteristically made himself the butt of the joke. But the story also underscores Pohl's position: even as city health officer, she was still a woman and was sent out to purchase a present for the boss's wife.

Pohl later recalled that her service as city health officer gave her essential lessons about the gendered nature of politics and "crystallized" her support for women's rights. "The commercial life (man's sphere?) and the home life (woman's sphere?) of a city are vitally affected by the health of that city," she noted. As city health officer, "it didn't take me long to see that when the commerce of the city . . . was threatened, the commercial bodies demanded protection, and immediate action on the part of the [city] council was the result." Yet when "the home . . . was in danger and the women of the city came as supplicants, the council took on a patronizing air and acted as though it did not want to be bothered with the business of women." For Pohl, her successful 1907–8 campaign against bubonic plague in Portland illustrated the workings of the commercial life and men's business in politics. "When that commerce-killing disease seemed imminent," she noted, "the action of the council was prompt and fairly adequate."[25] With Portland's business and profits threatened, male commercial interests and the business-oriented city council came together rapidly to provide the funds and the political will to assist the health department in preventing the spread of the disease.

In 1907 the bubonic plague was a frightening disease with an epic history. The Black Death had taken more than a quarter of the human population in the fourteenth century, with subsequent epidemic waves through the end of the eighteenth century. From the nineteenth through the early years of the twentieth century, the plague then reappeared globally, with outbreaks in Europe, Russia, and China, and in port cities of the Pacific, including in Honolulu and San Francisco. But by the time a new round of plague threatened the Pacific Rim in 1907, the science of bacteriology had provided answers to some of the mysteries of this ancient and deadly disease that took its victims quickly and terribly. The cause was the bacterium *pestis*, most often found in rats and other rodents and spread to humans by the bite of a flea. There was a significant difference between the battles against bubonic plague in 1900 and the new threats in 1907. Now there was a clear scientific understanding of the rat-flea-human dynamic. Solving the riddle of the what, why, and how of plague meant that public health officials such as Pohl could act to prevent its spread by regulating transportation, particularly shipping activities in ports, and by targeting, locating, and eradicating rats and cleaning up garbage and sewage in areas that might harbor rats and other rodents.[26]

As health officer of a port city on the Pacific, Pohl coordinated with national, regional, state, and local health organizations. Portland had a US Public Health and Marine Hospital Service office with a ward in St. Vincent's Hospital, and there were federal quarantine offices in Astoria, Oregon.[27] The State Board of Health was four years old, as was the revised and strengthened Portland Board of Health and city health office, all in place to respond.

In August 1907, a month after Pohl's appointment, bubonic plague struck San Francisco, and by October Seattle had reported its first case. Public health authorities across the West Coast urged cooperative preventative measures to avoid a spread and an epidemic.[28] In late August, officials at the Public Health and Marine Hospital Service quarantine station in Astoria issued a fumigation order for all vessels in the region, including Portland, and advised that the rats in the ports also be exterminated. Knowing the power of publicity, Pohl organized a tour of the Portland waterfront and invited along reporters and photographers from the *Oregon Journal*. The paper published a Sunday edition exposé, "Menace to City's Health," with images of rotting trash and open sew-ers.[29] "We have inspected the water front," Pohl reported to the board of health, "and find that many of the Front Street buildings discharge sewerage under the buildings into the river, or onto the ground, as the case may be." Some areas were "indescribably filthy, with their little rivulets of sewerage running out from under the buildings toward the river. Many people are employed in this part of the city, and there seems to be no good reason why these property holders should not be obliged to comply with the law and keep their premises clean."[30] The board supported Pohl's compliance with marine hospital regulations, her work on the waterfront, and her plans to ask for additional funding from the city council. Pohl also consulted with the city attorney to initiate a municipal executive order to require the cleanup of the waterfront, gathering the civic power to implement these policies.[31]

All of this was in preparation for Pohl's request for action at the next city council meeting on September 11, 1907. When speaking to the council members, who had, of course, followed her exposé in the newspapers, Pohl emphasized that the potential for an outbreak of bubonic plague in Portland was real, that science provided the answers for prevention policies, and that the city would be liable if it did not act. She outlined the role of rats and fleas in the spread of disease to humans, and the importance exterminating them and also of providing bacteriological examination. San Francisco, twice the size of Portland, with twenty plague cases reported so far, provided a cautionary tale. City officials there had ordered the burning of some homes and businesses, and contemplated burning the city and county hospital because of infection. San Francisco had strengthened its health office staff with "twelve extra medical inspectors, twenty-four sanitary inspectors, and scores of other people, among which are one hundred and twenty rat catchers." Pohl emphasized that immediate action in Portland could save the city from a similar fate and that inaction would amount to "criminal neglect." She and the health board recommended a series of measures to be taken at once: "That all garbage be placed in properly covered receptacles, that all wheat and other food stuffs upon which rats may feed be protected as far as possible. That rat catchers be employed, and that a disease peculiar to rats, known as 'rat typhoid' be introduced among them here, and that every measure be taken to prevent the introduction of bubonic plague, and to limit the possibility of its spread in case of its introduction into this city." A thousand dollars was essential immediately, "with the possibility of a request for more as the exigencies of the situation may arise."[32] The council approved the request and "gave City Health Officer Pohl to understand that five times that amount would be placed at her disposal if needed."[33]

In mid-September Pohl met with members of the city's Commercial Club and emphasized the "commercial importance of a clean water front free from vermin." While Pohl did not quote a specific figure in her report, Harry Lane frequently gave $500,000 as the price for restoring the city and its businesses should plague hit. Pohl reported "a general and very gratifying disposition on the part of those interested in that section of the city to co-operate with this department." A special committee from the Commercial Club visited the waterfront, and the Oregon Railroad and Navigation Company employed workers specifically to clean up their docks.[34] In October the board of governors of the Commercial Club wrote to the city council, noting that the "commercial and property interests [of the city] are in favor of a most vigorous campaign" and urging the council to give an additional and "larger appropriation for the use of the Board of Health." The club offered "every assistance within its power" to the city government and health board.[35]

Pohl secured an additional $2,500 appropriation from the city council for the work, and reported that the campaign "has met with the greatest encouragement from the Mayor and Council, the commercial and medical organizations, the press and the public." She concluded, with tremendous understatement, that "a general spirit of helpfulness has been manifested all along the line, instead of the opposition ordinarily met with."[36] By December the plague scare was essentially over, and Portland had had no reported cases of the disease. This cooperation between business and the city council was all the more significant because Portland and the nation were in the midst of a stock and banking crisis, the Panic of 1907, which affected Portland even before New York City. The Oregon Trust and Savings Company closed in August 1907 in reaction to a plunging stock market. In October officials closed Portland banks, like others in the nation, and then reopened them under a limited "clearinghouse system." Stability returned by December due to bailouts by the US Department of the Treasury and J. P. Morgan and Company of $25 million each to large banking trusts.[37]

The antiplague campaign demonstrated that male business owners and the men of the city council acted quickly when the commercial interests of the city were threatened. But it also suggests some important things about Pohl as she established her civic credentials and learned the political ropes. As an appointed office holder and city policy maker, Pohl embraced a Progressive Era vision held by many reformers in the nation. The city held a responsibility to protect not only businesses but citizens and consumers, and Pohl used her role as scientific expert to recommend the latest technology and policies to prevent the disease. She studied the issues, informed the public, took decisive action, and became the city's antiplague expert. Much of the press coverage of the campaign stressed Pohl's expertise, her sensible solutions, and her role as a scientific guide and leader of the city throughout the scare. She emphasized the need for prevention and highlighted the latest science. Resolute and strong in the face of the crisis, she demonstrated a leadership that had often been gendered as male. She understood the power of the press in shaping public and official opinion. During the autumn of 1907 she became a visible civic figure with an emerging voice in Portland.

One of Pohl's first acts was to engage the services of a rat exterminator for the city who had the authority of a special deputy on the health board.[38] Aaron Zaik had learned the trade as a young man in Odessa, a Black Sea port city with a long history of plague outbreaks. His credentials also included work in New York City, with businesses in Portland, and with Swift and Company in Seattle. The *Oregonian* emphasized Zaik's experience and his use of modern, scientific methods and chemicals, but also his art of rat catching, even his mastery of the "psychology and habits of the rodent tribe."[39] Zaik's initial work at the waterfront was so successful that after two weeks the city made his services available for free to any property holder.[40] While there were perhaps inevitable and unfortunate comparisons to the Pied Piper, and, in one *Oregon Journal* story, an attempt to portray his Russian accent, on the whole the press represented Zaik as a modern expert who would use technology and draw upon his considerable experience to help Portland avoid bubonic plague.[41] Pohl's selection of Zaik indicated to Portlanders that she was a strategic policymaker who was able to gather experts around her who could make the city safe.

By the end of October Pohl had the funding to offer Portlanders a bounty of five cents per rat. This was a policy that the health boards of San Francisco and other cities had developed as an incentive to maintain vigilance against the rodent population. Residents could assist in pre-

vention of plague by bringing "all rats, dead or alive" to the city crematory, handling them with care, to destroy fleas.[42] Pohl believed that it was
the civic duty of all residents to kill rats to prevent plague. "The five-cent
bounty on rats that has been offered has resulted in some being killed,
but we should not depend entirely on children to kill them for the money
there is in it," she told the *Oregonian*, with echoes of her own four-bits-
profit-per-skunk-liver childhood in Seabeck. According to Pohl, "Everyone in the city, rich and poor, should consider it his duty" to exterminate
rats. Referring to the current national and local financial crisis, Pohl
insisted that the "killing of rats is more important just now than the
closing of Oregon banks"[43] and praised residents and business owners
who did their part in the cleanup.[44] By December a new city ordinance
reflected this emphasis on the importance of community-wide action.
It required "wire screens or netting in all basements, warehouses, grain
elevators, docks, and packing-houses for the protection of all foodstuffs
from rats." In addition, the occupant of every building in the city had to
set at least one trap and check it and rebait it regularly, subject to city
inspection.[45]

The Portland Board of Health minutes list a total rat bounty of $458.10
paid from November 1907 to June 1908. At five cents per rat, this makes
a total of 9,162 rats.[46] Zaik and others contributed more carcasses in addition to those brought in by the bounty—in December Pohl estimated
that Zaik had personally brought in over 5,000 rats. As a result of all rat-
catching activities, the total number of rats destroyed at the city crematory in 1908 reached 16,179, with thousands more likely not reported.[47]
No infected rats were ever found, and Portland had no cases of bubonic
plague under Pohl's watch.

Pohl used the plague crisis and public sentiment it generated to lever-
age strategic support and funding for a badly needed city bacteriological laboratory.[48] In the first phase of the plague campaign, Pohl required
that every fifth rat brought to the city garbage incinerator was sent to
the office of the state bacteriologist for testing. By November she noted
that the "need of an adequate bacteriological laboratory daily becomes
more urgent. In this respect the city depends absolutely upon the State
[laboratory]. We go to the State for our diphtheria cultures; with our
rats; and only a day or two ago the aid of the State was required to settle
a dispute and determine whether or not several children in one of our
schools were afflicted with scabies or a noncontagious skin eruption."

A city laboratory was important for a variety of reasons, but it was the immediate antiplague sentiment that helped to win funding and support. The board hired Dr. Ralph Matson, the bacteriologist of the Oregon State Board of Health, on a separate city contract. Matson was a specialist and a lecturer at the University of Oregon Medical Department, and had recently returned from London, where he "took special courses in chemistry and bacteriology." Matson arranged for the city bacteriology office to be located at the medical school, where medical students could benefit from its activities. It was a win-win situation for everyone, and brought the latest science to Portland's city government.[49]

In their quest to eradicate unsanitary conditions during the plague scare, Pohl's health board predecessors had targeted immigrant communities, including Chinatown and the Russian settlement.[50] In San Francisco's disastrous experience with bubonic plague in 1900, business owners and politicians had covered up the disease and blamed it on Chinatown residents rather than supporting measures to eradicate it across the city. Health board policy there, as Alan M. Kraut points out, reflected "the basic assumption that the plague was primarily a Chinese problem."[51] And, as James Mohr has shown, during the 1900 plague epidemic Honolulu's health board quarantined Chinatown residents in detention camps. Many whites called for an all-out burning of Honolulu's Chinatown, and the board's controlled burn turned to tragedy when winds sent the flames across the Chinese district and destroyed it.[52] In Portland's antiplague campaign, Pohl's colleague, Oregon state bacteriologist Ralph Matson, blamed Asian immigrant communities for the disease. "A constant and unceasing guerilla warfare against the infected rat must be kept up as long as the Asiatic colonies and other places of like character are allowed to exist in American cities," Matson noted. "If we cannot compel the Hindu, chinaman and others to live up to our ideals of cleanliness," then "the coast will never be free of the danger of an incursion of the bubonic plague. If this result cannot be obtained by any other method than stringent exclusion of the Chinese, Hindus, Koreans, and Japanese, then I do not believe that exclusion is too high a price to pay."[53] In what Kraut has termed the "double helix of health and fear," many policymakers linked illness and germs with the "immigrant menace."[54]

By contrast, Pohl did not single out Chinatown or other residential communities but instead maintained that the entire city must be vigi-

Sarah A. Evans, market inspector, and Esther Pohl, city health officer, Portland City Hall, ca. 1907. Reproduced by permission of Oregon Health & Science University Historical Collections & Archives, Portland, Oregon.

lant. Her initial efforts focused on Portland's waterfront as a conduit for bubonic plague. Two months into the campaign, Pohl announced, "We have planned to begin an inspection of the Chinese quarters immediately, not with the idea that we expect to find any plague indications, but for the purpose of ascertaining what means the Orientals are using to prevent its propagation."[55] This did not prevent others from promoting fear of the Chinese American neighborhood; the *Portland Evening Telegram* published a lurid account of Pohl's visit, titled "Chinatown Pest Holes."[56] According to the *Oregon Journal*, when Pohl inspected Chinatown, she found the "front offices of the merchants" to be "orderly and unobjectionable," but behind the scenes, as in other markets, there were sanitary violations that endangered the city. Pohl objected to the fact that police were raiding gambling establishments in Chinatown, ostensibly being "careful of the morals of the Chinese," while not attending to sanitary affairs. She asked for city ordinances to be enforced in Chinatown as they were in other quarters of the city.[57]

Esther Pohl as Portland city health officer battling bubonic plague. From the *Portland Evening Telegram*, November 4, 1907, 1.

On November 4, 1907, the Republican *Portland Evening Telegram* featured Pohl in a front-page editorial cartoon. In "'Raus Mit the Rats" (Out with the Rats), Pohl heads a rowdy band of citizens, armed with guns, brooms, rakes, daggers, and clubs under the auspices of a "Board of Health" sign. Rats scurry away from the city, exclaiming, "This is worse than cats!" and "Plague on it!" A Chinese American man in a storefront comments in the *Telegram*'s idea of dialect, "Melican Man He Kille Alle

Lats." And Ralph Matson, in his laboratory, holds a menacing knife with the words "Will Carve the Rat." Pohl is at their head with sword in hand. While others are laughing, she is stern and resolute in her duty. She apparently took the cartoon all in good humor. A photograph of her sitting in the city health office clearly shows a copy of the cartoon on the wall above her desk.

Newspaper editors were not the only ones to praise Pohl's performance. The City and County Medical Society representing Portland and Multnomah County passed a resolution in their November 6, 1907, meeting congratulating Pohl and commending her successful work in the antiplague campaign.[58] Harry Lane praised Pohl and her department in his annual message to the city in January 1908: the work in the health department "has greatly increased during this past year," he said, "and at no time in the history of the Department has greater care or more intelligent effort been exercised in the conduct of the affairs entrusted to it."[59]

If the antiplague campaign epitomized what Pohl identified as the political business of men, the lessons of another campaign, this one for pure milk and dairy inspection in Portland, demonstrated the limits of women's political power to engender civic health. The pure milk campaign underscored the fact that to achieve civic health, women needed the vote so they could exercise real power in their communities. In this mass movement of which Portland took a leading role in the nation, Pohl drew on the power of a coalition of women's voluntary organizations. In her view, however, policymakers would never really attend to the "business of women" if those same women did not have the political clout of the vote and the consequent ability to hold elected officials accountable. Mobilization, education, and public awareness through women's organized activism for social justice and civic health were vital, but full civic rights were also needed to complete the job.

Portland led the way in a grassroots pure food and clean market movement that drew strength from the women's medical community and from the domestic science and "city beautiful" movements embraced by women's voluntary associations. These activists linked the changing methods of food production and distribution in the industrializing nation with new medical models of bacteriology, giving women as consumer-housewives increasing political power for "municipal housekeeping."[60] By 1905 a strong coalition had formed for a pure food movement in the city. It included the Portland Woman's Club, the Young Women's Christian Association, and the Civic Improvement League. Leaders invited newspaper reporters to visit Portland meat and food markets to document and publicize poor sanitary conditions, established a public "clean list" of establishments (just as the National Consumers' League was doing with the white label campaign for products made in healthy and safe factories), and compiled a list of shops to be boycotted.[61]

After a great deal of lobbying and publicity, a resistant city council finally authorized a market inspector position as part of the health board and in April 1905, with great fanfare, appointed Lillian Tingle, the candidate recommended by the activists, as the first market inspector in the nation.[62] But the reluctant city council had authorized a very low salary, and several months later, when Harry Lane became mayor, Tingle resigned because of it. The *Oregon Journal* noted, "[The] clean shop crusade is likely to languish."[63]

Sarah A. Evans stepped into the breach, and the new city health board elected her city market inspector on August 11, 1905, on the second day of Esther Pohl's tenure there.[64] As a charter member of the Portland Woman's Club and the Portland YWCA, Evans was the quintessential clubwoman. As one of the organizers of the Oregon State Federation of Women's Clubs in 1899, Evans lobbied successfully for legislative support for public libraries in Oregon and served as president of the Oregon Federation from 1905 to 1915. At the time of her appointment, Evans was editor of the weekly Women's Clubs section of the Sunday *Oregon Journal*. Despite the low salary, Evans recognized the importance of the office of market inspector, and she plunged into the work and made the job her own for thirty years, until her retirement in 1935.[65]

Evans's appointment as market inspector deepened her already strong friendship with Esther Pohl. Evans had sponsored Pohl's membership in the Portland Woman's Club in 1899, and she had assisted at the double wedding of Pohl's sisters Charlotte and Annie May in 1903. Evans was at her friend Esther Pohl's side at Freddie's death in 1908; it was she who provided information for the boy's death certificate as his mother grieved.[66]

As a clubwoman, health board member, and city health officer, Esther Pohl was a vigorous supporter of the clean market and pure food movement and helped to ensure its success. She put civic health before business interests. In her first annual city health report for 1907, Pohl noted, "The commercial value of a food industry to our city is not so important as whether or not the food product is wholesome or deleterious to the health of the community."[67] Local support led to state and national recognition for the campaign.[68] The Oregon branch of the National Consumers' League, best known for its advocacy for protective labor legislation for women, entered the Portland pure food campaign in 1906. The group provided additional energy for the local and state movement, and lobbied the national organization to take up pure food as a league concern.[69] In its 1907 biennial session, the Oregon State Legislature augmented the federal Pure Food and Drug Act of June 1906 with its own Pure Food Act "preventing the manufacture and sale of adulterated or misbranded or poisonous or deleterious foods" within the state and required accurate labeling, with fines and imprisonment as a consequence of violation.[70] Portland activists achieved their goal of a strong city ordinance to enforce clean markets in November 1907.[71]

In spite of these successes, problems with the quality of milk sold in Portland continued, and Pohl and other activists initiated a "war on bad milk." It was both a professional battle for Pohl as city health officer, and a poignantly personal one after her son Freddie's death in September 1908—caused, in her estimation and in the opinion of medical colleagues, by infected milk. The city council and the business community had responded to the plague scare, Pohl noted. But when "hundreds of little children had died from an impure milk supply," for "several years the women of this city were unable to secure any protection, for the reason that the commercial forces (dairymen), with sovereign power, were arrayed against the home forces (unenfranchised mothers), who at that time depended solely upon the beautiful, sentimental influence that we read about in the literature" of suffrage opponents.[72] Women's "influence" was not enough: they needed the power of the vote.

Pohl was vocal about pure milk from the first months of her tenure as city health officer. She recounted cases of watered down and adulterated milk and of cows fed from brewery mash, and called for better enforcement of current provisions and inspection. But her main focus became a new ordinance that would give the city health board, rather than the state dairy commissioner, the power to inspect dairies before licensing any milk vendor who wished to sell in the city. Dairies that supplied Portland were "sources of danger and death," and city health could be achieved only by "adequate dairy regulation and inspection" by the health board.[73]

To support the pure milk ordinance, Pohl drew upon and expanded the existing coalition of women's organizations that had built the office of market inspector. These included the Portland Woman's Club, the Oregon branch of the National Consumers' League, the Visiting Nurse Association and its formidable reform leader Millie Trumbull, and the Multnomah County Woman's Christian Temperance Union. Pohl spoke about the milk campaign before many of these groups and at other significant gatherings, including the 1908 Chautauqua at Gladstone Park.[74] In December 1907 the Pure Food Committee of the Oregon Federation of Women's Clubs, using an *Oregon Journal* reporter and photographer, made an investigation of outlying dairies, taking their cue from the successful market inspection and antiplague publicity campaigns. They reported "vile and foul" conditions, and vowed that their work had just begun. "They have proved up," the *Oregon Journal* reported, "and don't intend to shut up."[75]

Activists opposed Oregon state dairy and food commissioner J. W. Bailey, who denied that there was a problem with his inspections or enforcement. *Oregon Journal* editor Marshall Dana reported that Pohl went to Bailey's office with "a sample of milk" for him to test. Bailey agreed to test it, and, as Dana described it, "parted his walrus mustache, removed the cover from the container the city health officer handed him, tipped the bottle back and took a swig." Then, "swishing the swallow back and forth between his dentures he assumed a judicial pose. He pronounced the milk 'very good milk, yes, very good.'" That was the extent of his testing. Pohl thanked him for his opinion. "You see," she said, "that sample is mother's milk."[76] Dana's reconstruction of the event was no doubt exaggerated, but the act of bringing human milk to the dairy commissioner for testing certainly underscored Pohl's point about the lack of scientific testing, illustrated her sense of purpose, and demonstrated her skillful use of publicity for a cause.

City and state activists and members of the medical community continued to work to change the system.[77] In March 1909, Pohl's inspection and licensing ordinance passed the city council. In Pohl's estimation, the victory was "largely due to the efforts of the board and the women's clubs of Portland" versus dairy interests. A "council-chamber full of women" was there to support the ordinance.[78]

Pohl's first pure milk ordinance was an important initial step, but in late August 1909 the *Oregon Journal* published an exposé on local children's deaths due to bad milk, targeted commissioner Bailey as a "menace," and called for his removal.[79] The coalition of women's organizations again joined forces to push for a stronger bill.[80] At this point, Pohl, no longer city health officer, decided to contribute to the campaign in a very personal way. Pohl and her sister Charlotte had just returned home from a stay in St. Vincent's Hospital, and Pohl decided to share her own story with the press and the public. "I feel very strongly about this milk business," she said. "I was taken sick suddenly and so was my sister and we traced it to the milk. We were both delirious and wholly laid up. All the symptoms were of poisoning from milk." Then she discussed Freddie's death almost a year earlier. "Besides my own illness from an impure milk supply, I lost my boy for the same reason." "As a mother," she insisted, "I am vitally interested in this compelling of the dairy commissioner to do his paid duty. I have paid for this laxness by the life of my son." As a result, "No one could say anything that would show more interest. I say and I know that the milk supply of Portland is rotten, literally rotten. Commissioner Bailey doesn't pretend to do what he is paid to do. The consequence is, I've lost my boy."[81] Pohl's decision to speak publicly about her family tragedy meant that Freddie gave a face to the *Oregon Journal*'s figures about deaths from impure milk.

After Pohl spoke out, the board of trade, Portland Chamber of Commerce, and the state veterinarian and others joined this second pure milk campaign coalition. Charges and countercharges led to vigorous press coverage, angry letters to the state board of health, calls for Bailey's resignation, a grand jury investigation of Bailey that resulted in a "severe reprimand," and a new milk ordinance passed unanimously by the city council and the new Republican mayor, Joseph Simon, on November 24, 1909. With this, the food and dairy commission's control over the process ended.[82]

The pure milk campaign contributed to Pohl's progressive political philosophy about the nature of civic health and contributed to her gendered view of how politics worked. Milk was the quintessential "business of women." As the "most important food product in the world" and the "staple diet of infancy and childhood," nothing could replace it. "From the standpoint of child welfare, its milk supply is the most important matter with which a city has to deal." Children were a city's "little consumers," and "every city is expected to provide pure water for its adults," so, she reasoned, "why shouldn't it provide pure milk" for them? "Pure milk is a matter of politics unless one owns a cow." Contaminated milk was easier and cheaper to produce—formaldehyde preserved it more cheaply than ice, and brewery waste could be added for more profits. Men, Pohl said, were naturally interested in commercial matters. "From a man's standpoint dairying is a great industry that must be protected, and the prohibitive cost of pure milk must also be considered. But what doth it profit a woman to suffer for months and go down to the gates of death to produce one child if that child is to be sacrificed afterwards to the demands of trade?" This was not "men's business" but "a matter that pertains to the home, therefore, it is the business of women."[83] True to her progressive philosophy, Pohl also favored city ownership of dairies and milk depots.[84]

Some men crossed the gendered political line and supported the business of women. "At present there are men who maintain that pure milk is just such a [possible] dream, and they back their opinions with votes in our city councils and state legislatures." But women's "influence," significant though it was, could not compare with men's power to vote to make civic health a reality. Women activists backed dairy commissioner Bailey's opponent in 1908, but, Pohl insisted, "when the vote was counted the real value of that beautiful influence was apparent—it was nil."[85] Even a woman policymaker in appointed office, as Pohl was, with a "council-chamber full of women" active in pure food, market, and milk campaigns behind her, could not adequately address the business of women without a corresponding city full of women voters.[86]

Pohl's years on the health board and, in particular, her two years of service in appointed office as city health officer, honed and deepened her identity as a progressive Democrat. She added a gendered dimension to her progressive assault on special interests. Pohl cast the commercial world and "the interests" as male, and these male interests ignored or actively worked against the concerns of women. The coalitions of women's organizations that had achieved market and pure milk inspection were fighting an uphill battle. Pohl did not take their successes lightly; each was vital to the political process. But city health required the empowerment of women because male corporate and commercial interests did not respond to women as "supplicants." By going to dairy commissioner Bailey's office with a sample of breast milk, Pohl was making an emphatic and symbolic point about the conflict between gendered male interests and women's concerns and women's empowerment.

Pohl's developing theory of the "business of women" forged during her tenure as Portland city health officer dovetailed with other Progressive Era women's views about the nature of female citizenship and activism and how that compared to the "business of men." As Maureen Flanagan notes, activist Chicago women envisioned the city as a home, in contrast to the corporate interests of men. "Imagining the city as a shared home gave women a metaphor," she asserts, for an alternative "and rather more comprehensive set of priorities for city government."[87]

Pohl's final months as city health officer reemphasized the political battles of the Lane administration and her gendered position in appointed office. Pohl's annual reports for both 1907 and 1908 showed that Portland had the lowest death rate of any large city in the nation.[88] In January 1909 she requested additional funding from the city council. In response, council members accused her of spending too much money and praised her predecessor, Cortes H. Wheeler, for his ability to run the office with economy. Pohl defended her budget with data showing Portland's improved public health since she had taken office. "These things may all be due to the grace of God," she noted, and if so, "I earnestly thank him . . . but I think it is in part, at least, due to the work of the office." She contrasted current successes with Wheeler's failures, noting particularly his lax statistics and his poor job of enforcing quarantine.[89] But council members cut her request by almost a quarter and discussed reducing her salary, which they said had been increased "only upon the understanding that Dr. Wheeler would remain." With "all respect to Dr. Pohl," that salary was not "intended for her or for any other successor."[90]

In the aftermath of that contentious city council meeting, Pohl gave an interview to an *Oregon Journal* reporter. The "argument advanced by a newspaper [the *Oregonian*] and the evident opinion voiced by a few councilmen, that the health conditions in Portland are in no wise due to an efficient administration of the health office but to the effects of pure water and a balmy climate apply equally to all former administrations which have not been criticized as has mine," she noted. "Bull Run water and invigorating atmosphere have always been with us as will also the critics. It does seem to me, though, that there has been an attempt in some quarters to belittle the excellent record this department has made."[91] She had figures to show that more diseases had been reported under her watch but that the number of deaths was lower than when

Wheeler headed the office. "For my part," she said, "I prefer reports to deaths."[92]

In the midst of this dispute, Portland physician John Madden sent a letter to the *Oregonian* in an attempt to discredit Pohl as a female health officer. Madden was no stranger to criticizing the health department. In March 1906 city health officer Wheeler had charged him with failure to report a disease, and it was "diamond cut diamond" when the two met in municipal court and Madden lost his case, with a fine of twenty-five dollars.[93] In that instance, Madden had attacked the office; now he also attacked the woman in office. He began his letter by identifying Pohl as Portland's "lady health officer whom Mayor Lane's apotheosis of all womankind has placed at the head of the city's Health Department." She had the position, Madden suggested, because the mayor worshipped women, not because of her credentials or skill. After several long paragraphs in which he questioned the health department's handling of several of his cases, Madden closed with a specific attack on Pohl and on other women in public office with the power of enforcement: "Woman (God bless her!) is a sentimental and emotional critter. She is a great success as a homemaker and homekeeper; she is less of a success as a chief of police, and there are those who think that the performance of any sort of important police duties should not be given into her hands. You recall what the celebrated Dr. Johnson said about the woman preacher: 'A woman's preaching is like a dog standing on its hind legs. It is not that he ever does it well, but you are surprised that he is able to do it at all.'"[94]

At the end of April 1909 Pohl submitted her resignation, citing personal reasons and acknowledging that "the work has been hard and trying at times, and the criticisms often unjust . . . [and] in the meantime, the important work goes on unnoticed."[95] She had "private reasons for her action" she told the assembled board of health, whose members refused to accept her request. She agreed to "yield to the wishes of the members at this time, and remain indefinitely, if they so desired." Harry Lane reportedly "sighed and said, 'It isn't often that we receive a resignation we don't want to accept. . . . I wish I had a chance to accept those of some other public officers.'"[96] Amid additional talk by the city council of reducing her salary, Pohl continued to hold her position and to make and carry out policy. Her resignation remained on the table through the end of the Lane administration that summer. Lane did not run for reelection; lawyer and probusiness Republican Joseph Simon won the mayoral race in June, and the "Portland business community breathed a collective sigh of relief."[97] As one of his first official acts in office, Simon reappointed Cortes H. Wheeler as the new city health officer for Portland.[98]

Pohl left the health office to join the clinic of Coffey, Sears, Jones, and Joyce, headed by the renowned surgeon J. C. Coffey, to serve as head of obstetrics and gynecology. As she explained to her friend Anna Howard Shaw, "A coterie [of] specialists—men of the highest standing in the medical profession . . . have asked me to join them and devote my time exclusively to women's work. It is an association of which any medical woman in the west would be mighty proud, and I feel that it is a compliment to have been chosen."[99] Pohl continued her involvement in civic health. She served as the Oregon chair of the Public Health Education Committee of the American Medical Association, connecting vital local efforts with the national movement for public health.[100]

CHAPTER 5

Women, Politics, and Power

I N 1916 Chicago suffragist Ruth Hanna McCormick asked Esther Love-joy to answer the question "Why am I a suffragist?" Lovejoy responded by outlining her journey from experience to activism. For her, the ballot was intertwined with the discrimination she had first encountered in medical school, where she had not been eligible for an internship because she was a woman. Later, when bubonic plague threatened, the city council had supported her as Portland health officer, but it could not be bothered when women sought to protect the city from impure milk, something that she felt had brought about the death of her son Freddie.[1] Women needed the civic power to keep their homes and communities healthy and to help secure their equal place in education and the workplace. The ballot was a necessary tool for constructive resistance.

For forty-two years, from 1870 to 1912, Oregon activists campaigned for full voting rights for women in the state. The issue of votes for women was on the Oregon ballot six times, more than in any state in the nation—in 1884, 1900, 1906, 1908, 1910, and 1912.[2] In the 1906 and 1912 campaigns in particular, Oregon was in the vanguard of the votes for women movement, and served as an essential proving ground for the modern tactics involving mass media, organizing, and cooperative coalition building, what Sara Hunter Graham called the "suffrage renaissance" of the new votes for women movement.[3]

This renaissance began in 1905, when Portland hosted over a million and a half visitors at the Lewis and Clark Centennial Exposition.[4]

Suffrage Day at the Lewis and Clark Exposition, June 30, 1905, Portland, Oregon. Esther Pohl is on the second row on the right, standing to the left of tall Jefferson Myers. Oregon Historical Society Research Library, negative 59458, Portland, Oregon.

Many national organizations, including the National American Woman Suffrage Association (NAWSA) and the American Medical Association (AMA), decided to hold their annual meetings in the city during the fair. For Esther Pohl, the meetings were a strategic convergence. The NAWSA convention, held June 28 to July 5, preceded by days the AMA convention, held July 11 to 14, and some suffragists and women physicians attended both conventions.[5] As president of the all-female Portland Medical Club, a member of the Portland Woman's Club, and a worker on the NAWSA and AMA local arrangements committees, Pohl greeted both groups, gave speeches, organized activities, and facilitated networking across the two organizations.[6] She met and worked with national, regional, and local suffrage leaders. "Previous to this time I had been a passive or potential suffragist," she later wrote, "but the influence of the National

Woman's Suffrage Convention held at Portland in 1905 . . . crystallized my principles in a very short time."[7]

Organizers held Suffrage Day on June 30 at the Lewis and Clark Exposition grounds. National suffrage luminaries—including NAWSA's Susan B. Anthony, Anna Howard Shaw and Carrie Chapman Catt, Florence Kelley of the National Consumers' League, and writer Charlotte Perkins Gilman—joined local activists.[8] Pohl gave a speech as president of the Portland Medical Club and welcomed the suffragists: "We wish to express our gratitude to those courageous men and women living and to the memories of those who are gone who made our present honorable and profitable positions possible," she noted. After reviewing the situation of women in medical schools and in practice, Pohl closed with a considered reminder that, "because of the confidential relations [women doctors] hold with hundreds of families, they could exercise a considerable political power, if they chose to use their influence in securing votes for an individual or a cause."[9] Pohl also integrated visiting suffragists into the AMA convention and showcased suffrage among her AMA colleagues.[10] The overlapping conventions initiated a strategic working partnership and friendship between Pohl and NAWSA president Anna Howard Shaw, also a physician, which would last until Shaw's death in 1919.[11]

The Portland NAWSA convention launched a new generation of suffrage workers into the 1906 Oregon campaign for votes for women. These suffragists adopted a new philosophy, emphasizing a "fight in the open" rather than first-generation leader Abigail Scott Duniway's "still hunt" method of working quietly behind the scenes with influential leaders.[12] They also had a new tool in the political process to work with. In 1902, Oregon voters had passed legislation that allowed citizens who had gathered enough signatures to place an initiative measure on the ballot. Oregon votes for women activists were the first to use the initiative process in a sustained campaign.[13] Pohl joined other field workers, who began circulating petitions for the 1906 ballot initiative soon after the convention.[14] Women doctors in the Portland Medical Club, under Pohl's direction, "indorsed the equal suffrage movement by a unanimous vote" at their August meeting, and members began circulating petitions throughout the city."[15] Votes for women supporters established a state central suffrage committee "consisting of a leading member of the various women's organizations of the state" to harness the power of women's organizations to garner signatures.[16] Pohl represented the Portland

Medical Club on the committee.[17] By the end of December, the committee had enough signatures to place the votes for women initiative on the ballot for June 4, 1906.[18]

During the campaign, Pohl continued to emphasize the tangible results of the suffrage campaign for working and professional women. At a statewide suffrage conference in April, she discussed "the debt of the professional woman to the pioneer suffragists" and suggested that a good way to measure the debt was in earning power. The 7,300 women physicians in the nation, she noted, had an average income of perhaps $2,000 per year, which meant that medical women owed some fifteen million dollars to pioneer suffragists each year. But "what the world is indebted to the suffrage movement for, the [contributions] of the professional women, cannot be computed."[19] Pohl's letters to the editors of the *Oregonian* and *Portland Evening Telegram* in support of the cause argued for wage-earning women's need for the franchise and against the taxation of women without representation.[20]

Pohl also participated in the new fight in the open campaign style and the strategy attuned to the "language and methods of consumerism" in modern mass culture that Margaret Finnegan has termed "selling suffrage."[21] Workers placed new emphasis on reaching male voters through the mass media, popular culture, advertising, and the use of public space such as streets for parades and other gatherings for publicity. The 1906 campaign was one of the first to use these tactics; Oregon helped to pioneer what would become the successful tactical shift in twentieth-century suffrage campaigns, including Pacific Northwest victories in Washington in 1910, California in 1911, and Oregon in 1912.[22]

Pennsylvania suffragist and NAWSA organizer Ida Porter Boyer headed the press department at the Portland campaign headquarters in three rooms of the Stearns Building on 6th and Morrison Streets.[23] By February 1906, Boyer was sending out weekly articles to 223 newspapers across the state.[24] Oregon suffrage leader Sarah A. Evans reported that at the headquarters, "there daily went a stream of Portland women, often swelled by women from out of that City, who worked diligently from morning till night and many of them every day."[25] NAWSA's Alice Stone Blackwell, who came to Portland at the end of April, observed, "Typewriters are clicking busily, dictation is being taken down in short-hand, callers are being entertained, newspaper clippings are cut and pasted, letters written, routes laid out, reporters interviewed, and councils of war held with women from all parts of the city and State." At lunchtime "somebody appears with a basket of sandwiches, strawberries and other good things; for the Portland women hospitably provide refreshments." Then, "for an hour work is thrown aside and the air scintillates with fun."[26] Sarah A. Evans remembered the noon hours as "the social events of the campaign . . . and many business women acquired the habit of dropping in to help a bit and enjoy the delightful companionship of the women they found there."[27] Esther Pohl's medical office at the Failing Building was just around the corner, and the board of health offices in city hall were some seven blocks away. It is likely that Pohl, whom Blackwell called "a tower of strength" in the campaign, was there frequently.[28]

Pohl took woman suffrage work into the public streets when she arranged to have a suffrage float in the "Made in Oregon" parade. Sponsored by the Oregon Development League and Manufacturers' Association to boost local businesses and industry, the parade debuted a year before the Portland Rose Parade. The mile-long pageant on Friday afternoon, May 26, passed through the center of the city with more than one hundred floats and other decorated wagons and vehicles.[29] With several thousand visitors from inside and outside the state, this popular spectacle just over a week before the June 4 election provided unexcelled publicity. Pohl "secured a carriage, filled it with little boys and girls" (including her own four-and-a-half-year-old Freddie), and "put two older children at the outside to keep the younger ones from falling out." A placard read "Future Voters—Made in Oregon" and another group of young girls "distributed campaign literature" to the crowds.[30] Pohl's suffrage float was part of the campaign's new attention to mass culture and advertising.

Activists obtained permission to be poll watchers on June 4 to observe voting and to guard against any problems with the process, a first for any state suffrage campaign. Outside dozens of polling places in Portland, from hotels to office buildings to tents, suffragists distributed a final leaflet to men on their way to vote. They understood that being out in the streets in the rough and tumble of elections was an important test of women's willingness to participate in the political process. Supporters and opponents of candidates and ballot measures would be out in force for blocks around each location. Saloons were officially closed on Election Day, but by tradition beer and stronger drinks were always available. As polls stayed open until 7:00 p.m., poll watchers would need to observe vote counting into the night. Pohl estimated that there were "at least 500 women in Portland who were willing to volunteer their services."[31]

Pohl was charged with organizing and supporting those who would distribute literature as poll workers, and NAWSA's Kate Gordon was in charge of poll watchers. They organized teams by precinct.[32] Many women arrived an hour before the polls opened, and they needed umbrellas on this rainy June day in Oregon. "On election day it seemed as if the heavens had opened to pour floods upon us," Anna Shaw reported. "All day long Dr. Pohl took me in her automobile from one polling place to another. At each we found representative women patiently enduring the drenching rain while they tried to persuade men to vote for us." They "distributed sandwiches, courage, and inspiration among them . . . and tried to cheer me in the same way [as] the women [poll] watchers, whose appointment we had secured that year for the very first time."[33] The 3,000 women in Oregon who participated in poll watching and handing out literature included national organizers and local women; among them was Pohl's mother, Annie Clayson.[34]

Many women physicians, committed to the cause, were among the election workers in Portland. In addition to Esther Pohl, they included Amelia Ziegler, Katherine Gray, Gertrude French, Ella K. Dearborn, Eugenia Little, Florence Manion, L. Victoria Hampton, and Emma Maki.[35] Katherine Gray told a reporter that, "since it had been said the women generally were not in favor of the measure, she and her companions deemed it meet to show themselves and thus demonstrate the state of their feelings." Florence Manion noted, "We are . . . here to show the public that women are not contaminated by being with men on election day," a charge made by those who opposed women voting.[36]

Women doctors owed a debt to suffragists for their career opportunities, as Esther Pohl made clear in her suffrage speech at the Lewis and Clark Exposition, and on Election Day they were willing to risk those opportunities for the right to vote. Like other women who devoted time to the cause, they put their work at risk by taking time away for suffrage activities. And they placed their income at risk; as women whose work depended mostly on clients who were willing to see them, taking a controversial stand and taking public action could have negative consequences. Anna Shaw understood both. As she told Pohl, "I have never met such a grand and progressive lot of women doctors as there are here." "They have risked their bread and butter to take up this work."[37]

In spite of an effectively organized campaign, the measure received just 44 percent of the vote. Strong opposition came from well-financed liquor and business interests. Suffrage initiatives in 1908 and 1910 also failed. One reason was conflicts among local suffragists and with national leaders.[38] Abigail Duniway's loss of local and national support and her insistence on controlling the Oregon suffrage debate resulted in steady declines in support for the campaigns of 1908 and 1910. In 1910 Duniway put forward an initiative that would give tax-paying women the right to vote.[39] Socialists and Progressives, members of labor unions and other workers, and many women and men who considered themselves suffragists opposed the measure because of its class-based approach to voting power that privileged women who held property. Active work for the 1910 "taxpayer's suffrage" measure appears to have come only from Duniway and her dwindling number of supporters. Pohl was not an active participant in either the 1908 or 1910 campaigns.

The 1912 campaign, however, reversed this trend, with Esther Pohl Lovejoy and a diverse coalition of suffrage activists leading the way to victory. Over thirty years later, Nan Strandborg, who had been the executive secretary of the Portland Woman's Club Suffrage Campaign Committee and was in charge of publicity and press work in 1912, wrote to her friend about "those strange old days when you were our star speaker and chief money-raiser and I the one who chased after you with the handkerchiefs, parasol, pocket-books and other little impediments you were always leaving behind in the mad rush for luncheon clubs and anywhere else we could line you up for a platform blast!" Strandborg wondered "if we would have won that year without you. The bitter taste of the old line die harders like Abigail Scott Duniway was still in the mouths of the almighty males, through whose approval only could we gain the right to vote." But "you had the key to that and the courage to use it—giving courage to us all. Your witty and gay sallies with hard logical punches in between, and the purely feminine way in which your slim, daintily dressed figure leaned out appealingly when you were putting over your points, blotted out Abigail and her bitterness. You 'wowed' them. That's how it was done."[40]

Between the 1906 fight and the 1912 campaign, Esther Pohl advanced her medical and public health career and also experienced profound personal tragedy and transformation with the deaths of Freddie and Emil.

Throughout this period, she corresponded and visited with her suffrage mentor, Anna Howard Shaw, sharing her grief with a trusted friend and deepening their comradeship from the 1906 campaign. Pohl's 1910 medical studies in Vienna clinics broadened her outlook. On her return to the States, she stayed with Anna Shaw and her partner, Lucy Anthony, in Pennsylvania and attended suffrage gatherings in New York, where she strengthened friendships and networks.[41] Women physicians from many nations who were studying in Vienna celebrated Washington State's suffrage victory in 1910, Pohl recalled. There were also "rallies and banquets and all kinds of gratification meetings" in New York to celebrate, and Pohl was feted as a daughter of Washington State. The connections among the local, regional, national, and transnational movements for civic rights for women were clear, and Pohl learned "how much a single state gaining suffrage meant all over the world."[42]

In the midst of her work for the ballot in 1912, Esther Pohl met George Albert Lovejoy, an insurance executive with the Guarantee Fund Life Association. An early member of the suffrage society in Spokane, George moved to Portland in 1911. Active in fraternal organizations and in the Progressive Business Men's Club of Portland, he supported the votes for women campaign in Oregon.[43] The press made much of the couple's private trip to British Columbia for their July 30 marriage.[44] "George A. Lovejoy and Dr. Esther C. Pohl will henceforth work for the suffrage cause in double harness," the *Oregonian* revealed. "They have been doing so for some time, unknown to their friends, for they spirited themselves away from the city on July 29, being married the following day at Victoria, B.C." The couple "returned in secret to Portland, but the news leaked out through friends of the bridegroom, who could not understand why he did not re-engage his rooms at the Commercial Club."[45] The couple returned to Portland and made their residence at Esther's 393 Williams Avenue home.

Emil had been dead for over a year, Freddie for almost four. Esther had been to Vienna and the East Coast, and had talked with Anna Shaw about the scars that would not heal. George was ten years her junior, thirty-three to her forty-three. They shared an interest in Democratic politics and woman suffrage, and both were involved in community organizations. Esther did not leave many records of her time with George in her papers, but it appears that their shared interests and a hopeful desire for happiness were enough to establish a bond.

George A. Lovejoy. From the *Oregon Voter*,
December 30, 1922, 99.

By 1912 the votes for women movement had also changed, and the
national US political scene was in ferment. Important developments in
the long history of women's quest for voting rights in Oregon and the
nation suggested the possibility of a successful campaign. Oregon women
had what Esther Lovejoy called a "local grievance": they were voteless
but surrounded by states where women could cast a ballot. Women had
achieved the vote in Idaho (1896), Washington (1910), and California
(1911), and it appeared that the Republic of China would grant suffrage
to women.[46] And, in the recent Washington and California campaigns,
attention to popular culture and the mass advertising techniques pio-
neered in Oregon in 1906 had been effective.[47] At the national level, progressives and radicals vied with conservatives for the power to direct the
nation's policies and economy: progressive Robert La Follette challenged
William Howard Taft for the Republican nomination; Theodore Roosevelt left the Republicans to run as a Progressive third-party candidate;
Socialist Eugene Debs received over 900,000 votes; and Woodrow Wilson articulated a Democratic Progressivism in his winning platform.[48]
In Oregon, as in other western states, strong Socialist and Progressive
movements invigorated electoral politics and "helped to bring renewed
gains for women's political rights."[49]

Coalitions blossomed in 1912 because Abigail Scott Duniway was ill for much of the year, because there was no strong central organization, and because many workers were dissatisfied with Duniway's previous campaigns and her still hunt. Activists had to appeal to male voters, and they established suffrage leagues tailored to specific groups. These included the Colored Women's Equal Suffrage Association, the Chinese American Equal Suffrage League, and a Men's League of Multnomah County in Portland. Neighborhood, religious, and occupational groups joined in support of the cause—some twenty-three in Portland alone, and over seventy across the state. The State Federation of Labor, the Civic League and the Woman's Christian Temperance Union, Portland's Central Labor Council, the Socialist Party of Oregon, the Oregon State Grange, and the State Woman's Press Club all endorsed suffrage, lending strength, legitimacy, and publicity to the campaign.[50]

Esther Pohl was a founding member of the Portland Woman's Club Suffrage Campaign Committee, organized in January 1912. Anna Shaw chose to work with her trusted suffrage allies Esther Pohl and Sarah A. Evans through this organization, contributing two hundred dollars each month from an anonymous NAWSA donor to the club committee for suffrage work. Pohl worked throughout the campaign with the Woman's Club Suffrage Campaign Committee, sponsoring events such as the publicity-generating Octogenarians for Suffrage forum that April.[51] She also joined the Portland branch of the College Equal Suffrage League and the Portland Equal Suffrage League.[52]

In September 1912, Esther Lovejoy organized Everybody's Equal Suffrage League as a tangible symbol of the importance of coalitions and collaboration in the campaign and also as a jab to the competition and conflict that had been a part of suffrage politics. Everybody's League was "free from all cliques and class distinctions and open to all," and its "members scorn any rules and regulations." Wage-earning women had told Lovejoy that subscriptions for other suffrage societies, sometimes at several dollars per month, were out of their reach, but that they wanted to participate. Anyone could be a life member of Everybody's League for a subscription of twenty-five cents, and everybody who was a member automatically became a vice president.[53] According to the *Oregon Journal*, the "notable thing about the league is its democracy, the membership includes both men and women, young and old, and from the humblest walks of life up to and including United States senators and supreme

Members of the Portland Woman's Club Suffrage Campaign Committee, April 1912. Left to right: Elizabeth Eggert, Grace Watt Ross, and Esther Pohl visiting suffrage supporter Francis X. Matthieu. Reproduced by permission of Oregon Health & Science University Historical Collections & Archives, Portland, Oregon.

[court] judges."[54] Everybody's League principles struck a chord with many Oregonians, and the group enjoyed favorable press—including news of the subscription of New York suffragist and society leader Alva Belmont—and took credit for some six hundred members by the close of the campaign.[55]

As a speaker and an organizer, Pohl emphasized collaborative coalition building. Early in the campaign she established a twice-monthly suffrage forum in the Olds, Wortman, and King department store auditorium that brought a variety of groups together, and she was a frequent forum speaker.[56] Pohl spoke on suffrage at a University of Oregon alumnae dinner, and she also addressed the Portland Transportation Club (with "unique invitations in the form of a prescription signed by Dr. Pohl"), the members of the Grange, and the Colored Women's Equal Suffrage Association of Portland.[57] In her speeches Pohl voiced the themes central to her own suffrage philosophy: woman suffrage was just and equitable, and women needed suffrage to make laws for a better community. Oregon needed to catch up with Idaho, Washington, and California, and grant the vote to its women.[58] The vote was vital for wage-earning and professional women to make workplaces safe, wages fair, and occupations and training accessible.[59] In particular, she stressed that women needed the vote to maintain healthy communities. She asked members of the Oregon Grange, for example, if a woman "is compelled to drink infected water because the city in which she lives empties its sewage into the river at one point and takes its drinking water out of it at another, is she not just as apt to die from Typhoid as the man who approves of the system? If she is too poor to pay the water rate fixed by the city government," Pohl asserted, "the water is promptly turned off, though she may have a half dozen thirsty children waiting at the faucet." Women, she said, should have a voice in "making those laws."[60]

In May 1912, Ernst Hofer, editor of the Salem *Capital Journal*, invited Pohl to contribute to a symposium on woman suffrage. She responded with "An Argument for Woman Suffrage." "Above and beyond the claims which men and women have in common," she wrote, "there are reasons why women should vote which are associated with the divine function of motherhood to which no man can lay the slightest claim." A woman was motivated by love to sacrifice and protect her children, for whom "she has labored and suffered the ordeal of blood and pain, and gone down to the gates of death to bring into this world." Alternatively, a man was "moved by self-interest to guard the thing for which he has labored, the work of his head and hand, if you please, which is usually represented by the symbol $."[61]

Women needed the vote to fight "the interests." While other progressives defined "the interests" as banks, trusts, and corporations only, Pohl defined these same powerful combinations specifically as *male* interests. Antisuffragists, she wrote, maintain that "a woman's place is in her home," and Pohl agreed with the premise, but "bitter experience" demonstrated that "the despoiler of the home usually comes through the water faucet, or in the milk bottle, or with unclean or adulterated food, or in some other way that, as a domestic fixture, [a woman] is powerless to prevent but as an active participant in the franchise she might effect by her influence on municipal and state laws." Moreover, "predatory man has invaded her sphere" and taken "away her washing," sending women "to follow it into the laundries or starve." Male interests took away spinning and food preservation, and women had to follow them to factories, meat-packing plants, and canneries "until eight million women have been obliged to follow their work into the world." There they traded the "home rule of the mother" for "the factory rule of the master." Women needed the ballot to defend themselves and their families in these new industrial conditions. "No man who thinks, and is imbued with the spirit of justice, will deny their petition."[62]

Male corporate interests had achieved "marvelous results . . . since they invaded Woman's Sphere and appropriated her profitable industries. They have systematized all kinds of women's work . . . with a progressive genius." One need only look, Pohl said with tongue in cheek, at the food industry. "Their embalmed sausages are enough to turn the mummy of King Ptolemy green with envy"; processed meats have "realized the most optimistic dreams of the old alchemists, and their tomato catsup compounded of turnips and analine dyes has proved the practical value of modern commercial chemistry." It was a shame, Pohl continued, "that these ingenious enterprises should have been hampered by the pure food law, backed by the organized but unenfranchised women of the land." Pohl called for the intelligent cooperation of both men and women for protection of "the family home, the home city, the home state and the home nation." All were directly or indirectly affected by politics and required women's empowerment through the vote.[63]

Lovejoy increased her use of the methods of mass advertising and popular culture in the 1912 campaign. From headquarters in the Rothchild Building, she and her Woman's Club Suffrage Committee colleagues managed an inventory of "votes for women" buttons, banners, flags, and leaflets in the yellow suffrage colors—an estimated 165,000 pieces of literature and 50,000 buttons across the campaign.[64] The State Central Campaign Committee, of which Everybody's League and the Woman's Club Committee became a part, arranged for a giant "Votes for Women" sign to be hung on the left-field fence of the new Portland baseball grounds during the opening game of the Pacific Coast League in April.[65] The committee convinced Portland department stores to advertise suffrage and to have suffrage window displays.[66] Lovejoy helped to sponsor suffrage slide shows at Portland motion picture theaters. W. M. "Pike" Davis of the Men's League purchased advertising space on the drop curtains at Portland's Orpheum and Empress Theaters, and by the end of the

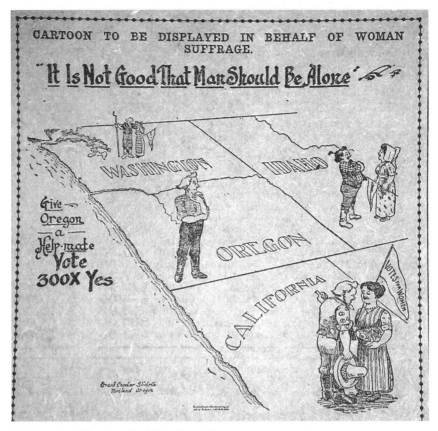

"It Is Not Good That Man Should Be Alone." From the *Oregonian*, October 21, 1912, 10.

campaign, suffrage groups, including Everybody's League, had lantern slide shows in over thirty movie houses in Portland and vicinity.[67] "One of the notably striking ones shows the states of California, Washington, and Idaho with portraits of a man and woman in the center surrounded by the products of the states," the *Oregon Journal* reported. "The state of Oregon is represented by a lonely, dejected man. The lesson is obvious."[68]

Lovejoy headed up a suffrage "flying squadron," another of the popular new tactical innovations that would become a standard tool for campaigning.[69] "In an automobile, a flying trip is made through some territory selected," the *Oregonian* noted, "and in the wake of the 'flying squadron' the signboards, crossroads stores, and private mail boxes along the rural routes blossom with a burden of suffrage literature." Lovejoy and her group drove a wide "circle of seventy miles out of Portland" through adjacent Clackamas County to small towns and larger communities such as Estacada, Milwaukee, and Oregon City. "Signs were tacked in convenient places, and a veritable storm of literature was precipitated upon the people in the district through which the party passed."[70]

Esther Pohl took advantage of the Portland Rose Festival in June 1912, one of the best opportunities for mass advertising in the city. Working with W. M. "Pike" Davis of the Men's League, who was one of the festival organizers, Pohl and members of the Woman's Club Campaign Committee sponsored a suffrage lunch wagon. Each day of Rose Festival week, they prepared and sold sandwiches, doughnuts, ice cream, and sodas from 12:00 until 2:00 on the downtown streets. They decorated what the press called a "Ballyhoo Wagon," donated by the Speedwell Auto Truck Company, with "bunting, festoons of rose and green, votes for women flags, and signs that bring home the Pacific Coast Suffrage slogan: 'Oregon Next.'"[71] Pike Davis rode along as the "spieler," and the lunch wagon attracted interested throngs.[72] The group invited Hilda Keenan, an actor then performing at the Orpheum Theater, to lend her celebrity to the cause. Keenan won spectators' acclaim as she tossed a sandwich to a sailor who was watching the festivities atop a telephone pole. When the occasional antisuffragist booed or hissed the wagon along the route, suffrage workers rang a dinner bell and smiled, and the crowd responded with applause.[73] It was all spectacle and street performance—ballyhoo that made for unequaled and unforgettable publicity. The suffrage lunch wagon drew festivalgoers and spectators by the thousands and provided entertainment and suffrage publicity throughout the week.[74] Holding the giant Votes for Women umbrella on the suffrage lunch wagon, surveying the bunting and flags festooning the converted Speedwell truck, Esther Pohl epitomized the modern suffrage campaigner.

Perhaps the most strategic success for Lovejoy was her facilitation of the widely successful campaign visit of her friend and NAWSA president Anna Howard Shaw in September 1912.[75] Shaw launched the Oregon segment of her trip at the second annual Pendleton Round-Up on September 27, with Lovejoy there to greet her.[76] At the Round-Up, Shaw spoke from an automobile, "holding the meeting at night on the street in which thousands of horsemen—cowboys, Indians, and ranchmen—were riding up and down, blowing horns, shouting, and singing." People cheered, stopped to talk and shake her hand, and threw flowers. Her one regret, Shaw said, was that she had arrived too late to see the cowgirls com-

Suffrage Lunch Wagon, Portland Rose Festival, June 1912. Esther Pohl holds the umbrella, with her sister Charlotte standing next to her. Courtesy of Amy Khedouri.

pete.[77] Ten carloads of suffrage supporters greeted the entourage with banners and cheers at the Union Depot in Portland. Shaw spoke from Lovejoy's car at Fifth and Alder Streets for an hour and a half to a crowd of six hundred. The *Oregonian* described her "instant appeal" to the audience, and the *Oregon Journal* claimed that she held "complete sway over those within the sound of her voice."[78]

Shaw's nonstop pace and her enthusiastic reception in Portland continued for two more days, with speeches, a luncheon in her honor at the Hotel Portland with some 500 guests, an address to the Portland Equal Suffrage League, and a mass meeting at the Multnomah Hotel Ballroom.[79] From Portland Shaw traveled to the college campuses at Corvallis and Eugene, then to community events in Roseburg, Grants Pass, Ashland, and Medford. The benefits of her visit to the Oregon campaign were incalculable. As Lovejoy and the Woman's Club committee reported, "The number and enthusiastic spirit of those attending these affairs has given a marked stimulus to the campaign and been a splendid means of advertising."[80] In later years Lovejoy summed up this portion of the 1912 campaign this way: "Dr. Shaw—Let 'er buck."[81]

"Selling suffrage" took vision and coordination—and money. Antisuffragists spent $5,213.40 to defeat the measure. Supporters outspent them by almost two to one, with $10,119.07. This included the $200 per month from Anna Shaw as well as other funds from the Portland Woman's Club Suffrage Campaign Committee led by Esther Lovejoy ($2,298.06), contributions from the Oregon State Equal Suffrage Association ($1,704), the College Equal Suffrage League ($2,716.41), and the Portland Equal Suffrage League ($2,911.70). W. M. "Pike" Davis contributed $488.90 as an "Individual, advocating Equal Suffrage Amendment."[82]

For Esther Pohl Lovejoy, the important thing about the suffrage victory in November 1912 was not the close vote—the measure passed by 52 percent, a margin of just 4,161 votes—but the impressive turnaround from the 1910 vote and the ability of Oregon suffragists to reverse the results of the adverse campaigns that had preceded this one. The numbers, she wrote, "demonstrate that the decision may be reversed in a very short time," with the hard work of a broad coalition of suffrage workers.[83] This powerful result, this positive application of the Oregon initiative system, and this impressive victory for equality was due, in her view, to the strength that came from diverse organizations, from suffragists working with "neither head nor tail to the campaign." Lovejoy's Everybody's Equal Suffrage League epitomized the success of collaborative suffrage activism. The victory was attributable to the tactics of modern mass media and advertising for the cause used by these diverse suffragists and their organizations to such good effect, and to Lovejoy's relationship with Anna Howard Shaw and NAWSA leaders. Coalition politics also created limited but noteworthy bridges across racial lines with cooperative work among white, African American, and Chinese American suffragists.

After the achievement of woman suffrage in 1912, Esther Lovejoy and other Oregon women were conscious of the power of their right to the ballot and of the opportunities for women to act politically, including participating in party politics, lobbying, elections, and office holding. As residents of one of the nine western states where women had full voting rights, Oregon women also claimed an important role in the practical political strategies of the national suffrage movement and in the vision of what was possible for women across the nation. After the 1912 elections, suffragists at the national level were enmeshed in conflicts about strategies and tactics. This led to a split between NAWSA, chaired by Anna Howard Shaw, and after 1915 by Carrie Chapman Catt, and the Congressional Union (CU) led by Alice Paul and Lucy Burns.

After 1912 Lovejoy continued to build coalitions across organizations in Oregon with Everybody's Equal Suffrage League and, in 1916, with the Oregon Equal Suffrage Alliance. In the post-1912 debate Lovejoy stood strongly and actively for NAWSA and, with Anna Shaw and Carrie Chapman Catt, against the Congressional Union. And she took an active role on the national suffrage stage, serving as the Oregon State representative to the NAWSA Congressional Committee in 1916 and on a special suffrage "Emergency Corps" in 1920. Lovejoy defined her political identity as a member of the progressive Democratic Party in Oregon. She had held office as a Democratic appointee, was now a voting party member, and hoped to hold elective office in the future.

As the election of 1914 neared, Alice Paul and Lucy Burns and members of the CU believed that the Democratic Party, in the majority in the US Congress, was responsible for congressional failure to enact a woman suffrage amendment. They advised enfranchised women to vote against all Democratic candidates for Congress. Having been schooled in British politics, where the parliamentary party could be held accountable far more readily than in the United States, Paul and Burns believed that holding the party in power responsible for suffrage would demonstrate the political clout of women voters as a bloc and would result in action on votes for women at the national level. The policy would even be in force in states such as Oregon, where Democratic US senators George Chamberlain and Harry Lane were strong suffragists. As Alice Paul wrote to Chamberlain, who was up for reelection, "While we feel no opposition to you as an individual and appreciate whatever service you may personally have rendered to the suffrage movement, it is apparent that your individual interest in suffrage can avail us little as long as your party, which is now in control of Congress, continues its unfriendly attitude toward our resolution."[84]

For many NAWSA members, with their history of nonpartisanship and carefully cultivated relationships with many Democrats in Congress, the strategy seemed incredibly destructive.[85] Esther Lovejoy, Sarah A.

Evans, and many others in Oregon felt that opposing the reelection of suffrage supporter George Chamberlain to the US Senate went against all of the political work that they had done over years of campaigning. To Lovejoy, the strategy was an insult to her political identity as former Democratic office holder, party member, and hopeful office seeker.

In September 1914 the CU sent organizers to work against the reelection campaigns of congressional Democrats in western states. It was nonpartisan action, Alice Paul said, "We have no more of a grievance against the Democratic Party than the Republican Party. It is our purpose to oppose any party in power that uses such power to oppose the enfranchisement of the women of America."[86] New York activist Jessie Hardy Stubbs became the lead CU organizer for Oregon, joined by North Carolina suffragist Virginia Arnold.[87] With headquarters in the new Pittock Building in Portland, built on property held by *Oregonian* owner and business magnate Henry Pittock, Stubbs began to make contacts, gave interviews, and arranged for literature and other printed materials. She set up her first mass meeting at the Portland Central Library.[88] Seeking to establish common ground, Stubbs wrote a letter to Esther Lovejoy requesting a personal meeting. "Your name was given to me in Washington as a woman suffragist who could be counted on at all times. . . . I am a widow of a physician and a trained nurse, so that I can well appreciate that you are a very busy woman. However, I am especially eager to lay the work of the Congressional Union, its hopes and aims before you."[89]

Lovejoy accepted Stubbs's invitation and also attended Congressional Union meetings to learn about their views first hand. Stubbs reported to Alice Paul that Lovejoy was "putting up a pretty stiff fight against me" and sent along newspaper clippings to prove it. But, Stubbs acknowledged, "she really is a very bright woman and an admirable opponent, in that she comes quite frankly to me and tells me to my face what she thinks of my whole campaign." Lovejoy, she told Paul, "is an ardent admirer of Dr. Shaw's and was quite prepared—I think—to find me wearing horns. She was broad minded and liberal enough to come and see me and convinced herself that this was not so." In Stubbs's view, Lovejoy's position stemmed not only from her support for and loyalty to Anna Shaw and NAWSA but also from her partisan hopes and her place in pragmatic Oregon politics. Lovejoy "has had a Democratic appointment," she wrote, "and expects more favors at the hands of that party."[90]

In Oregon, Democrats and Republicans supported woman suffrage as a political reality after 1912, and the Socialist, Progressive, and Prohibition Parties had provided longstanding support. Progressive Democrats Harry Lane and George Chamberlain had both been early supporters. The Congressional Union's goal of defeating Democratic candidates was, for Lovejoy, nothing short of "political treason"[91] against Democratic candidates in Oregon who had supported suffrage and against Oregon women who supported those candidates. In addition, Lovejoy could not shake her belief that the CU's plan was partisan because it distinguished among parties and targeted particular party members regardless of their support for suffrage. Lovejoy believed that, to be nonpartisan, suffrage work must be done outside of party politics. Western women voters such as Lovejoy faced the practical dilemma of a voting women's bloc versus women's individuality in political participation far earlier than women whose votes came with the 1920 federal amendment.[92]

If Congressional Union supporters "are going to repay public men who work for suffrage by this sort of ingratitude," Lovejoy told the *Oregon Journal*, "it will discourage men from working for equal suffrage in other states.[93] When Chamberlain returned to Oregon to campaign at the end of October, after the close of the congressional session, Lovejoy helped organize a rally at the Portland Commercial Club and spoke alongside Chamberlain at a Democratic women's meeting at the Central Library.[94] "These women are telling, boasting, how they antagonize Congress with the threat of the potential power of 4,000,000 women votes in the west," she said at the Chamberlain meeting. "They would have us believe that they control these votes. But the women of the west will cast their ballot as they want to, and not according to the dictates of the east."[95] Lovejoy was particularly incensed at what she considered Stubbs's patronizing attitude during her suffrage "chalk talks" at the Pittock Building. At the CU headquarters there, Stubbs and Arnold "had a nice little school-room with about fifty seats and a real black-board," Lovejoy told Anna Shaw, and they invited voting women to come learn about politics.[96] Resolutions passed at a meeting of Everybody's Equal Suffrage League protested the CU's policy, "which, in effect, is to shoot a close friend to spite a distant enemy," and was "unworthy of Oregon women." League members concluded, "We resent these efforts to lead the women of Oregon and other states into a position of ingratitude to the men through whose help they now enjoy the right to vote.[97]

Lovejoy also asked determined questions about contributions to the CU campaign, because, in her view, this was the most solid evidence of the union's partisanship. Stubbs had written to Alice Paul, "These wonderfully beautiful headquarters were given to us rent *free*." Mr. Kelly, rental agent for the new Pittock Building, was "a close personal friend" of R. A. Booth, the Republican candidate for the US Senate running against George Chamberlain. Kelly gave the CU "a suite of five rooms all around the most prominent corner" of the building for their use during the campaign without charge. But, she wrote, "It is a secret that we got the headquarters *free, absolute!*"[98] But the situation was obvious to Lovejoy. She knew how hard it was to raise funds for a nonpartisan suffrage campaign in Oregon, she wrote to Anna Shaw, "and it seems strange that these women from Washington [DC] could afford commodious quarters in the finest building in the city." But "the fact that the Pittock Block belonged to Mr. Pittock, who owns and controls the *Oregonian*, which was strongly supporting the candidacy of Mr. Booth . . . together with the fact that this building is controlled by Whitmer-Kelley Co. and that Mr. Kelly was a member of the Booth-Kelly Lumber Company, gave rise to the suspicion that the quarters had been provided by those interested in the campaign of Mr. Booth." Here were "the interests" indeed.[99]

Throughout the fall 1914 campaign and beyond, Lovejoy tried to follow the Congressional Union's money. In her first published press interviews, Stubbs emphasized that the CU had some $15,000, and in her enthusiasm indicated, "We will raise a lot more."[100] Lovejoy wanted to know, she told the *Oregon Journal*, "the source of this $15,000 Mrs. Stubbs says she has to spend in this state. . . . I think she is getting this money from certain interests that want to defeat the Democratic administration." In a number of speeches and interviews, Lovejoy accused the union of using the "cloak of suffrage to cover their designs."[101] She was so relentless in her queries about funding that Portland CU member Mary Cachot Therkelsen threatened Lovejoy with legal action for damages.[102]

At the end of October, Jessie Stubbs responded to Lovejoy in a public forum. The money, Stubbs said, "came from the generous contributions of such women as [Alva] Belmont and hundreds of others." Most of these women had previously given donations to NAWSA, including funds for the 1912 Oregon campaign, she said. Lovejoy and the Portland Woman's Club Suffrage Campaign Committee "received regularly a goodly sum toward the campaign. . . . by many of the same women who today prefer to show their support" for the Congressional Union. "Money from the East was welcome in those strenuous campaign days," Stubbs said. "In the great battle for National woman suffrage, what is the difference between 1912 and 1914? None at all."[103] Stubbs did not mention the Pittock Building arrangement but instead emphasized women's individual contributions and put the question back on Lovejoy. Lovejoy had accepted Eastern money and support in 1912 and was rejecting it in 1914. What was the difference?

George Chamberlain won reelection to the Senate with 46 percent of the vote, to his Republican opponent R. A. Booth's 36 percent, something Lovejoy termed an "astonishing majority" given that Republican James Withycombe had won the governorship with 48 percent. She believed that the CU campaign had been helpful to Chamberlain's victory and considered the results to be a vindication of her position and of the independence of western women voters.[104] For her part, Jessie Stubbs took heart that Chamberlain's advertising in the last week of the campaign had used the slogan "He fought for National Woman Suffrage." She believed that this meant that their work had made woman suffrage a national issue.[105] National CU leaders echoed Stubbs's view. The union had worked against forty-three incumbent Democrats for the US House, Senate, and governorships; twenty-three were not reelected.[106] This meant that both Stubbs and Lovejoy could claim victory for their work and for their positions in the campaign.

Lovejoy continued to oppose CU strategies and actions. She protested at the Women Voters' Conference in San Francisco in September 1915, which was hosted by the CU, and claimed her place and her voice as a western woman voter. She raised the question of representation of all western women voters, including those who did not support the Congressional Union, and a "sharp dispute" ensued.[107] Alice Paul eventually stepped in and made a ruling that since the Congressional Union had organized the convention and paid for it, only union members would be able to vote there. The San Francisco *Examiner* reported that the women "opposed to the Congressional Union policy will present a resolution . . . opposed to the 'cut and dried, autocratic' programme, which, according to Dr. Lovejoy, was all ready to be put through before the convention was called."[108]

Lovejoy's allegiance to NAWSA's strategies and to the national Democratic Party in these suffrage conflicts led her to embrace a policy that compromised the coalitions she had built across racial lines in her activism. At the San Francisco meeting, Lovejoy asked why suffragists there opposed NAWSA's willingness to work with Democrats in the South. "In view of the fact that the South is against National woman suffrage . . . will we not get National suffrage sooner if we work on a measure acceptable to them?"[109] Members of both NAWSA and the CU, as well as most white suffragists, as historian Rosalyn Terborg-Penn has demonstrated, "virtually abandoned" African American women in their quest for the vote.[110]

A change of leadership brought important transformations to NAWSA, and Esther Lovejoy's suffrage activism moved beyond the West. At the 1915 NAWSA convention in Washington, DC, members elected Carrie Chapman Catt to be the new president of the organization. Anna Howard Shaw, released from active leadership, was named honorary president. Catt brought with her a strong organizational style and skills in dealing with conflicts and factions. Her Winning Plan focused on strong and organized action for the federal amendment, with particular attention on lobbying and publicity, and efficient organization at both the state and national levels. There was room for state suffrage action in the Winning Plan, but within the context of this larger effort. NAWSA formed a congressional committee, and in 1916 Lovejoy became its Oregon representative.[111]

Lovejoy embraced the Winning Plan nationally and worked to transform local and regional suffrage activism to support the federal suffrage amendment. She remained a loyal friend to and correspondent with Anna Howard Shaw but also began to work with Carrie Chapman Catt. Lovejoy conferred with Catt and Shaw on plans for a new suffrage organization in Oregon that would affiliate with NAWSA. Under Lovejoy's leadership, the Oregon Equal Suffrage Alliance was formed in December 1916.[112] In a state where women could vote, it was a challenge to create a group that would not be associated or identified with a political party, and Lovejoy worked to achieve a balance. "It was not so easy to get the right women officers," she wrote to Catt. "I found it quite impossible to please everybody. Partizan [sic] politics was hard to eliminate," with "every one declaring for non-partizanship and yet partizan to the tips of her toes."[113]

Lovejoy and the Oregon Equal Suffrage Alliance remained solidly in the NAWSA camp during the First World War. When Carrie Chapman

Catt visited Portland as the United States entered the war in the spring of 1917, Lovejoy presided at a luncheon attended by some six hundred people sponsored by the alliance.[114] Oregon Equal Suffrage Alliance members followed Catt's planned dual role during the war by adopting a program to support food conservation as a war effort. Lovejoy spoke at an organizing meeting, and alliance members set up headquarters in Portland as a "clearing house for all women who want to take an active hand" in war work.[115]

On June 4, 1919, Congress passed federal woman suffrage legislation, and the next step would be for thirty-six state legislatures to ratify the measure to place the Nineteenth Amendment into the federal constitution. By March 1920, thirty-five had done so, including Oregon in special session on January 12, 1920.[116] As attention turned to Connecticut as a possible last state to ratify, NAWSA sent Lovejoy and other activists to that state in May in a suffrage "Emergency Corps." Although the Emergency Corps did not convince the Connecticut governor to hold a special session to consider the matter, the *Woman Citizen* named Lovejoy as a "western woman of more than national prominence" representing Oregon in the corps.[117]

In August 1920, Tennessee became the final state needed to ratify the federal suffrage amendment. Lovejoy and other Portland suffragists celebrated this final step on a long journey with a victory luncheon at the Crystal Room of the Benson Hotel. At noon on August 28, 1920, Portlanders celebrated by blowing whistles and ringing bells. Lovejoy urged women to look to the future, making "a plea for independence of thought and action, declaring that if women fail to stand together then they will not achieve the great things that lie before them."[118]

CHAPTER 6

The First World War and Transnational Activism

F OR Esther Lovejoy, the First World War was a vital bridge leading her from local and national feminist activism to organization and activism on a transnational scale. The conflict was also a turning point in Lovejoy's understanding of the effect on women of war and militarism. From this understanding, she created a new vision of the possibilities of social change and constructive resistance. From September 1917 to February 1918 Lovejoy went to France as a representative of US women's organizations to study the public health needs of women and children in devastated areas. In France she found that wartime violence against women took the form of rape, dislocation, poverty, and disease, and she developed a strong critique of militarism and war. Lovejoy's experiences and observations also underscored her belief that women were capable, equal citizens with men and that women could cross national, class, and professional divides to unite for progressive action. When she returned to the States, Lovejoy developed her ideas across several speaking tours, in written reports and published articles, and in her book *The House of the Good Neighbor*, published by Macmillan in a first edition in 1919, with a second edition with a foreword by Herbert Hoover in 1920. At the close of the war, Lovejoy used these ideas to build a postwar program for action by helping to organize and direct visionary new transnational organizations for medical women and medical relief.

For many US women, including Esther Lovejoy, the First World War was a watershed in the struggle to define and claim the full rights of female citizenship.[1] While the war brought opportunities for many groups of women to extend their progressive activism, it was also a time of severe repression of civil liberties, anti-immigrant sentiment, and continuing violence against Americans of color. In the period from 1912 to 1920, Portland and Oregon saw challenges to the established order and increasingly harsh crackdowns on radicals and on those suspected of radicalism.[2] And, with the coming of the war and the Russian Revolution, fears of disloyalty and an emphasis on "100 percent Americanism" led to a series of federal and state acts that trampled constitutional protections and to the repression of even moderate reformers in Oregon and in the nation.[3]

Lovejoy's mentor, Harry Lane, who represented Oregon in the US Senate, was one of six in that body who opposed the United States entering the war. The Oregon press printed inflammatory headlines and political cartoons showing Lane goose-stepping in a German uniform before the Kaiser. Most Oregonians condemned Lane for his position and called for his resignation or recall, but there were some who supported him, including many in organized labor, Socialists, and Ada Wallace Unruh of the Woman's Christian Temperance Union.[4] The *Oregonian* interviewed a wide array of people from various political and activist circles, including Esther Lovejoy, on their reactions to Lane. Lovejoy did not condemn and censure Lane outright, but she hesitated to support him openly in this repressive climate. She took a safer road and compromised her loyalty to the man who had mentored her in Democratic city politics. "I don't really feel like giving any expression of opinion at this time, although I have a very strong opinion," she told the reporter. "There may be something about it that we don't understand yet. I prefer to reserve my opinion until I know all about it."[5] With the stress of this virulent opposition, Lane's poor health worsened, and he died in California while returning home to Portland in May 1917.

Lovejoy provided more active support for her Portland medical colleague Dr. Marie Equi, who was imprisoned in San Quentin for speaking out against the war. When Equi was working for parole in 1921, Lovejoy followed the case, was in contact with Equi's attorney, Helen Hoy Greeley, and took action to free her colleague. Writing to Portland attorney C. E. S. Wood in the spring of 1921, Equi told Wood that Lovejoy was aware that Justice Department officials had tried to block Equi's parole. Lovejoy worked with other women physicians to send a petition to the

Department of Justice on Equi's behalf that June. It appears that Love-joy was also in communication with the Justice Department regarding the progress of Equi's parole. A friend told Equi that Lovejoy "had a letter from D. of J. saying the parole was awaiting the signature of Daugherty. The Women's Medical Society has taken action yesterday [and] we hope for results."[6]

Unlike Lane and Equi, but like many other progressives, Lovejoy initially gave her wholehearted support to a war that could "make the world safe for democracy."[7] True to her suffrage politics and alliances, she continued to support the National American Woman Suffrage Association, whose local and national leaders chose to support the war effort. And, as a woman physician, Lovejoy believed that the war offered an opportunity to showcase the medical work and skill of the nation's 6,000 women physicians. When the United States entered the conflict, Lovejoy, now forty-eight, took steps to get to France, using medical, suffrage, and other networks to accomplish her goal.

Lovejoy was an active member of the Medical Women's National Association (MWNA), which was founded in 1915 as a professional development and advocacy organization for women physicians.[8] Over the course of the war, through a registration of women doctors, petition drives, and test-case applications, members of the MWNA led a strong although ultimately unsuccessful fight for officer status for women in the US Army Medical Corps. Arguing that women physicians were prepared citizens eligible for such service, MWNA members pushed for a fuller female civic role in the context of wartime service.[9]

At the second annual meeting of the MWNA in New York City on June 5 and 6, 1917, Lovejoy made a strong case for the involvement of women doctors in wartime medicine. The group noted that women doctors in the warring nations were providing wartime medical care and they hoped to organize US women physicians to serve. They decided to establish a War Service Committee, headed by Dr. Rosalie Slaughter Morton, and held an organizational meeting on June 9.[10] Some in attendance believed that "since the majority of women doctors specialize in maternity cases, they would be of little use in war work." But Lovejoy disagreed, insisting that the "greatest service that can be rendered a nation is the propagation of the race either for war or peace and the second greatest service is the proper care of women about to bear and bearing children." And since male physicians were engaged in military service, she argued, "the work of caring for the maternity cases in the allied countries is naturally left to the women."[11] Members selected Lovejoy to chair a Committee on Maternity Service as part of the new MWNA War Service Committee. Lovejoy volunteered to go to France, and the MWNA authorized her to "go to Europe as the official representative of the War Service Committee" if she would pay her own expenses. Lovejoy was to survey "conditions affecting women before, during, and after childbirth," and then to "determine what women physicians might advantageously do in the way of relief work" in France.[12]

Lovejoy conferred with her friend and mentor Anna Howard Shaw, the newly appointed chair of the Woman's Committee of the Council of National Defense, about the work of her committee and the possibilities for partnership.[13] The women's branch of this wartime organization became an umbrella group for women's activities.[14] Shaw called a meeting of presidents of women's organizations on June 19 in Washington, DC, under the auspices of the Woman's Committee. Lovejoy and her colleague Dr. Eliza M. Mosher represented the MWNA at the meeting, joining women from over fifty other associations. Lovejoy reported that her obstetrics section of the MWNA's War Service Committee was going to investigate "if the needs of prospective mothers in the devastated regions of France are such" that the MWNA could "send to them trained medical women obstetricians to give them expert assistance, and to conserve the lives of the babies and little children." Lovejoy would then report back "to the women of this nation."[15] As the meeting concluded, Mosher pointed out that "a committee of men had been sent to France by the Red Cross to look into the physical needs of the people," and introduced a resolution, adopted unanimously, that Lovejoy be added as an official member and the first woman of this American Red Cross Commission to France. The women and their organizations, Mosher said, should all send telegrams to the Red Cross asking that Lovejoy be included. "The idea," she told them, "is to give her the authority to find out exactly what the condition is."[16] The Woman's Committee later sent a letter of recommendation and endorsement to the American ambassadors of France and England on Lovejoy's behalf and a "general letter concerning her work for maternity cases."[17]

In the meantime, Lovejoy was in contact with others who might help move her official visit to France along, and she did not hesitate to use her political and medical networks. Her Portland medical colleague K. A.

J. MacKenzie wrote a general letter of introduction for her, and senator George Chamberlain wrote directly to Jean Jules Jusserand, the French ambassador to the United States, introducing Lovejoy as his "warm personal friend."[18] Lovejoy also wrote to acting chair of the Red Cross Eliot Wadsworth and to Ambassador Jusserand himself. She outlined her plan and told Jusserand about the upcoming meeting of the Woman's Committee of the Council of National Defense. "Not fewer than two million women will be represented at this meeting. I shall present this matter to them and I should like your opinion regarding this proposed service before that time."[19] Jusserand indicated that he needed to cable the request to France; Lovejoy left word for Wadsworth and Jusserand that she would be returning to Portland and asked them to contact Anna Shaw with any updated information.[20]

Lovejoy saw gender discrimination at work in the delays. Writing to her friend, department store owner and reformer Edward Filene, she complained that, in spite of her endorsements and the fact that "the mission is not going to cost the Red Cross anything it seems strange that my credentials are not forthcoming." The organization, she said, could even give her a special commission if there were objections to her membership on the regular roster with the seventeen men already serving in France. "I talked with Mr. Wadsworth and didn't get anywhere. If I had been a man talking about the work and the needs of men, it might have been different, but with the greatest respect to Mr. Wadsworth, I doubt if he knows any more about the needs of women than I know about the needs of men—not as much, perhaps, because I have worked in hospitals among sick men." She informed Filene that she had also written to Ellis Meredith, the Colorado newspaper reporter and suffrage activist, now in Washington, DC, about the matter. Lovejoy told Filene that Meredith "has the reputation for getting results among women, but I don't know how she would get along with the men of the Red Cross."[21]

Lovejoy did not want the Red Cross delays to prevent her from going to France, and so she arranged for a place with the American Fund for French Wounded headed by Dr. Alice Barlow Brown in Paris and sailed for France on August 28. By September 14 Lovejoy was in Paris and the bureaucratic wheels had been sufficiently greased to secure her employment at the Children's Bureau of the Red Cross with a salary of $182 per month.[22] "There are delays and disappointments here," she wrote to her husband George Lovejoy, "but growth is rapid, and anyone with a capac-

Marie-Jeanne Bassot of the
Résidence Sociale, Paris.
Legacy Center, Drexel University College of Medicine,
Philadelphia, Pennsylvania.

ity for development will grow more here in a year than he could possibly grow in ten at home. In other words, me for France until the end of the war, if possible." It was, she said, "a big job for a woman, and I must make good."[23]

Lovejoy's expectations about her big job centered on finding a way for American women physicians to provide medical relief to French mothers and children. What she found was that French women, including social workers, doctors, and midwives, were capable and active participants in their own medical and relief work and welcomed her as a partner. Just as in the United States, her colleagues in France were engaged in social medicine. Lovejoy found immediate familiarity and formed strong bonds with French women as a result.

Lovejoy's most important relationship was with Marie-Jeanne Bassot, who administered the Résidence Sociale, a settlement house in the working-class factory district of Levallois, just northwest of Paris. Bassot recalled the October 1917 day she met Lovejoy at the local lyceum. "You wished, at once, to come and see our home, and in a quarter of an hour you had decided to come and live with us."[24] Like Chicago's Hull House and the Neighborhood House in Portland, this first of the French settlement houses, founded by Bassot in 1909, focused on providing social services to working and poor urban residents.[25] Its role intensified with the transformation of Levallois in wartime. Industrialists retooled prewar automobile and perfume factories there to manufacture munitions and airplanes, and employed women workers, many of whom were single or whose husbands or partners were at the war front. The staff of the Résidence provided day care and after-school care for children, established an employment office, and contracted with the French war department for local women to sew pajamas and shirts for soldiers by the piece at home while caring for their small children. Résidence staff established networks with other agencies such as the Red Cross to provide Levallois women and their families with subsidized milk and food. Visiting nurses established an antituberculosis campaign, and the staff provided other public health care through dispensary work in the community, with a focus on prenatal, childbirth, and early childhood care and nutrition.[26]

Chicago's Hull House founder Jane Addams asserted that settlement houses provided two important benefits to society. Their "objective value" was to administer services to urban residents in need, and their "subjective value" was to give women and men the chance to serve their communities by working in settlement houses.[27] Lovejoy found both at the Résidence Sociale, the settlement house she called "The House of the Good Neighbor." Bassot and her colleagues, Lovejoy noted, "were among the first to engage in this kind of work with the idea that the greatest good could be accomplished by living in the poor quarters of the city and developing connections with the different communities based upon personal association, common interest, sympathetic understanding, and affection."[28]

Lovejoy wrote *The House of the Good Neighbor* in 1919 in large part as a tribute to Bassot and the Résidence Sociale, and she connected the settlement house with donors in the States from groups such as the Port-

The Résidence Sociale, Paris. Photo by the author.

land Woman's Club.[29] At the close of the war, Lovejoy promoted a successful fund-raising campaign for the Résidence Sociale that included a visit from Marie-Jeanne Bassot to the States and a needs-assessment report presented to a variety of groups.[30] "Mlle. Bassot has been able to enlist a large co-operation among French people," Lovejoy asserted, "and I believe that the center in Paris is likely to become as great a health and social center as the Henry Street Settlement or the Hull House in Chicago."[31] Lovejoy maintained her partnership with Bassot and her financial support for many years thereafter, being herself a beneficiary of the "subjective value" of this pioneering social settlement as the Résidence continued to thrive as a Paris institution.

Lovejoy's investigation of conditions for women in France also took her outside the circle of the Résidence Sociale. She observed the Paris Maternity Clinic on the nearby Port Royal Boulevard and reported on food and milk canteens for single mothers. She visited munitions factories in and around Paris that employed many women workers, including André Citroën's showcase plant on the Quai de Javel in Paris.[32] In these factories she found women producing seventy-five-millimeter shells and other weapons, and noted that the skin of many women exposed to chemicals became bright yellow with toxic jaundice. She observed that the "industrial face of the nation had changed." With France "literally bustling with munition plants . . . modern woman had found her place in modern warfare."[33] Lovejoy also stayed at the refugee center established at the French resort city of Evian-les-Bains across Lake Geneva from Lausanne on the Swiss border. Here repatriated French citizens returned from exile and captivity in the occupied north, most of them women and children, and many in need of medical and surgical care.

With these observations, Lovejoy formed strong opinions about the powerfully gendered question of declining birthrates. As Susan Grayzel demonstrates, with the long-term falling birthrate and the death toll of the war, English and French pronatalists and nationalists "seized the opportunity that the war provided to launch intensified campaigns about the necessity of women performing the vital service of replenishing— reproducing—the nation." In France, especially, ethnic and national arguments centered on Germany's "superior birthrate" and therefore that nation's ability to outstrip others in war or peace. Policymakers paid attention to women and children during the conflict, Grayzel finds, but "rhetoric was not matched by substantive action." In essence, France and Germany "promoted motherhood and regulated women."[34] The birthrate question also connected to fears of "race suicide" in the United States, as white women had fewer children than immigrant women or women of color.[35]

Lovejoy had come to France to study the needs of women and children from a feminist standpoint of support. The "greatest service that can be rendered a nation is the propagation of the race either for war or peace and the second greatest service is the proper care of women about to bear and bearing children" she had told her medical women colleagues that summer. But those who saw wartime relief as an opportunity to investigate and "resolve" the declining birthrate, including some of Lovejoy's male medical colleagues from the United States, had different goals entirely. One example was Fred Lyman Adair, an obstetrician at the University of Minnesota Medical School, who volunteered for service in France with the Red Cross in 1918. Dr. William P. Lucas, head of the Children's Bureau in France, assigned him to "investigate and report on the Obstetric Situation in Paris with special reference to Prenatal Care." This placed Adair in France in the same department and at the same time as Lovejoy. Adair made an extensive study of French birth and death rates, with recommendations for a "campaign against abortion," the development of Red Cross prenatal clinics in Paris, and a program of maternal welfare work.[36] Adair asserted that the plan "was especially important for France because of the low and diminishing birthrate, the high percentage of sterility, the large number of abortions, and great number of still births and high infant mortality especially in the first two weeks of life."[37]

Adair tried to implement this plan by convincing Paris officials to give him the names of women who had applied for the city's prenatal allotment benefit and by visiting French homes (something, he said, about which the French were "very skeptical"). He recognized the need for providing adequate housing and food in addition to medical care, but felt that "those who occupy a low social and economic [status] have other needs than spasmodic material relief and . . . such relief should only be given after proper investigation and study." He also recommended creating a new and "different type of consultation for pregnant women where the women would be periodically observed by a well-trained medical man and not by a sage-femme (midwife)."[38] Lovejoy saw things very differently. "Wherever two or three scientific-looking men, or well-fed, well-groomed, prosperous-appearing gentlemen beyond the military age, were gathered together in earnest and solicitous communion of thought," she wrote, "the chances are they were discussing the birth-rate."[39] This kind of "maternalism" was not about supporting mothers but rather producing babies as a national cause, and Lovejoy made a strong distinction between this and her own social justice argument. She was changing her mind about her assertion that the "greatest service that can be rendered a nation is the propagation of the race either for war or peace."

France's birthrate had indeed been falling, Lovejoy wrote, "undoubtedly due in large measure to voluntary sterility maintained for the purpose of escaping . . . the suffering, danger, personal sacrifice and economic burden incident to child-bearing and child-rearing." The war made everything worse. "Food was scarce; milk was hard to obtain; and fuel was out of the question." During the wartime crisis "there was no class of women who needed work so much as the mothers of helpless children," but they had a hard time finding wage work, and, if pregnant, often lost their employment. They were "confronted with a choice of evils. If they worked in the factories their children were neglected, and if they did not work their children were hungry." Before and during the war, the "bare necessities of life were precarious, and the future so uncertain that prudent women—the kind that make good mothers—were unwilling to leave paid positions and face the inevitable tragedy of helpless motherhood." The State wanted more babies, she continued, "but from the standpoint of the average woman this involved a personal calamity and a crime against the unbegotten too terrible to contemplate."[40]

The "vital topic" of the birthrate was a gendered issue for Lovejoy. It "was discussed by men as an abstract national problem, but a prospective, over-burdened, or bereaved mother was not likely to get the national point of view. She knew from experience that the nation did not share the suffering or responsibility. That was her problem, and there was nothing abstract about it." Lovejoy put her confidence in the women. They were "not mathematicians, but they knew just how much money they could earn when they were well, and just how much was required to support their families. They also knew that if they were sick or disabled, their incomes would be lost and the children they already had would go hungry." With tongue in cheek, Lovejoy concluded, "And so they took a limited, feminine view of this grave question that was treated in a broad, abstract way by men of means to whom it was a problem of impersonal patriotism."[41]

Similar views about trusting women came through in Lovejoy's official recommendations. Lovejoy's primary goal in France and her charge from the women's organizations that sponsored her was to observe conditions among women and children and to recommend how US women physicians and others might provide the most effective assistance. In her official report to women's groups, Lovejoy was careful to recommend cooperation and respectful working relationships with French women midwives, nurses, physicians, and social workers, not a medical takeover on the order of Adair's plan. "The need for American women physicians in the maternity field in France is not urgent," she concluded in her official report. There were some 1,300 midwives in Paris, she noted, and they delivered most of the routine births in Paris and some 95 percent in the rest of the nation. The sage-femme was "popular with the French people . . . and in most cases her services would be preferred to those of foreign women physicians who are unable to speak French." Indeed, Lovejoy observed, the "favor with which French women physicians have been received, and which is also accorded to American women physicians, is probably because the French people regard these professional women as a higher order of their beloved sage-femmes."[42]

American women and other women physicians could provide valuable assistance to French medical workers. There was an important role for public health in the devastated areas, and they could help to raise funds and to create a structure for necessary support. "While the child-bearing women of France are not in need of maternity service" because they preferred French midwives and physicians, they "are in need of almost everything else" Lovejoy reported.[43] US women physicians could provide essential public health services and connect refugees and civilians with vital medical relief. They would not supplant French physicians and midwives but could work in cooperation with them to assist women in need.

In January 1918 the Red Cross asked Lovejoy to return to the States as a special representative and speaker for a spring fund-raising drive, and she left France in February.[44] She was so successful that the organization extended her stay, and she did not return to service in France during the conflict. Her full schedule connected her with many people across the nation with whom she shared her wartime observations. When she arrived in New York in early February 1918, she first reported to the Medical Women's National Association and then spent time in Washington, DC, briefing the Woman's Committee of the Council of the National Defense and other women's organizations.[45] On May 8 she spoke to the assembled representatives of the General Federation of Women's Clubs at their biennial convention in Hot Springs, Arkansas, and then went to the Midwest for the Red Cross, with stops in Chicago and various Michigan towns. For the rest of May through early June 1918, Lovejoy toured Florida and Georgia for the Red Cross Southern Division fund drive. She also made a report to her medical colleagues at the third annual meeting of the Medical Women's National Association in Chicago on June 10 and 11. She returned to Oregon on June 20 and embarked on a regional speaking tour for the Red Cross Pacific Division and for the YMCA to army logging camps and shipbuilding facilities across the region. From September 8 to 14 she was the featured speaker in the Fourth Liberty Loan Drive on a tour of southern and central Oregon, and then went to New Orleans for a tour of the South for the Red Cross. The influenza pandemic affected the scope of this last Red Cross campaign, which was stalled for most of October. Lovejoy participated in emergency public health work in New Orleans during that month and then resumed her Red Cross lectures to audiences in Louisiana and Arkansas at the end of November and through December 1918.[46]

LIBERTY LOAN

Rally Tonight
High School Auditorium
8 O'CLOCK   8 O'CLOCK

DR. ESTHER POHL LOVEJOY
Hear a Message Direct From
FRANCE
Special Music by the Liberty Chorus
Tues. Evening   Sept. 10 '18

Esther Pohl Lovejoy, Liberty Loan speech poster, 1918. Reproduced by permission of Oregon Health & Science University Historical Collections & Archives, Portland, Oregon.

Lovejoy contracted influenza that December and spent several months recuperating in Washington, DC. By April 1919 she was active again and won notoriety for her successful fund-raising for the Women's Liberty Loan. She reportedly raised more than $100,000 throughout the campaign and was featured in several Liberty Loan promotional airplane flights around Washington, DC.[47]

Writing enabled Lovejoy to reach an even wider audience. The Woman's Committee of the Council of National Defense mimeographed her written report of the situation in France and sent it to the over fifty national organizations under the council's umbrella as "Council of National Defense Circular 113." Lovejoy's report also went to the Red Cross. The Medical Women's National Association published the report in full in the May 1918 issue of *Woman's Medical Journal*. And that same month the popular *Ladies' Home Journal* published Lovejoy's account of the French women and children refugees repatriated at Evian.[48] Her chapter on "Democracy and Health" appeared in the edited volume *Democracy in Reconstruction*, and the *Woman's Medical Journal* ran a full copy of the chapter in its June 1919 issue.[49] Lovejoy also used this time to

Esther Pohl Lovejoy on Liberty Loan promotional flight, 1919, Washington, DC. Reproduced by permission of Oregon Health & Science University Historical Collections & Archives, Portland, Oregon.

develop and complete *The House of the Good Neighbor.* Reviewers praised the book, and the editors of the *Medical Women's Journal* serialized many of its chapters for readers during 1920.

From her extensive speaking tours, published reports and articles, and in *The House of the Good Neighbor,* Lovejoy developed four major conclusions about the effect of war on women. Her first was that wartime highlights women's capabilities and contributions and demonstrates their fitness for citizenship and equality with men. Her second point emphasized that wartime experience enabled women to transcend class, cultural, and professional differences and to unite for progressive action. Third, she demonstrated that wartime and war's violence affected women in a different way than it did men and therefore deserved specific attention. And fourth, Lovejoy mounted a critique of the destructive role of militarism and war in the modern state and called for an end to war as an instrument to resolve conflict between and among nations.[50]

In her speeches and writing Lovejoy emphasized women's contributions to the war and underscored their equality with men. "Compared with the usual apprenticeship period of a beginner in the different industries, these women developed remarkable efficiency in an unbelievably short time," she wrote of munitions workers. They made 90 percent of the seventy-five-millimeter shells for the French contribution to the Allied war effort.[51] In *The House of the Good Neighbor* Lovejoy used parallel examples of women's and men's service during wartime to emphasize their equality. "If a man fell at his gun, his place was filled and the fight went on. If a woman failed at her lathe, her place was filled and the work went on. Men might die and France might be lost, but not for the want of munitions, if her women could help it.[52] For Lovejoy the "manner in which women en masse have stepped under and lifted the burden of labor from the shoulders of men has amazed the world."[53]

Lovejoy also emphasized that wartime conditions called upon women to transcend the barriers of class, nationality, and professional status that divided them, to unite for progressive action. Cooperative work for the war effort, Lovejoy insisted, had created a "new aristocracy of service" rather than social class. Women factory workers and "women who have been deprived by generations of wealth in America" were finding common ground.[54] The elite women who founded the Résidence Sociale, she said, "realized that the exclusive circles from which they had escaped had succeeded in excluding the best part of life. . . . They wanted to be strong enough to help themselves and to help others . . . they had had enough tea and macaroons to last forever." And, more importantly, she observed, the "fight against established customs which these women had made for their own freedom of action, the right of self-determination and self-development," meant that they were also willing to grant to the working-class women at the Résidence Sociale the "independence of thought and action they had demanded for themselves."[55] Marguerite de Witt Schlumberger, the president of the French suffrage society, was surprised at the progressive opinions of the women workers at the Résidence. She gave a "mild" presentation on votes for women, "carefully restraining and modifying any opinions she considered too radical for her audience," Lovejoy noted. But afterward, Schlumberger told Lovejoy that she realized that, without having heard from the women at the Résidence, she was "not keeping abreast of all the phases of the woman movement."[56]

Lovejoy insisted that women suffered the violent effects of war differently than men experienced them. Women were victims of rape and experienced a loss of control over their bodies and their lives. In her speeches and in her published accounts, Lovejoy wrote of her experiences at the refugee center at Evian, where she had confronted what she considered to be the ultimate horror of war's violence. At the time of invasion, the Germans had "sorted out" the residents of northern French villages. "Those without military value were robbed of their earthly possessions, evicted en masse from their native towns and villages, herded together, and finally deported," she wrote, but "those with military value were detained by their conquerors." People who could fight, those who could labor, and those who could bear children, Lovejoy said, had military value to the Germans and were kept in the occupation zone.[57] Families were separated by the German policy of keeping "strong boys over fourteen" for labor value and "strong girls over sixteen" and "strong young women" with "less than one child" for labor and "breeding" value.[58] Men fought and worked, and women worked and were exploited sexually and economically. As a result, the Germans did not allow young women to be repatriated from occupied areas, "to prevent most of the children born to young French or Belgian women by German fathers" from leaving German territory.[59] The Germans "separated the women they could use for breeding and other purposes in Northern France and Belgium, just as though they were so many cattle."[60]

Lovejoy emphasized that women suffered the consequences of war not only by being raped by the "brutal soldier who breaks down the door with the butt of his rifle," but also from the soldier who "comes in kindness with a loaf of bread for her and her children and who actually affords her protection against all save himself."[61] Wartime exposed the lie in the traditional construction of men as the protectors and women as the protected. "The women who had been most carefully protected by their husbands and fathers were the most helpless," she wrote. "Under such circumstances," she believed, the "cumulative power of fear and want is harder to resist" than rape.[62] Women suffered the consequences of invasion, violence, rape, desperate impoverishment, and disease, and some, Lovejoy said, could turn only to the enemy for "protection." "Warfare is much worse for women than for men. Men have the right of death and they die fighting gloriously for their ideals. But women must live and be confiscated with the goods and the chattels."[63]

These observations and experiences led Lovejoy to a general critique of modern warfare and militarism and a call for an end to war. One of her strongest assertions came in her speech to the General Federation of Women's Clubs when she asked her audience to consider the effect of "military rule" on soldiers regardless of their nationality. "Suppose in this country (we all respect our troops, they are the highest type of men), suppose next to our military camps there was a village and the order went out to make this place as horrible as possible, the military order was no door shall be locked in this village; would that village be a safe place for women and girls?" Rather, such an order "makes that town the property of the soldiers."[64] The German private soldier, so often seen as the enemy, was in reality the "pathetic victim" of "military values."[65] Militarism was a process and a deadly power that trapped participants on all sides of the conflict. And the price of modern war was too great. Lovejoy argued that the "vital participation of women in this war means that war must cease between nations, or men must fall lower than beasts. There is no beast that will attack the female of its own species, and the successful conduct of future wars means the wholesale killing of the women of the enemy as well as the men."[66] Nations, Lovejoy believed, created a false "camouflage of holiness" for the "unholy sacrifices" of wartime."[67]

Lovejoy valued her US speaking tour and time to write, but she wanted to return to France. The November 11, 1918, armistice that ended the conflict, and the influenza pandemic that fall and winter, made it difficult for Americans to get clearance to go to France. One hopeful avenue Lovejoy had for a return was service with the MWNA War Service Committee, now renamed the American Women's Hospitals (AWH). In the last year of the war, the AWH had staffed two all-female medical units in France, to strong acclaim. Two of Lovejoy's Oregon colleagues, Mary McLaughlin, MD, and Mary Evans, MD, were in service with the AWH at Luzancy.[68] Lovejoy was in line to serve in the AWH in an anticipated fourth medical unit, but this was cancelled in late 1918 as the war concluded.[69] Lovejoy worked to secure another Red Cross assignment, which did not materialize. In April 1919 she wrote to Marie-Jeanne Bassot at the Résidence Sociale that she wanted very much to return to France, but wanted to "come without being connected with any organization" and without being "under orders. . . . I am far from rich, but I want to come back for a time, and I would rather pay my own expense and be free."[70]

As she worked to return to France, Lovejoy chafed at the regulation that prevented US women from serving overseas if they had husbands, sons, or brothers serving abroad. She considered the policy a blatant double standard that threatened her own wartime service and denied all women full citizenship rights. The US government withheld the passports of women with male relatives in the American Expeditionary Force, preventing them from engaging in any sort of overseas military service or even voluntary service abroad with organizations such as the Red Cross. The original Selective Service Act, which put military conscription into action in May 1917, drafted eligible men aged twenty-one to thirty. This age span was in place when Esther embarked for France in September 1917 and meant that the thirty-eight-year-old George Lovejoy did not have to register. And because he chose not to volunteer, Esther's service was unhampered by the rules. But in August 1918 Congress voted for an expansion of the draft age to between eighteen and forty-five, which meant that George was now eligible and would have to register.[71]

Lovejoy was concerned about how this would affect her own service and possibilities for work in France. In early September 1918 she contacted the Red Cross. "Mr. Lovejoy will register under the new draft, and I am a bit anxious about my passport," she wrote. "I have learned that it will be about two months before he [will likely be] inducted into the service, and that the rules regarding passports to wives have been relaxed somewhat. It is not likely that he will have the luck to be sent abroad . . . but I want to know whether my passport is safe in any case." She was booked for two months of work in the States, "but I don't want to lose my job in France and if my passport is in danger I must leave the country while I am able to do so." She asked for a response about her standing as soon as possible.[72] Significantly, she did not intend to obey the rule and stay home but to leave for France before George could be sent abroad. The war concluded before she had to test the policy.

In an undated speech from this period, Lovejoy outlined the civic double standard that this policy created for women's war service. "From the beginning of the war in 1914 it has been easy for a man to get into service," she said. "Age and physical condition permitting, all he had to do was to go to Canada and enlist. But service abroad for American women has been a coveted honor and privilege mighty hard to secure." The male relative rule was detrimental to women and also prevented trained and effective war workers from serving abroad. "Qualified and experienced married nurses are standing by wondering what there is in matrimony that depreciated the value of their service overseas." The young woman "who is shut out because of the existence of a strange half-brother, the issue of a second marriage" after her parents' divorce "twenty-five years ago, wishes she had been born an orphan." Lovejoy acknowledged that "personal preference does not cut much figure with a truly patriotic woman," but women wanted to know the real reasons for the ban. "Throughout the length and breadth of the land questions along this line are insistently being asked which nobody seems able to answer." For women, "glory and gratitude is their rightful portion, but even while the nation is singing their praises and calling them blessed, it is withholding the blessings of citizenship from them in a heartbreaking way in some instances. The world," she said, "has been weeping intermittently for many years over the story of 'A Man without a Country.'" Yet here was a policy that stripped women of their own rights of citizenship and left them without a country in the fullest sense.[73]

Lovejoy found that her great acclaim and her growing reputation among medical colleagues led to new administrative roles. At the third annual meeting of the Medical Women's National Association held in Chicago in June 1918, president Bertha Van Hoosen announced that "the usual order of business would be suspended and Dr. Esther Lovejoy's address be given precedence above all else." Lovejoy presented information about her wartime service, with emphasis on the French refugees in Evian. The *Woman's Medical Journal* reported that "her intense feeling, together with a great deal of natural eloquence and dramatic power, held her audience of several hundred women physicians spellbound, and there were few dry eyes when she had finished."[74] The *Journal* reprinted Lovejoy's article about refugees at Evian, titled "A Tragic Line of Rapatriés," in the same issue.[75] At this 1918 meeting, colleagues elected Lovejoy as first vice president of the organization, and returned her to that post at the next meeting in June 1919.[76] At the 1919 meeting, the new president, Etta Gray, asked Lovejoy to take on the chair of the MWNA's American Women's Hospitals (AWH), formerly the War Service Committee, which was now expanding its wartime program to include postwar medical relief. Lovejoy accepted with the understanding that she could also complete her Red Cross work.[77] Several months later, Gray agreed to serve with the AWH in Serbia, and Lovejoy, by virtue of her position as first vice president of the MWNA, became the acting president of the association.[78] Gray also asked Lovejoy to serve an additional year as chair of the AWH. In February 1920 Lovejoy wrote to colleague Mathilda Wallin, "I had not intended remaining longer than my year in that service. Indeed, as you know, I have felt that I could

American Women's Hospitals personnel (Esther Pohl Lovejoy at right), ca. 1919. Reproduced by permission of Oregon Health & Science University Historical Collections & Archives, Portland, Oregon.

not afford to do the work any longer on account of its being practically volunteer service for me, but if Dr. Gray is willing to stay on the job in Serbia for another year, I ought to be willing to stay on the job in New York for another year."[79]

During the World War, women physicians on both sides of the conflict provided medical care in hospitals and clinics and with voluntary organizations, and formed all-female medical units like the ones associated with the American Women's Hospitals.[80] One result of this shared identity and experience was the five-week International Conference of Women Physicians attended by more than one hundred medical women from over sixteen nations. They convened in New York City from September 15 to October 24, 1919, to discuss a range of topics relating to women's health, including conditions for working women and birth control. Delegates created a series of resolutions supporting working women's health, maternity leave, accident and sickness insurance, and sex education, among others.[81] Lovejoy, as acting president of the Medical Women's National Association, presided over a reception and dinner for the international guests and a "welcome home" event for American Women's Hospitals personnel. The dinner was a who's who of more than 150 medical women from Europe, the United States, Canada, Asia, and Latin America. Many of the medical women gave short remarks, recalling wartime medical service and calling for additional cooperative work in the future. Marie-Jeanne Bassot, Lovejoy's colleague and friend from the Résidence Sociale, represented social service workers at the dinner and conference.[82]

Having shared wartime experiences and having spent over a month together sharing common concerns for women's health and debating ideas and programs, the assembled group saw the "importance of conferring together regarding matters affecting national and international health" and the possibility of an "international association of women physicians."[83] During the war years, women in the United States and Great Britain had organized national women's medical associations, in 1915 and 1917, respectively.[84] At the reception hosted by Lovejoy and the MWNA, Norway's Kristine Munch "made an eloquent appeal for the formation of an International Association of Medical Women."[85] At the close of the conference, the assembled women doctors organized the Medical Women's International Association (MWIA) as an "outgrowth of the war and reconstruction activities of medical women of different nationalities" to provide the structure to continue their shared work.[86] Those present selected Esther Lovejoy to serve as the first president of the association, and the executive board included nine members from Europe (England, France, Holland, Italy, Norway, Scotland, Serbia, Sweden, and Switzerland), two from South America (Argentina and Uruguay), two from East Asia (China and Japan), one from Canada, and four from the United States.[87]

Members from Great Britain included Jane Walker, a founder and first president of the Medical Women's Federation of Great Britain who had campaigned for officer rank for British women physicians during the war.[88] Louisa Martindale served on the executive committee of the National Union of Suffrage Societies and worked to open medical education and practice to women in Britain. She was a founder of the Medical Women's Federation of Great Britain, and during the war provided medical care at the Scottish Women's Hospitals at the Royaumont Abbey outside of Paris.[89] Christine Murrell was active for votes for women in the Women's Social and Political Union, provided medical care to suffragists on hunger strikes, and chaired the postwar Women's Election Committee to advocate for the election of women to the House of Commons. During the war she was a medical officer in the Women's Emergency Corps, a voluntary aid organization established by the National Union of Suffrage Societies.[90]

French physician Lucie Thuillier-Landry was an active member of the Union Française pour le Suffrage des Femmes (UFSF) and the International Woman Suffrage Alliance and was the founder of the French Medical Women's Association.[91] Germaine Montreuil-Straus was a pioneer in sex education in France and a member of the Counseil National des Femmes Françaises (CNFF) and the International Woman Suffrage Alliance.[92] Sweden's Alma Sundquist was an expert in venereal disease who worked at the Stockholm free clinic and helped to develop Sweden's sex education program for public schools.[93]

Founding members outside of Western Europe and the United States included Grace Ritchie England of Canada, suffragist and public health activist, provincial vice president of the National Council of Women, and a Canadian representative to the International Congress of Women.[94] Paulina Luisi, the first woman in Uruguay to receive a medical degree and a pioneer in sex education and working women's rights, was organizer of the Alianza Uruguaya de Mujeres para el Sufragio Femenino (Uruguayan Alliance for Woman Suffrage) in 1919 and a delegate to the International Woman Suffrage Alliance.[95] Alicia Moreau was a leading Argentinean socialist feminist, suffragist, and public health activist, author of *Feminism in Social Evolution* (1911) and *The Civil Emancipation of Women* (1919).[96] Tomo Inouye, a 1901 graduate of the University of Michigan, was medical director for girls in the Tokyo public schools and a founder of the Japanese Medical Women's Society.[97]

Esther Lovejoy had much in common with these other founding leaders of the Medical Women's International Association. They shared an identity as women physicians and had had similar experiences with organizing and activism before the war, and many had engaged in wartime medical service. They advocated for women's complete citizenship as they envisioned a postwar world of progressive public health. As

Leila Rupp has found regarding other groups of women working across national borders, "Identity politics of such organizations sometimes served as an alternative—or at least a complement—to national identity."[98] In this postwar world, Lovejoy shared a transnational identity with other women physicians working for social justice outside national borders that motivated them to take action.

CHAPTER 7

Candidate Lovejoy
and a Shopgirl's Rise

O N Election Day, November 2, 1920, many women throughout the
United States made history by exercising their first opportunity
to vote after the ratification of the Nineteenth Amendment that
August. Their Oregon sisters voted too, but they had been voting since
achieving the franchise in 1912. Yet, when Esther Lovejoy placed her ballot in the box with a check mark next to her own name at her Portland
precinct's polling place that day, she was also making history. Lovejoy
was the first woman in the state to be a candidate for representative to
the United States Congress in a general election.

Esther Lovejoy was uniquely prepared to mount her campaign in
1920. She was a veteran of partisan politics in appointed office as Portland's city health officer and experienced in the political process from
her suffrage activism. This included the nuts and bolts of get-out-the-
vote organizing and considerable fundraising skills. Lovejoy had honed
her talent for public speaking, and she knew how to harness the power
of popular culture and mass campaigning to reach constituents with a
direct message. Wartime service mattered in this first election after the
conclusion of the First World War, and Lovejoy was well known for her
work with the Red Cross in France, her national speaking and fundraising tours, and as the author of *The House of the Good Neighbor*.[1] Her executive ability as the director of the American Women's Hospitals and as
organizer and president of the Medical Women's International Association also counted. And she possessed the cachet of national and interna-

tional service and experience. Lovejoy's supporters emphasized that she embodied both male and female characteristics: experience, toughness, and decision-making ability, combined with advocacy for health, social justice and women's issues, and a woman's determination to "clean up" politics. Lovejoy was a confident person who worked to achieve her goals. As journalist Fred Lockley noted, "No one has ever accused Dr. Lovejoy of lack of ambition or loafing on the job."[2]

When Lovejoy made her run for Congress, Oregon women had been or were currently candidates for fifty-six statewide offices, from the 1914 general election (the first statewide election after the achievement of the vote in Oregon in 1912) to the present contest in 1920. This included runs for the state legislature, state treasurer, superintendent for public instruction, and delegates to party conventions and presidential electors. Almost half of these were Democrats like Lovejoy. Of the fifty-six, twenty-two were Democratic, twelve Socialist, nine Republican, seven Prohibition candidates, four members of the Progressive Party, and two Independent.[3] Two women had served in the 1915 Oregon legislature, the first opportunity for women to do so since suffrage: Marian Towne, Democrat from Jackson County, and Kathryn Clarke, Republican from Douglas County.[4] Sylvia McGuire (Mrs. Alexander) Thompson won the seat to represent Oregon's Twenty-Ninth District (Wasco County) in the 1917 state legislative session, and voters reelected her in 1918. Dozens of women were candidates for and some had been elected to local offices around the state.[5] Like their colleagues in California, Washington, and other suffrage states in the West prior to the federal amendment, Oregon women had been testing the boundaries of elected office before other women in the nation could do so in 1920.[6]

Candidate Lovejoy had proven herself a party stalwart defending the Democratic Party and George Chamberlain against the Congressional Union. Her loyalty to Harry Lane had wavered during his opposition to the war but was tempered by gratitude for his mentoring and principles in the long run. Lovejoy's political identity developed locally and grew through the tumultuous local and national political debate among suffragists, Progressive Era politics, and the coming of the First World War. Lovejoy was a progressive Democrat in an overwhelmingly Republican state. Republican party registration levels in the state were "two to three times as large" as Democratic ones in this period. "Democrats rarely controlled more than a handful of seats during the first three decades of the twentieth century" yet were "able to win the governor's race in five differ-ent elections during that same period" by coalition building with other progressives.[7] And Democrats had sent George Chamberlain and Harry Lane to the Senate. Given this, Lovejoy and her progressive supporters had reason to be hopeful for victory in 1920.

In February 1920 Esther Lovejoy returned to Portland from her American Women's Hospitals work in New York amid rumors that she might make a run for the Democratic nomination for US Congress from the Third District (Portland and Multnomah County).[8] On her way home, Lovejoy joined Effie Comstock Simmons, president of the Oregon Equal Suffrage Alliance, to represent Oregon at the "victory convention" of the National American Woman Suffrage Association held in Chicago. With federal suffrage having been achieved, this convention marked the transition of NAWSA to the new League of Women Voters. Lovejoy next joined Simmons in Portland to help launch the local Oregon league.[9]

As principal speaker at a special luncheon of the city's Democratic Jackson Club on March 11, Lovejoy announced her candidacy. "I did not make up my mind until this morning, but I am going to run for con-gress," she said. "I am going to win if I can. But whether I win or not, I am going to have a fine time running." Her lunchtime topic before her announcement had been the children of France. "I think it is a woman's job to take care of the children, her own first, if she has them . . . I have no children of my own," but "I have taken care of the children of Portland in many ways. Since I have been away, I have been doing what I could for the children of the world. I want to continue to do that." Some people, Lovejoy said, believed that women should keep out of the "sorry mess" of politics. But if politics were a mess, "then it is the place of the women to get into politics and help make it clean. That is woman's work. She is the greatest cleansing agent in the world."[10]

By the first of April, Lovejoy was the only Democratic candidate in the primary for representative from the Third District. She worked with supporters to establish a campaign organization and then returned to New York so that she could catch up on AWH business and prepare for the upcoming Medical Women's National Association convention to be held in New Orleans on April 26 and 27. She presided at that meeting as acting president and reported as chair of the AWH.[11] Unopposed at home, Lovejoy's plan was to return to Portland after the primary for hard campaigning in the general election. Democratic women in Multnomah

County began organizing in her absence.[12] Lovejoy arranged to have her platform presented for her in absentia at April meetings of the Women's Democratic Club and the Portland Women's Research Club.[13] And party activist Alice McNaught organized a Lovejoy for Congress Club at the end of March "to membership in which all Democratic women of Multnomah County have been invited."[14]

But on April 13, Sylvia McGuire Thompson, a two-term Democratic state representative and current president of the Portland Federation of Women's Clubs, declared her candidacy. With Thompson in "the arena against her sister candidate," the *Oregon Journal* predicted that a "real feminine battle will be staged, with the democratic nomination as the prize."[15] Thompson's Democratic platform was similar to Lovejoy's: postwar support for veterans and approval of Woodrow Wilson's Treaty of Versailles and League of Nations, and support for development of Oregon resources and workers.[16] Because of the candidates' similar positions, Democratic voters would principally be considering the different kinds of experience and preparation that each candidate brought to the contest, as well as the less tangible characteristics of the candidates themselves.

Sylvia Thompson brought experience and visibility in local politics and club work to her campaign.[17] Having been elected as a state representative from Hood River and Wasco Counties in 1916, she was the third woman to serve in the Oregon legislature following the single terms of Marian Towne and Kathryn Clarke in the 1915 session. She was the only woman in the legislature throughout her service, including her initial term in the 1917 session, and, after her reelection in 1918, she served in the 1919 regular session and the special session of January 1920.[18] In that special 1920 legislative session, Thompson had sponsored House Joint Resolution 1, which became Oregon's ratification of the Nineteenth Amendment to the US Constitution for woman suffrage at the federal level.[19] However, there were rumors that Thompson planned to switch parties and become a Republican. She was also part of a faction hostile to Democratic senator George Chamberlain. So in this contest she presented problems for many Democrats.[20]

Lovejoy altered her original plan and returned to Portland on May 11, ten days before the primary election, and conducted a vigorous in-person campaign. The Democratic *Oregon Journal* predicted as much as a 60 percent turnout of registered voters and reported that "the anti-

Chamberlain contest and the Lovejoy-Thompson congressional race have aroused the Democratic voters of the county to a greater degree than for several years."[21] Lovejoy won by 57 percent of the Democratic vote and outspent her opponent by almost three to one, with her supporters investing $1,134 to Thompson's $385.[22] A week later, at a meeting of the Jackson Club, Lovejoy thanked her supporters and let them know that she was going to leave for New York to complete work with the American Women's Hospitals. Confident in her ability to succeed in November, she would return to Portland in July "to wage an aggressive campaign for election."[23]

If the primary brought two progressive women with significant experience together for voters to assess, the general election would be a referendum on Progressive Era policies versus corporate interests and forces of reaction to progressivism. The contest showcased the continuing fears of radicalism, feminism, and change engendered by the war and by postwar demobilization. Republicans charged that Lovejoy and her supporters were "Reds" and Bolsheviks, even "common cattle"; the Lovejoy coalition accused her opponent of being a reactionary unfit for legislative service. It was also an intensely gendered campaign, setting a male incumbent against a well-qualified and popular woman activist, former appointed office holder, and executive. It was at once a unique local campaign and one with familiar echoes across the nation.

In the general election, J. T. Johns ran as the Industrial Labor and Socialist candidate, but Lovejoy's main contest was with Republican incumbent Clifton N. "Pat" McArthur. Active in student athletics and student affairs as an undergraduate at the University of Oregon from 1896 to 1901, McArthur read law and was admitted to the Oregon State Bar in 1906. He won election to the Oregon House of Representatives from Multnomah County for the 1909 and 1913 sessions, and served as speaker of the house for each. Elected to the US Congress from the Third District in 1914, voters returned him to Washington in 1916 and in 1918.[24] McArthur built an antilabor and antiprogressive record, particularly during the First World War. In 1918 the National Security League, a preparedness and home-defense organization that increasingly moved to the far right as members advocated reactionary policies against progressives and radicals, gave McArthur a grade of 100 percent "right" on his votes for their wartime legislation.[25] As a member of Congress, McArthur had been equivocal on the question of Prohibition, a stance that angered prohibitionists and many women voters, including many in his own Republican party.

Lovejoy returned to Portland on August 15, 1920, to begin her campaign.[26] Events on the national stage coincided with her first weeks in the city and reinforced her credentials. On August 18 Tennessee became the thirty-sixth and final state to ratify the Nineteenth Amendment. Lovejoy celebrated with other suffrage activists, and in interviews linked the victory to the next steps for women in politics, including office holding.[27] She also won the campaign-boosting assignment of introducing Democratic vice-presidential candidate Franklin D. Roosevelt to some 5,000 supporters on his Portland campaign stop at the city's Municipal Auditorium on Saturday, August 21.[28]

By 1920 many Portlanders were anxious to defeat McArthur, and a coalition of citizens across party and activist lines gathered to support Lovejoy. As one editor phrased it, the "qualities of the Lovejoy campaign are both positive and negative; positive in support of Lovejoy and negative toward McArthur."[29] Lovejoy gained the endorsements of the Multnomah Prohibition Party and the Woman's Christian Temperance Union (WCTU), the Central Labor Council, and most union locals in the city.[30] The Oregon Popular Government League formed as an umbrella nonpartisan organization "representing the progressive thought of the city," and "its sole work" was "to elect Dr. Lovejoy."[31] The league represented the Portland Labor Council and the Oregon State Federation of Labor, the Portland Federation of Churches, public school teachers, railroad workers, "farmers and progressives and liberal thinkers from the general public."[32] League members urged Portlanders to organize "a Lovejoy meeting" in their neighborhoods, made literature available, and mailed over 40,000 campaign cards with a pledge to vote for Lovejoy.[33] Delegates from the Central Labor Council, under league auspices, met each Sunday afternoon to organize the work of registering wage-earning women and men to vote.[34]

Democratic women precinct workers held weekly meetings to organize for the Lovejoy cause, and a sizable group of Republican women soon joined them. The *Oregon Journal* reported that McArthur was "'in bad' with the women of Multnomah county" because he had been equivocal on Prohibition, and many were "skipping over the traces" to join the Lovejoy campaign.[35] Bertha Mason Buland organized the Central Republican Women's Lovejoy Club, with "large numbers" of Republican women supporters and a plan to "carry the organization into every section of the district at once, with branch chapters in strategical places."[36] Other influential Portland women joined the campaign, including League of Women Voters president Effie Simmons, clubwoman Nan Wood Honeyman, author Anne Shannon Monroe, labor activist Lizzie Gee, president of the Oregon State WCTU Mary Mallett, and Prohibition leader Ada Wallace Unruh.[37]

The Lovejoy campaign tried to reach all progressive voters before the November election. Here Lovejoy combined the successful strategy of coalition building that had brought victory to the suffrage campaign in 1912 with the possibilities of cross-party progressive unity against McArthur in the present contest. Hers was a broad social justice platform that welcomed supporters across party lines. Lovejoy's speaking schedule provides strong evidence not only of hard campaigning but also of her appeal to a large number and variety of groups. From Franklin Roosevelt's Portland visit at the end of August to the eve of the election, Portland newspapers reported that Lovejoy spoke at seventy-three campaign events.[38] This no doubt underrepresents the extent of her campaigning; the *Portland News* reported in mid-October that Lovejoy was making as many as six campaign speeches per day.[39] She spoke at community gatherings at schools and the central library, at major events sponsored by the Popular Government League and by labor groups, to granges and women's clubs, and at county fairs.

Lovejoy reached across religious and racial lines. She addressed Protestant church groups, the Catholic Women's League, and the Daughters of the Covenant of B'nai B'rith, a Jewish service organization.[40] She addressed at least two African American organizations in Portland during the campaign. The Rosebud Club, formed during the war to knit for soldiers and conserve food on the home front, invited Lovejoy to speak at the home of club leader Cora Bunch on September 28. Lovejoy linked her own service in wartime France with that of African American soldiers. She "spoke at length" about their service and "gave them unstinted praise for their part, which she declared was a large one, in winning the war." She also spoke at the African American Baptist Association at the Mount Olivet Baptist Church.[41] While Lovejoy was certainly making the most of extending her campaign to all groups, her invitations from the Rosebud Club and the Mount Olivet Baptist Church suggest some commitment to coalition building across racial lines and a link to successful suffrage organizing in 1912 with the Colored Women's Equal Suffrage Association.

Lovejoy's platform focused on the importance of progressive programs of social justice based on support for the people and on the general welfare versus that of "the interests." One way that she and her campaign strategists developed this theme was to emphasize the "possibilities in democratic America" embedded in her own life story of "a shopgirl's rise."[42] The Lovejoy for Congress Club noted that Lovejoy had been "a salesgirl in the city of Portland at the age of seventeen" and was "now a woman of International position and a credit to the state of Oregon."[43] Journalist Fred Lockley, in five installments of his popular *Oregon Journal* column, used the same narrative when he recounted Lovejoy's struggles as a department store clerk to work her way through the University of Oregon Medical Department.[44] And speaking to building trades union members, Lovejoy noted, "I formed early in life a strong, deep sympathy for the working class . . . and stand ready if elected to assist in the enactment of such measures as will promote their interests."[45]

Other aspects of Lovejoy's career mattered in the campaign. The *Oregon Labor Press* reported that Lovejoy "promised, if elected, to employ the same tactics that transformed the health office from an easy berth to a place of activity, and added that she knew of no institution that needed stirring up more than Congress does at the present time.[46] At a crowded campaign gathering, a woman passed Lovejoy an envelope that contained a fifty-dollar liberty bond. Earlier in her career the doctor had provided the woman with medical service without charge, and she now wanted to contribute to her campaign.[47] Backers also publicized the letter of support Lovejoy received from Marie-Jeanne Bassot and the staff of the Résidence Sociale.[48] All connected Lovejoy's personal story with the people and their needs.

Lovejoy also addressed the "the interests" directly in her speeches and interviews. "As I see things," she told an audience of railroad workers, "what this country needs more than anything else just now is simple social justice. The people are downtrodden, cannot obtain their full rights, and people who work hard are not receiving in return their just share of the products of their labors."[49] Calling wealthy elites "peacetime slackers" and decrying wartime profiteers, Lovejoy advocated "demillionairizing some of our millionaires" and criticized Congress for failing to pass adequate legislation to support veterans.[50] "A good many peo-

"Lovejoy for Congress" campaign card, 1920. Reproduced by permission of Oregon Health & Science University Historical Collections & Archives, Portland, Oregon.

ple who shout the loudest . . . are simply hiding behind the folds of our flag," she noted. Among them are "such beasts of prey as the modern profiteer[s], who, while the world was embroiled in war and since, grasp every dollar possible regardless of consequences, [and] are among our most vehement shouters when it comes to waving the flag."[51] Speaking at a meeting of the Meat Cutters' Union on October 13, Lovejoy declared, "I stand for the whole people . . . and not for the special vested interests. I am not going to congress to legislate for the big moneyed interests of this country as against the whole people. I shall be guided by my conscience and the best progressive thought of the entire country in my actions if elected." She pledged to work for the general welfare. "If any considerable number of the members of congress and of the other legislative and official bodies of the world had been doing that for all these years we should never have been afflicted as we are with wars and civil strife with fighting between capital and labor and class against class." Social justice, Lovejoy declared, was the "best means of restoring good feeling between the workers and their employers." Humanitarian legislation that would "give to the masses relief from profiteering and from the predatory interests, will make a better country of this land of ours."[52] Reform, not revolution, was the answer.

Yet Lovejoy's affiliation with and courting of labor voters led her away from social justice when it came to immigration policy. From the time of her official declaration of candidacy that spring, Lovejoy established a platform of immigration regulation and restriction.[53] In speeches she announced her opposition to "the unrestricted immigration of foreign races and especially to those that are unassimilable."[54] Her platform as outlined on her campaign cards advocated "measures regulating immigration and excluding unassimilable races."[55]

In her evolving philosophy of what she termed national health, Lovejoy expanded her views of civic health forged during her work as Portland city health officer, in the suffrage campaigns, and during her wartime service. National health would be based on democratic social justice principles that would enable citizens to thrive, creating national well-being and security. "Practical education, woman suffrage, prohibition—these are fundamental health measures. They work together against poverty, illiteracy, vice, and disease."[56] And "poverty," Lovejoy insisted, "is the disease which claims most victims prematurely."[57] In the "social creed" printed on her 40,000 campaign cards, she noted, "I believe that moral, mental, physical, political, and economic disease is due largely to social dishonesty and poverty introduced by ignorance, vice, intemperance, greed, and profiteering, and that social justice is the rational remedy."[58] "Social justice is the best cure," she said, "for the dissatisfaction which exists in large proportions throughout the United States and the world today."[59]

Lovejoy's program for national health included support for the prohibition of alcohol. It does not appear that she was ever a member of the Woman's Christian Temperance Union, even though many of the women with whom she worked in Portland reform circles were active in the cause.[60] Yet some evidence suggests that Lovejoy was a supporter before taking up the issue on the campaign trail. Certainly her life experience with her father, who drank up the proceeds of various family enterprises, was a cautionary tale. In "Democracy and Health" (1919), Lovejoy linked Prohibition with her evolving views of national health, asserting, "Prohibition is the greatest health measure ever adopted by a nation."[61] Lovejoy's campaign rhetoric about Prohibition echoed this hopeful national health theme. She told 300 members of the Portland Women's Research Club that "the saloon door was the direct route to poverty lane."[62] In a speech to the members of the Sunnyside WCTU Lovejoy insisted that "as a citizen and as a physician I regard the prohibition of the liquor traffic as the greatest forward step we have ever taken as a health measure and as a measure which will, if given fair administration, in a generation or so rid this country of the taste for liquor. It will put us in the front rank economically and every way and will eventually lead to a dry world, for no other nation can compete with us which permits its people to be poisoned by liquor."[63] Perhaps the editors of the *Oregon Journal* captured Lovejoy's relationship to Prohibition in the most accurate way: "She has come in close contact with vice, debauchery, and disease, and she knows how closely these things affect the public weal. She is an advocate of clean living and clean thinking," they noted. "That is why she won the nomination of the Prohibition party without being a party prohibitionist."[64]

If her congressional campaign was "positive in support of Lovejoy," it was also "negative toward McArthur." W. T. McElveen, pastor of Portland's First Congregational Church, characterized McArthur as "a subservient tool of a do-nothing, boss-ridden congress."[65] Ada Wallace Unruh, a Prohibition supporter in the Lovejoy coalition, the reverend E. C. Hickman, and G. W. McDonald, representing the Oregon Popular Government League, all criticized McArthur's "belated pledge" to support Prohibition, now a federal law, and insisted that he could not be trusted to enforce it.[66] Lulu M. Horning, vice president of the Multnomah County WCTU, noted, "Congressman McArthur is commonly regarded as being so conservative that he is reactionary."[67] Chaplain Frederick Kendall Howard of the Good Samaritan Hospital in Portland "pointed out that republicans, democrats, prohibitionists and all shades of opinions and beliefs are represented in the Oregon Popular Government League, which seeks to retire from congress a member whose record . . . has not been in the interests of the mass of people."[68] Lovejoy noted that, if elected, she "would be the first person to be elected to congress from this district in six years . . . the present incumbent was not elected, but just climbed onto the [Republican] elephant and rode in."[69]

Supporters of Lovejoy and McArthur clashed over a postwar debate regarding the nation's railroads that became a symbol of the larger politics of the Red Scare in their election contest. During the war, the federal government had taken some control of the nation's economy and production, including railroads, communication, and shipbuilding for the war effort. In December 1917, Woodrow Wilson had established the United States Railroad Administration, a wartime agency that managed the industry and its policies and, under pressure, made some improvements in wages and working conditions.[70] Wartime legislation for the Railroad Administration was set to expire in 1920, and many Americans, including workers and organized labor, farmers, progressives, and radicals, saw the opportunity to build on wartime gains, while Republicans, business interests, and railroad owners hoped to return railroads to private hands. In 1919, Chicago labor lawyer Glen Plumb proposed that the government purchase all railroad property and lease it to a new corporation to be administered equally by representatives of labor, management, and the public. The Plumb Plan League soon garnered many supporters in Oregon and in the Pacific Northwest and the rest of the nation. But in the postwar backlash against progressivism and labor in the midst of the climate of fear created by the Red Scare, opponents immediately branded the Plumb Plan as Bolshevism and supported legislation that would return the railroads to private hands.[71] Business leaders and bankers in Portland were solidly behind this legislation, as were the editors of the *Oregonian* and the *Portland Evening Telegram*.[72] In Congress, C. N. McArthur voted for the Esch-Cummins Bill, also known as the Transportation Act of 1920, which returned railroads to private ownership. Although the bill recognized collective bargaining in principle, "such recognition proved a token gesture."[73]

For Lovejoy and her supporters, McArthur's vote was a betrayal of workers in favor of business interests. For his part, McArthur called the Plumb Plan "simply a step toward Socialism and soviet government."[74] He insisted that Lovejoy and "all of the radical forces of the community" were "arrayed" against him.[75] According to the editors of the *Portland News*, "McArthur rants on radicalism and tells his auditors that he loves his country. Dr. Lovejoy says that the only way to cure ultra radicalism is to remove the cause for labor unrest. She demonstrated her love of country during the war while McArthur was helping a few rich men get richer by voting as he was commanded. McArthur openly defied labor and he now seeks to class the rank and file of the workers with the 'radicals.' Anybody who is for progressive things is a 'radical' in McArthur's stereotyped vocabulary."[76] The editors of the *Oregon Labor Press* believed that McArthur's "only defense is calling his opponents radicals and undesirable citizens and in waving the American flag, which he defended by keeping his seat in Congress and voting measures for the enslavement of the American people."[77] Lovejoy supporter J. C. Hannan agreed. "When we need food, clothing, fuel, houses, and adequate transportation facilities in order to restore sanity to this country, all McArthur can say is 'All who oppose me are traitors.'"[78] McArthur responded with a letter denying the charges and noting that Hannan was "the secretary-treasurer of the Plumb Plan of this city . . . which seeks to raid the public treasury for the purpose of setting up [a] soviet railroad system in the United States."[79] Throughout the campaign, B. A. Green, the secretary of the Oregon Popular Government League, quoted an affidavit from Hannan that no Plumb Plan funds had been "spent to elect Dr. Lovejoy or to defeat McArthur."[80]

Lovejoy supporters were outraged when, less than two weeks before Election Day, they learned that McArthur forces had pressured a large Portland department store and a bookstore to take down their sales displays of Lovejoy's *The House of the Good Neighbor*. Speaking to a large audience of the Central Labor Council, Lovejoy explained that she had evidence that "pressure was brought to bear on the stores" by McArthur supporters to take down a large display of her books next to her picture. She then went to the bookstore and "found that a display which had been promised to be kept a week had been dismantled after two days." The editors of the *Oregon Labor Press* believed that after Lovejoy's contributions to the war and her warm welcome back in the States, "it remained for political hucksters of her home town to stoop to the level of retarding the sale of her book which is not political for fear that the voters might be impressed with her ability and unselfishness and elect her to Congress, retiring one of the most reactionary members of a reactionary Congress." Lovejoy contested "McArthur's charge that her supporters are reds, radicals, small Americans and common cattle."[81]

These exchanges also underscore the continuing importance of the strategic use of popular culture and mass media in campaign advertising. At rallies, parades, and Lovejoy's numerous speaking engagements, bands played and crowds sang the "Lovejoy Special" campaign song.[82] Supporters flooded the district with her 40,000 two-sided campaign cards that featured her picture, history, and platform. Her campaign advertised widely, including in the city's foreign-language newspapers such as *La Tribuna Italiana*.[83]And, at the close of the campaign, the Lovejoy coalition planned two large-scale advertising blitzes for local newspapers, one against McArthur's record and one supporting Lovejoy's platform.

For the anti-McArthur advertisements, the Lovejoy campaign made use of materials produced by the National Voters' League, which was organized in 1913 as a progressive reform organization reporting to citizens on the votes and "attitudes" of their representatives and senators. The league was headquartered in Washington, DC, and Oregon reformer William S. U'Ren served on its executive board and likely connected the group to the Lovejoy campaign. In 1916 the League coined the acronym MAWSH ("Might as Well Stay Home") in its journal the *Searchlight on Congress*. MAWSH referred to members of Congress whose lackluster work did nothing to free the nation from "pork and spoils and petty politics," and who served the interests of big business and finance.[84] In the October 1916 issue editors published a roster grading all of the members of the US House of Representatives as either a machine member, an independent, or a MAWSH, with the latter predominating. The League graded C. N. McArthur as a MAWSH.[85]

Members of the Lovejoy for Congress campaign used McArthur's MAWSH status in a series of five newspaper advertisements published from October 22 to October 27. Titled "'The Third District in Congress': Five Reel Comedy Featuring MAWSH McArthur," each installment detailed McArthur's voting and policy record with a fifth and final "climax" reel summarizing "The Real Mawsh." The advertisements stressed McArthur's support for banking interests against a postal savings system, his opposition to farm loan support, and national unemployment insurance. They critiqued his vote for the Esch-Cummins Transportation Act (against the Plumb Plan), his vote against an eight-hour day for railroad workers, and his support for a bill that would have penalized workers for striking during wartime. He was an eleventh-hour opportunist, they said, when it came to woman suffrage. "He voted for the suffrage amendment. But ask some of those who worked from 1905 to 1912 for suffrage in Oregon how much help they got out of Pat." He "stood in the way . . . just as long as he could, just as long as he deemed there were votes to be gotten thereby." The same was true, the campaign insisted, for Prohibition. "Now he will vote dry. He will get him a starched collar and a velvet Fauntleroy suit and a blue ribbon right away. O Pat, quit your kidding! Anything on the hip, Pat?"[86]

The series began at the same time as McArthur supporters were using their influence to remove *The House of the Good Neighbor* displays in town, and they also moved to squelch the MAWSH advertising campaign in the Republican-backed *Oregonian*. Popular Government League manager B. A. Green reported that the campaign had paid the *Oregonian* for all five installments of the advertisement; the first had been printed and the other four accepted. But then the editors of the *Oregonian* notified Green that "orders were given to 'kill' the advertisements," but that he would be able to get back the money that the campaign had paid. Lovejoy committee members believed that they were "being unfairly treated, particularly in view of the fact that the matter contained in the five advertisements merely consisted of a relation of McArthur's official record during his service to congress."[87] The *Oregon Journal* printed the MAWSH series.

In the "positive in support of Lovejoy" series that followed from October 27 to November 1, Lovejoy addressed her coalition in six installments of "Your Candidate and Her Work," directed at different groups of supporters. The first spoke to business people, emphasizing that Lovejoy had "built up her own business" as a physician and would support the development of Oregon resources and infrastructure. The second was addressed "To the Women of Multnomah County" and emphasized women's political power. "You have been enfranchised. You are now ready to make your influence felt in political life. You have wiped out the saloon. You have almost abolished child labor. You have fought for high morals in the home and cities. You have made our schools what they are." But "sinister forces" prevented women from having their full voice in civic matters. "Make your influence felt by sending one of your own to congress," Lovejoy urged; Congress needed the "humanizing influence of womankind." "What a wonderful thing for the freedom of Oregon to be able to say 'From Cash Girl to Congress Woman.'" The campaign addressed other installments to parents, to the "moral forces of Multnomah County," and to "Believers in True Democracy." The final advertisement on the day before the election contained signatures from Lovejoy for Congress members and a long list of signatures of war veterans supporting her. The series concluded: "In the name of the womanhood of America, in the name of the children of America, in the name of the moral forces of America, in the name of those who fought for their ideas in the World War, in the name of those who toil with hand or brain, your country needs your vote on November 2 for Esther Pohl Lovejoy."[88]

Mass advertising campaigns required money, and the Lovejoy coalition outspent the McArthur forces by more than two and a half times its advertising dollars, $3,609 to $1,380. Lovejoy contributed $750 of her own funds, while the Oregon Popular Government League put in $2,173, and a Special Committee in Behalf of Esther Lovejoy headed by Prohibition activist Lee Paget donated $686. The McArthur campaign ran the standard advertisements in local newspapers and distributed other literature. McArthur contributed $177 of his own money, and the Republican Congressional Campaign Committee spent $1,203 on his campaign.[89]

An analysis of the representation of candidate Lovejoy in press reports and speeches suggests that Lovejoy and her supporters also created a specific image of a winning contender who possessed both male and female qualities, making her the ideal choice for office. The editors of the *Portland News* endorsed Lovejoy this way: "Appeal is constantly being made to the prejudices of women at election time," they wrote. "Women voters are urged to support this or that measure because it embodies some idea that women favor. They are asked to cast their ballots for certain candidates because these have supported measures for which women have always fought. Frequently some woman has aspired to a public office and has the suffrage of her companions because of the fact that she is a woman." However, "the newly enfranchised sex has at this coming election a chance to place in office a woman who has demonstrated her ability in fields covered by a man." Lovejoy "has thoroughly demonstrated her innate sympathy for the common people and [is] one who at the same time has shown her ability to cope with problems that many men could not solve."[90]

Other reports echo this theme. In an editorial endorsing Lovejoy's candidacy, the *Oregon Journal* editors noted, "Dr. Esther Pohl Lovejoy is an executive and a leader. She has a woman's fineness and tenderness and a man's courage and strength."[91] The *Portland News* recalled Lovejoy's "ride in a bombing plane" during her successful liberty loan work during the war, concluding that she "doesn't lack real nerve for anything" and should be elected.[92] After reviewing Lovejoy's career for the audience at the meeting of the Prohibition Party in Multnomah County, a speaker referred to Montana representative Jeannette Rankin's alleged tears at the congressional vote to authorize US entrance into the First World War in 1917: "We have had a woman in Congress who simply wept when matters of grave importance were before that body." But "in Dr. Lovejoy we will have a representative . . . who will work and not weep."[93]

Many supporters also contrasted Lovejoy's strengths with McArthur's weaknesses in gendered language. The *Portland News* characterized Lovejoy as a successful doctor and "a woman of abundant energy, culture and high ideals." By contrast, "McArthur turned to politics when he failed to make a living at the law."[94] Another editorial asserted that, "while Pat McArthur was sauntering up and down the rue de Pennsylvania or preening himself at tea parties in our fair capital during the time when the war was at its height, Dr. Lovejoy . . . was over in France administering to the wants of the sick and wounded."[95] After McArthur's declaration that Lovejoy supporters were radicals, Popular Government League secretary B. A. Green invited him to a public debate. "Your constituents are interested in facts and . . . votes are not won by calling names. Schoolboys may settle arguments in this manner, but we would suggest that in this campaign we appear before the public as full grown-ups."[96] At a meeting of the Portland Women's Research Club on October 25, McArthur shared the platform with Lovejoy, and she asked him to repeat the preamble to the Constitution. "McArthur rose and said, 'I don't know; let's see if I remember it.' And then he stood and repeated it, 'Just like a little school boy obeying teacher.'"[97]

If supporters emphasized Lovejoy's male and female qualities, the front page of the *Oregon Journal* on November 2, Election Day, reminded readers that women were active contenders and partners in the political field. Esther Lovejoy voted that morning at the Rosenfeld garage at 221 Vista Avenue. The page-one photograph of Lovejoy placing her ballot in the box, with an unidentified woman poll worker looking on, emphasized that Oregon women were on all sides of the ballot box and the civic power it represented: as voters, election workers, and candidates.[98]

Lovejoy's strong showing of 44 percent of the vote was not enough to win the election, but it was a significant achievement. In Oregon and the nation, Republican forces scored victories in the 1920 election. At the national level, Republican Warren Harding had one of the largest margins of victory in the history of the nation, some 60 percent, compared to 34 percent for the Cox/Roosevelt Democratic ticket and 3.4 percent for Eugene Debs's Socialist ticket. But voter turnout nationwide was the lowest in US history, "the first presidential contest in which less than a majority of eligibles voted."[99] In Oregon, voter turnout was much higher: 66 percent of those registered voted in Multnomah County's Third District contest between Lovejoy and McArthur, and 70 percent voted in the presidential contest. There were more votes for Democrats and Socialists in Lovejoy's Third District: the Democratic Cox/Roosevelt ticket received 36 percent of Multnomah County votes, Debs and the Socialists, 5 percent, and Republican Harding, 58 percent.[100]

Because Oregon county clerks recorded voter registration by party and by sex, we can see that Esther Lovejoy garnered a wide number of votes beyond her party and beyond the women's vote.[101] Lovejoy received 31,853 votes, 44 percent of the total. Democratic women made up just 10 percent of the total registered voters. And if percentages of actual voters were similar to those who had registered, it means that Lovejoy received 14 percent or more of her total votes from Republicans. In the presidential race, Multnomah voters gave the Democratic Cox/Roosevelt ticket 27,854 votes and the Prohibition Party candidate Aaron S. Watkins 846 votes, meaning that Lovejoy's candidacy surpassed the votes received by the national party candidates at the same election by almost 3,000 votes. Among Republican voters, Harding received 44,806 votes to McArthur's 37,884. Eugene Debs, the Socialist Party candidate, received 3,488 votes in Multnomah County, more than the vote for Third District Socialist candidate J. T. Johns, who had 3,252 votes.[102] All of these figures suggest that Lovejoy had success with male voters, made inroads into the Republican camp with both female and male voters, and had success with voters outside the Democratic and Republican Parties.

How did Lovejoy take the outcome? Visiting the Central Labor Council two days after the election, she spoke of the "Republican wave" that had influenced the election. She also speculated that some women had voted Republican, against the Democratic League of Nations, because they were concerned that their "fathers, sons, husbands and brothers" might be called to fight in another conflict.[103] But Lovejoy told the group that she "would much rather be defeated with the forces which supported her than to have won the election with the support of others." She joked that "her trade as surgeon might make her eligible to membership in the

Meat Cutters union," and "kept the delegates laughing by her humorous references to campaign incidents."[104] The Central Labor Council and State Federation of Labor gave Lovejoy letters of introduction and union credentials in appreciation of her support.[105]

Lovejoy had put her political faith and fate in the power of coalition building, following a strategy that had brought victory in the 1912 campaign for woman suffrage in Oregon. But some within the Democratic Party in Multnomah County, including leaders posturing for their own candidacies, found Lovejoy's independence a disturbing betrayal of the party process and power. One of her outspoken opponents was her medical colleague, Dr. C. J. Smith, a former state senator and 1914 gubernatorial candidate. Smith had been planning a run for the Third District seat before Lovejoy, "without consulting the party . . . jumped in with both feet" and announced her own bid for the office at the Jackson Club meeting. In an interview with the *Oregonian* a week after the election, Smith said that he and his advisers decided not to contest her, but that they "didn't like Dr. Lovejoy's method." And they were appalled by the Lovejoy for Congress coalition. "The first thing the democratic managers knew Lovejoy's campaign was being managed by a republican labor leader and a republican prohibitionist" who "filled her speaking engagements." Smith believed that he could have won the seat with the votes of "the democrats and republicans who wanted to defeat McArthur but who would not vote for a woman to go to congress."[106] Reading through the personal and party jealousy, it seems quite possible that Lovejoy would not have received the Democratic nod for her candidacy, and that the only way she had achieved it was by announcing independent of party oversight.

George Lovejoy does not appear in any of the press reports or archival materials relating to Esther Lovejoy's 1920 congressional campaign. The two were waging a private battle that became a public one just after the conclusion of the election, a dispute that would soon end their marriage. When Esther Lovejoy was at work directing the American Women's Hospitals in New York and contemplating a possible run for US Congress in early 1920, George Lovejoy was in Oregon organizing a business venture associated with a proposed tuberculosis sanitarium in Winchester, near Roseburg, in southern Oregon. Both George and Esther owned separate acreage in Winchester; for Esther this was land dating from investments before Emil's death. George asked her to join in his investment by selling land and becoming a partner, confident that the sanitarium would be a moneymaker. Esther was in New York and initially thought the sale would be a good way to raise needed funds for her campaign and beyond. But when she learned the particulars, she actively opposed the project.[107]

She had two major objections to the proposed sanitarium. The first was that the site would include land on the North Umpqua River above the Winchester Dam, the source of Roseburg's water supply.[108] Lovejoy feared that tubercular patients would contaminate the water supply, spreading the disease to humans and animals in the watershed.[109] Her second objection concerned the questionable therapies planned for the sanitarium and the lack of credentials of George Lovejoy's partner. "Dr." Vern I. Ruiter had no formal medical training or license but had been running a tuberculosis hospital in Roseburg for five years and held several patents on electric healing devices.[110] Ruiter proposed to use "a system of electrotherapy utilizing a special bath cabinet" as a cure for tuberculosis at the new sanitarium.[111] George Lovejoy was a believer and claimed that he had "seen demonstrations of remarkable success from [Ruiter's] electrical bath treatments."[112] Ruiter claimed that he had cured himself of tuberculosis with the device.[113] Esther Lovejoy saw Ruiter as a quack with no credentials and no credibility, and did "not wish her place in the medical profession imperiled through any connection of her name with an institution of this sort."[114]

After her return to Portland in May 1920, Esther Lovejoy drew on her network within the state public health system for assistance. She contacted state, county, and city health officers, and in September the Oregon State Board of Health notified the Douglas County health officer that the board opposed the sanitarium project because it would pollute the North Umpqua River watershed and public drinking supplies.[115] George Lovejoy and his partners, however, refused to stop construction. And so, as Esther Lovejoy carried on with the final weeks of her congressional campaign in the fall of 1920, she also worked with a growing coalition of supporters to secure an injunction against George Lovejoy and Vern Ruiter. On November 10, just over a week after the election, Esther Lovejoy addressed the Roseburg City Council at a special meeting. Sadie Orr Dunbar, the secretary of the Oregon State Anti-Tuberculosis Association, came with her, as did the attorney for the state board of health. Lovejoy explained her position in detail and told the council, "I cannot understand how the people of Roseburg can sit by and see their water supply polluted and made unfit for use." The sanitarium would be a "disgrace to the community" and a "blotch upon her personal name and record," and she would "fight the battle single-handed if no help can be secured." Dunbar told council members that a county tuberculosis sanitarium was very important but that this one should not be built, and cited concerns about water contamination. The health board attorney emphasized that "the city and county health officers and the state board" had the power to stop construction, and "assailed the promoters of the plan and branded it as a purely money making scheme." Douglas County district attorney George Neuner, who had worked on legislation to protect the watershed of the North Umpqua, also spoke in support of the ban and informed council members that the county was joining in the complaint.[116] The council adopted a resolution to join the state board of health to "restrain and prevent the construction" of the sanitarium.[117]

The "sanitarium fight" became front-page news in the Roseburg *News-Review,* and the Portland *Oregonian* and *Oregon Journal* also covered the story through mid-November and December of 1920. The papers aired personal disputes between Esther Lovejoy and George Lovejoy in the midst of the controversy. For his part, George Lovejoy sent a letter to the editor of the *News-Review* just after the first city council meeting, and continued to make his objections to the press. He said that he had no plans to make money on the sanitarium, asserting that he saw "no promise of even compensating profit." He noted that the group had taken "every precaution" to dispose of sewage safely and that the sanitarium would "accomplish a great good." He challenged those who were attacking his "motives" and "character as a business man." He defended Ruiter even though Ruiter "assumes to combat disease in other than the manner prescribed by the accepted ethics of the profession." George Lovejoy saved particular criticism for his wife. She "was not actuated by humanitarianism in her opposition to the hospital site," he said, but "feared for its effect upon the value of adjacent property owned by her." He produced a series of telegrams showing that she talked of selling "up to a few weeks before the election."[118]

Esther Lovejoy responded to her husband's charges and provided an explanation that linked the situation to the delicate public perception of a female candidate during a campaign. "I greatly dislike to discuss further the personal phases of this fight for the public health," she told an

Oregonian reporter. She wanted to "make it clear that as soon as I knew the actual purpose to which the property was to be put, I was against it and have been against it ever since." She learned the full "nature of the plan" when she came to Portland from New York in May, for the primary, and "since then my opposition has been constant." She telegraphed "early in June, after I had returned to the east," that she would not sell. Members of the state board of health, she said, could "testify that I have been consistently against it since that time." It was true, she said, "that my later telegrams continued the offer to sell, if the health board could be persuaded to approve, but I knew—none better—that they would not advise it." As a candidate, Esther Lovejoy weighed the damage a public airing of this conflict could do to her prospects for election. "My promise to Mr. Lovejoy was nothing more than an attempt to keep our relations cordial," she said, "though by subterfuge."[119]

The State Board of Health authorized a formal injunction suit against George Lovejoy and Ruiter on November 29.[120] On December 15 a coalition including the Oregon State Board of Health, the Douglas County health officer and Douglas County, the Roseburg city health officer, the mayor and city council, Esther Lovejoy, and Steve Pearson, a local landowner, all filed suit for injunction against the Winchester Hospital.[121] By February 2, 1921, the Douglas County Circuit Court issued a default judgment in favor of Esther Lovejoy and the other plaintiffs because George Lovejoy, Ruiter, and their partners had not responded to the injunction suit, nor had they appeared. The court "restrained them from proceeding or attempting to proceed" with the construction of the Winchester tuberculosis sanitarium.[122] George Lovejoy dissolved the sanitarium corporation later that month.[123]

In November 1920, as she waged the "sanitarium fight" in city council chambers and newspaper columns, Esther Lovejoy took steps to divorce George Lovejoy. Her attorney was B. A. Green, manager of the Popular Government League supporting her congressional candidacy. On November 24 the couple formalized arrangements to settle all property rights, with Esther Lovejoy's mother Annie acting as trustee.[124] That same day Esther Lovejoy filed for dissolution of marriage. The complaint focused on her reputation and her finances. She charged that George Lovejoy had, "with the intent to profit by the use of [her] reputation," formed the sanitarium venture, and "advertised by implication and otherwise that this Institution would be known as the 'Lovejoy Sanitarium,'" and "endeavored in every possible way to give the general public the impression" that Esther Lovejoy "was to be connected therewith . . . to capitalize [on her] professional reputation for his own use and benefit." George Lovejoy "gave no consideration to [her] professional or personal name and reputation" but sought "his own personal enrichment." The sanitarium project would have threatened the water supply, and George Lovejoy "intended . . . to prey upon the credulity and helplessness of suffering people, without rendering them service of any value." Further, while Esther Lovejoy was in wartime service, she had "entrusted her property" to her husband "for management, all of which was mismanaged to [her] material injury."[125] She also charged that he had "for a long time been a stock salesman and repeatedly tried to sell oil and other stocks to her, and when she refused to buy them would become surly and morose and would not speak to her sometimes for weeks at a time."[126]

Esther Lovejoy filed the complaint in faraway Baker County in Eastern Oregon in the court of judge Gustav Anderson, a personal friend. She wanted the case handled discreetly and without publicity, given the context of the "sanitarium fight" and also because of the negative effects the publicity of a divorce would have on her career.[127] George Lovejoy waived any additional time and did not appear in court, and Anderson ruled in Esther Lovejoy's favor with a decree of divorce on December 10.[128] Anderson's letter, written to her that same day, confirms their friendship, Lovejoy's desire for privacy, and the wide reach of her network. "It was a very pleasing surprise to me to hear your voice the other day over the 'phone, but I also felt a touch of sorrow upon learning of the unpleasant features. . . . You unquestionably took the proper course, and I sincerely hope all the future will be full of happiness and blessings to you, for you deserve the very best." There was no newspaper coverage of the divorce, Anderson wrote, and "to-day when I handed the papers together with the decree to the clerk I asked him again if he would be sure to so handle them that there would be no publicity, and he said, 'I most certainly will.' He heard you when you spoke here at the high school auditorium, and when I acquainted him with the situation before the papers came, he assured me he would take every precaution, and it appears that he has truly kept his word."[129]

There was no press coverage until George Lovejoy confirmed the divorce to the *Oregon Journal* in July 1921 as he developed a relationship with Ethel McIntosh of Portland. The couple married in December

1921.[130] Esther Lovejoy was by then back at work in New York. There is little information about George Lovejoy's side to the controversy beyond the press reports of the "sanitarium fight."[131] Perhaps, in addition to these financial disputes, Esther Lovejoy's ascending star in local, national, and international affairs was too challenging for him to live with. An additional stress on the relationship may have involved his aspirations for elected office in the context of her candidacy. He ran successfully as Democratic state representative from Multnomah County in 1922 but was not reelected in 1924. He and Ethel moved to Seattle in 1927, where he won election to the Washington State senate in 1932 and again in 1934. He died in Seattle in 1944; Ethel survived him until her death in 1966.[132]

CHAPTER 8

The Quay at Smyrna and Beyond

I N the fall of 1922, as an eyewitness and participant on the quay at the port city of Smyrna at the close of the Greco-Turkish Civil War, Esther Lovejoy found herself at the center of a devastating postwar humanitarian crisis. Her work in Smyrna helped to transform the American Women's Hospitals (AWH)—created during the First World War to showcase the work of medical women as they pressed for inclusion in the military medical corps—into a medical humanitarian organization that would reach around much of the globe during her lifetime. "Plans for terminating the program were under consideration," Lovejoy later wrote, "when suddenly this unprecedented disaster calling for medical service changed the course of the American Women's Hospitals and our most important work began."[1] With Lovejoy at the helm for almost fifty years, from 1919 to 1967, the AWH become a precursor to later non-governmental organizations such as Doctors Without Borders. Positioned as a leader of both the AWH and the Medical Women's International Association (MWIA), one of Lovejoy's major contributions would be to combine the visions and work of both organizations to create a feminist approach to transnational medical activism.

As president of the MWIA, Esther Lovejoy organized and facilitated the organization's second annual meeting in the first week of September 1922 in Geneva, Switzerland. Her colleagues, physicians and AWH executive board members Eliza Mosher, Grace Kimball, Elizabeth Thelberg, and Sue Radcliff, were also there. American Women's Hospitals field physicians Etta Gray and Mabel Elliot joined the group to discuss the work the two of them were directing in Serbia and Soviet Armenia.[2] The question of the ongoing medical work of the group in Greece was also on the agenda. The three-year-old civil war between Turkey and Greece was concluding and Turkish nationalists were overthrowing the Ottoman Empire, part of a long history of conflict in the region. Lovejoy and her colleagues learned that the Aegean port city of Smyrna on the Anatolian coast, occupied by the Greeks since 1919, had been taken by Turkish troops. Smyrna had been a cosmopolitan city of Greeks, Armenians, Turks, Jews, Europeans, and Americans. But now, in the charge and countercharge of power after the First World War, Turkish troops and "irregulars" had attacked, raped, and killed Smyrna's Greek and Armenian residents, the city was burning, and refugees were gathering. Smyrna residents were now "trapped between three deadly elements: fire, sword and water."[3]

The AWH board sent Lovejoy to Constantinople, where, as she later recalled, "in this unprecedented emergency the American relief organizations pooled their resources and operated as the Disaster Relief Committee."[4] She was with the refugees at Smyrna for the last week of September, then left for Europe and the United States to raise funds for AWH operations before returning to the field. American Women's Hospitals staff members responded to the continuing refugee crisis by establishing hospitals, dispensaries, and quarantine stations.[5] In the months and years that followed, in her speeches, interviews, congressional testimony, articles, and, ultimately, her 1927 book *Certain Samaritans*, Lovejoy recounted her experiences in Smyrna to stimulate people to action. Once again women were experiencing the violent consequences of war and militarism, here within the context of ethnic, religious, and military strife, and war affected them differently that it did men. The solution was for citizens of all nations to work together in the short term to provide immediate relief, and in the long term to end war and empower women in their communities.

Lovejoy left Constantinople for Smyrna in mid-September with an American war photographer on a derelict old ship, the *Dotch*, loaded with food supplies for the city.[6] Initially some Allied ships had taken on refugees from Smyrna as passengers and transported them away from the crisis. Lovejoy reported that those refugees had paid for their passage. But no ships had returned, and Allied vessels under orders of neutrality could not now officially assist the hundreds of thousand of others who fled to the landing quay during and after the burning of the city, which began on September 13.[7]

Lovejoy's work with the refugees during the last week of September, "Evacuation Week," as she called it, took place in desperate circumstances in a context of complex transnational political and economic relations of which she was highly critical.[8] "The greatest crime against humanity with which I am personally familiar," she wrote, "was committed on the Smyrna Railroad Pier during the last week of September, 1922."[9] Greece had been part of the Allies during the First World War and had controlled the city of Smyrna during the three-year civil war with Turkey and the emerging Turkish nationalist movement. The conflict had been "fought on Turkish territory," with support for the Greeks coming from Britain and other Western nations.[10] US postwar foreign policy, and the postwar policies of Britain, France, and Italy, increasingly focused on oil reserves in the region, leading to declarations of neutrality in the Smyrna refugee crisis. The American high commissioner admiral Mark Bristol had become, in Peter Balakian's characterization, "in effect a public relations man for American business in Turkey" with an emphasis on oil.[11] Bristol believed that the Greek occupation of Smyrna had been a "British plot to extend her sphere of influence into the richest area of Turkey." Bristol provided support for US refugees living in Smyrna but gave orders that "no American official should be seen to help the Greek or Armenian communities" and told US soldiers not to act to assist others.[12] "Neutrality," Lovejoy wrote, "was a strange and terrible word to the people on that quay. It meant that warships would not take any more of them away; that they were at the mercy of their traditional enemies, and it meant outrage, slavery and death."[13]

Asa Jennings, a US staff member of the Smyrna YMCA, worked against this official neutrality on all sides. He commandeered two structures that had survived the fire to serve as an emergency maternity hospital and to house food and supplies for refugees. He tried to break through the Allied refusal to provide additional ships without success, except for an Italian transport of 2,000 people. According to author Giles Milton, by courage and bluff Jennings convinced the Greek government, fearful of Turkish reprisals, to authorize Greek ships in the Aegean harbor of Mytilene to sail to the rescue of refugees.[14] With this authorization in place, the Turkish commanders agreed to a window of escape for some of the refugees. Those who were not men of the military age of seventeen to forty-five years could leave Smyrna if they did so by September 30. The men of military age were, by Lovejoy's account, "to be detained and deported to the interior." After the September 30 deadline, "all refugees, regardless of age or sex, remaining in Smyrna . . . were to share this terrible fate" of deportation.[15]

The situation meant that the 300,000 refugees Lovejoy found when she arrived in Smyrna would have to be evacuated by September 30 or face death. They had been waiting for almost two weeks in conditions of fear, overcrowding, deprivation of basic needs, and growing danger of disease in accumulating human waste. They were unwilling to leave the packed quay for fear of reprisals. Many of the men had already been taken, leaving women and children behind. By September 25, nine ships had sailed, but no more were on the horizon. Thereafter just four days remained until the deadline for escape.

Nineteen Greek ships arrived in the early morning of September 26, signaling a "terrible struggle" as they began to dock at the end of the railroad pier. Refugees would have to pass through a long, narrow gauntlet to reach the safety of the ships. "The quay was separated from the pier by two iron picket fences about seventy yards apart," Lovejoy reported. "These fences had narrow gates. The pier extended a long distance out to deep water, and three more fences with narrow gates had been improvised by placing heavy timbers across the piers about two or three hundred yards apart." Turkish forces would use this gauntlet to "carefully scrutinize" all of the refugees and then pull all men of military age out of line. Lovejoy called this "walking the plank."[16]

Lovejoy focused her feminist curiosity on the devastating plight of the women of Smyrna in the wake of war's violence. During the evacuation week, and especially in the last desperate days, families passed through the inspection gauntlet, and men would be taken at gunpoint, with women "weeping, praying, and begging for mercy" and then being driven "toward the ships, [soldiers] pushing them with their guns, striking them with straps or canes, and urging them forward like a herd of animals."[17] Some women were separated from their children and defied soldiers to reach them. In the "strength of madness," some climbed the fences and braved the butts of rifles.[18] During the night, women shrieked for the searchlights to protect them from assault on the quay. Those "deported to the interior," Lovejoy noted, would endure a "fate worse

Esther Lovejoy (at right above "X") on the quay at Smyrna, September 1922. Reproduced by permission of Oregon Health & Science University Historical Collections & Archives, Portland, Oregon.

than death, because it is preceded by slavery on the part of the men and even worse [indicating rape] on the part of girls and women."[19] Lovejoy herself was assaulted on the quay. "A Turkish soldier, mistaking her for a Greek woman, struck her heavily with the butt end of a rifle and left a mark."[20]

Pregnant women were inducted into a "terrible motherhood," Lovejoy recalled. "Three-quarters of the crowd were women and children, and never have I seen so many women carrying children," she said. "It seemed that every other woman was an expectant mother." And "there were many premature maternity cases" because of the "crushing and rushing" at the pier. Lovejoy estimated that over a hundred women were in labor across the five days of the evacuation week. British and US sailors, now with permission from Turkish authorities to assist the movement of the refugees to the ships, got to know Lovejoy and put her in contact with maternity cases. She assisted with many of the births. One woman, "who had been in the crush at the first gate for hours, finally staggered through holding her just-born child in her hands."[21] Some women delivered their children "while standing. Some of the infants died within an hour from exposure, but the mothers clung piteously to the bodies."[22] Here were the themes of *The House of the Good Neighbor* in a new location and a new conflict, with the same consequences for women.

Lovejoy also recognized a broader context in the history of the conflict, which for her meant an indictment of all militarism and war. During the First World War, while Turkey was fighting on the side of the Central Powers, the "Christian population within her borders, encouraged to believe that the success of the Allies would mean a religious and national freedom for them, probably aided and abetted these forces whenever they got the chance."[23] On a speaking tour of the United States, Lovejoy spoke of a "travesty of national and international responsibility. The Christian nations," she said, "by their actions and reactions, created conditions that made this holocaust inevitable." She noted that they provided munitions to the Turkish forces and wrote treaties that were mere "scraps of paper." The "Turkish soldiers moved in and the Greek soldiers marched out, and then the Christian nations responsible for the whole wicked business held up their hands and maintained neutrality while the Turks wrecked their vengeance on the non-combative peoples of Smyrna, most of whom were women and children."[24] Lovejoy's "faith in Christianity" had been shaken. "The nations should have found a way to have stood together for humanity's sake."[25]

In her study of Lovejoy's and Dr. Ruth Parmalee's medical work for the AWH in Greece, historian Virginia Metaxas makes the important point that medical women working in relief organizations in this period "shaped a narrative of motherhood to be shared with the American public in which childbirth and maternal responsibilities were described as relentless, even in the face of disaster, thus justifying their presence as helpers in sometimes horrific situations." By combining "Christian imagery or language" that had been used in previous missionary endeavors in the region "with the universal experience of motherhood and childhood," AWH personnel rendered "'exotic' Greek and Armenian children" to be more like the Americans they hoped would then donate to the cause.[26] In Lovejoy's case, the lessons at the quay at Smyrna also became part of her philosophy of women's relationship to the state. Women's political power and activism were essential to bringing an end to the atrocities of war, an end to the militarism that affected them so powerfully.

Lovejoy used her speeches and writings about Smyrna and the relief work that followed to condemn the hypocrisy of power and the excess

Esther Lovejoy (right) and Marian Cruikshank with refugees in food line. Legacy Center, Drexel College of Medicine, Philadelphia, Pennsylvania.

of plenty in consumer society. One officer on hand she characterized this way: "He seemed like a man with a kind heart and a strong defense reaction against this weakness in himself." Other representatives of neutral political and military power she described less kindly. With the "power of life and death in their hands," one of their number might say, she mused, "'I forbid this ship to sail. We must maintain neutrality no matter what happens to these women and children. Pooh! What an odor! It makes me sick at the stomach. Come in to the Consulate, let's get a drink.'"[27] Leaving the quarantine island of Macronisi, with its thousands of refugees, its epidemics, and a shrinking AWH purse in the wake of the Smyrna disaster, Lovejoy reached the Hotel Grande Bretagne in Athens as dinner service began. "Corps of waiters were passing down the aisles with loads of food gathered from the land and the sea." She described the onslaught of "course after course . . . hors d'oeuvres and cocktails to stimulate flagging appetites, followed by

American Women's Hospitals Camp D, quarantine on Macronisi Island in the Aegean, 1923.
Legacy Center, Drexel University College of Medicine, Philadelphia, Pennsylvania.

soup, fish, fowl, meat, desserts and all sorts of trimmings along the way, finished with coffee, cigarettes and liquor served in the lounge." The contrast with her refugee work was stark. "The room seemed full of hungry children. Their living faces looked out of the clouds [painted] on the ceiling, as real as the frescoes of great artists, and in my mind's eye, that long line of wretched human beings was moving down the rear wall of the dining room toward the mush pots of the American Women's Hospitals." She saw "enough jewelry displayed in that dining room (some of it secured from refugees) to have fed the outcasts on [Macronisi] Island for a month."[28]

Before the Smyrna disaster in the summer of 1922, AWH board members had been discussing an end to the work; now Lovejoy was directing a thriving medical relief organization. In the immediate aftermath of Smyrna, the AWH operated nineteen hospitals in Greece, with additional dispensaries, milk depots, and relief stations.[29] One of the most visible parts of this work was the establishment of the AWH quarantine station for refugees on Macronisi Island. American Women's Hospitals physician Olga Stastny directed the work of nine separate camps for various diseases requiring quarantine, including smallpox and typhus, with "tents, bedding, fuel, fresh water and food" being shipped in to the small, barren island. From January to June 1923, the AWH received some

13,000 refugees in these tent camps, with "canvas-covered pavilions and large tents, hard to manage during storms," serving as hospitals with a daily schedule of clinics.[30] Lovejoy's successful facilitation of the scope and logistics of this work was the basis for a transformation of the AWH into a medical humanitarian relief organization with expanding agility and resources to respond to crises across the globe.

By 1927, AWH personnel had staffed thirty-seven hospitals and many more clinics, and had provided support to orphanages in the Balkans.[31] Continuing requests for assistance came from private individuals, from other relief agencies such as the Red Cross and the Near East Relief, and from heads of governments and government agencies.[32] The AWH provided medical support in Soviet Armenia and Russia after the revolution, sent assistance after earthquakes shattered Tokyo in 1923, and provided vital relief before and during the Second World War in Europe, China, and the USSR, and expanded its reach after the conflict.[33]

As the destitution of the Great Depression spread in the early 1930s, the AWH also responded to public health needs within the United States by establishing a "home service."[34] Residents in poor, rural districts faced an epidemic of pellagra, a disease of malnutrition and vitamin deficiency on the rise as a result of the Depression. Rural poverty, in particular, led to increasing health needs.[35] In 1931 the AWH established public health centers in North and South Carolina, and the next year in Kentucky, Tennessee, and Virginia. By means of a "healthmobile" made up of a car and a trailer, a doctor, dentist, nurse, and nutrition specialist staffed an AWH dispensary "carrying health to the country." With educational and nutritional programming; prenatal, maternity, and well-baby clinics; and general dispensary work, the AWH continued the work throughout the Depression and after.[36]

Esther Lovejoy directed the AWH until just months before her death at ninety-eight in 1967. By that time, the AWH had provided medical relief in twenty-eight nations: France, Serbia, Armenia, Turkey, Greece, Macedonia, Thrace, the Soviet Union, Albania, Japan, China, Great Britain, Australia, Finland, The Netherlands, Norway, Germany, the Philippines, Haiti, Korea, India, Taiwan, Thailand, Vietnam, Bolivia, Chile, Niger, and Togo; in the US states of Tennessee, Florida, South Carolina, North Carolina, Kentucky, Virginia, Alaska, and New Jersey; and contributed to various women's hospitals in the United States. Hundreds of thousands of people had received support in clinics, refugee centers, orphanages, dispensaries, and mobile hospitals. And hundreds of medical personnel and staff had worked and trained with the group.[37]

It took skilled organization and diplomacy to lead the AWH. Lovejoy took the chair in 1919 in the midst of conflict and controversy about her predecessor, Rosalie Slaughter Morton, and Lovejoy later referred to herself as the "referee of the fight."[38] Morton, an 1897 graduate of the Woman's Medical College of Pennsylvania, came from a long line of male physicians in a genteel Virginia family. She served as a special commissioner for the Red Cross in Serbia and studied war work among women in Europe in 1916 with a plan to build a program for US women's service. Morton, as historian Ellen S. More has noted, "dearly wanted to act heroically," but her skills did not lay in administration.[39] Yet at the 1917 meeting of the Medical Women's National Association, Morton accepted the chair of the new War Service Committee, which would become the American Women's Hospitals, after "the pressure brought to bear was too strong even for her determination."[40] Morton was "over-extended and overtired" with a variety of duties.[41] She did not provide strong leadership or organization to the new group, her communication with the MWNA board was sporadic, and her fundraising behind schedule. Committee finances were at best unclear, at worst in disarray. MWNA president Bertha Van Hoosen was particularly concerned about the situation, and corresponded with Morton and others about the urgent need for communication, organization, and financial clarity and transparency.[42]

By the time of the June 1918 meeting of the MWNA at which Esther Lovejoy reported her wartime service to great acclaim, many of the group's leaders were concerned about Morton's role as chair of the AWH. Morton was "unable to be present because of illness."[43] At the meeting, as Bertha Van Hoosen recalled, "a motion was made to the effect that Dr. Morton be made Chairman of the American Women's Hospitals War Service Committee, for life" by one of her supporters. Van Hoosen said that the motion was unconstitutional, as it fell to the MWNA president to appoint committee chairs each year. "Speakers for and speakers against took the floor and held it, a dozen at a time." Van Hoosen adjourned the meeting to end the bickering, and the group reached no resolution.[44] Just over a week later, Morton submitted her resignation, stating that illness would prevent her giving "the time and strength to the committee which it has a right to expect," and expressing her deep appreciation "to the loyalty of my friends." Dr. Mary Crawford, corresponding secretary of the AWH, agreed to take the chair for the year.[45]

"Dr. Morton's friends remained loyal," Van Hoosen later recalled, and at the June 1919 meeting, "another stampede of 'Morton for life' was started."[46] Esther Lovejoy did not remember a stampede so much as the solitary march of one of Morton's chief supporters. "The wonderful fight in 1919—who could ever forget it. That was twenty years ago and I still chuckle every time I think of it. I have a moving picture in my mind of Emily B[arringer] coming down the aisle in ground-shaking shoes ready for the fray."[47] In the end, Lovejoy agreed to chair the AWH for one year, and, at the strategic suggestion of Chicago's Dr. Rachelle Yarros, the MWNA sent Morton "on a fully paid tour of inspection to the European theater of war."[48]

Across the next several decades, the Morton controversy simmered and occasionally boiled over in MWNA and AWH politics as Lovejoy built a strong reputation for directing the organization during crises and economic hard times. At the 1922 MWNA meeting, questions about the founding of the AWH and Morton's role again emerged. Morton and a colleague wanted to have her name put on the AWH stationery as the founder of the organization. Outgoing president Martha Tracy asked three members of the AWH board, Drs. Eliza Mosher, Sue Radcliff, and Mathilda Wallin, to research the matter and report to the group at the 1923 meeting. Their "Origin of the American Women's Hospitals: Report of Committee" concluded that the AWH was founded by the MWNA, not one individual, and was therefore under its organizational authority.[49]

Morton did not accept the findings, and worked to establish her own version at the same time that she tried to discredit Esther Lovejoy. Feelings ran high on both sides.[50] As Morton worked on the manuscript for her 1937 autobiography *A Woman Surgeon,* she wanted to provide what she considered the correct interpretation of her importance to the origins of the AWH.[51] She wrote to protest when Inez Haynes Irwin, in her 1933 book *Angels and Amazons: A Hundred Years of American Women,* wrote that the AWH was established by the War Service Committee of the MWNA.[52] Morton also corrected portions of Kate Campbell Mead's projected second-volume history of medical women, placing herself as founder.[53]

Morton revealed much about her attitude toward Esther Lovejoy in a letter she sent to Mead with these revisions in 1934, a letter that also suggests Lovejoy's outsider status in some medical women's circles. "It takes no glory from later workers that I, being on the ground in Europe, had the gumption to form a plan and the energy to use my time off duty in what interested me intellectually and what turned out to be also a benefit to the Medical Women's National Association in providing an immediate plan for war work plans," Morton told Mead:

> Dr. Lovejoy's attitude can only be excused on the basis that her heredity is emotional. A woman doctor from Portland, Oregon told me that Dr. Lovejoy's mother had been for years in an insane asylum and her father was known as a bar room orator and died a drunkard. This work was her first chance to give her life importance, outside a market inspector position in Seattle. She has done good work but I cannot understand, nor can hundreds of other women, why, when she has been paid a good salary, supplied with an apartment and given royal perquisites in traveling expenses, etc., etc., that she would be almost deified and demand adulation while you and I, and other women, who have done equally valuable work, [have contributed] with all our soul and energy to the progress of medical women and humanity, without any salary.[54]

Morton's claim that Lovejoy's "heredity is emotional" was matched by her own quite passionate reactions to the situation. She repeated gossip about Lovejoy's parents in an effort to discredit and even shame her antagonist. She also cast them with Lovejoy far away in an obscure Pacific Northwest, where Portland and Seattle were interchangeable and Lovejoy was a market inspector rather than city health officer, living a life of little importance. Lovejoy's AWH salary and "royal" benefits (which Morton misrepresented) and her reputation that approached "deification" were all the more inexplicable in someone emerging from her "humble" (and, one might conclude from Morton's accusations, "defective") origins. It is suggestive to note that Morton corresponded with Abigail Scott Duniway's son Clyde in 1924 and 1928, and apparently met with him. She may have been interested in learning more about Lovejoy's clashes with Duniway in Oregon suffrage days.[55]

Morton engaged in a campaign to investigate Lovejoy and the finances of the AWH from the mid-1930s until the time the United States entered the Second World War. She charged that Lovejoy had used AWH funds to rent her apartment, and to pay for lavish entertainment and unnecessary trips abroad, and that she had paid the way of family members who had traveled with her, all claims that appear to have no basis in budgetary fact. Morton also proposed numerous drafts of a resolution to take to the MWNA to investigate and audit Lovejoy and the organization.[56] And she continued to promote her version of AWH history. At the 1934 American Medical Association meeting in Cleveland, supporters led by Emily Dunning Barringer hosted a banquet for Morton and awarded her a "handsome loving cup" recognizing her "distinguished services during the World War as first chairman of the War Service Committee of the Medical Women's National Association known as The American Women's Hospitals."[57] When Morton stated in her 1936 entry for *Who's Who in America* that she had been "'presented with a loving cup' by the American Medical Association in 1934 'in commemoration of having been founder of the Am. Women's Hospitals,'" and suggested the same in her 1937 autobiography, Lovejoy and the AWH board felt that they had to act.[58] They responded with a detailed report in 1937 titled "American Women's Hospitals Organized by War Service Committee of the Medical Women's National Association" and concluded that the AWH had been founded not by one person but by a committee. This 1937 report provided references to AWH files, minutes, and auditor statements, and the board unanimously reaffirmed the conclusions of the 1923 report.

This controversy and its consequences, born early and long-lived, suggest some crucial things about Esther Lovejoy and her style of leadership. Lovejoy was used to adversaries, and she responded with constructive resistance. From the beginning of her tenure as chair of the AWH, she insisted on scrupulous accounting and auditing of the AWH books each year.[59] She realized the importance of a tight budgetary ship, all the more so because Morton had not been a good accountant when in her tenure as chair and continued to make unsubstantiated claims about Lovejoy's use of AWH money. Lovejoy also authored no-nonsense reports and broader organizational histories that emphasized accomplishments and spread the credit among the workers involved.[60] The Morton controversy also demonstrates just how successful the American Women's Hospitals was becoming and the evolution of its importance for women physicians and the broader public thereafter.

This is not to say that Lovejoy was always easy to work with or approachable to everyone. Far from it. Her executive secretary, Estelle Fraade, described her this way: Lovejoy "had a dominant personality—

sometimes domineering—and it was a brave soul who opposed her, largely because she was always sure of her facts and figures before she took a position and those who might want to oppose her were rarely as well prepared or informed. This was true even in her early nineties."[61]

Lovejoy took great pride in her ability to steer the AWH. She had been an outsider, and some colleagues, including Morton, continued to see her as one. But Lovejoy had prevailed. Writing to suffrage leader Carrie Chapman Catt in November 1940, she recalled the early days: "The American Women's Hospitals group were having all kinds of internal troubles . . . after the manner of human beings, both men and women," she wrote. "And for this reason a dark horse from the Pacific Coast was put in control for a short time in order to establish peace, if possible. I was the dark horse and am still on the job." And, she continued, "in this connection I should say, in defense of my sex, that while we do not always agree, our quarrels are not as violent as those of the opposite sex."[62] Lovejoy wrote in much the same vein in 1958 to Mary Crawford, MD, who had directed the AWH in the interim after Morton's resignation. "It was my privilege to build on the work which was started by you and others who worked with me for years. . . . I shall never forget the meeting at Atlantic City in 1919 and I am sure you will be glad to know that since I took over that year we have worked without interference by people who did not know what they were about." She was hoping, Lovejoy said, "that some woman doctor of your age and mine during the First World War will appear and build upon the foundation that has been established."[63]

Lovejoy directed AWH operations from a New York City office that, after 1934, was located in Rockefeller Center. The AWH office served as the headquarters of the Medical Women's International Association during the early 1920s and as the headquarters of the Medical Women's National Association (renamed the American Medical Women's Association, AMWA, in 1937) from 1919 to 1950.[64] The AWH executive board was a group of women doctors with a relatively stable membership who were active in the national association. They met together monthly to set policy and respond to requests. Lovejoy worked with doctors and nurses in the AWH employ, established and maintained institutional and governmental relationships, facilitated the establishment of new fields of work, and oversaw annual fund-raising drives and other revenue-generating matters, including the day-to-day finances of the group. She traveled to AWH locations frequently to make arrangements, study problems, and

American Women's Hospitals executive board meeting dinner at the home of Dr. Mathilda Wallin, New York, 1940. Clockwise from bottom left: Dr. Mathilda Wallin, Dr. Bertha Van Hoosen, Dr. Tipton Mullins, Dr. Elizabeth Mason Hohl, Mrs. Estelle Fraade (AWH executive secretary), Dr. Helen Walbridge, Dr. Harriet F. Coffin, Dr. Esther Lovejoy, Dr. Inez Bentley, Dr. Catherine MacFarlane, Dr. Nellie Noble, and Dr. Mabel M. Akin. Reproduced by permission of Oregon Health & Science University Historical Collections & Archives, Portland, Oregon.

work with local staff and other administrators. Lovejoy won reappointment to her post each year by each successive president of the MWNA/AMWA, and held the post of MWNA president consecutively with her chair of the AWH in 1932–1933. She reported to the full membership at each annual meeting of the MWNA/AMWA, wrote interim reports, and worked to publicize the work of the AWH in the United States and abroad for medical, women's, and general audiences.

In the mid 1930s, Estelle Fraade, a graduate of Barnard College, joined the staff as executive secretary, a post she held for over forty years. She took on a great deal of the administrative work of the organization, "making sure the money out was not more than the money in," her daughter Amy recalled. She "kept in touch with the clinics abroad, and received their appeals for money, wrote the brochures and letters, sent them to contributors, made the brochures, kept the record of contributors, and arranged board meetings." Lovejoy and the women physicians on the board had a vision of women helping women, and Fraade's steady presence enabled the group to make that vision a reality.[65]

Lovejoy was committed to supporting communities and medical personnel through locally identified needs rather than by what we might term relief imperialism. She urged all women physicians to become involved in the medical relief work of the AWH. "Let us get acquainted with the medical women and men of Russia and of other countries and help them in their time of great need," she suggested in 1922. Let us "help them, not by sending English and American physicians at English and American salaries to do their work, but by making it possible for them to live through the winter and work in their own countries."[66] American Women's Hospitals relief efforts in the Greco-Turkish conflict included the employment of fifteen refugee physicians and some forty-five other medical personnel, including nurses, on the refugee and quarantine islands of Chios and Mytilene in 1923. "Russian, Greek and Armenian physicians, both men and women, have been employed by the American Women's Hospitals," Lovejoy reported. We have "been able to save a great many of our well qualified colleagues in war stricken countries from the bread line, by making it possible for them to work among their own people."[67] In Shanghai, China, during the late 1930s, the AWH financed the salaries of Dr. Lydia Hsü and the three women physicians on her staff for their hospital for refugees of the Japanese occupation.[68] American Women's Hospitals funds to Great Britain and France during the Second World War went directly to the women physicians of those nations, who then decided how best to use them.[69]

From the beginning of her tenure with the AWH, Lovejoy fought to maintain the group's separate status from other humanitarian and medical relief groups. She saw the pragmatic value of collaboration but did not want to have the work of the AWH subsumed, silenced, or made invisible within a larger organization. With its postwar medical work, the AWH became a part of a coalition of relief agencies called the American Committee for Armenian and Syrian Relief, later renamed the Near East Relief.[70] The organization also worked with the International Red Cross, the American Friends Service Committee, and the American Board of Commissioners for Foreign Missions. Lovejoy insisted that the AWH work independently in all possible situations. She did this by maintaining strict accounting of separate funds. Cooperation was necessary and desirable in many situations. The Red Cross, for example, could provide food and milk to clinics and orphanages, while the AWH had full control of medical matters. In all of these cases, the AWH accepted donations from other relief agencies for equipment and supplies, but Lovejoy maintained direct control over salaries to preserve independence of action.[71] "We do not contribute toward any organization," Lovejoy wrote, "but we do pay for work we undertake in cooperation with other organizations."[72]

Lovejoy worked tirelessly, and, in some people's minds, relentlessly, to publicize the work of the AWH. Certainly this was to raise needed money for the group, but she also wanted to emphasize the independent work of the AWH to make sure that the staff and their accomplishments were recognized. Some characterized this as arrogance or ambition. In 1940 British physician Janet Campbell noted in frustration that, along with relief funds, Lovejoy had sent armbands with the AWH logo "to be worn, for publicity purposes, by any doctor or nurse shown in a photograph as being in charge of sick children!"[73] But this was also a fierce determination, by a woman with experience in how women's accomplishments could be silenced and erased, to make sure that the AWH mattered and received credit for its work. It was something worth fighting for, something substantial about which a true history mattered. In her first annual report to the AWH executive board in 1920, Lovejoy noted that in the two months since sending out a newsletter, the AWH had raised over $14,000. "These letters are of value not only from the standpoint of financing our work but from the standpoint of letting the country know what medical women are capable of doing."[74] In her fundraising efforts and her many interviews, speeches, articles, and books throughout her AWH tenure, Lovejoy would write medical women and their transnational work into history.

Lovejoy acknowledged that there was both a medical and a financial side to the AWH, and she had learned how to adapt to each. "As Health Officer of a large city, it had formerly been my practice to observe people closely for signs of disease," she wrote. But now, in AWH service, she observed people "for signs of wealth and human sympathy."[75] She did not hesitate to publicize her practice of traveling by the least expensive steerage rates aboard ship so that the AWH "relief work should get 100 cents on the dollar." Donors were generous, she said, in a front-page, publicity-generating story about her accommodations in the *New York Times*, and "I refuse to stand by and let this money be used for joy-riding."[76] From the first, Lovejoy brought successful modern campaign advertising techniques to the work. She produced newsletters with eye-catching images of AWH activities and built a list of donors.[77] Brochures, mailings, and presentations became a feature of the AWH public relations work each year. And she used the new medium of film. "When in Greece recently, Dr. Lovejoy had several reels of films made showing the AWH work in Athens, Crete, [Macronisi], and vicinity," the *MWNA Bulletin* announced in 1923. "These admirable motion pictures were shown by Dr. Lovejoy" at the American Medical Association annual meeting. "The combination of Ancient Greek glory and the misery today made a striking contrast and gave food for serious thought on the trend of human progress."[78]

As an author, Lovejoy publicized the work of the AWH, and her books generated publicity and donations. *Certain Samaritans* (1927, 1933) and *Women Physicians and Surgeons* (1939) were filled with anecdotes, excerpts from letters by AWH staff, Lovejoy's own wit and pathos, and countless images of the AWH in action. Lovejoy donated the proceeds from the books, multiplying their financial impact on the AWH.[79] American Women's Hospitals financial reports attest to the spike in donations after Lovejoy made major publicity campaigns or after these books were published. For example, the 1923 report "Donations in Cash for Work in Serbia, Armenia, Macedonia, and Greece in Undesignated Funds" listed donations of $252,316, almost seven times the $37,507 received the year before. By December 1928, after the 1927 publication of *Certain Samaritans*, donations were $94,831, almost double those of the previous year.[80] By 1952 Lovejoy estimated that "between forty and fifty thousand dollars in gifts and legacies were directly connected with *Certain Samaritans*, in addition to royalties passed to the AWH and books sold through the office."[81] Fundraising plus strict accounting also paid dividends. Lovejoy was proud to steer the AWH through the Great Depression of the 1930s with funds intact when many organizations were failing.[82] Fundraising for the American Women's Hospitals reached $4,334,593 by Lovejoy's death in 1967.[83]

Lovejoy sought material for her books aggressively. The author Rose Wilder Lane considered Lovejoy to be ruthless. Lane worked with the Red Cross after the First World War, and observed and wrote about the Greco-Turkish Civil War.[84] In 1923 she was working in Greece and Alba-

Esther Lovejoy and Medical Women's National Association colleagues in the 1930s. Left to right: Dr. Esther Lovejoy, Dr. Elizabeth Bass, Dr. Martha Tracy, Dr. Helena Ratterman, Dr. Anna Blount, and Dr. Mary Elizabeth Bates. Reproduced by permission of Oregon Health & Science University Historical Collections & Archives, Portland, Oregon.

nia, writing magazine articles and completing her book *The Peaks of Shala* (1923). Lovejoy was with the AWH gathering material for what would become *Certain Samaritans*. Lane befriended relief workers, including those working for the Near East Relief, "the Red Cross crowd," and the staff of the American Women's Hospitals. In Athens in mid-February, several weeks after sending her completed manuscript for *Peaks of Shala* to the publisher, Lane and her friend and photographer Peggy Marquis twice had coffee with Lovejoy and AWH nurse and business manager Marian Cruikshank.[85] Marquis accompanied Lovejoy to several nearby cities, and Lane noted in her diary, "Dr. Lovejoy tried to get away with Peggy's [photographic] plates and prints and did get one." Lane later cabled her agent: "Imperative Lovejoy must not see [my] Armenian manuscript writing."[86]

Esther Lovejoy's overlapping worlds of the American Women's Hospitals, the Medical Women's National Association/American Medical

Women's Association, and the Medical Women's International Association were sites of work and activism but also of collegial development and friendship. "The friends I have among medical women are the best friends I have in the world, and without the National Association I should never have come in contact with them," she confided to Portland colleague and friend Mabel Akin.[87] In her presidential address to the MWNA in 1932, Lovejoy outlined some of the ways that these vital networks operated. "Personal acquaintance with women physicians doing good work in different states and nations inspires us to greater efforts in our own fields," she noted. "There is so much to be gained by attending the national and international meetings—professionally, educationally, socially and from the standpoint of travel, recreation, and personal relations." Women doctors could "visit great cities at home and abroad" and "hospitality committees are waiting at the gates. Private cars are at our service and our guides are prominent citizens pointing with personal pride to the wonders of their cities instead of tourist agents" working for businesses. The rewards were substantial: "enduring friendships . . . loyalty is fostered, toleration developed, and ethics among women physicians take on a finer, more personal meaning."[88]

Across these years, Lovejoy continued her feminist curiosity about the lives of women in areas where the AWH worked. It was a curiosity that included questions about women's social, cultural, and economic lives in addition to their medical ones as Lovejoy advocated for measures to empower women's health and well-being. In the 1920s in Constantinople, for example, Lovejoy noted that women who worked as street cleaners were war widows and had been appointed to this work by the Turkish government during the First World War. "Men who wanted the jobs asked the government to dismiss the women," she noted. "After all earthly argument had been exhausted these men put forth the unanswerable argument that it was unseemly in the sight of Heaven for women to be seen in public places cleaning streets. To meet this objection, the friends of the war widows decided that the women street cleaners should be disguised in men's clothes in order that they might hold their jobs and still not compromise Constantinople in the sight of Heaven." Lovejoy and AWH business director in Greece, Marian Cruikshank, had their picture taken with one of the women street cleaners.[89]

Building on this feminist curiosity, Lovejoy continued to develop her theory of women's citizenship, empowerment, and social justice. On Sep-

Esther Lovejoy (left) and Marian Cruikshank (right) with a woman street cleaner in front of the Italian Military Headquarters in Constantinople, 1920s. Reproduced by permission of Oregon Health & Science University Historical Collections & Archives, Portland, Oregon.

tember 23, 1928, she gave a speech titled "Woman's Big Job" on the New York National Broadcasting Company's WJZ Radio program *Twilight Reveries*. In it she outlined her belief that women's greater civic power was working to bring an end to war. Many progressive transnational activists who shared Lovejoy's view about an end to war worked to support the Kellogg-Briand Pact in 1928. Originally brokered by Frank Kellogg, the United States secretary of state, and Aristide Briand, the French foreign minister, as the Pact of Paris, and signed on August 27, 1928, over fifty nations ultimately adopted this agreement to renounce the use of war as an "instrument of national policy," in effect to "outlaw war."[90] Lovejoy, who was in the midst of positive publicity from her 1927 first edition of *Certain Samaritans*, added her voice and her take on the treaty in her radio speech.

Lovejoy began by establishing her credentials: service in France in the World War, and ten years' medical and refugee work with the American Women's Hospitals in the Russian famine, the Greco-Turkish War, and the recent conflict in China. She was a woman who knew war, had observed it and been in the midst of it. And war was always gendered. In these "Wars, Revolutions, [and] Resultant Dislocation of populations and settlement of refugees," she said, "I have seen long lines of men carrying guns and long lines of women with their children in their arms fleeing from the wrath of men organized into armies and navies for the destruction of their fellowmen." And "during these destructive outbursts," she continued, "normal woman instinctively seeks safety in flight" and life for her children at "any price." Human survival is their goal, something more important "than that the power of the world should be exercised by any one set of men."[91] Lovejoy identified a cycle, "a repetition on a colossal scale" in which nations prepared for war. "Men built ships and guns . . . women delivered the soldiers" and then war mowed down millions of young men as soldiers and millions of children due to wartime hunger and disease. Then the cycle repeated itself. "As soon as a new crop of boys in the neighboring countries were old enough to kill and be killed, war was declared, and they were set at it, hammer and tongs, fire and sword, burning pitch and boiling tar." Nations have always created a "camouflage of Holiness" to mask these "unholy sacrifices" in order to perpetuate the cycle.[92]

But things were changing. All women were "instinctively against war" and were using their increasing civic power to prevent it. When the World War began, most women were not enfranchised, but during and after the conflict this began to change. "Since the enfranchisement of women, in the most favored nations, a political passion for permanent peace is developing." Witness, Lovejoy said, the Kellogg-Briand Pact of Paris. "I am not claiming that this movement is entirely due to women in politics," she continued. "Without the enfranchisement of women, these things may have come to pass, but in all the ages that men have fought and died, or lived and made treaties, nothing of the kind has ever happened before. Therefore I am justified in the opinion that the passion for permanent peace moving the world at the present time is due, in large measure, to the collective moral influence of women in politics." Secretary of State Kellogg had negotiated the Pact of Paris "with but little talk . . . [and] there was no need for talk. The nations were already convinced. For ten years, in pulpits, women's clubs, conferences and elsewhere, the talking, writing and general agitation necessary to produce the Pact of

Esther Lovejoy in the late 1920s, about the time of her "Woman's Big Job" speech. Library of Congress, Washington, DC.

Paris has been going on in every city, town and hamlet throughout the civilized world. Why work the churn after the butter has come?"[93]

Lovejoy believed that if such peace were to be achieved, it would require social justice to maintain it. "Wars between great nations are probably evils of the past, unless Asia should break loose in some unexpected manner," she noted, "but revolutions and local hostilities will doubtless continue intermittently." The new technologies of war, she insisted, made armed conflict too dangerous. Nations must reduce armaments, settle the debts of previous conflicts, and "set their young men free from military slavery . . . to work out their individual genius." The "elimination of poverty, child welfare, relief of farmers, prohibition and equality of opportunity are on the air in these campaigning days. Poverty is the fundamental evil. Ignorance and Vice are the bartenders of Poverty, serving Crime, Disease and Death." "'Equality of Opportunity' sounds well on the air," she told her listeners, "but these are empty words while one man is born in a good home with every care that money can buy, and another is born in a tenement where his mother dies of neglect." We are "bound together" as a people, Lovejoy insisted, "and it is the moral duty of every woman in the land to protect her own home by using her political power to improve conditions in the homes of other women."[94]

Esther Lovejoy utilized her feminist curiosity and embodied her commitment to "Woman's Big Job" in her work for the American Women's Hospitals. The AWH, Lovejoy noted, "extending from country to country, has encircled the globe" on behalf of women.[95] And as Alma Dea Morani, MD, who succeeded Lovejoy as director of the AWH in 1967, affirmed, the achievements of Lovejoy and the AWH demonstrated that the "care of the needy sick has become an aspect of social justice and not just an image of charity."[96]

CHAPTER 9

Feminist Transnational Activism and International Health

I N her presidential address to the Medical Women's International Association in Geneva, Switzerland, in September 1922, Esther Lovejoy urged her colleagues to embrace feminist transnational health activism. Lovejoy believed that the three-year-old MWIA could unite the ten thousand women doctors of the world for positive action "in matters pertaining to international health." She defined international health as the abolition of "pestilence, which passes from country to country, and all the causes of pestilence, chief among which stands war," and as "the prevention of disease, which is due in large measure to destitution resulting from social and economic injustice and war between nations." Lovejoy hoped that medical women in the MWIA, partnering with enfranchised women across the globe and acting in concert with the relief work of the American Women's Hospitals, could work to achieve this progressive postwar vision that linked feminism and international health with social justice and peace.[1]

Women physicians associated with the MWIA and the AWH were a relatively small group compared to other organizations, such as the Women's International League for Peace and Freedom, but Lovejoy's organizing concept of international health and the structures she established to implement it were vital transnational responses to war, disease, and medical and humanitarian emergencies. Lovejoy facilitated a feminist "without borders" philosophy for international health that was similar to the ideologies of later medical relief organizations such as Doctors Without Borders. Such groups, according to medical sociologist Renée Fox, link "medical humanitarian and human rights action, within the larger framework of what has been termed a 'without borders' movement." This involves challenging state policies and politics with programs "premised on the conviction that medical care, service, and relief is a humane form of moral action, with the capacity to bind up wounds that are more than physical, to 'heal the body politic' as well as the human body."[2] Lovejoy's "without borders" activism through the AWH and MWIA was also strengthened by a feminist vision of the role of medical women in international health and a commitment to social medicine as a method to effect change in international affairs and to create strong and healthy communities. Medical women shared many elements of a common identity and program, what Lovejoy called the "friendly and practical relations of women doctors in different countries."[3] They were "writing treaties of peace," Lovejoy noted, "not on scraps of paper, but in the hearts of thousands of children, the men and women of tomorrow."[4]

Not long before Lovejoy's death, a colleague summed up her philosophy as a simple but profound one: "Hoping that internationally cooperating professional women could prove a potent instrument for friendship, understanding, and the peace they all cherish."[5] To achieve this, Lovejoy and her colleagues designed the MWIA to support three major transnational goals: to promote medical education and careers for women, to provide opportunities for women physicians to form collegial partnerships for action across and above national boundaries, and to formulate health policies that would promote and support healthy, safe, and secure communities for all women.[6] In the process they created an alternative to traditional state and international policymaking that focused on the military, diplomacy, and power relations.[7] They challenged what J. Ann Tickner has identified as the "concepts central to international relations theory and practice such as power, sovereignty, and security . . . framed in terms we associate with masculinity." Instead, Lovejoy and her colleagues developed the theory and practice of international health with a feminist perspective, from margin to center, from local to global, starting from the experiences of women to formulate transnational policies and programs for action.[8]

Over eighty delegates from twelve nations refined these goals at the second general convention of the MWIA, held in Geneva the first week of September 1922, while the Third Assembly of the League of Nations

Esther Lovejoy (at center with cape) at the Geneva Meeting of the Medical Women's International Association, 1922. Legacy Center, Drexel University College of Medicine, Philadelphia, Pennsylvania.

was in session. Delegates attended the opening session of the League, passed policy resolutions for the League's consideration, and attended conference sessions on a range of themes, from birth control to venereal disease to the status of women physicians in various nations.[9]

It was at this important conference, in her presidential address, that Lovejoy articulated her vision for the global activism of medical women and international health.[10] Lovejoy arrived at the conference directly from her AWH relief work in the Balkans, where she was "in daily contact with conditions which should move the medical women of the world, out of pity for the suffering of other women, to unite together and do their utmost in order that the objects of this organization may in some small measure be attained."[11] The association stood as an "instrument wherewith we can make our corporate intelligence and medical training available for service in matters pertaining to international health." The MWIA could support efforts to gain political rights for all women so that they could participate in formulating health policies in their communities. Enfranchised women, Lovejoy noted, "are responsible for health conditions in their own homes and in addition to these high duties they greatly influence city, state and national legislation and policy." Medical women should support these women voters and policymakers "in an educational way," as it was "important that their ideas along health lines should be sound." Lovejoy also wanted the association to assist with setting international health policy and to have a role in advising the League of Nations.[12] The MWIA, she said in a later interview, "was formed in order that the women of the world might stand together to advance health measures, and that means doing away with war."[13]

Medical Women's International Association members were part of a growing number of transnational activists following the First World War, including groups such as the International Woman Suffrage Alliance, the Women's International League for Peace and Freedom, the International Labor Organization, and the International Congress of Working Women.[14] Like other activists, MWIA members experienced frustration with the League of Nation's "dismal record on the inclusion of women"[15] but continued to press for involvement. The League formed a permanent Health Committee in 1923, with commissions to investigate and assist in medical emergencies such as epidemics, to keep statistics and issue reports, and to hold conferences and interchange visits for medical specialists. A number of women physicians participated in these interchange visits.[16] Two MWIA members, Swedish physician Alma Sundquist and Danish physician Estrid Hansen-Hein, served on the League of Nations Advisory Commission for the Protection of Women and Children Traffic in Women and Children Committee.[17] In the interwar period, the MWIA took steps to strengthen women physicians' roles in other organizations by creating liaison officers who would represent the MWIA at meetings of the League, the International Labor Organization, and the International Red Cross. The MWIA exchanged publications with international health organizations, publicized employment opportunities in its journal and other venues, and encouraged women physicians to prepare themselves in their local work for a future in transnational service.[18]

As a transnational group, the MWIA helped women physicians consult with and support one another so that they could take on strong policymaking roles in their communities and home nations, and so that they might contribute to international organizations by establishing health policies. The MWIA adopted a dual membership structure after Lovejoy suggested it. It included physicians who were members of an established national association, such as in the United States, and also individual members from nations that did not have an organized women's association, such as Turkey. Membership grew from several hundred in the early 1920s to 2,000 in 1924 and over 3,600 by 1929.[19] Medical Women's International Association conferences in these years featured topics such as women and cancer, working women and health, birth control, sex education, and physical education, and provided a forum for women to share research, strategies, and information. The MWIA journal featured reports on women physicians' activities in their respective nations, as well as information on international organizations and global health issues, and reprinted conference papers. Thus, while MWIA members continued to work for a larger role in national and transnational policymaking, they were also achieving results by assisting in the development and professionalization of women physicians in a variety of nations. Because the MWIA was a professional organization as well as a potential policymaking one, Lovejoy and MWIA members counted solid accomplishments in strengthening women physicians' roles and networks as a foundation for future achievement in the transnational policy arena.

Esther Lovejoy's work with Soviet public health pioneer Vera Pavlova Lebedeva is one notable example of her facilitation of effective connections between the AWH and the MWIA, and the potential that a shared identity as women physicians held for a feminist "without borders" philosophy and practice. The partnership of these two women was particularly significant given that Allied nations, including the United States, had participated in military operations against the Bolsheviks in Russia in 1918–1919 and that a virulent Red Scare raged in Western nations in the 1920s. In public, Lovejoy could use medical relief as both the motivation for the work and as some protection from criticism. The fact that the AWH was in the Soviet Union was not the concern of medical women, Lovejoy asserted. "We were there," she said, "to care for the sick."[20]

Lebedeva combined medical and revolutionary activism throughout her life. Born in poverty 1881 in Nizhnii Novgorod, Russia, she secured a place for her education in the gymnasium with the assistance of a charitable organization, worked as a rural schoolteacher, and in 1901 enrolled at the Women's Medical Institute in St. Petersburg. Expelled for distributing revolutionary materials, Lebedeva returned home to Nizhnii

Esther Lovejoy with health workers at Buzuluk, Soviet Union, 1923. Left to right: Nurse Berdenuk, Nurse Kazan, and Dr. Saukie (all Russian staff members); Igor Kazan; AHW staff members M. C. Phillips, Dr. Effie Graff, and Dr. Esther Lovejoy; and Alec Pavlov, interpreter. Reproduced by permission of Oregon Health & Science University Historical Collections & Archives, Portland, Oregon.

Novgorod and worked for the Bolshevik Party by assisting political prisoners during the 1905 Revolution. Here she met and married the revolutionary author Pavel Lebedev-Poliansky. The couple worked in exile in Finland and Switzerland, then she returned to her medical studies in St. Petersburg, graduating in 1910. Fired from her first position as a *zemstvo* (local district) physician for revolutionary activity, Lebedeva joined Pavel in Geneva, where she combined work in a women's clinic with activism in association with Vladimir Lenin and other Russian exiles.[21]

Lebedeva returned to Russia in May 1917 and, following the October Revolution of 1917 that brought the Bolsheviks to power, became the director of the new Soviet Department for the Protection of Maternity and Infancy (OMM). As director of the OMM, Lebedeva combined her medical training and public health concerns with her views about women's roles and her ideological identification with the new Soviet state to develop comprehensive services. Women would no longer be lone individuals who needed to find medical and child care in isolation, and who bore the double burden of wage work and domestic work. Women would achieve liberation as workers who were also mothers. Lebedeva's goal was to establish women's clinics and child care centers and to provide prenatal and pediatric health education across the new nation. These goals were "based on the picture of woman in the work process," she asserted, "which we keep constantly before our mind's eye."[22]

In 1922 Lebedeva began to work with Esther Lovejoy and other medical women in the AWH and was soon involved in the MWIA. The Soviet Union was emerging from severe famine and the ravages of civil war, and beginning in 1921 the AWH provided salaries for Dr. Effie Graff and Mabelle Philips in their work with the American Friends Service Committee in Buzuluk, in the province of Samara. As part of their discussion about possible AWH work in Moscow, Lebedeva extended an invitation to Lovejoy to visit in the spring of 1923. Visa delays postponed Lovejoy's plans to meet with Lebedeva directly, but the two corresponded about ways that the AWH might work with the OMM. Lovejoy also sent information and materials about the MWIA, including a copy of her 1922 Geneva presidential address. The "fraternal spirit engendered" at the Geneva conference, she wrote, "gave us all new hope for a closer union for international service in the future. . . . There are only a few thousand medical women in the world, but united for action they might render a comparatively large service in their chosen field."[23]

The following year Lebedeva accepted Lovejoy's invitation to represent the Soviet Union as a councillor to the 1924 London meeting of the MWIA and to present a paper about her work. This was at a time when conflict between Lebedeva's nation and the West severely hampered most other transnational relations.[24] In "Mothers' and Children's Welfare in Soviet Russia," Lebedeva articulated her public health theory and reported on Soviet accomplishments. First, she said, "we consider Mothers' and Infants' Welfare as a task of the state" and a "social function," and "absolutely exclude from our work any suggestion of philanthropy." In the Soviet state women were first workers, then mothers. "In organizing institutions to alleviate the burden of motherhood, we consider the woman always as a working force in the process of work."[25] Lebedeva presented information on the development of institutions and services within her department. These included *crèches* (nurseries and day-care centers), consultation centers, Homes of Mother and Child to support women during the two-month maternity leave, milk canteens, and legal services—some 1,350 institutions in all. Lebedeva also highlighted the establishment of the Scientific Institute of Mothers' and Infants' Welfare in Moscow, a teaching hospital that trained "physicians, pediatrists, midwives, and nurses" with the latest developments in obstetrics, gynecology, pediatrics, diet and nutrition, and a center for the development of public health educational resources and dispensaries. The work, Lebedeva noted, combined the "experience gained by Western scientific thought" with Soviet "social principles."[26]

Yet, even as Lebedeva shared her hopes and accomplishments with Lovejoy and colleagues in London in 1924, her vision of a new society based on the liberation of women and the redefinition of motherhood and the family in the Soviet Union was disintegrating. As Wendy Goldman demonstrates, the period from 1917 to 1936 in Soviet politics saw a "complete reversal" from a commitment to women's liberation and the "withering away" of the family in the early years of the Soviet state to restrictions and reversals of progressive policies and a "repressive strengthening of the family unit."[27] The Soviet Women's Party, the *Zhenotdel*, which provided vital advocacy for women's issues, was severely weakened in the 1920s and abolished in 1930. The Soviet adoption of the New Economic Policy in 1921 shifted support for Lebedeva's clinics and *crèches* to local districts that had little if any financial support to spare. It also caused grave unemployment for many women, further eroding women's ability to support themselves and their families. In the mid-1920s, women earned 65 percent of what men earned because they were "concentrated in unskilled, menial jobs at the bottom of the pay scale."[28] Lebedeva provided a strong voice of opposition to these changes and insisted that the dismal economic situation, combined with the decrease in state funding, challenged women's very survival.[29]

As a result, both Soviet state policies and international fears of the USSR were strong barriers to women's transnational medical work and to the achievement of the goals of social medicine. In these challenging years following the London conference, however, Lebedeva continued to work with Lovejoy and other medical women outside the Soviet Union. The AWH provided $1,000 to fund public health publications and educational work in the Soviet Union.[30] Lebedeva left the OMM in 1931, but the foundation for cooperative work had been established. There was little contact between the AWH and Soviet women doctors during the 1930s, given that Lebedeva was no longer in the OMM, that Stalinism strengthened many barriers, and that economic depression hampered

fund-raising for relief. But during the Second World War, women physicians in the USSR identified sulfa drugs and other medicines as top
priorities for AWH funding for wartime medical relief work in their
nation.[31] Thus the cooperative work established by Lovejoy and Lebedeva
formed a foundation for later support and stood as an important transnational achievement throughout the interwar and war years.

Lovejoy, however, walked a fine line and risked support for her organizations when she linked the AWH and the MWIA with Lebedeva and
Soviet medical women, particularly before the US and Soviet alliance during the Second World War. Even old allies deserted Lovejoy to distance
themselves from supposed radicalism. In January 1925, former NAWSA
president Carrie Chapman Catt organized a Conference on the Cause and
Cure of War in Washington, DC, involving major women's organizations,
including the League of Women Voters and the General Federation of
Women's Clubs. Alice Hamilton, a pioneer in industrial medicine, wrote
to Jane Addams, her colleague in the Women's International League for
Peace and Freedom, that Catt had kept any information about the activities of the American Women's Hospitals out of the conference. She had
"refused to let the Women's Hospitals literature—the Near-East and
Russian relief work, you know—be shown."[32]

The power of Lovejoy's vision for transnational medical women's net-
works is also apparent in the case of Austrian physician Dora Teleky.
Born in Vienna in 1879, Teleky graduated from the University of Vienna
Medical School as one of the first women graduates and one of Sigmund
Freud's first female students.[33] In the years before the First World War,
Vienna was an international center for postgraduate clinical studies, and
Teleky served as assistant in gynecology and obstetrics in the two leading women's clinics in the city. It was in this context that she first met
and worked with women physicians who came to Vienna's postgraduate clinics from many nations, including Esther Lovejoy.[34] Following the
war, Teleky organized and directed a birth control clinic in Vienna and
continued her medical and surgical work. Her research and scholarship
in gynecology and urology led to her election as the first woman in the
Austrian medical scientific society the Gesellschaft der Aerzte.[35]

Teleky shared the transnational impulse of many women physicians
following the First World War, but her Austrian nationality and her
wartime service in an Austrian military hospital had made her a former
enemy of Allied nations. In 1922 Lovejoy, as president of the MWIA, chal-

lenged such notions. She invited her colleague from Vienna clinic days to the MWIA Geneva conference and introduced Teleky personally to her colleagues at the banquet that marked the close of the gathering. Teleky said that "she had not hoped ever again to be received so warmly" and that the reception she received at the conference "would give heart to her colleagues in Vienna." Lovejoy responded, "If women had a larger place in the affairs of nations the world war would never have come."[36] Teleky "made the most beautiful speech on the peace of the world I ever heard anyone make, because she made it from the depths of her heart and soul," Lovejoy recalled later. "I believe that woman had more influence than perhaps any other one woman at that meeting, because all the others felt friendly, even those who had entertained some ill spirit, perhaps, from other countries—it all seemed to pass away after Dr. Teleky spoke that night."[37]

Teleky emerged as a dedicated transnationalist after this conference. In 1924 the one hundred members of the five-year-old Austrian Women's Medical Society she had founded elected Teleky as a delegate to the MWIA meeting in London. Teleky became the MWIA corresponding secretary and board member for Austria, a post that she held until 1938. She joined the editorial board of the *Medical Woman's Journal* in 1923 and continued to serve through the Second World War.[38] Teleky and the Austrian Women's Medical Society hosted the fifth council meeting of the MWIA in Vienna in 1931, and Teleky presented a report on birth control at the eighth general meeting of the MWIA in Stockholm in 1934.[39]

In the interwar years, Austrian state policies challenged Teleky's status as a woman physician and threatened her life as a Jewish woman. Following the annexation of Austria by Germany in 1938, Teleky wrote that the Austrian medical women's association had been dissolved and that she could no longer serve as MWIA corresponding secretary. She was proud to have collaborated with her colleagues from other nations, she wrote, "all of whom were so capable and so devoted to our common work."[40] As Austria became an increasingly dangerous place for Jewish citizens, Teleky and her husband, Ernst von Brücke, worked with international colleagues to find ways to leave the country. Von Brücke, also of Jewish descent, lost his position as a prominent faculty member at the University of Innsbruck in 1938. He secured a position as research associate at Harvard University through the effective support and lobby-

The Medical Women's International Association Meeting at Stockholm's City Hall, 1934. In Esther Lovejoy, *Women Physicians and Surgeons: National and International Associations* (New York: Livingston Press, 1939), 14. Reproduced by permission of Oregon Health & Science University Historical Collections & Archives, Portland, Oregon.

ing efforts of his colleague, Alexander Forbes, and arrived in Boston in August 1939, just two weeks before the Nazi invasion of Poland.[41]

To leave Austria, Teleky drew upon her transnational relationships with women physicians. In July 1938, when her assets as a Jewish woman were claimed by the Reich, she found refuge for some months with her British MWIA colleagues, staying first in London and then south of the city in Surrey. She came to New York in September 1939.[42] Esther Lovejoy visited Teleky upon her arrival in New York, and by November 1939, Teleky was in Boston, where her husband was conducting laboratory research at Harvard Medical School. After Ernst von Brücke's death in June 1941, Teleky remained in Boston, secured her state medical license, and pieced together medical work and eventually built a practice. She retired to Switzerland in 1950 at the age of seventy-one and lived in retirement until her death in 1963. [43]

Lovejoy and other women physicians worked to assist Teleky and refugee colleagues, and coordinated their activities with other women's and refugee groups. The MWIA formed a joint committee with the International Federation of University Women to provide support for medical and professional women, and former MWIA president Lucie Thuillier-Landry was the organization's liaison to the International Committee for the Assistance of Refugees in Geneva.[44] Esther Lovejoy and the AWH provided funds for refugee medical women and worked with Thuillier-Landry, MWIA president Louisa Martindale, the French Association of Medical Women, and the French Association of University Women.[45] The Danish and Swedish medical women's associations raised funds to assist refugee colleagues. MWIA honorary secretary Germaine Montreuil-Straus "kept an up-to-date list of all these women doctors of whom they were notified, and made contact with those countries which were, it was believed, able to accept them."[46] The American Medical Women's Association formed a refugee committee in July 1938, directed by Rita S. Finkler, a 1915 refugee from Russian pogroms. And the women's medical associations of various US states also formed committees. Initial efforts involved individual sponsorship of medical colleagues from Austria and Germany, including Dora Teleky. Many groups then began fund-raising.[47] Montreuil-Straus characterized the process: "England and France were for some of the refugees mainly transit countries from which they made their way to the U.S.A., where a Committee of Welcome, headed by Dr. Finkler, helped them to re-establish themselves."[48] This transnational work to support refugee women physicians, Montreuil-Straus believed, demonstrated that "solidarity was not an empty display of words."[49]

Refugee women physicians encountered many challenges in relocation and in the reestablishment of their careers that underscored the importance of support from transnational medical women's networks. Nativism, anti-Semitism, and fears of competition in a decade of international economic depression operated against male and female physician refugees. But, as historian Atina Grossmann has noted, women physicians faced added burdens and a situation "highly complicated by gender."[50] The "general committees set up to help refugee physicians" were "unsympathetic to the substantial number of women who hoped to reestablish their medical careers."[51] Immigration laws in many European nations and in the United States were restrictive before the conflict, and, combined with adverse bureaucratic practices, created a "world of barriers" with the coming of persecution and war.[52]

The MWIA's Germaine Montreuil-Straus noted, "In actual fact, with the exception of Great Britain, where fifty German and Austrian doctors, and fifty Czech doctors, after passing their examinations, were allowed to practice," and the United States, where other women were able to study and pass medical examinations, "our unfortunate colleagues had no means of resuming professional activities outside their own countries."[53] Some European nations, such as The Netherlands, Sweden and France, had limited options for temporary stays on tourist visas, but the possibility of permanent residency was severely limited.[54] In the United States, strict quotas for immigration were in force, and states and state medical societies also restricted medical licenses. By 1940 twenty-seven states required applicants for the medical licensing examination to be US citizens, and eighteen required applicants to have taken out "first papers" of intention to become citizens. Twenty-seven states also required applicants to hold a medical degree from approved US and Canadian medical schools.[55] Barriers to practice and licensing meant that women physicians often had to turn to alternative means of making a living.[56] The transnational medical women's networks of support were therefore crucial for many refugee women physicians and countered not only Nazi policies based on anti-Semitism but other repressive restrictions against Jewish women physicians in other nations, including the United States.

These examples are part of a larger pattern of AWH and MWIA transnational action to foster international health. Lovejoy and other physicians came to know Tomo Inouye as Japan's representative to the MWIA, and Lovejoy and Inouye corresponded throughout the early 1920s. When a powerful earthquake devastated much of Tokyo in 1923, Inouye headed a committee that directed AWH funds and supervised Japanese medical women and medical relief for earthquake victims. Lovejoy and Inouye were able to act quickly to put the aid in place because of their networks and relationship.[57] The AWH executive board directed Lovejoy "to write to Dr. Inouye expressing our delight upon hearing from her, reminding her that there are members of the Board who remember her personally, and requesting her to write us as frequently as she can."[58]

During the Second World War, in addition to supplying Soviet women physicians with medicine, Lovejoy and the AWH provided other requested support through networks established with women physicians in the MWIA. Over the course of the war, the AWH contributed over $51,000 to a fund administered cooperatively with members of the British Medical Women's Federation to provide civilian and refugee relief and to resupply hospitals that had been bombed.[59] Sixty-four British medical women who had received assistance signed a "round robin" document of thanks in 1944.[60] The AWH contributed $50,000 to China during the war, which went toward salaries for Chinese women physicians, nurses, and medical supplies. And, in France, with the cooperation of Germaine Montreuil-Straus and the Women's Medical Service Committee, the AWH sent $200 per month until the fall of Paris and then contributed $300 per month for reconstruction and refugee services in France in 1945. The AWH worked with the Committee of Social Work of Resistant Organizations (COSOR), formed as part of the resistance to Nazi occupation, in cooperation with the French Medical Women's Association.[61]

In postwar Norway, Lovejoy and the AWH partnered with Dr. Irmelin Christensen and members of the Norwegian Medical Women's Association to determine the priorities that Norwegian women doctors had for public health relief, and jointly funded a new water system for the rebuilding of the town of Televåg, which had been destroyed during the conflict. The Norwegian women physicians placed particular emphasis on assisting women of the village with clean and plentiful water supplies for family and community health.[62] In 1951 the AWH, in cooperation with the Philippine Medical Women's Association, established a prenatal and children's clinic in Manila, and by the mid-1950s the clinic provided preventative medical care to all ages, public health classes, and home visits.[63] In the immediate aftermath of the Hungarian uprising of 1956, the AWH worked with the Austrian Women's Medical Association and its president, Dr. Lore Antoine, to provide medical supplies and food for refugees from the crisis. Because the AWH worked directly with Austrian women physicians and sent supplies "directly to the association nearest to the troubled area," it "made us better known," Antoine said, "and will help to start more useful work here." Antoine reported that "this service had enormously increased the standing of women doctors in her country, both in the medical profession and outside of it."[64]

Esther Lovejoy explained this process of building international health to suffrage leader Carrie Chapman Catt in 1940. She urged Catt to read her book *Women Physicians and Surgeons* to understand the relationship between US women physicians and women doctors abroad. "You will be able to see at once how easy the International makes it for us to carry on relief in foreign countries. Because of that organization and the conferences held from time to time, we have become personally acquainted with many women physicians overseas." This meant "it is not necessary for us to send American women into foreign countries to conduct medical service because we can do a better job at a far lower cost by work-ing through the medical women of those countries."[65] As Estelle Fraade noted, the AWH practice of listening to the priorities of local person-nel and providing support permitted women physicians "to serve their own people as they might otherwise be unable to do, and in addition has advanced the status of women doctors in their own countries."[66]

Working through the MWIA and the AWH, Lovejoy engendered her vision of international health by supporting, not supplanting, women doctors in their own communities. And, in so doing, women physicians could help to empower and educate women around the globe. In a with-out borders challenge to traditional policies, Lovejoy and the organiza-tions she fostered worked to achieve social justice and peace as women supporting women above and across national boundaries. This was a part of Lovejoy's continuing effort at constructive resistance, now on a transnational scale.

Conclusion

A LEGACY OF CONSTRUCTIVE RESISTANCE

S she directed the American Women's Hospitals from the 1920s to the Cold War amid escalating global strife, poverty, the rise of fascism and militarism, and other forms of social injustice, Esther Lovejoy did not lose her vision of the power of feminist transnational organizing and international health, nor of "Woman's Big Job" and the importance of constructive resistance. One of Lovejoy's major contributions in her later years was her continuing commitment to preserving and recording the history of women in medicine. She served as an expert on women's medical history at conferences and in articles and reports, authored two additional books, and contributed to public history commemorations, placing medical women and their activism at the center of her analysis and showcasing their contributions.

In *Women Physicians and Surgeons: National and International Organizations* (1939) Lovejoy linked the stories of the three major medical associations with which she was associated: the American Medical Women's Association (formerly the Medical Women's National Association), the American Women's Hospitals, and the Medical Women's International Association. As with *Certain Samaritans,* she preserved the records and activities of these groups with images, letters, excerpts from official reports, and an overriding chronological narrative of her own to create a "record of high achievement and adventure."[1] Written during the Great Depression, when raising money was a particular challenge, Lovejoy's goal for *Women Physicians and Surgeons* was also to capture the interest of readers and then to create donors. And as with the publication of *Certain Samaritans* before it and *Women Doctors of the World* that followed, Lovejoy donated the profits back to the American Women's Hospitals.

In 1940 Lovejoy contributed to two public history projects that gave her the opportunity to emphasize the achievements and activism of women doctors. The National Broadcasting Company asked her to consult with scriptwriters for the "Women in Medicine" segment of the NBC/WJZ Radio series *Gallant American Women* in 1940. Coordinated by journalist Eva Hansl and supported by the US Department of Education and the New Deal's Federal Works Progress Administration, it was one of forty-seven segments in a two-part series on women's accomplishments broadcast in 1939 and 1940. The series included women from a variety of professions and activities, women in the arts, education, industry, and government. "Women in Medicine" included scenes on early women practitioners and pathbreakers such as Elizabeth Blackwell, but when it aired on March 12, 1940, it focused its twentieth-century coverage on the American Women's Hospitals.[2]

Lovejoy also assisted Carrie Chapman Catt, former president of the National American Woman Suffrage Association, in making medical women and their history a part of the Woman's Centennial Congress, a three-day meeting of women in New York City November 25–27, 1940. The group gathered to commemorate "The Woman's Century, 1840–1940," beginning with the 1840 London Anti-Slavery Convention attended by Lucretia Mott and Elizabeth Cady Stanton that was a catalyst for the organized movement for woman suffrage in the United States.[3] A decade after Catt had refused to have AWH literature at the Conference on the Cause and Cure of War in 1925, the two leaders from suffrage days reconnected and in the fall of 1940 Lovejoy agreed to represent women physicians on the Centennial Congress program.[4]

Lovejoy used this opportunity to showcase women's accomplishments in medicine and the importance of their national and transnational organizing and activism. She outlined the history of early women medical leaders and the successful struggle to gain access to medical education that had led to the over 8,000 women working in the profession in the United States that year. Lovejoy stressed the importance of the organization of the Medical Women's National Association in 1915, now the American Medical Women's Association, "for the purpose of promoting the interests of women physicians, participating in constructive movements, and cooperating effectively with the medical profession throughout the country." She also underscored the vital role of transnational activism and the Medical Women's International Association, "with the result that the leading women physicians of the world are personally acquainted." As the world plunged into war, she noted, "it has been the privilege of the American group, during this time of stress, to help their associates in China, Finland, France, and particularly in England, and to carry on a special service in Greece for the care of civilian sick and injured."[5] As ever, Lovejoy saw the work of the AWH and MWIA dovetailing for effective action.

In her final book, *Women Doctors of the World* (1957), completed when she was in her late eighties, Lovejoy provided a compendium of women's challenges and accomplishments in medicine, from the Greeks to the mid-twentieth century.[6] It was a statement of her continuing faith that medical women, cooperating across national borders, in concert with the enfranchised and active women of all nations, could change, and indeed had changed, the world. Her chapters were chronological, geographical, and biographical, ranging from the United States, Great Britain, Australia and New Zealand, the Balkans and the Near East to Russia, Asia, Africa, and Latin America. Seeking to make medical women visible in their historic actions and contemporary accomplishments, Lovejoy created a collective biographical account of the profession that became the standard reference work in the field. She wanted to restore women to the history of the profession: "Little is said about the work of women in the histories of medicine," she wrote in the preface.[7]

Lovejoy's goal for *Women Doctors of the World* was inclusion and breadth, and she gathered and presented information on the professional medical accomplishments of women of all nations. In some cases this involved challenging racism that prevented women from training and excelling as physicians and impeded medical women from working together. Lovejoy outlined the accomplishments of diverse women physicians who broke barriers, including Rebecca Lee, the first African American woman to graduate from medical school (New England Female Medical College 1864); Eloiza Diaz Insunza and Ernestina Perez Barahona, who shared the distinction of being Chile's first medical women graduates in 1887; Mary Susan Malahlele, the first Bantu woman to graduate from medical school in South Africa in 1947; and Mildred Fay Jefferson, Harvard's first African American woman graduate in 1951.[8]

In her discussion of a 1930s MWIA committee that collected data about women and children's health in India and Africa, Lovejoy addressed the committee's problematic use of the term "exotic" to refer to the women and children of these communities. "'Exotic' as a descriptive term was criticized on the ground that foreign women doctors were just as 'exotic' to the indigenous peoples of Central Africa and other remote places as those peoples were to them," she wrote, "and the name of the committee was changed."[9]

Lovejoy viewed the publication of *Women Doctors of the World* as a way to make the archives of women in medicine available to the public, casting herself in the role of archivist and historian:

> The office of the American Women's Hospitals in New York City was the headquarters of the Medical Women's International Association during its formative years when I was president and the headquarters of the American Medical Women's Association from 1919 to 1950. Articles and books by women doctors as well as official publications of medical societies passed over my desk in this office, which became a center of information about women in medicine.
>
> Questions from writers and from young college women considering medicine as a career were sometimes hard to answer. They wanted facts. And searching for the facts I was rewarded by a wealth of authentic information regarding the work of women in the medical profession. This material, supplemented by personal observation in various countries, became the basis for *Women Doctors of the World*.[10]

Esther Lovejoy's *Women Doctors of the World*, *Women Physicians and Surgeons*, *Certain Samaritans*, and *The House of the Good Neighbor* are indeed chronicles of medical women's history, accomplishments, and transnational work. They are also Lovejoy's personal memoirs, critiques of national and international policies, and statements against war and for cooperative activism. But these were just some of the products of Lovejoy's historical work. She also used fiction, speeches, autobiographical writing, and even radio drama to commemorate and interpret the history of women. As a historian of women, Lovejoy incorporated each of the four major stages of women's history identified by historians Gerda Lerner, Linda K. Kerber, and Jane De Hart.[11] She engaged in compensatory history by collecting, conserving, and publishing major archival

Esther Lovejoy signing *Women Doctors of the World*, ca. 1957. Reproduced by permission of Oregon Health & Science University Historical Collections & Archives, Portland, Oregon.

Right: Esther Lovejoy (left of wreath), with Philippine and US medical women, Ninth Congress, Medical Women's International Association, Manila, 1963. Reproduced by permission of Oregon Health & Science University Historical Collections & Archives, Portland, Oregon.

information about women physicians and women's transnational medical activism. She produced contribution history by telling of medical women's involvement in traditional historical categories such as the First World War. Yet she also rewrote the traditional historical narrative in a variety of ways. She emphasized medical women's alternative goals to address violence against women and to challenge military barriers to medical women's officer status, and focused on twentieth-century transnational activism with the American Women's Hospitals and the Medical Women's International Association. She also incorporated the concept of gender as a social construction and category of analysis, detailing the gendered nature of wartime roles, emphasizing the possibilities of international health as an alternative to war, and the possibilities of connecting diverse women and their communities through transnational activism as an alternative to traditional state diplomacy.

In addition to her work as a historian, the rhythms of Lovejoy's later years continued to be set by the various conferences and gatherings she attended and by a wide web of communication across the globe. At the end of her long life, Lovejoy had amassed many honors: medals from

Greece, France, and other grateful nations; honorary degrees in law and public health, the Elizabeth Blackwell Medal; and a Medical Woman of the Year award. In 1963, in association with the MWIA annual meeting in Manila, the Philippine Medical Women's Association dedicated Esther Lovejoy Hall in their Quezon City building with a mural in which Lovejoy stands at the center of Philippine women physicians against a backdrop of world flags.[12]

A vital reason that Lovejoy was able to stay active and traveling for so much of her long life was the dedicated service of Estelle Fraade, the AWH executive secretary. Fraade's facilitation of travel plans increasingly included accompanying Lovejoy to conferences. Fraade's steady presence and encyclopedic knowledge of the work of the American Women's Hospitals enabled Lovejoy to maintain her role as director.[13] Family members, fortunate nieces, nephews, and then grandnieces and grandnephews also accompanied Lovejoy around the world as she traveled to conferences. Correspondence kept her up to date with Portland events.[14] And by establishing a scholarship fund in the names of Frederick and Emil Pohl at what is now the Oregon Health & Science University, Love-

Esther Lovejoy, visiting Portland City Health Office, August 1963, next to her picture as city health officer. Reproduced by permission of Oregon Health & Science University Historical Collections & Archives, Portland, Oregon.

joy's generosity guided hundreds of women and men to the field of medical practice in Oregon.[15] At ninety-three, vigorous and with her sense of humor intact, Lovejoy revisited the city health offices at Portland City Hall. "I'm the only woman who was ever health officer here," she noted.[16] In a photograph of that visit she is seen pointing energetically to her picture on the wall in a line with other city health officers. She remained vitally interested in medical women's affairs and in righting wrongs. "I am old and a little weary," she wrote to a friend. "But when I sense dirty work in any quarter, it is like a shot in the arm. It renews my youth."[17]

The American Women's Hospitals was such a central part of Lovejoy's life that she was reluctant to leave it. She told colleague Elizabeth Mason

Hohl, "For several years I have noticed that whenever I am invited to speak at different places special mention is made of my advanced years, as though it were the wonder of the world, and I sometimes feel that I have already attended my own funeral service and listened to my obituary over and over again."[18] Jessie Laird Brodie, MD, felt that Lovejoy "could not bring herself to give up the authority which she had carried for so many years in this, her personal organization."[19] Supporters on the AWH executive board created contingency plans and, when Lovejoy was ready, accepted her resignation on May 1, 1967.[20] It was almost exactly fifty years since she had met with the assembled women physicians of the Medical Women's National Association and offered to represent them on a fact-finding mission to France to study the needs of women and children.

Esther Lovejoy died on August 17, 1967. Estelle Fraade returned to Portland with her ashes for a small ceremony at Lone Fir Cemetery. Her marker is now visible.[21]

This study of Esther Clayson Pohl Lovejoy's life and work emphasizes the connections among the various strands of her ideas and her activism, and suggests the importance of understanding those connections for a more complete analysis of women's civic, economic, and medical activism from the late nineteenth century to the present. It affirms the importance of studying the personal and the political aspects of a life of constructive resistance. It centers on the life of one woman who influenced a complicated century, from 1869 to 1967, a woman who had what women's studies scholar Cynthia Enloe calls the feminist curiosity to observe and understand women and their particular lives and concerns as she built a life dedicated to social justice and social change.[22]

Esther Clayson Pohl Lovejoy carried with her the experiences of the girl who waited tables at the family's Bay View Hotel in Seabeck, and the young woman who worked in department stores to pay her way through medical school. Lovejoy's suffrage activism and her partisan political philosophy and engagement developed with this working person's consciousness at the core. Like her progressive Democratic mentor Harry Lane, Lovejoy stood in opposition to "the interests"—both political and economic—that thwarted city health and democracy. She also embraced an evolving feminist standpoint vis-à-vis the interests. In her work for woman suffrage, she outlined why women, particularly, suffered at the hands of male interests that had robbed them of an economic role in society outside the factory doors, and of a male political system that denied them a voice in making their communities healthy and workplaces safe. And as she moved into national and transnational activism during and after the First World War, Lovejoy continued to battle these interests—political and economic institutions, nations, and an unchecked capitalist system that prevented women from exercising their full civic and economic citizenship.

The Federal Bureau of Investigation apparently has no files on Lovejoy,[23] even though she worked in Soviet Armenia and with Soviet physician Vera Lebedeva and wrote of herself in *Certain Samaritans* as having Bolshevik-like sentiments about power. With her AWH colleague Marian Cruikshank, Lovejoy wished for "an instantaneous exchange of populations" by which "refugees should take the places of all the people in the world whose personal and political schemes tend to create refugees." True to form, her list of the "refugee makers" included "representatives making up all the countries making up the League of Nations . . . from the governing bodies of all the great states of the world, members of commissions, a few relief workers and other missionaries."[24] Lovejoy deflected criticism by claiming that medical humanitarianism was not political, and she appears to have evaded official government scrutiny. The American Women's Hospitals does not appear in the infamous 1924 "Spider Web Chart" that identified women's organizations and leading women considered subversive by conservatives and government agencies.[25] But Carrie Chapman Catt and other women facilitating the Cause and Cure of War conference shunned Lovejoy and the AWH as being too radical.

As with her view of work and workers, for Lovejoy the right and obligation to vote encompassed one facet of a much broader vision of women's citizenship. Her capacious view also included office holding, both appointed and elective; economic citizenship (women physicians with their salaries had suffrage leaders to thank, she said, but she also risked that salary with her activism); and the right of women to serve the state in wartime independent of their male relatives. Women had the right to be mothers, which was also a service to the state, but only when the state provided them with affirming social and economic conditions and systems. Women had the ultimate right to control their own bodies. And all women citizens had the right and the obligation to develop

Esther Lovejoy at the University of Oregon Alumni Association dinner, Portland, 1957. Reproduced by permission of Oregon Health & Science University Historical Collections & Archives, Portland, Oregon.

healthy communities. One of Lovejoy's most vital contributions to twentieth-century feminist thought was the development of this ultimately transnational vision of civic health, the political view that women and all citizens required the civic power of the vote to shape healthy communities with policies ranging from clean food and pure milk to an end to war and the promotion of social and economic justice.

An analysis of Lovejoy's views and actions regarding female citizenship also expands our understanding of the movement for woman suffrage in Oregon, in the West, and in the nation. Her work in the 1905–1906 "suffrage renaissance" and the successful 1912 campaign helps us to understand that this was a broad-based movement that included many workers. With her Oregon colleagues, Lovejoy used the new tactics of mass advertising and campaigning and built coalitions that sometimes crossed ethnic and racial boundaries in limited but important ways. Lovejoy's role as a partisan Democratic woman voter in the western states shaped her reaction to the Congressional Union's strategy of holding the party in power responsible for the lack of action on the federal amendment. It complicates the story and underscores the importance of Oregon and the West to our analysis of the national suffrage narrative. And, by locating Lovejoy's work in the votes for women movement within the broader context of her activist life, we may see the importance of suffrage ideas and activism not only in her long life's journey for change but also in the history of and continuing quest for complete human rights.

Esther Lovejoy's constructive resistance was also based on an increasingly expansive and pragmatic vision of social justice that emphasized the need for humans to act to make their world a healthier and safer place, one of equality and empowerment. This philosophy had no place for hypocrites or for those who would not act. Esther Pohl had noted that Portland was a healthier place under her watch as city health officer; as she told the hostile city council, "[It] may all be due to the grace of God," and if so, "I earnestly thank him . . . but I think it is in part, at least, due to the work of the office." After her sojourn on the quay at Smyrna, she told a Portland audience that "only one formula is needed to eliminate war: just putting into practice the Christian principles we profess." But the "Christian nations are responsible for the burning of Smyrna just as truly as if they had set fire to the torch."[26]

Although not an active follower of organized religion, Lovejoy's grandniece Nancy Snook Frankovic remembered Lovejoy having a Bible by her bedside in her New York apartment from which she read at night.[27] Perhaps it opened from frequent use to the New Testament book of Luke and the story of the Good Samaritan. In Portland, Lovejoy had been a member of the Women of Woodcraft, a women's mutual benefit association affiliated with the Woodmen of the World. The Women of Woodcraft referred to each other as "neighbors," and their initiation ritual included induction into the group facilitated by a "Guardian Neighbor." The center of the ritual involved a recitation of the story of that certain Samaritan who had stopped to help a man who had been robbed and beaten along the road when others had passed him by. The "grandest answer" to the question "Am I my brother's keeper" the script reads, is "in practical and homely deeds of sympathy, friendship and material aid." The "answer which the Women of Woodcraft give is recorded in the lives of little children, saved from want and crime and ignorance; in the hearts of lonely widows, whose paths have been smoothed and burdens lifted; in homes surrounded and protected."[28] Lovejoy proved to be a transnational guardian neighbor in theory and in action, and she named her colleagues *Certain Samaritans*.

Esther Clayson vowed never to be trapped in a relationship like her mother's marriage, and she continued to work for women's right to create and maintain their own lives. Esther Clayson Pohl established an extended household in which her mother provided care for her son Freddie. She made her home in Portland as Emil continued to live and work in Alaska, keeping her own priorities in what later generations would term a "commuter marriage." She went to France and toured the nation while married to George Lovejoy, and she ended the relationship when he crossed the boundaries of her professional life. Esther Lovejoy continued to build friendships, relationships of support and service, and collegial and institutional ties, but did so by maintaining the independence and freedom of movement necessary to travel to AWH locations in a variety of nations and to many conferences and meetings of medical women each year. Her rich friendships were with medical women and in the cause of transnational medical relief. The letters that remain suggest that those friendships accompanied an increasing devotion to the American Women's Hospitals, making it difficult to pass the baton of the organization in her later years.

As she prepared her autobiography, Lovejoy gave only a general hint of another romantic relationship in her life. "There are parts of my story—glowing memories that are forever mine alone," she wrote. "These cannot be spread on paper without losing their beauty. A pressed orchid leaves an ugly stain." And so, "thank God for a good forgettery, and if there were tales to tell I wouldn't tell them. Even if I had a right to tattle on myself, these things involve a second party, a comparatively honorable and innocent one, if he holds his tongue . . . I don't know much about men," she concluded, "but the woman who kisses and tells has missed the supreme experience of life. She has never been in love."[29]

Lovejoy's freedom to build her life in medical and civic activism also came in part because she had liberated herself from her father, from his physical presence and from his words published in the *Patriarch* as arrows designed to wound her, and also from the broader patriarchal structures that bound all women. All of her life she worked to achieve women's liberation from such structures and from gender-based discrimination that prevented women from achieving full civic and economic citizenship and health. Her work also stemmed from her own ambition to succeed. In her 1912 "Argument for Woman Suffrage," she noted that "it falls largely upon the high-spirited girl who has the luck or ill-luck to resemble a [dominant] father. She cannot squeeze into her mother's mold [if she is a weak woman] because she is her father's daughter and there isn't a slavish cell in her system." There were "many responsible women," she wrote, who "chafe and fret because they are denied the right to do their full duty."[30]

Lovejoy's ambition meshed with her insistence on the rightness of her cause, muting the personal and stressing work on the behalf of others, a more acceptable vision of female activism.[31] This was true in her early years of suffrage and city health, and when she brought the Oregon State Board of Health to her side in her dispute with George Lovejoy over the Winchester Tuberculosis Sanitarium. And it continued in her transnational work when cultural constructions of women's political and leadership roles were constrained by gendered rules. Tapping her toes impatiently in 1917 with her ambition to go to France, she sought to expedite French ambassador Jean Jules Jusserand's permission by urging him to act before the upcoming meeting of women's groups with Anna Howard Shaw's Woman's Committee of the Council of National Defense. And she also took on the League of Nations. In a 1922 letter from Geneva to her family just before convening the meeting of the Medical Women's International Association, she wrote in frustration that the League "has chosen the same day on which to open their opposition show. . . . We decided on Monday, Sept. 4 at least a year ago and announced our intentions and subsequently the League of Nations decided on the same day regardless of the congestion of the city and shortage of rooms." Believing that the League should recognize the importance of her new transnational organization of women doctors, she had apparently complained. "Anyhow the League of Nations is trying to make peace with our association by inviting us to attend the opening session and reserving special seats for our delegates and showing us other courtesies later in the week."[32]

Lovejoy channeled her considerable ambition into organizing, directing, and defending the institutions she helped to construct and define. She first developed institutions of support for women at the local level, including her collaboration with women colleagues in the Portland Medical Club, her work to define city health in Portland, her effective advocacy of votes for women through Everybody's Equal Suffrage League and the Portland Woman's Club Suffrage Campaign Committee, and her campaign as a Democratic candidate for US Congress in 1920. Like Jane Addams of Hull House and Marie-Jeanne Bassot of the Résidence Sociale, who established settlement houses in the center of neighborhoods of need, Lovejoy developed the American Women's Hospitals and the Medical Women's International Association into institutions of medical, cultural, and economic support for refugees and local medical professionals, a transnational federation of settlement houses and institutions of medical activism strongly tied to her theory of international health. The umbrella she had held so resolutely over the heads of suffrage workers riding in the Suffrage Lunch Wagon in Portland was much bigger now; Lovejoy subsequently unfurled a metaphorical umbrella over the federated work of hundreds of AWH and MWIA sites of medical humanitarian relief and coalition building for international health across many borders.

Like Jane Addams, Lovejoy understood and experienced the objective and subjective dimensions of the clinics, dispensaries, orphanages, and hospitals under this umbrella. These dimensions included the support the institutions could bring to refugees and others in need, and also the opportunities for medical practice and personal enrichment they provided for medical staff (and directors). Several years before her death, Lovejoy concluded, "The AWH is more than a medical service. Conducted in cooperation with women doctors and nurses in one country after another for over forty years, it has contributed to friendship and good will of inestimable value."[33] The "great reward" for Lovejoy was "the enrichment of lives by work worth doing in countries where epochal movements were in operation . . . [and] an intimate acquaintance with people of different nationalities—not only with the dominant races of Western Europe, but those of older lands."[34] She spoke of herself as well as others when she emphasized the transformative nature of "an intimate acquaintance with people of different nationalities." Lovejoy had been raised with the privilege of whiteness from her early years in Seabeck. In some ways she had crossed the boundaries of that privilege in her Oregon years, by not scapegoating Portland's Chinatown in her fight against bubonic plague, and by addressing the Colored Women's Equal Suffrage Association in 1912 and the Rosebud Club in 1920. But in her 1920 candidacy for Congress, she opposed immigration of the "unassimilatable." And her advocacy for a state-by-state solution to national woman suffrage left Southern states free to discriminate against African American women. In her transnational work with women physicians across boundaries and her contact with women in clinics and in wartime need, Lovejoy's feminist curiosity enabled her to find increasing common cause with women across racial and ethnic boundaries. It would appear that on her journey from Seabeck to transnational organizing, she increased her capacity to value inclusion and to exchange white privilege to some degree with gendered solidarity.

Today the American Women's Hospitals Service, under the continuing organizational rubric of the American Medical Women's Association, funds transnational clinics in Haiti, Uganda, Vietnam, India, Barbados, South Africa, and Nepal. The AWHS supports clinics in the United States in Racine, Wisconsin; Clearfield, Tennessee; and Washington, DC. The organization also provides a travel grant for medical students who have been accepted into an overseas clinical program.[35] The Medical Women's International Association continues as a transnational non-governmental organization with international congresses and general assemblies every three years. With members across the globe in affiliated national associations and as individual members in the larger group, women physicians in coalition build programs for international health.[36]

The continuing crises of war, revolution, famine, and natural disasters in the twenty-first century challenge this quest for international health. Lovejoy's theoretical blueprint and her strategies for its implementation contribute to the ongoing work to resolve these barriers to healthy lives. At the 1995 United Nations Fourth World Conference on Women in Beijing, delegates reiterated Lovejoy's vision for a just and healthy society and outlined the steps to achieve it in their "Platform for Action." They affirmed this platform at the Beijing + 5 meeting in 2000, Beijing + 10 in 2005, and most recently at Beijing + 15 in New York in 2010:

> Women have the right to the enjoyment of the highest attainable standard of physical and mental health. The enjoyment of this right is vital to their life and well-being and their ability to participate in all areas of public and private life. Health is a state of complete physical, mental and social well-being and not merely the absence of disease or infirmity. Women's health involves their emotional, social, and physical well-being and is determined by the social, political and economic context of their lives, as well as by biology. However, health and well-being elude the majority of women. A major barrier for women to the achievement of the highest attainable standard of health is inequality, both between men and women and among women in different geographical regions, social classes and indigenous and ethnic groups. In national and inter-

national forums, women have emphasized that to attain optimal health throughout the life cycle, equality, including the sharing of family responsibilities, development and peace are necessary conditions.[37]

As governments, non-governmental organizations, and other transnational and international groups recognize the importance of women's empowerment in global health and development in the twenty-first century, Esther Lovejoy's story and the active policies and practices she worked for take on even more relevance as a model for change, full human rights, and international health achieved through social justice.

CHRONOLOGY

November 16, 1869	Esther Clayson is born in Seabeck, Washington Territory, to Annie Quinton and Edward Clayson, Sr.
1870s	Esther attends school in Seabeck and works in the family's Bay View Hotel.
1880	Esther Clayson christens the ship the *State of Sonora* in Seabeck.
November 1882	"The Getaway": Esther, her mother Annie, and her sister Annie May escape Seabeck and Edward Clayson Sr., and find a temporary haven in Portland.
1883 to 1886	Esther and her family live in Portland, Oregon; Esther works at the family's Golden Rule Hotel.
1886 to 1888	Esther works on the family's Clackamas County, Oregon, farm.
March 1888	Annie Clayson sues her husband Edward successfully for divorce, and Esther and her brothers Ted, Will, and Fred and her sisters Annie May and Charlotte live without him in Portland.
1888	Esther begins department store work in Portland.
1890	With advice from her mentor, Callie Charlton, MD, Esther matriculates at the University of Oregon Medical Department in Portland.
April 1891	Esther Clayson uses all of her funds for medical school and returns to full-time department store work for eighteen months at Lipman and Wolfe and then Olds and King. She continues private study with Dr. Frank Blaney Eaton.
October 1892	Esther returns for her last two years of medical school.
April 2, 1894	Esther Clayson graduates from the University of Oregon Medical Department as the recipient of the Wall Medal for her studies; because she is a woman,

the faculty deny her the internship that customarily accompanies such academic achievement.

April 25, 1894	Esther Clayson marries her former classmate Emil Pohl, MD.
April 1894	Esther Pohl begins her medical practice, riding a bicycle to cases and answering maternity calls from the Russian German neighborhood of Portland.
1897	Esther Pohl enrolls at the West Chicago Post-Graduate School and Polyclinic and the Chicago Clinical School for postgraduate training.
July 30, 1897	Emil Pohl and Esther's brother Frederick Clayson depart Portland for the Klondike Gold Rush. Many Clayson family members migrate for a time to Skagway, Alaska.
Spring 1898	Esther and Emil Pohl offer medical care during a cerebrospinal meningitis epidemic in Skagway and environs. Esther returns to medical practice in Portland. She returns to Alaska intermittently over the next years, as Emil divides his time between Portland and various Alaska towns.
1899	Esther Pohl joins the Portland Woman's Club. She is active in club work and social medicine throughout her years in Portland.
December 25, 1899	Esther's brother Frederick Clayson is murdered while returning to Skagway.
1901	Esther's father Edward Clayson, Sr., begins publication of his weekly newspaper the *Patriarch* in Seattle.
December 26, 1901	Esther and Emil's son Frederick Clayson Pohl is born in Portland. Annie Clayson provides child care for Freddie as Esther builds her medical practice.
1904	Esther Pohl travels to Vienna for clinical postgraduate work; visits Elizabeth Blackwell, MD, in East Sussex, England; and tours Jerusalem and Egypt, writing reports for the *Oregon Journal* back home.
July 1905	As president of the all-female Portland Medical Club, Esther Pohl welcomes delegates to the annual meetings of the National American Woman Suffrage Association and the American Medical Association,

	held in Portland in conjunction with the Lewis and Clark Centennial Exposition.
August 1905 to July 1907	Portland progressive Democratic mayor Harry Lane appoints Esther Pohl to the Portland Health Board, where she serves for two years.
1906	Esther Pohl takes a leading part in the Oregon woman suffrage campaign of 1906 and adopts the new tactics of popular culture and mass campaigning of the "suffrage renaissance."
July 1907 to July 1909	Esther Pohl serves as Portland City Health Officer, battles bubonic plague, and fights for pure food and pure milk legislation. She develops a progressive Democratic political identity.
September 11, 1908	Freddie Pohl dies in Portland from what Esther and her colleagues consider to be tainted milk, spurring on her campaign for pure milk.
1910 to 1911	Esther Pohl travels to Vienna for additional medical and clinical study. She stays on the East Coast with suffrage mentor Anna Howard Shaw and her partner Lucy Anthony, and then with her sister Charlotte, who is matron of the Idaho State Penitentiary in Boise.
May 11, 1911	Emil Pohl dies of spinal meningitis in Fairbanks, Alaska.
July 30, 1912	Esther Pohl marries Portland businessman George A. Lovejoy.
1912	Esther Pohl Lovejoy leads the Portland Woman's Club Suffrage Campaign Committee, establishes Everybody's Equal Suffrage League, and works for the successful ballot measure enfranchising Oregon women on November 5, 1912.
1914 to August 26, 1920	Esther Lovejoy works with the National American Woman Suffrage Association and local suffrage groups to achieve nationwide suffrage. She opposes the campaigns of the Congressional Union to hold the Democratic Party responsible for the failure of the federal amendment.
September 1917 to February 1918	Esther Lovejoy represents US women's organizations in France. She lives and works at the Résidence Sociale, a settlement house administered by Marie-

	Jeanne Bassot and her staff in the working-class factory district of Levallois just northwest of Paris. She also visits refugees in Evian.
1918 to 1919	Esther Lovejoy tours the United States for the Red Cross and Liberty Loan drives. She also writes articles and the manuscript for *The House of the Good Neighbor*, published in 1919, with a revised edition in 1920.
June 1919	Esther Lovejoy takes the chair of the American Women's Hospitals, the War Service Committee of the Medical Women's National Association.
October 1919	Esther Lovejoy helps to organize the Medical Women's International Association.
1919 to 1924	Esther Lovejoy serves as the first president of the Medical Women's International Association. She continues attending meetings and being active in policymaking for the rest of her life.
November 2, 1920	Esther Lovejoy gains 44 percent of the vote for representative to US Congress, Third District, Oregon, losing the election to Republican opponent C. N. McArthur.
December 10, 1920	Esther Lovejoy obtains a successful divorce from George A. Lovejoy.
September 4–7, 1922	Esther Lovejoy presides at the second annual meeting of the Medical Women's International Association and delivers her presidential address "The Possibilities of the Medical Women's International Association" outlining her concept of international health.
September 24–30 1922	Esther Lovejoy provides medical relief on the quay at Smyrna through the American Women's Hospitals.
1922 to 1967	Esther Lovejoy continues to chair the American Women's Hospitals and expands the organizations' "without borders" role across twenty-eight nations. She travels extensively and attends national and international women's medical association conferences.
1920s	Esther Lovejoy works with Soviet public health pioneer Vera Lebedeva.

1927	Lovejoy's *Certain Samaritans* is published, with a revised edition in 1933.
September 23, 1928	Esther Lovejoy delivers her antiwar address "Woman's Big Job" on a New York radio station.
1932 to 1933	Esther Lovejoy serves as president of the Medical Women's National Association.
1939	Lovejoy's *Women Physicians and Surgeons: National and International Organizations* is published.
1939 to 1945	Esther Lovejoy facilitates American Women's Hospitals support for wartime medical relief projects in China, England, France, and the Soviet Union. Lovejoy and members of the American Women's Hospitals and the Medical Women's International Association assist Jewish and other refugee women physicians, including Dora Teleky.
March 12, 1940	Esther Lovejoy contributes to the "Women in Medicine" segment of the radio program *Gallant American Women*.
November 25–27, 1940	Esther Lovejoy showcases the work of women doctors at the Women's Centennial Congress in New York.
1957	Lovejoy's *Women Doctors of the World* is published.
May 1, 1967	Esther Lovejoy resigns from the chair of the American Women's Hospitals.
August 17, 1967	Esther Clayson Pohl Lovejoy dies in New York City at the age of ninety-eight.

ABBREVIATIONS

Works frequently cited have been identified by the following abbreviations:

AWH Records
: American Women's Hospitals Historical Materials, AWH Historical Materials, 1917–1982, Legacy Center, Archives and Special Collections on Women in Medicine and Homeopathy, Drexel University College of Medicine, Philadelphia, Pennsylvania.

CPBH
: City of Portland Board of Health Minutes, 1903–1909, City of Portland Archives and Records Center, Portland, Oregon.

EPL 2001–004
: Accession 2001–004, Esther Pohl Lovejoy Collection, Historical Collections & Archives, Oregon Health & Science University, Portland, Oregon.

EPL 2001–011
: Accession 2001–011, Esther Pohl Lovejoy Collection, Historical Collections & Archives, Oregon Health & Science University, Portland, Oregon.

HWS
: Elizabeth Cady Stanton, Susan B. Anthony, Matilda Joslyn Gage, Ida Husted Harper, eds., *History of Woman Suffrage*, 6 vols., reprint of the 1881–1922 ed. (New York: Arno Press, 1969).

PWC
: Portland Woman's Club (Oregon), Records, 1895–1995, MSS 1084, Oregon Historical Society Research Library, Portland, Oregon.

SWS
: Esther Pohl Lovejoy, "Salt Water and Sawdust," box 4, folders 23–31; box 5, folder 32, accession 2001–011, Esther Pohl Lovejoy Collection, Historical Collections & Archives, Oregon Health & Science University, Portland, Oregon.

NOTES

INTRODUCTION

1   Allissa Franc Keir first used the term in her 1926 article on Lovejoy when she referred to "Dr. Lovejoy's constructive resistance against what fate deals out to her." Keir, "A Daughter of Pioneers," *Everybody's Magazine* 54, no. 3 (March 1926): 34–35, 168–72, quote 168. In later notes for her autobiography, Lovejoy wrote, "As someone later said of her she learned at an early age constructive resistance against what fate deals out to her." Esther Pohl Lovejoy, handwritten notes for an autobiography, 3, box 3, folder 19, EPL 2001–011.

2   This is Joyce Antler's term. Joyce Antler, "Feminism as Life-Process: The Life and Career of Lucy Sprague Mitchell," *Feminist Studies* 7, no. 1 (Spring 1981): 134–57.

3   See Linda K. Kerber, *No Constitutional Right to Be Ladies: Women and the Obligations of Citizenship* (New York: Hill and Wang, 1998); and Alice Kessler-Harris, *In Pursuit of Equity: Women, Men and the Quest for Economic Citizenship in Twentieth-Century America* (New York: Oxford University Press, 2001).

4   Scholars are contributing important work to this field, including Rebecca J. Mead, *How the Vote Was Won: Woman Suffrage in the Western United States, 1868–1914* (New York: New York University Press, 2004); Rebecca Edwards, *Angels in the Machinery: Gender in American Party Politics from the Civil War to the Progressive Era* (New York: Oxford University Press, 1997); Edwards, "Pioneers at the Polls: Woman Suffrage in the West," in *Votes for Women: The Struggle for Suffrage Revisited*, ed. Jean Baker (New York: Oxford University Press, 2002), 90–101; and Gayle Gullett, *Becoming Citizens: The Emergence and Development of the California Women's Movement, 1880–1911* (Urbana: University of Illinois Press, 2000).

5   Nancy Cott, *The Grounding of Modern Feminism* (New Haven, CT: Yale University Press, 1987), 85.

6   See, for example, Erika K. Kuhlman, *Of Little Comfort: War Widows, Fallen*

Soldiers, and the Remaking of the Nation after the Great War (New York: New York University Press, 2012); Ingrid Sharp and Matthew Stibbe, eds., *Aftermaths of War: Women's Movements and Female Activists* (Leiden, The Netherlands: Brill, 2011); and Jay Winter, *Remembering War: The Great War between Memory and History in the Twentieth Century* (New Haven, CT: Yale University Press, 2006).

7 Alan Dawley, *Changing the World: American Progressives in War and Revolution* (Princeton, NJ: Princeton University Press, 2003), 297–304; Leila Rupp, *Worlds of Women: The Making of an International Women's Movement* (Princeton, NJ: Princeton University Press, 1997).

8 Kimberly Jensen and Erika K. Kuhlman, eds. *Women and Transnational Activism in Historical Perspective* (Dordrecht, The Netherlands: Republic of Letters, 2010), 1.

9 Cynthia Enloe, *The Curious Feminist: Searching for Women in a New Age of Empire* (Berkeley: University of California Press, 2004).

10 Esther Lovejoy, "Women's [*sic*] Big Job Is Man—His Creation, Care, and Preservation," 1–2, typescript of speech, [1928], box 1, folder 5, EPL 2001–011.

11 Erika K. Kuhlman, *Reconstructing Patriarchy after the Great War: Women, Gender and Postwar Reconciliation between Nations* (New York: Palgrave Macmillan, 2008).

12 Rupp, *Worlds of Women*.

1. LESSONS IN CONSTRUCTIVE RESISTANCE

1 With any autobiography, historians must consider the author's purpose for publication and any bias, and must consult as many other sources as possible to deepen the analysis beyond one perspective. Many physicians of Esther Lovejoy's generation published their memoirs, and Lovejoy tried without success to publish her own. There are several versions of her autobiography in the Esther Pohl Lovejoy Collection at the Oregon Health & Science University Historical Collections & Archives, with corrections made in several hands, including most probably those of Estelle Fraade, Lovejoy's administrative assistant. I have tried to use material that appears consistently across the versions. It also appears that Lovejoy wished to provide her version of events to refute the account made by her father. Estranged from most of his family in later life, and living in Seattle, Edward Clayson, Sr., published his own versions of the Seabeck years, including a weekly newspaper titled the *Patriarch,* in which many Seabeck stories appeared. In 1911 he published the book *Historical Nar-*

ratives of Puget Sound, Hoods Canal, 1865–1885: The Experience of an Only Free Man in a Penal Colony (Seattle: R. L. Davis, 1911; reprinted with an introduction and historical notes by Glen Adams, Fairfield, WA: Ye Galleon Press, 1969), with excerpts from these serialized Seabeck narratives. The area was known as Hood's or Hoods Canal but is Hood Canal today.

2 Annie Mary Clayson, certificate of death, November 28, 1924, box 76, "Death Certificates Multnomah 1924," folder 26, "Multnomah County (September 1–December 31)," accession 91A-17, Oregon State Board of Health, Oregon State Archives, Salem, Oregon.

3 SWS, box 4, folders 23, 18, and 57; Esther Pohl Lovejoy, "Our Historical Novel," loose pages, box 1, folder 7, EPL 2001–011.

4 Edward Clayson, Sr., certificate of death, January 2, 1915, box 32, "Death Certificates, Lane–Multnomah 1915," folder 37, "Multnomah County (January 1, 1915–January 3, 1915)," accession 91A-17, Oregon State Board of Health (copy from King County, Washington), Oregon State Archives, Salem, Oregon; Fred Lockley, interview with Will Clayson, "Fred Lockley's Impressions," Oregon Journal, August 18, 1946, 16A; SWS, 1–13.

5 SWS, 26, 16.

6 Ibid.

7 Clayson, Narratives, 10, 25.

8 Lockley interview with Will Clayson; Clayson, Narratives, 12, 62; United States House of Representatives, 41st Congress, 2nd Session, Executive Document 314, Report of the Postmaster General no. 4 (Washington, DC: Government Printing Office, 1870), 263.

9 Fred C. Blanchard to Glen C. Adams, April 27, 1964, box 3, folder 22, EPL 2001–011; SWS, 77–78.

10 SWS, 78–79.

11 Ibid., 56–57.

12 Ibid., 65.

13 Ibid., 66–67.

14 Ibid., 66.

15 "Ex-Mayor of Anchorage Dies at Portland Home," Oregonian, September 30, 1950, 7.

16 SWS, 321.

17 William G. Robbins, Colony and Empire: The Capitalist Transformation of the American West (Lawrence: University Press of Kansas, 1994), 128–29.

18 Thomas Frederick Gedosch, "Seabeck, 1857–1886: The History of a Company Town" (master's thesis, University of Washington, 1967); Thomas R. Cox, Mills and Markets: A History of the Pacific Coast Lumber Industry to 1900 (Seattle: University of Washington Press, 1974), 110–16.

19 Robert E. Ficken, *The Forested Land: A History of Lumbering in Western Washington* (Durham, NC: Forest History Society / Seattle: University of Washington Press, 1987), 31, 34.

20 United States Department of Commerce, Bureau of the Census, *Tenth Census of the United States, 1880* (Washington, DC: United States Bureau of the Census, 1880), section for Seabeck, Washington Territory; copy at Seabeck Conference Center Archives, Seabeck, Washington.

21 Gedosch, "Seabeck," 83–91.

22 Edmond S. Meany, Jr., "The History of the Lumber Industry in the Pacific Northwest to 1917" (PhD diss., Harvard University, 1935), 314.

23 Gedosch, "Seabeck," 64.

24 SWS, 57.

25 Gedosch, "Seabeck," 111–12; Clayson, *Narratives*, 65.

26 SWS, 82–83.

27 Ibid., 101–2.

28 Ibid., 165–67; Esther Pohl Lovejoy, abstract for *Salt Water and Sawdust*, box 3, folder 20, EPL 2001–011. Lovejoy referred to the hotel as the Bayview, but other records indicate that the name was Bay View.

29 Proceedings of County Commissioners, Kitsap County, also Record of Liquor Licenses, Bonds, Etc., vol. 1, 1858–1874: March 6, 1871, 160; November 13, 1872, 178; November 4, 1873, 187; May 4, 1874, 194; November 12, 1874, 199; May 7, 1873 (out of order in bound volume), 288; and vol. 2, 1875–1901: May 3, 1875, 7; June 7, 1876, 23; November 5, 1877, 61; May 6, 1879, 97; November 1, 1880, 127 (here H. J. Quinton, Annie's brother, applied for and received the license); May 3, 1881, 140; November 11, 1881, 151; May 2, 1882, 162; November 6, 1882, 167; Kitsap County Auditor's Office, Port Orchard, Washington.

30 Clayson, *Narratives*.

31 Gedosch, "Seabeck," 91–94; Proceedings of County Commissioners, Kitsap County, vol. 2, 1875–1901: May 3, 1881, 138–39; Clayson, *Narratives*, 25–28.

32 Gedosch, "Seabeck," 77–82; SWS, 187–91.

33 SWS, 193–95; Gedosch, "Seabeck," 94–96. This included writing to the Department of the Interior to expose the mill. United States Senate, *Executive Documents, First and Second Sessions of the Forty-Fifth Congress, 1877 and '78*, vol. 1, no. 9, doc. 306D (Washington, DC: Government Printing Office, 1877), 160; and "Seabeck Items," *Rebel Battery* 1, no. 1 (October 1878): 3.

34 "The Bay View Hotel," *Rebel Battery* 1, no. 1 (October 1878): 3. This first number is the only extant copy of what appears to have been a longer publishing run.

35 SWS, 255–56, 195.

36 Ibid., 84–85.

37 Ibid., 219–23, 111–12.

38 Steven Mintz, *Huck's Raft: A History of American Childhood* (Cambridge, MA: The Belknap Press of Harvard University Press, 2004), 133–53, quote 152.

39 Elliott West, *Growing Up with the Country: Childhood on the Far Western Frontier* (Albuquerque: University of New Mexico Press, 1989), 73–98, quote 74.

40 SWS, 214.

41 West, *Growing Up with the Country*, 82.

42 SWS, 214–15.

43 Ibid., 214.

44 Ibid., 219–24.

45 The book is in the collection of the Seabeck Conference Center, and was published in Boston by Lee & Shepard, with no date listed. The publisher released several editions from the 1850s to the 1870s. There is a signature "Esther C. Pohl" on the second leaf, and, on the first, in Esther Lovejoy's handwriting, "Borrowed by Edward Clayson from the Seabeck Library about 1875, and passed by his daughter Esther Clayson Pohl Lovejoy to the Kitsap County Historical Society in 1953." "Seabeck Public Library" is stamped in ink.

46 West, *Growing Up with the Country*, 180–84; Robert E. Ficken, *Washington Territory* (Pullman: Washington State University Press, 2002), 36; Clayson, *Narratives*, 3.

47 SWS, 217–18.

48 Ibid., 226.

49 West, *Growing Up with the Country*, 190–91, 194.

50 Clayson, *Narratives*, 38–48.

51 *Laws of the Territory of Washington Enacted by the Legislative Assembly in the Year 1873, Together with Joint Resolutions and Memorials* (Olympia, WA: C. B. Bagley, Public Printer, 1873), 427.

52 *Laws of the Territory of Washington Enacted by the Legislative Assembly in the Year 1877* (Olympia, WA: C. B. Bagley, Public Printer, 1877), 274; West, *Growing Up with the Country*, 200.

53 Angie Burt Bowen, *Early Schools of Washington Territory* (Seattle, WA: Lowman and Hanford, 1935), 21–23.

54 Bowen, *Early Schools*, 538–39; Clayson, *Narratives*, 3.

55 SWS, 228–29. A shitepoke is a type of heron but also a colloquial term for a bag of manure.

56 Peggy Pascoe, *What Comes Naturally: Miscegenation Law and the Making of Race in America* (New York: Oxford University Press, 2009).

57 Alexandra Harmon, *Indians in the Making: Ethnic Relations and Indian Identities around Puget Sound* (Berkeley: University of California Press, 2000), 103–5.

58 Harmon, *Indians in the Making*, 106; Gedosch, "Seabeck," 61.

59 SWS, 141.

60 Henry Zenk with Tony A. Johnson, "A Northwest Language of Contact, Diplomacy, and Identity: Chinuk Wawa/Chinook Jargon," *Oregon Historical Quarterly* 111, no. 4 (Winter 2010): 444–61.

61 SWS, 209–12.

62 Ibid., 300–301.

63 SWS, 141, 149.

64 Gedosch, "Seabeck," ix, 61–62, 120–21; Art Chin, *Golden Tassels: A History of the Chinese in Washington, 1857–1992* (Seattle, WA: Chin, 1992), 40–54.

65 SWS, 104–5.

66 Ibid., 105–6.

67 Sophonisba P. Breckinridge, "Separate Domicil for Married Women," *Social Science Review* 4, no. 1 (March 1930): 37–52, quote 37; and Nancy Cott, *Public Vows: A History of Marriage and the Nation* (Cambridge, MA: Harvard University Press, 2000).

68 J. H. Jellett, *Pacific Coast Collection Laws* (San Francisco: Bacon and Company, 1876), 271; Northwest Women's Law Center Legal Voice, "Brief *Amici Curiae* of History Scholars, 12–14, *Andersen et al. v. King County, Washington,* and *Castle et al. v. State of Washington*, Supreme Court of the State of Washington, nos. 75934–1 and 75956–1," http://nwwlc.org/pdf/Historians_Brief.pdf, accessed September 10, 2011.

69 SWS, 78.

70 Ibid., 78–80.

71 Ibid., 80.

72 Ibid., 80.

73 Ibid., 128.

74 Ibid., 129–31. Parents had the legal right to use "moderate" physical punishment to enforce their authority in this period, but Esther emphasized her father's excess. David Peterson del Mar, *Beaten Down: A History of Interpersonal Violence in the West* (Seattle: University of Washington Press, 2002), 81–82.

75 SWS, 167–68.

76 Candice Lewis Bredbenner, *A Nationality of Her Own: Women, Marriage, and the Law of Citizenship* (Berkeley: University of California Press, 1998), 15.

77   Sophonisba P. Breckinridge, *Marriage and Civic Rights of Women: Separate Domicil and Independent Citizenship* (Chicago: University of Chicago Press, 1931), 21–22.

78   Edward Clayson, Declaration of Intention, vol. 2 (1862–1871), 110, Jefferson County, Washington, Naturalization Records, Washington State Archives, Olympia, Washington.

79   Grand and petit juror list, May 16, 1871, *Proceedings of County Commissioners, Kitsap County*, vol. 1, *1858–1874*, 163; payment for jury service, August term of Third Judicial District Court, November 7, 1871, vol. 1, *1858–1874*, 170; grand jury list, May 1, 1876, vol. 2, *1875–1901*, 24; and payment for jury service, December 5, 1876, vol. 2, *1875–1901*, 39; "Edward Clayson, 'Patriarch,' Dead," *Seattle Post-Intelligencer*, January 3, 1915, 10.

80   SWS, 174–79.

81   Robert Straus, *Medical Care for Seamen: The Origin of Public Medical Service in the United States* (New Haven: Yale University Press, 1950), 60–74, 94–98; Fitzhugh Mullan, *Plagues and Politics: The Story of the United States Public Health Service* (New York: Basic Books, 1989).

82   SWS, 169.

83   Meribeth Meixner Reed, "Describing the Life Cycle of U.S Marine Hospital #17, Port Townsend, Washington, 1855–1933," *Military Medicine* 170, no. 4 (April 2005): 259–67; Mullan, *Plagues and Politics*, 14–15.

84   Reed, "Life Cycle," 261; Christine A. Neergard, "Dr. George V. Calhoun," *Washington Historical Quarterly* 25, no. 4 (October 1934): 286–93.

85   Reed, "Life Cycle," 261–62; Kit Oldham, "Dr. Thomas T. Minor" (August 13, 2004), HistoryLink.org, http://www.historylink.org/index.cfm?DisplayPage=output.cfm&file_id=5730, accessed September 10, 2011.

86   Reed, "Life Cycle," 262.

87   Jacob Hauptly diary, 1872–1899, June 23 and 24, and November 14, 1881, typewritten transcript, Kitsap County Historical Society Archives, Bremerton, Washington; Proceedings of County Commissioners, Kitsap County, meeting of February 2, 1880, vol. 2: *1875–1901*, 112; meeting of May 4, 1880, vol. 2: *1875–1901*, 116; meeting of January 5, 1883, vol. 2: *1875–1901*, 169.

88   Nancy Rockafellar and James Havland, eds., *Saddlebags to Scanners: The First One Hundred Years of Medicine in Washington State* (Seattle: Washington State Medical Association, 1989), 77–78, 215–16.

89   Esther Pohl Lovejoy, "Our Historical Novel," box 1, folder 7, EPL 2001–011.

90   SWS, 71; Janet Farrell Brodie, *Contraception and Abortion in Nineteenth-Century America* (Ithaca, NY: Cornell University Press, 1994); Andrea

Tone, *Devices and Desires: A History of Contraceptives in America* (New York: Hill and Wang, 2001).

91 *Tenth Census of the United States, 1880,* Seabeck schedule; Judith Walzer Leavitt, *Brought to Bed: Childbearing in America, 1750–1950* (New York: Oxford University Press, 1986).

92 SWS, 279.

93 Ibid., 117–119.

94 Clayson, *Narratives,* 14–15.

95 SWS, 71–72.

96 E. W. Wright, ed., *Lewis and Dryden's Marine History of the Pacific Northwest* (New York: Antiquarian Press, 1961), 278.

97 SWS, 310–11.

98 Clayson, *Narratives,* 92–94; *Patriarch,* October 7, 1911, 2.

99 SWS, 311–13.

100 Ibid., 313–15.

101 Esther Pohl Lovejoy, notes for autobiography, box 5, folder 35, EPL 2011–011.

102 SWS, 308, 266–73.

103 Ibid., 322.

104 Ibid.

105 Hauptly diary, e.g., May 31, 1873, and February 28, 1877; SWS, 264–66.

106 Hauptly diary, April 8, 1881. My thanks to David Lewis for assistance with Chinuk Wawa definitions.

107 Hauptly diary, November 30, 1882, and December 1, 1882.

108 SWS, 324–25.

109 Ibid., 329.

110 "During the separation of personal and hotel property" at the time of the lease and their departure, Esther recalled, "a precious box of papers, including leaflets, manuscripts, and copies of the *Rebel Battery* disappeared." SWS, 329.

111 Esther C. P. Lovejoy, with introduction by Bertha Hallam, "My Medical School, 1890–1894," *Oregon Historical Quarterly* 75, no. 1 (March 1974): 7–35.

112 *Portland City Directory, 1884* (Portland, OR: J. K. Gill, 1884), 40.

113 Lovejoy, "My Medical School," 18; Lovejoy, "Our Historical Novel," 226.

114 Fred Lockley, interview with Esther Lovejoy, "Observations and Impressions of the Journal Man," *Oregon Journal,* September 25, 1900, 6; Lovejoy, "Our Historical Novel," 12–18.

115 Lovejoy, "Our Historical Novel," 288–89.

116 Ibid., 289.

1   Esther C. P. Lovejoy, with introduction by Bertha Hallam, "My Medical School, 1890–1894," *Oregon Historical Quarterly* 75, no. 1 (March 1974): 7–35, quote 14. Belle Schmeer graduated from Willamette University Medical Department in 1886. "College of Medicine, Willamette University Alumni Register, Who's Who 1920," *Willamette University Bulletin* 13, no. 1 (January 1920), 46.

2   Lovejoy, "Medical School," 14.

3   "College of Medicine Alumni Register," 44; *Portland City Directory, 1885* (Portland, OR: R. L. Polk, 1885), 442, 553.

4   *Portland City Directory, 1889* (Portland, OR: R. L. Polk, 1889), 196; Lovejoy, "Medical School," 15.

5   H. K. Hines, *An Illustrated History of the State of Oregon* (Chicago: Lewis Publishing, 1893), 973–74.

6   Lovejoy, "Medical School," 15.

7   Lovejoy, "Medical School," 17–18.

8   Many thoughtful scholars have addressed these topics in important detail. See Regina Markell Morantz-Sanchez, *Sympathy and Science: Women Physicians in American Medicine* (Chapel Hill: University of North Carolina Press, 2000); Ellen S. More, *Restoring the Balance: Women Physicians and the Profession of Medicine, 1850–1995* (Cambridge, MA: Harvard University Press, 1999); Mary Roth Walsh, *Doctors Wanted: No Women Need Apply: Sexual Barriers in the Medical Profession, 1835–1975* (New Haven, CT: Yale University Press, 1977); Thomas Neville Bonner, *To the Ends of the Earth: Women's Search for Education in Medicine* (Cambridge, MA: Harvard University Press, 1992); Steven J. Peitzman, *A New and Untried Course: Woman's Medical College and Medical College of Pennsylvania, 1850–1998* (New Brunswick, NJ: Rutgers University Press, 2000); Anne Taylor Kirschmann, *A Vital Force: Women in American Homeopathy* (New Brunswick, NJ: Rutgers University Press, 2004); Eve Fine, "Women Physicians and Medical Sects in Nineteenth-Century Chicago," in *Women Physicians and the Cultures of Medicine,* ed. Ellen S. More, Elizabeth Fee, and Manon Perry (Baltimore: Johns Hopkins University Press, 2009), 245–73; John S. Haller, Jr., *Medical Protestants: The Eclectics in American Medicine, 1825–1939* (Carbondale: Southern Illinois University Press, 1994).

9   Walsh, *Doctors Wanted*, 178–85; Morantz-Sanchez, *Sympathy and Science*, 64–89; Peitzman, *New and Untried Course.*

10   Robert A. Nye, "The Legacy of Masculine Codes of Honor and the Admission of Women to the Medical Profession in the Nineteenth Century,"

in More, Fee, and Perry, *Women Physicians and the Cultures of Medicine*, 141–59, quote 143.

11 Kirschmann, *Vital Force*, 119.

12 United States Office of Education, "Statistics of Schools of Medicine for 1893–94," *Report of the Commissioner of Education for the Year 1893–94*, vol. 2, parts 2 and 3 (Washington: Government Printing Office, 1896), 2045–50.

13 Medical education in Oregon involved the development of two competing and conflicting institutions. The first was the Willamette University Medical Department (WUMD), located in Salem from 1867 to 1878, in Portland from 1878 to 1895, and again in Salem from 1895 to 1913. In 1887, amid "acrimonious" conflict over teaching and credentialing issues, many of the leading faculty at WUMD resigned their positions and established the rival University of Oregon Medical Department in Portland (UOMD, renamed the University of Oregon Medical School in 1913, now Oregon Health & Science University). After clashing for some twenty-five years, the WUMD closed in 1913 and merged with the UOMD, with the new name of the University of Oregon Medical School. In Oregon, therefore, women students had just one coeducational school from which to choose until 1887, and two thereafter, until the merger in 1913. There were no homeopathic medical schools and no female medical colleges to provide alternatives for the medical education of women, as was the case in other regions. Willamette University Medical Department Records, accession 1999–01, Historical Collections & Archives, Oregon Health & Science University, Portland, Oregon; Olof Larsell, *The Doctor in Oregon: A Medical History* (Portland: Bindfords & Mort for the Oregon Historical Society, 1947), 341–400; Robert Moulton Gatke, *Chronicles of Willamette: The Pioneer University of the West* (Portland, OR: Binfords & Mort, 1943), 254–56, 426, 494–95. Sawtelle graduated from the Women's Medical College of New York in 1872. "Mary Priscilla Avery Sawtelle, 1835–94," in Jean M. Ward and Elaine A. Maveety, eds. *Pacific Northwest Women, 1815–1925: Lives, Memories, and Writings* (Corvallis: Oregon State University Press, 1995), 200–208.

14 Lucy I. Davis, "History of Women Graduates of Oregon Medical School," *Twenty-Fifth Annual Meeting and Directory of the Alumni Association, University of Oregon Medical School* (Portland, OR: Alumni Association of the University of Oregon Medical School, 1937), 17–20.

15 "List of Graduates," *Eighth Annual Announcement of the Medical Department of the University of Oregon, Session of 1894–1895* (Portland, OR: A. Anderson, 1894), 24–25.

16 See the *Portland City Directories* for these years.

17 Esther Pohl Lovejoy, notes for autobiography, 6, box 3, folder 19, EPL 2001–011.

18 *Fourth Annual Announcement of the University of Oregon Medical Department for the Session of 1890–1891* (Portland, OR: David Steel, 1890), 18; Larsell, *Doctor in Oregon*, 343–76. The three-year course of study was common for the period. Paul Starr, *The Social Transformation of American Medicine* (New York: Basic Books, 1982); Kenneth Ludmerer, *Learning to Heal: The Development of American Medical Education* (Baltimore: Johns Hopkins University Press, 1996).

19 Lovejoy, "Medical School," 18–19.

20 Ibid., 23, 26, and "List of Graduates," *Eighth Annual Announcement*, 24–25.

21 Susan Porter Benson, *Counter Cultures: Saleswomen, Managers, and Customers in American Department Stores, 1890–1940* (Urbana: University of Illinois Press, 1986), 12–27, quote 27.

22 Ibid., 266.

23 Glenn Arthur Ridley, "The Causal Factors in the Development of Olds, Wortman, & King into a Modern Department Store," (master's thesis, University of Oregon, 1937), 8–9.

24 Lovejoy, "Medical School," 15, 25; Benson, *Counter Cultures*, 163; United States Department of Commerce, Bureau of the Census, "Average Annual Earnings in All and Selected Industries and in Occupations, 1890–1926," *Historical Statistics of the United States: Colonial Times to 1970*, part I (Washington, DC: US Government Printing Office, 1975), 168.

25 Larsell, *Doctor in Oregon*, 176.

26 Lovejoy, "Medical School," 24–25.

27 Ibid., 15.

28 Ibid., 25.

29 Ibid., 25–26; "She Kept 'Em Laughing," *Old Oregon* 37 (August–September 1957): 15.

30 Nell Irvin Painter, *Standing at Armageddon: The United States, 1877–1919* (New York: Norton, 1987), 110–40; E. Kimbark MacColl, with Harry H. Stein, *Merchants, Money, and Power: The Portland Establishment, 1843–1913* (Portland, OR: Georgian Press, 1988), 306–14.

31 Lovejoy, "Medical School," 28–29; MacColl, *Money, Merchants, Power*, 311.

32 Morantz-Sanchez, *Sympathy and Science*, 92–93.

33 Bertha Van Hoosen, *Petticoat Surgeon* (Chicago: Pellegrini & Cudahy, 1947); Emily Dunning Barringer, *Bowery to Bellevue: The Story of New York's First Woman Ambulance Surgeon* (New York: Norton, 1950); Rosalie Slaughter Morton, *A Woman Surgeon: The Life and Work of Rosalie Slaughter*

Morton (New York: Frederick A. Stokes, 1937). For Bates, see Wilbur Fiske Stone, *History of Colorado,* vol. 2 (Chicago: S. J. Clarke, 1918), 452–57; and for Potter, see More, *Restoring the Balance,* 99–105.

34 Carla Bittel, *Mary Putnam Jacobi and the Politics of Medicine in Nineteenth-Century America* (Chapel Hill: University of North Carolina Press, 2009), 15–31, quotes 24 and 30; Mary Putnam Jacobi, "Woman in Medicine," in *Woman's Work in America,* ed. Annie Nathan Meyer (New York: Henry Holt & Co., 1891), 199; Gloria Moldow, *Women Doctors in Gilded-Age Washington: Race, Gender, and Professionalization* (Urbana: University of Illinois Press, 1987), 117.

35 Moldow, *Women Doctors,* 115.

36 United States Department of Commerce, Bureau of the Census, *Tenth Census of the United States, 1880,* Portland, Multnomah County, Oregon, roll T9–1083, Enumeration District 101, 7–296. Schmeer was "keeping house" with two children.

37 Larsell, *Doctor in Oregon,* 415.

38 Census of Chehalis Washington, 1871, roll V228–1, Washington Territorial Census, 1871, Olympia, Washington. The Portland city directories for 1890 and 1891 list Scammon as a student.

39 "Death Takes Dr. Sara Hill," *Oregonian,* September 21, 1957, 7.

40 Lovejoy, "Medical School," 27–28.

41 In 1890–1891 the female members of the student body were Esther Clayson, Clara M. Davidson (who graduated from the Woman's Medical College of Pennsylvania in 1893), and Helena Scammon; in 1892–1893, Esther Clayson, Inez DeLashmutt, Lucy Mowdy, Helena Scammon (who graduated that year, becoming the first woman to graduate from UOMD), and Mrs. A. Whitney; in 1893–1894, Dicie E. Baird, Esther Clayson (who graduated that year), Jessie Fremont Davis, Tillie Dittenhoeffer, and Olive Hartley. See the volumes of the *Annual Announcement of the Medical Department of the University of Oregon* for the years 1890–1906. For women students before 1889, see Bertha Hallam to Esther Lovejoy, September 25, 1952, box 1, folder 3, EPL 2001–004.

42 *Sixth Annual Announcement of the Medical Department of the University of Oregon, Session of 1892–1893* (Portland, OR: Lewis & Dryden, 1892), 6.

43 Emily Loveridge, "As I Remember," typescript, 5, 12, item 16, box 1, Linfield—Good Samaritan School of Nursing Archives, Linfield College, McMinnville, Oregon.

44 *Seventh Annual Announcement of the Medical Department of the University of Oregon, Session of 1893–1894* (Portland, OR: A. Anderson, 1893), 6–7, 8–12, 16.

45 Ibid., 16.

46 John Harley Warner and James M. Edmonson, *Dissection: Photographs of a Rite of Passage in American Medicine, 1880–1930* (New York: Blast Books, 2009), 15.

47 Notebook, pad 3 of 7, 79–82, box 8, EPL 2001–011.

48 See Nye, "Masculine Codes of Honor," and Michael Sappol, *A Traffic of Dead Bodies: Anatomy and Embodied Social Identity in Nineteenth-Century America* (Princeton, NJ: Princeton University Press, 2002), 217–18.

49 Lovejoy, "Medical School," 21; "She Kept 'Em Laughing," *Old Oregon* 37 (August–September 1957), 15.

50 Lovejoy, "Medical School," 21–22.

51 Ibid., 21.

52 *Seventh Annual Announcement*, 7–8.

53 Lovejoy, "Medical School," 34.

54 Ibid., 33.

55 Ibid.

56 William Thompson Lusk, *The Science and Art of Midwifery,* 4th ed. (New York: D. Appleton and Company, 1892). Chapters include "The Management of Pregnancy" and "The Physiology and Management of Childbed."

57 Morantz-Sanchez outlines these elements in *Sympathy and Science.*

58 Lovejoy, "Medical School," 33–34.

59 "University of Oregon, Medical Department," *Medical Sentinel* 2, no. 5 (May 1894): 200–202.

60 Esther Pohl Lovejoy to Mrs. Medill McCormick, n.d. (ca. 1916), Amy Khedouri Materials, Scottsdale, Arizona.

61 Morantz-Sanchez, *Sympathy and Science*, 165–78; Walsh, *Doctors Wanted*, 219–22; and Starr, *Social Transformation*, 123–24.

62 Adelaide Brown, "The History of the Children's Hospital in Relation to Medical Women," in *Who's Who Among the Women of California,* ed. Louis S. Lyons and Josephine Wilson (San Francisco: Security Publishing, 1922), 171–72; Rickey Hendricks, "Feminism and Maternalism in Early Hospitals for Children: San Francisco and Denver, 1875–1915," *Journal of the West* 32, no. 3 (July 1993): 61–69.

63 Other institutions with internships open to women were the New England Hospital in Boston, the Woman's Hospital of Philadelphia, the West Philadelphia Hospital for Women, the Woman's Hospital and Foundling Home in Detroit, the New York Infirmary for Women and Children, and the Chicago Children's Hospital. Walsh, *Doctors Wanted*, 221. Helen MacMurchy, "Hospital Appointments: Are They Open to Women?" *New York Medical Journal*, April 27, 1901, 712–16.

64 Richard D. Scheuerman and Clifford E. Trafzer, *The Volga Germans: Pioneers of the Northwest* (Moscow: University Press of Idaho, 1980), 170–71; Center for Volga German Studies, "The Volga Germans in Portland," Concordia University, Portland, Oregon, http://www.volgagermans.net/portland, accessed September 15, 2011.

65 Lovejoy, notes for autobiography, 8–10.

66 Esther Pohl Lovejoy, "The Luck of Some Women," n.d., typescript, box 1, folder 5, EPL 2001–011.

67 Nan Strandborg to Esther Pohl Lovejoy, January 24, 1964, box 3, folder 18, EPL 2001–011.

68 Larsell, *Doctor in Oregon*, 409.

69 Ibid., 409–12; William Harvey King, *History of Homeopathy and Its Institutions in America,* vol. 1 (Chicago: Lewis Publishing Company, 1905), 412–13; "Oregon Homeopathic Medical Society," *Medical Sentinel* 2, no. 5 (May 1894): 204–5; "The Homeopathic Medical Society of the State of Oregon," *Pacific Coast Journal of Homeopathy* 4, no. 12 (December 1896): 490; Larsell, *Doctor in Oregon*, 412–13; "The Eclectic State Society of Oregon," *Medical Sentinel* 2, no. 5 (May 1894): 204; "Oregon," *Eclectic Medical Journal* 54, no. 7 (July 1894): 337.

70 Oregon State Board of Medical Examiners, *Medical Register of Oregon* (Salem: State Medical Board and Oregon State Printer, 1898).

71 See the *Portland City Directory* for these years.

72 Marie Rose Wong, *Sweet Cakes, Long Journey: The Chinatowns of Portland, Oregon* (Seattle: University of Seattle Press, 2004), 166; Office of the City Auditor, Portland Historical Timeline, Portland Archives and Records Center, http://www.portlandonline.com/auditor/index.cfm?a=284518&c=51811, accessed September 15, 2011.

73 William M. Bowen, "The Five Eras of Chinese Medicine in California," in *The Chinese in America: A History from Gold Mountain to the New Millennium,* ed. Susie Lan Cassel (New York: Rowman & Littlefield, 2002), 174–92.

74 Judith Walzer Leavitt, *Brought to Bed: Childbearing in America, 1750–1950* (New York: Oxford University Press, 1986); Charlotte G. Borst, *Catching Babies: The Professionalization of Childbirth, 1870–1920* (Cambridge, MA: Harvard University Press, 1995).

75 Many advertised in Portland's daily newspapers in these years.

76 Regina Morantz-Sanchez, "Female Patient Agency and the 1892 Trial of Dr. Mary Dixon Jones in Late-Nineteenth-Century Brooklyn," in *Women Physicians and the Cultures of Medicine,* ed. Ellen S. More, Elizabeth Fee, and Manon Perry (Baltimore: Johns Hopkins University Press, 2009),

69–88; Regina Morantz-Sanchez, *Conduct Unbecoming a Woman: Medicine on Trial in Turn-of-the-Century Brooklyn* (New York: Oxford University Press, 1999).

77 Esther Clayson Pohl, MD, certificate, West Chicago Post-Graduate School and Polyclinic, April 1, 1897; and Esther Pohl, certificate, Chicago Clinical School, December 7, 1897; both in box 3, "Diplomas, Licenses, Honors, and Certificates," EPL 2001–004.

78 Thomas Neville Bonner, *American Doctors and German Universities: A Chapter in International Intellectual Relations* (Lincoln: University of Nebraska Press, 1963), 69–82; Esther Pohl Lovejoy, *The House of the Good Neighbor* (New York: Macmillan, 1919), 111–12; Dr. E. C. Pohl, American Medical Association of Vienna membership card no. 1409, box 1, folder 1:3, AWH Records.

79 Esther Pohl Lovejoy, speech, n.d., n.p., box 2b, folder 19, "Lovejoy, Esther Pohl, Posthumous Papers and Biographical Information," AWH Records; "Bright Portland Woman Writes Interestingly from Abroad," *Oregon Journal*, April 17, 1904, 33; "Portland Club Woman's Adventures en Route to Europe," *Oregon Journal*, March 27, 1904, 32; Esther Pohl, "A Portland Woman in Egypt," *Oregon Journal*, November 13, 1904, and 29 and November 20, 1904, 33.

80 Lovejoy, notes for autobiography, 8–10.

81 Ibid., 21.

82 Motor Vehicle Registration Record, 1905–1910, Record of Statements and Certificates Issued to Owners of Automobiles, Index of Automobile and Motorcycle Licenses Issued, Office of the Secretary of State, Oregon State Archives, Salem, Oregon.

83 Maureen A. Flanagan, *Seeing with Their Hearts: Chicago Women and the Vision of the Good City, 1871–1933* (Princeton, NJ: Princeton University Press, 2002); Daphne Spain, *How Women Saved the City* (Minneapolis: University of Minnesota Press, 2001); John C. Putman, *Class and Gender Politics in Progressive-Era Seattle* (Reno: University of Nevada Press, 2008); Gayle Gullett, *Becoming Citizens: The Emergence and Development of the California Women's Movement, 1880–1911* (Urbana: University of Illinois Press, 2000).

84 Morantz-Sanchez, *Sympathy and Science*, 282. Ellen S. More, in *Restoring the Balance*, characterizes this as "maternalist medicine."

85 Nancy Cott, *The Grounding of Modern Feminism* (New Haven, CT: Yale University Press, 1987); Noralee Frankel and Nancy S. Dye, eds., *Gender, Class, Race, and Reform in the Progressive Era* (Lexington: University Press of Kentucky, 1991); Sandra Haarsager, *Organized Womanhood: Cultural Poli-*

tics in the Pacific Northwest, 1840–1920 (Norman: University of Oklahoma Press, 1997); Gloria E. Myers, *A Municipal Mother: Portland's Lola Greene Baldwin, America's First Policewoman* (Corvallis: Oregon State University Press, 1995).

86 Spain, *How Women Saved the City*, 24–27.

87 "Personals," *Medical Sentinel* 4, no. 10 (October 1896): 476; Lucia H. Faxton Additon, *Twenty Eventful Years of the Oregon Woman's Christian Temperance Union, 1880–1900* (Portland, OR: Gotshall Printing, 1904), 47–52.

88 People's Institute and Free Dispensary, Records, accession 2008–010, Historical Collections & Archives, Oregon Health & Science University, Portland, Oregon; Emily Stuckman, "More Than a Sign of the Times: Progressive Era Educational Efforts of the Portland Section, National Council of Jewish Women," paper presented at Game Changers and History Makers: Women in Pacific Northwest History Conference, Spokane, Washington, November 2010; "Quarterly Meeting Held," *Oregonian*, November 6, 1906, 12.

89 *Portland City Directory, 1907–1908* (Portland, OR: R. L. Polk, 1907), 148, 152,

90 Kimberly S. Moreland, *History of Portland's African American Community, 1805 to the Present* (Portland, OR: Bureau of Planning, 1993), 41.

91 Florence Crittenton Refuge Home, Portland, Oregon, minutes, December 22, 1903, Board of Managers, 1903–1906, bound volume, accession B 90, University of Oregon Special Collections and Archives, Eugene, Oregon.

92 Florence Crittenton Refuge Home, minutes, January 12, 1904, 17.

93 Florence Crittenton Refuge Home, minutes, January 10, 1905, 96. They included doctors Mae H. Cardwell, Gertrude French, Edna Timms, Amelia Ziegler, Sarah Whiteside, Kittie P. Gray, and Angela Ford Warren.

94 Florence Crittenton Refuge Home, minutes, April 12 1904, 34. Katherine G. Aiken, *Harnessing the Power of Motherhood: The National Florence Crittenton Mission, 1883–1925* (Knoxville: University of Tennessee Press, 1998), 128–29.

95 "Woman's Club Meeting," *Oregonian*, May 10, 1902, 7; *Fourth Annual Announcement of the Woman's Club of Portland, Oregon, 1899–1900*, 16; "The Woman's Club Season of 1901–1902," 8; *Woman's Club of Portland, Oregon, 1909–1910, Thirteenth Annual Announcement*, 14; *Woman's Club of Portland, Oregon, 1912–1913, Sixteenth Annual Announcement*, 6, all in box 12, folder 1, PWC.

96 Cora Bagley Marrett, "Nineteenth-Century Associations of Medical Women: The Beginning of a Movement," *Journal of the American Medical Women's Association* 32, no. 12 (December 1977): 469–74; "On the Evolution

of Women's Medical Societies," *Bulletin of the History of Medicine* 53, no. 3 (Fall 1979): 434–48.

97 Mae H. Cardwell notebook, "Early Women Physicians of Oregon, Excerpted by K. C. Mead, January 1930," 25, Lucy I. Davis Phillips, Collection on Oregon Women Medical School Graduates, accession 2004–030, Historical Collections & Archives, Oregon Health & Science University, Portland, Oregon.

98 Estelle B. Freedman, "Separatism as Strategy: Female Institution Building and American Feminism, 1870–1930," *Feminist Studies* 5, no. 3 (Fall 1979): 512–29, reprinted with additional commentary in Freedman, *Feminism, Sexuality, and Politics: Essays by Estelle B. Freedman* (Chapel Hill: University of North Carolina Press, 2006). Ella J. and Angela Ford, Oregon's first women graduates, gained admittance to the three-year-old Oregon State Medical Society in 1877, and Esther Pohl joined in 1899. Gendered barriers limited their full participation in holding office and presenting papers at the annual meeting. Mae H. Cardwell, "The Oregon State Medical Society—An Historical Sketch," *Medical Sentinel* 13, no. 7 (July 1905): 193–94. The influential Portland City Medical Society barred women from membership until 1902. Mae H. Cardwell, "Portland City Medical Society—A Resume," *Medical Sentinel* 13, no. 7 (July 1905): 212–23.

99 Morantz-Sanchez, *Sympathy and Science,* 181.

100 Medical Society of the State of California, *Official Register and Directory of Physicians and Surgeons in the State of California: To Which Is Added a Directory of Physicians and Surgeons in Oregon and Washington and a Directory of California State Nurses' Association* (San Francisco: Medical Society of the State of California, 1905), 282–307.

101 Mae H. Cardwell, "Medical Club of Portland—Historical," *Medical Sentinel* 13, no. 7 (July 1905): 223–26.

3. GOLDEN HOPES FOR FAMILY AND CAREER

1 Esther Pohl Lovejoy, manuscript for autobiography, n.p., n.d., box 3, folder 19, EPL 2001–0011; Esther C. P. Lovejoy, with introduction by Bertha Hallam, "My Medical School, 1890–1894," *Oregon Historical Quarterly* 75, no. 1 (March 1974): 34.

2 United States Department of Commerce, Bureau of the Census, *Tenth Census of the United States, 1880* (Washington, DC: United States Bureau of the Census, 1880), Kewaunee, Kewaunee County, Wisconsin, Ross 1431, Enumeration District 52, p. 229A; Emil Pohl, certificate of death, May 11, 1911, accession 91A17, box 16, "Death Certificates, Marion 1911–

Multnomah 1911," folder 63, "Multnomah County, 1911 (May 10–May 12)," Health Division, Oregon State Archives, Salem, Oregon.

3 Lovejoy, "Medical School," 21; "Well-Known Doctor Dies in Fairbanks," *Oregon Journal*, May 13, 1911, 5; William Harvey King, *History of Homeopathy and Its Institutions in America,* vol. 1 (New York: Lewis Publishing, 1905), 412–13; Olof Larsell, *The Doctor in Oregon: A Medical History* (Portland: Bindford & Mort for the Oregon Historical Society, 1947), 358, 438.

4 Albert Pohl, probate case file #1709, accession 92A-24, box 42, folder 4, Probate Case Files, Multnomah County, Oregon State Archives, Salem, Oregon; "Meeting of Stockholders," *Oregonian*, April 19, 1887, 5.

5 *Portland City Directory, 1886* (Portland, OR: R. L. Polk, 1886), 369; *Portland City Directory, 1887* (Portland, OR: R. L. Polk, 1887), 381; *Portland City Directory, 1888* (Portland, OR: R. L. Polk, 1888), 438; *Portland City Directory, 1889* (Portland, OR: R. L. Polk, 1889), 452; *Portland City Directory, 1891* (Portland, OR: R. L. Polk, 1891), 520.

6 Albert Pohl, probate case file.

7 Lovejoy, "Medical School," 21; "Doctor Dies in Fairbanks," 5.

8 "Got Their Diplomas," *Oregonian*, April 4, 1893, 8.

9 Lovejoy, "Medical School," 21.

10 *Portland City Directory, 1894* (Portland, OR: R. L. Polk, 1894), 485, 630. LaMoree graduated from the Albany (New York) Medical College in 1870; Oregon State Board of Medical Examiners, *Medical Register of Oregon* (Salem: State Medical Board and Oregon State Printer, 1898), 18. Albany Medical College was the first "regular" medical school to welcome homeopathic physicians to its teaching staff in the 1840s. John S. Haller, *The History of American Homeopathy: The Academic Years, 1820–1935* (New York: Pharmaceutical Products Press, 2005), 140.

11 Lovejoy, "Medical School," 34; Oregon Marriage License Index and Record, December 1885–June 1895, Multnomah County, microfilm reel 2, vol. 10, p. 205, Oregon State Archives, Salem, Oregon.

12 All are listed in Alumni Association of the University of Oregon Medical School, *Twenty-Fifth Annual Meeting and Directory of the Alumni Association of the University of Oregon Medical School* (Portland: Alumni Association of the University of Oregon Medical School, 1937). "Death Takes Dr. Sara Hill," *Oregonian*, September 21, 1957, 7. For Schmeer McDonald, see "Personal and General," *Oregonian*, October 28, 1888, 8.

13 Carla Bittel, *Mary Putnam Jacobi and the Politics of Medicine in Nineteenth-Century America* (Chapel Hill: University of North Carolina Press, 2009); Emily Dunning Barringer, *Bowery to Bellevue: The Story of New York's First Woman Ambulance Surgeon* (New York: Norton, 1950).

14 Regina Morantz-Sanchez, *Sympathy and Science: Women Physicians in American Medicine* (Chapel Hill: University of North Carolina Press, 2000), 135–37.

15 Wenzel Pohl, probate case file #3917, accession 92A-24, box 103, folder 2, Probate Case Files, Multnomah County, Oregon State Archives, Salem, Oregon.

16 *Title Guarantee Company v. Wrenn*, 35 Or. 1899, 62–75.

17 Esther Pohl Lovejoy, notes for autobiography, box 1, folder 7, EPL 2001–011.

18 Alan Derickson, *Workers' Health Workers' Democracy: The Western Miners' Struggle, 1891–1925* (Ithaca: Cornell University Press, 1988), 107.

19 *Portland City Directory, 1896* (Portland, OR: R. L. Polk Publishers, 1896), 515; "Dr. Emil Pohl, Course Certificate, Chicago Policlinic, May 2, 1896," and "Emil Pohl, License to Practice Medicine, British Columbia Medical Council, September 4, 1896," both in box 3, "Diplomas, Licenses, Honors, and Certificates," EPL 2001–004; Lovejoy, notes for autobiography;" "Personals," *Medical Sentinel* 5, no. 6 (June 1897): 312. Information on Emil and Esther as attending physicians at births locates them in Portland at several points in this chapter. See Portland Birth Index, accession 77A-46, register 3 of 7, birth index, June 1893–July 1899, City of Portland, Health Division, Oregon State Archives, Salem, Oregon.

20 "The Elder Filled Up," *Oregonian*, July 28, 1897, 1, 6; "Getting the Elder Ready," *Oregonian*, July 29, 1897, 1; "Off in Gold's Quest," *Oregonian*, July 31, 1897, 1, 6, quotes 1.

21 "Ex-Mayor of Anchorage Dies at Portland Home," *Oregonian*, September 30, 1950, 7; United States Department of Commerce, Bureau of the Census, *Twelfth Census of the United States, 1900* (Washington, DC: United States Bureau of the Census, 1900), Skagway, Southern Supervisors District, Alaska, roll T-623 1831, 88B, Enumeration District 7; "May Have Been Murdered," *Oregonian*, January 19, 1900, 8.

22 *Twelfth Census of the United States, 1900*, Skagway, 88B.

23 Lovejoy, notes for autobiography, n.p. "Skaguay" is an earlier spelling taken from the indigenous Tlingit.

24 Lovejoy, notes for autobiography, 22; Catherine Holder Spude, "Bachelor Miners and Barbers' Wives: The Common People of Skagway in 1900," *Alaska History* 6, no. 2 (Fall 1991): 17–29, quote 20.

25 Kathryn Morse, *The Nature of Gold: An Environmental History of the Klondike Gold Rush* (Seattle: University of Washington Press, 2003).

26 Lovejoy, notes for autobiography, 11–12.

27 Morse, *Nature of Gold*, 140, 182.

28 "May Have Been Murdered."

29 Lovejoy, notes for autobiography, 22.

30 *Standard Medical Directory of North America, 1902* (Chicago: G. P. Engle-hard, 1901), 733; Board of Medical Examiners, *Medical Register of Oregon*, 21; "Emil Pohl, License to Practice Medicine, British Columbia Medical Council," and "Emil Pohl, License to Practice Medicine in the North-West Territories of Canada, February 24, 1898," both in box 3, EPL 2001–004.

31 Emil Pohl, MD, "Cerebro-Spinal Meningitis," *Medical Sentinel* 14, no. 11 (November 1906): 529–31, quote 529.

32 Lovejoy, notes for autobiography, 22; Howard Clifford, *The Skagway Story* (Anchorage: Alaska Northwest Publishing Company, 1975), 30; D. C. New-man, MD, "On the Status of Medical Affairs in the Klondyke," *Medical Sentinel* 7, no. 1 (January 1899): 33–34.

33 Fred Lockley, interview with Esther Lovejoy, "Observations and Impres-sions of the Journal Man," *Oregon Journal*, September 25, 1920, 6; Emil Pohl, "Cerebro-Spinal Meningitis," 529.

34 Morse, *Nature of Gold*, 162–63.

35 "Personals," *Medical Sentinel* 6, no. 6 (June 1898): 249; *Portland City Direc-tory, 1898* (Portland, OR: R. L. Polk Publishers, 1898), 406; *Portland City Directory, 1899–1900* (Portland, OR: R. L. Polk Publishers, 1899), 804; "Amelia Ziegler, Biography 1937, Notes of Dr. Kate Mead Sent for Com-parison by Lucy Davis," box 1, folder 9, Lucy I. Davis Phillips Collection on Oregon Women Medical School Graduates, Historical Collections & Archives, Oregon Health & Science University, Portland, Oregon.

36 Portland Birth Index, June 1893–July 1899.

37 Terrence Michael Cole, "A History of the Nome Gold Rush: The Poor Man's Paradise" (PhD Diss., University of Washington, 1983), 86–87; *Standard Medical Directory of North America*, 41.

38 "Personals," *Medical Sentinel* 7, no. 9 (September 1899): 431; "Physicians and Surgeons," *Nome News*, November 1, 1899, 4; Cole, "History of Nome Gold Rush," 88–89, 112; "Medical Society Meeting," *Nome News*, Novem-ber 18, 1899, 1.

39 "City Treasurership," *Nome Gold Digger*, February 7, 1900, 1; "Passes the Plums," *Nome Gold Digger*, February 7, 1900, 2; "Senate's Hot Time," *Nome News*, February 17, 1900, 3; Cole, "History of Nome Gold Rush," 89–90; "News Nuggets," *Nome Gold Digger*, January 11, 1900, 4.

40 Lovejoy, notes for autobiography, 15.

41 Spude, "Bachelor Miners," 20.

42 "Life at Skagway," *Oregonian*, February 14, 1898, 3; "May Have Been Mur-dered"; "Sourdough Reunion Recalls Strange Slaying in Alaska," *Orego-nian*, August 3, 1931, 3.

43 Esther Pohl Lovejoy to "My Dear Nephew," October 30, 1923, box 1, folder 2B, EPL 2001–011.

44 "May Have Been Murdered"; "Sourdough Reunion Recalls Strange Slaying"; Henry Woodside, "The Great Yukon Murder Case," *Wide World Magazine* 8, no. 44 (December 1901): 154–62; "Dawson Men Murdered," *Nome Gold Digger,* March 14, 1900, 4; Allan Curtis, "Christmas Day Murders," *Canadian West* 13 (Fall 1988): 81–85, and 14 (Winter 1988): 126–33; Ed Ferrell, *Frontier Justice: Alaska 1898: The Last American Frontier* (Westminster, MD: Heritage Books, 2007), 5–11.

45 Esther Pohl Lovejoy, autobiography draft, 290, box 1, folder 7, EPL 2001–011. For Arctic Brotherhood, see Ferrell, *Frontier Justice,* 11.

46 Portland Birth Index, accession 77A-46, register 4 of 7, Birth Index, August 1899–May 1905, City of Portland, Health Division, Oregon State Archives, Salem, Oregon.

47 Emil Pohl, "Cerebro-Spinal Meningitis," 530–31; "Personals," *Medical Sentinel* 10, no. 11 (November 1902): 530.

48 "Beloved Physician Dies Very Suddenly," *Fairbanks News-Miner,* May 12, 1911, 3.

49 "Catalogue of Students for Session 1900–1901," *Fifteenth Annual Announcement University of Oregon Medical Department, Session 1901–1902* (Portland: University of Oregon Medical Department, 1901), 28.

50 *Portland City Directory, 1901–1902* (Portland, OR: R. L. Polk Publishers, 1901), 209.

51 Marriage License Index and Record, July 1895–October 1903, Multnomah County, Oregon State Archives, reel 3, vol. 15, 166, 168; "Blanchard-Snook-Clayson," *Oregonian,* February 1, 1903, sect. 3, p. 18; Hiram T. French, *History of Idaho: A Narrative Account of Its Historical Progress, Its People, and Its Principal Interests,* vol. 2 (Chicago: Lewis Publishing, 1914), 685–87.

52 Esther Pohl Lovejoy, handwritten autobiography, 17, box 3, folder 19, EPL 2001–011.

53 Ibid., 21.

54 "Drs. Pohls' Son Dead," *Oregonian,* September 12, 1908, 9.

55 Lovejoy, handwritten autobiography, n.p.

56 "Dr. Pohl's Son Dies at St. Vincent's," *Oregon Journal,* September 11, 1908, 5; Frederick Clayson Pohl, certificate of death, September 11, 1908, accession 91A17, box 8, "Death Certificates, Multnomah 1908–Yamhill 1908," folder 8, "Multnomah County, 1908 (September 1–September 11)," Health Division, Oregon State Archives, Salem, Oregon; telegram from George F. Wilson, Portland, to Dr. Emil Pohl, Fairbanks, September 11, 1908, and telegram from Esther Pohl, Portland, to Emil Pohl, Fairbanks, September

13, 1908, both in box 5, folder 38, EPL 2001–011; "Death Due to Impure Milk," *Oregon Journal*, August 30, 1909, 1.

57 "The Funeral of Little Fred Clayson Pohl," *Oregon Journal*, September 14, 1908, 7.

58 Telegram from Esther Pohl to Emil Pohl, September 13, 1908.

59 *Portland City Directory, 1909* (Portland, OR: R. L. Polk Publishers, 1909), 1105.

60 "Beloved Physician Dies Very Suddenly," 3; United States Department of the Interior, *Report of the Territorial Mine Inspector to the Governor of Alaska for the Year 1915* (Washington, DC: Government Printing Office, 1916), 12, 16; Alfred H. Brooks et al., *Mineral Resources of Alaska: Report on Progress of Investigations in 1914, United States Geological Survey Bulletin 622* (Washington, DC: Government Printing Office, 1915), 230–31, 235.

61 Anna Howard Shaw to Dr. E. H. [*sic*] Pohl, Idaho State Penitentiary, Boise, Idaho, January 10, 1911, Amy Khedouri Materials, Scottsdale, Arizona.

62 Emil Pohl to "My Dear Wife Het," June 20, 1910, box 1, folder 2A, EPL 2001–011.

63 Emil Pohl to "My Dear Wife Het," November 15, 1910, box 1, folder 2A, EPL 2001–011.

64 Ibid.

65 Ibid.

66 "Beloved Physician Dies Very Suddenly," 3; Emil Pohl, death certificate, May 11, 1911, accession 91A17, box 16, "Death Certificates, Marion 1911–Multnomah 1911," folder 63, "Death Certificates, Multnomah County, May 10–May 12, 1911," Health Division, Oregon State Archives, Salem, Oregon; transit permit no. 228, July 27, 1911, Washington State Board of Health, box 16, "Death Certificates, Marion 1911–Multnomah 1911," folder 63, "Death Certificates, Multnomah County, 5/10–5/12 1911," accession 91A17, Health Division, Oregon State Archives, Salem, Oregon; Emil Pohl, "Certificate of Safety to Transport Remains," Fairbanks, Alaska, July 6, 1911, box 16, "Death Certificates, Marion 1911–Multnomah 1911," folder 63, "Death Certificates, Multnomah County, 5/10–5/12 1911," accession 91A17, Health Division, Oregon State Archives, Salem, Oregon.

67 "Well-Known Doctor Dies in Fairbanks."

68 "Beloved Physician Dies Very Suddenly," 3.

69 Transit permit no. 228, and "Certificate of Safety to Transport Remains."

70 "Divorce Matters," *Oregonian*, March 28, 1888, 3.

71 William Hughes Clayson, Probate Court Estate 360, Clackamas County, Probate Files, box 6, folder 24, Oregon State Archives, Salem, Oregon; *In RE Clayson's Will*, 24 Or., 1893, 542–49.

72 *Seattle City Directory, 1893* (Seattle: Polk's Seattle Directory Company, 1893), 297; *Seattle City Directory, 1899* (Seattle: Polk's Seattle Directory Company, 1899), 266; *Seattle City Directory, 1901* (Seattle: Polk's Seattle Directory Company, 1901), 78, 334.

73 Quoted in Ferrell, *Frontier Justice*, 11.

74 *Clayson v. Clayson*, 66 Pacific Reporter, 1902, 410–11.

75 "Mrs. Clayson Sues Again," *Oregon Journal*, April 16, 1909, 9; "Mother Sues Her Son," *Oregonian*, July 15, 1916, 7.

76 "Populist Party," *Patriarch*, May 28, 1904, 3; "Clayson a Candidate," July 30, 1910, 2; and "Candidate," January 11, 1913, 1. "Edward Clayson, 'Patriarch,' Dead," *Seattle Post-Intelligencer*, January 3, 1915, 10.

77 "Convention of Husbands and Fathers," *Patriarch*, June 25, 1904, 1; "Female Barbers," *Patriarch*, November 18, 1905, 2.

78 Clayson published the self-referential weekly from 1901 to 1914, and most advertisers were brewers and liquor retailers. Lovejoy, "Our Historical Novel," 289. John C. Putman notes that few Seattle suffragists took him seriously. Putman, *Class and Gender Politics in Progressive-Era Seattle* (Reno: University of Nevada Press, 2008), 104–5.

79 "Seattle Cuckold Mill," *Patriarch*, June 27, 1903, 2; "Divorce Compass," *Patriarch*, June 27, 1903, 3.

80 "He Pleads Guilty," *Seattle Republican*, January 16, 1903, 3. The first extant copy of the *Patriarch* begins with May 16, 1903, so we don't have a record of what Edward published or had to say about the libel suit.

81 "The Fall of Esther," *Patriarch*, July 22, 1905, 3.

82 "Dr. Harry Lane," *Patriarch*, February 29, 1908, 4.

83 "Professional Ethics of an Official She," *Patriarch*, June 5, 1909, 3.

84 "A Woman-Suffrage-Prohibition Combination," *Patriarch*, November 5, 1910, 2.

85 Edward Clayson, death certificate, January 2, 1915, and Washington State Transportation of Corpse Permit 4, January 2, 1915, accession 91A17, box 32, "Death Certificates, Lane 1915–Multnomah 1915," folder 37, "Death Certificates, Multnomah County, January 1, 1915–January 3, 1915," Health Division, Oregon State Archives, Salem, Oregon; Lovejoy, "Our Historical Novel," 289–90.

86 "Membership Roll and Dues Records 1901–7," 348, box 6, folder 1, PWC; "Mrs. A. M. Clayson," *Oregonian*, November 29, 1924, 16; Anna Shaw to Esther Pohl, January 7, 1907, 4, Khedouri Materials.

87 Esther Pohl Lovejoy to Bertha Hallam, July 25, 1947, box 1, folder 1B, EPL 2001–004; Annie Mary Clayson, certificate of death, November 28, 1924, box 76, "Death Certificates Multnomah 1924," folder 26, "Mult-

nomah County (September 1–December 31)," accession 91A-17, Oregon State Board of Health, Oregon State Archives, Salem, Oregon; "Mrs. A.M. Clayson"; "Anna M. Clayson Dead; Mother of Portland Doctor," *Oregon Journal*, November 29, 1924, 5.

88 "Het" [Esther Lovejoy] to Lottie [Charlotte Snook], "On Board the Steamship *Scythia*," n.d., box 1, folder 2B, EPL 2001–011.

89 Annie May is buried with this death date in Lone Fir Cemetery in Portland. "Mrs. Snook, Eighty-Five, Dies in Hospital," (Salmon, Idaho) *Recorder-Herald*, January 29, 1970, 7.

90 "Ex-Mayor of Anchorage Dies," 7.

91 United States Department of Commerce, Bureau of the Census, *Fourteenth Census of the United States, 1920* (Washington, DC: United States Bureau of the Census, 1920), Portland, Multnomah, Oregon, roll T625 1502, Enumeration District 151, 4B; and Oregon Death Index 1942–50, microfilm reel "Oregon Death Index A-Kl," Oregon State Library, Salem, Oregon.

4. CITY HEALTH AND THE BUSINESS OF WOMEN

1 "Will Take Office with Clean Hands," *Oregon Journal*, May 10, 1905, 12; Paul S. Holbo, "Senator Harry Lane: Independent Democrat in Peace and War," in *Experiences in a Promised Land: Essays in Pacific Northwest History*, ed. G. Thomas Edwards and Carlos A. Schwantes (Seattle: University of Washington Press, 1986), 242–59; E. Kimbark MacColl with Harry H. Stein, *Merchants, Money, and Power: The Portland Establishment, 1843–1913* (Portland, OR: Georgian Press, 1988), 372–420; Jewel Lansing, *Portland: People, Politics, and Power, 1851–2001* (Corvallis: Oregon State University Press, 2003), 262–73; Robert D. Johnston, *The Radical Middle Class: Populist Democracy and the Question of Capitalism in Progressive Era Portland* (Princeton, NJ: Princeton University Press, 2003), 29–46.

2 MacColl and Stein, *Merchants, Money, and Power*, 387; Lansing, *Portland*, 262, 267, 269, quote 267.

3 Marshall N. Dana, *Newspaper Story: The First Fifty Years of the Oregon Journal, 1902–1952* (Portland, OR: Binfords & Mort, 1951); and George S. Turnbull, *History of Oregon Newspapers* (Portland, OR: Binfords & Mort, 1939).

4 "General Session, Opening Address," *Transactions of the Thirty-Fourth Annual Meeting of the Oregon State Medical Association,* July 1908, 23.

5 "Harry Lane, Mayor, to the Honorable City Council," May 22, 1908, Portland City Council minutes, May 27, 1908, vol. 28, "April 22, 1908–October

20, 1908," microfilm reel 52, Portland Archives and Records Center, Portland, Oregon. Lane married Lola Bailey in 1882. They had two daughters and adopted a third. He was elected to the US Senate from Oregon in 1912 and died in office in 1917. "Senator Lane Succumbs in San Francisco," *Oregon Journal*, May 24, 1917, 1, 10.

6 Lovejoy, notes for autobiography, "Handy Note Book," box 8, EPL 2001–011.

7 Charter provisions, "Article V of Charter of the City of Portland, Oregon, Filed in the Office of the Secretary of State, January 23, 1903," CPBH; Olof Larsell, *The Doctor in Oregon: A Medical History* (Portland: Binfords & Mort for the Oregon Historical Society, 1947), 474–85; Paul Starr, *The Social Transformation of American Medicine* (New York: Basic Books, 1982), 184–85; Lansing, *Portland*, 250–51.

8 "Suspense Ends: Mayor Announces List of Appointments," *Oregonian*, January 24, 1903, 10.

9 Oregon State Board of Health, *First Biennial Report of the Oregon State Board of Health, 1905* (Salem: Oregon State Printer, 1905).

10 Special meeting, Portland Board of Health, August 11, 1905, 87, CPBH; "City Doctors Bad Actors," *Oregon Journal*, August 9, 1905, 1, 6; "Lane Calls Health Board Careless," *Oregonian*, August 10, 1905, 16.

11 Harry Lane to "Dear Doctor," August 7, 1905, "Lane, Harry," subject files B, Board of Health, 1905, box 1, folder 1, accession A2000–003, City of Portland Archives and Records Center, Portland, Oregon; "Board of Health Won't Pay the Bill," *Oregon Journal*, July 1, 1905, 2.

12 "City Doctors Bad Actors," 6.

13 Larsell, *Doctor in Oregon*, 177, 362, 481. "Plan to Increase Pay and Give Wheeler Place," *Oregon Journal*, December 9, 1905, 4; Regular meeting, Portland Board of Health, February 1, 1906, 117, CPBH.

14 Special meeting, Portland Board of Health, July 11, 1907, 219, CPBH; "Wheeler Hands in Resignation," *Oregon Journal*, July 9, 1907, 4; "Board to Accept: Resignation of Dr. Wheeler Will Stand," *Oregonian*, July 10, 1907, 11.

15 "Board to Accept," 11.

16 Special meeting, Portland Board of Health, July 11, 1907, 219–20, CPBH.

17 "Woman Is Health Officer," *Oregonian*, July 12, 1907, 10; "Woman Is Elected City Health Officer," *Oregon Journal*, July 11, 1907, 1; "Woman Takes Wheeler's Place: Board Appoints Dr. Esther C. Pohl Health Officer," *Portland Evening Telegram*, July 11, 1907, 1; "A Woman as Health Officer," *Northwest Medicine* (Old Series) 5, no. 8 (August 1907): 244; "Personal," *Journal of the American Medical Association* 49, no. 5 (August 3, 1907) 423;

"Dr. Esther C. Pohl," *Woman's Medical Journal* 18, no. 1 (January 1908): 14.

18 "Dr. Bertha V. Thompson," *Woman's Medical Journal* 6, no. 12 (December 1897): 367; "Greeley Names Woman for City Physician," *Woman's Medical Journal* 15, no. 10 (October 1905): 220; "Dr. Eliza Cook," *Woman's Medical Journal* 14, no. 7 (July 1904), 160.

19 "Women Physicians—Public Health Boards," *Medical Woman's Journal* 9, no. 8 (August 1899): 283–84; "Dr. Kate P. Van Orden," *Woman's Medical Journal* 14, no. 4 (April 1904): 87; "Dr. Minnie C. T. Love," *Woman's Medical Journal* 15, no. 5 (May 1905): 111.

20 "Dr. Emma Johnston Lucas," *Woman's Medical Journal* 4, no. 7 (July 1895): 191; "Dr. Mary Breen," *Woman's Medical Journal* 9, no. 8 (August 1899): 305; "Dr. Mary R. Butin," *Woman's Medical Journal* 12, no. 9 (September 1902): 215; "A Woman as Health Officer," *Woman's Medical Journal* 13, no. 5 (May 1903): 94; "Madera (Cal.) Health Officer," *Woman's Medical Journal* 13, no. 11 (November 1903): 227.

21 S. Josephine Baker, *Fighting for Life* (New York: MacMillan, 1939); Judith Walzer Leavitt, *Typhoid Mary: Captive to the Public's Health* (Boston: Beacon Press, 1996), 44.

22 Rosalie Slaughter Morton, MD, "Woman's Place in the Public Health Movement," *Woman's Medical Journal* 22, no. 4 (April 1912): 83–87.

23 Baker, *Fighting For Life*, 64–65.

24 Harry Lane to Nina Lane, September 7, 1907, folder 3, "Harry Lane Correspondence, 1879–1911," Nina Lane Faubion Papers, accession Ax 185, University of Oregon Special Collections and Archives, Eugene, Oregon.

25 Esther Pohl Lovejoy to Mrs. Medill McCormick, n.d. (ca. 1916), Amy Khedouri Materials, Scottsdale, Arizona.

26 William H. McNeill, *Plagues and Peoples* (New York: Anchor Books, 1976); Marilyn Chase, *The Barbary Plague: The Black Death in Victorian San Francisco* (New York: Random House, 2004); James C. Mohr, *Plague and Fire: Battling Black Death and the 1900 Burning of Honolulu's Chinatown* (New York: Oxford University Press, 2005); Frank Morton Todd, *Eradicating Plague from San Francisco: Report of the Citizens' Health Committee and an Account of Its Work* (San Francisco: C. A. Murdock, 1909).

27 Fitzhugh Mullan, *Plagues and Peoples: The Story of the United States Public Health Service* (New York: Basic Books, 1989); *Portland City Directory, 1907–8* (Portland, OR: R. L. Polk, 1907), 170.

28 "The Plague Agitation," *Northwest Medicine* (Old Series) 5, no. 9 (September 1907), 280; Todd, *Eradicating Plague from San Francisco*; L. D. Fricks, *Review of Plague in Seattle (1907) and Subsequent Rat and Flea Surveys* (Washington: US Government Printing Office, 1936).

29 "Menace to City's Health," *Oregon Journal*, September 1, 1907, 18.

30 Regular meeting, Portland Board of Health, September 3, 1907, 229–30, CPBH.

31 "Waterfront to Be Swept Clean," *Oregon Journal*, September 12, 1907, 1.

32 Esther C. Pohl, City Health Commissioner, to the Honorable Mayor and City Council, Portland, Oregon, September 11, 1907, Portland City Council minutes, vol. 26, "March 20, 1907–October 9, 1907," 605, microfilm reel 51, Portland City Archives and Records Center, Portland, Oregon. San Francisco's population in 1910 was 416,912, and Portland had 207,214 residents that same year. "San Francisco Population," from *1990 & 1960 Census of Population*, vol. 1, *Characteristics of Population*, part 6, *California*, US Department of Commerce, Bureau of the Census, at http://www.abag.ca.gov/abag/overview/datacenter/popdemo/sanfran.html, and "Portland Timeline 1902–1951," Portland Archives and Records Center, at http://www.portlandonline.com/auditor/index.cfm?a=284506&c=51811.

33 "Guards Against Plague," *Oregonian*, September 11, 1907, 10.

34 Regular meeting, Portland Board of Health, October 1, 1907, 239, CPBH; "Must Clean River Front," *Oregon Journal*, September 13, 1907, 6; "Rats' Death Knell Rings," *Oregon Journal*, September 14, 1907, 3.

35 "Tom Richardson, Manager, Portland Commercial Club, to Honorable Mayor and Common Council of the City of Portland," October 28, 1907, Portland City Council documents 1907 (F-I), series 2001–09, box 92, folder 3, "Health," City of Portland Archives and Records Center, Portland, Oregon; "Club Will Fight Plague," *Oregonian*, October 29, 1907, 16.

36 "Report to Honorable Mayor and Board of Health, December 12, 1907, from Esther Clayson Pohl, Health Officer," 6–7, box 10, "Annual Reports, Harbor-Health," folder 4, "Annual Reports, Health, Board of, 1905–12, 1918," City of Portland Archives and Records Center; special meeting, Portland Board of Health, November 16, 1907, 249, CPBH; "Council Guards Against Plague," *Portland Evening Telegram*, November 14, 1907, 18.

37 MacColl and Stein, *Merchants, Money, and Power*, 408–9; "Oregon Trust and Savings Company Closes Its Doors," *Portland Evening Telegram*, August 21, 1907, 1; "Portland Banks to Open Today: Clearing House System Is Adopted," *Oregonian*, October 30, 1907, 1.

38 Regular meeting, Portland Board of Health, October 1, 1907, 240, CPBH. Zaik received forty-eight dollars for a month of work. Special meeting, Portland Board of Health, November 6, 1907, 244, CPBH.

39 "Kills Rats for a Living? No, He Does It as An Art," *Oregonian*, September 15, 1907, 8.

40 "Will Kill Rats Gratis," *Oregonian*, September 25, 1907, 9.

41 "Russian Royal Rat Killer Puts Kibosh on Portland's Rodents," *Oregon Journal*, September 27, 1907, 9.

42 "Bounty on Rats," *Oregonian*, October 22, 1907, 9; "Guard Against the Plague," *Oregonian*, October 23, 1907, 16; "No Plague in Portland," *Oregonian*, October 26, 1907, 9.

43 "Should Kill Rats," *Oregonian*, October 30, 1907, 10.

44 "Fight All Chances of Epidemic," *Oregon Journal,* October 26, 1907, 1, 2.

45 "Taps for the Rats," *Oregonian*, December 5, 1907, 9.

46 See Board of Health minutes from November through June, 1908, CPBH.

47 Special meeting, Portland Board of Health, January 30, 1909, CPBH.

48 Esther Pohl, "The Health Department, Its Activities, and Its Needs," type-script speech [1909], box 1, folder 8, EPL 2001–004.

49 Special meeting, Portland Board of Health, November 6, 1907, 245, 247, CPBH; Special meeting, Portland Board of Health, November 16, 1907, 249, CPBH; Larsell, *Doctor in Oregon*, 383; "Microbe Fight Is Inaugurated, *Oregon Journal*, October 22, 1907, 7; "Continues War on Rats," *Oregonian*, November 17, 1907, sect. 2, p. 2.

50 "Town Topics," *Oregon Journal*, August 7, 1905, 5; "Health Officers Find Unspeakable Filth in Portland Chinatown," *Oregon Journal*, November 9, 1905, 6.

51 Alan M. Kraut, *Silent Travelers: Germs, Genes, and the "Immigrant Menace"* (Baltimore: Johns Hopkins University Press, 1994), 84–96, quote 89.

52 Mohr, *Plague and Fire*, 125–41.

53 "Breeders of Plague," *Oregon Journal*, December 30, 1907, 14.

54 Kraut, *Silent Travelers*, 1–9.

55 "Extermination of Rats a Necessity," *Oregonian*, October 28, 1907, 4.

56 "Chinatown Pest Holes Must Go," *Portland Evening Telegram*, October 28, 1907, 3.

57 "Chinatown Is in Awful Condition," *Oregon Journal*, October 29, 1907, 16.

58 "Portland City and County Medical Society, Nov. 6, [1907]," *Medical Sentinel* 16, no. 1 (January 1908): 34; "Plague War Must Not Become Lax," *Oregon Journal*, November 7, 1907, 13.

59 Harry Lane, "Annual Message of the Mayor," January 8, 1908, p. 246, Portland City Council minutes, vol. 27, "October 23, 1907–April 13, 1908," microfilm reel 51, Portland City Archives and Records Center.

60 Nancy Tomes, *The Gospel of Germs: Men, Women, and the Microbe in American Life* (Cambridge, MA: Harvard University Press, 1998); Margaret Rossiter, *Women Scientists in America: Struggles and Strategies to 1940* (Baltimore: Johns Hopkins University Press, 1982); Suellen Hoy, *Chasing Dirt: The*

American Pursuit of Cleanliness (New York: Oxford University Press, 1995).

61 Meeting of March 12, 1901, folder 4, "Secretary's Book of the Home Department," Portland Woman's Club, "October 1900–November 1901," box 1, "Minutes, 1895–1995," PWC; Women Favor Pure Food," *Oregon Journal*, January 20, 1903, 4; "Some Suggestive Plans for Woman's Civic League," *Oregon Journal*, March 19, 1905, 14; "Women's Campaign for Clean Markets," *Oregon Journal*, April 12, 1905, 2.

62 Special meeting, Portland Board of Health, April 24, 1905, CPBH; "Clean Markets Crusade's Object: Miss Tingle Prepares for Hard Fight against Dirt and Disease," *Oregon Journal*, April 24, 1905, 5.

63 "Salary Too Small for Miss Tingle," *Oregon Journal*, July 1, 1905, 2.

64 Special meeting, Portland Board of Health, August 11, 1905, 87, CPBH.

65 *Encyclopedia of Northwest Biography*, ed. Winfield Scott Downs (New York: American Historical Company, 1943) s.v. "Evans, Sarah Ann (Shannon)," 220–23; Sandra Haarsager, *Organized Womanhood: Cultural Politics in the Pacific Northwest, 1840–1920* (Norman: University of Oklahoma Press, 1997), 291–300; "Sarah A. Evans First Inspector," *Oregonian*, June 23, 1935, 1:2; Jim Scheppke, "The Origins of the Oregon State Library," *Oregon Historical Quarterly* 107, no. 1 (Spring 2006): 130–40.

66 "Portland Woman's Club Membership List, 1904–1925," box 6, folder 2, PWC; "Blanchard-Snook-Clayson," *Oregonian*, February 1, 1903, 3:18; Frederick Clayson Pohl, certificate of death, September 11, 1908, accession 91A17, box 8, "Death Certificates, Multnomah 1908–Yamhill 1908," folder 8, "Multnomah County, 1908 September 1–September 11," Health Division, Oregon State Archives, Salem, Oregon.

67 Pohl, "Report to Honorable Mayor and Board of Health," 1907.

68 Lillian Tingle, "Clean Market Day in Portland: The Story of How a City's Meat Markets Were Reformed," *Good Housekeeping* 47, no. 1 (July 1908): 99–102.

69 Maud Nathan, *The Story of an Epoch-Making Movement* (New York: Doubleday, 1926), 198–205; "Consumers' League Meet," *Oregonian*, March 29, 1906, 7.

70 "An Act Preventing the Manufacture and Sale of Adulterated or Misbranded or Poisonous or Deleterious Foods," 1907, Or. Laws 318–22 (February 25, 1907).

71 Regular meeting, Portland City Council, November 27, 1907, 70, Portland City Council minutes, vol. 27, "October 23, 1907–April 13, 1908," microfilm reel 51, Portland Archives and Records Center, Portland, Oregon.

72 Esther Pohl Lovejoy to Mrs. Medill McCormick, n.d. (ca. 1916), Khedouri Materials.

73 Special meeting, Portland Health Board, November 6, 1907, 247, CPBH; Pohl, "Report to Honorable Mayor and Board of Health," 1907, 8–9; Pohl, "Report to Honorable Mayor and Board of Health," 1908, 4, 5; "Dr. Pohl Declares Need of Emergency Hospital," *Oregon Journal*, July 16, 1908, 4.

74 "Dr. Pohl Declares Need," 4.

75 "Portland Dairies That Breed Disease," *Oregon Journal*, December 22, 1907, 2:8.

76 Dana, *Newspaper Story*, 100.

77 "Wants Milk Law," *Oregonian*, December 12, 1908, 16; "Let Us Be Sure of Pure Milk," *Oregon Journal*, October 29, 1908, 8.

78 "Better Milk Bill Passed," *Oregon Journal*, March 24, 1909, 2; Esther Pohl, "Milk Is the Most Important Food Product in the World," typescript speech, [1912], 3, box 1, folder 8, EPL 2001–004; "Ordinance No. 19090, An Ordinance Relating to the Maintenance of Dairies and to Regulate the Selling of Milk..." box 1, folder 8, EPL 2001–004.

79 "Milk Plague Gathers in the Babies," *Oregon Journal*, August 29, 1909, 1.

80 Stella Walker Durham, "The Portland Pure Milk War: The Story of a Victory Won by a City's Housewives," *Good Housekeeping* 50, no. 4 (April 1910): 518; Nathan, *Epoch-Making Movement*, 200.

81 "Death Due to Impure Milk: Dr. Esther C. Pohl Blames Poor System of Inspection for Disease Which Killed Her Son and Sent Herself and Sister to Hospital," *Oregon Journal*, August 30, 1909, 1.

82 "Health Board Leads Milk Crusade," *Oregon Journal*, September 14, 1909, 1; "Bailey's Duty Is to Clean Dairies," *Oregon Journal*, September 22, 1909, 1, 3; "Nurses Will Aid Milk Crusade," *Oregon Journal*, September 27, 1909, 2; "Milk Supply Shown to Be Very Bad," *Oregon Journal*, September 30, 1909, 1, 4; "Grand Jury Inspects Dairies," *Oregon Journal*, November 24, 1909, 1; "Council Passes Pure Milk Ordinance at Morning Session," *Oregon Journal*, November 24, 1909, 1.

83 Pohl, "Milk Is Most Important," 4, 5.

84 Esther Lovejoy, "Democracy and Health," in *Democracy in Reconstruction*, ed. Frederick A. Cleveland and Joseph Schafer (New York: Houghton Mifflin, 1919), 189–90.

85 Pohl, "Milk Is Most Important," 2.

86 Ibid.

87 Maureen Flanagan, *Seeing with Their Hearts: Chicago Women and the Vision of the Good City, 1871–1933* (Princeton, NJ: Princeton University Press, 2002), 86.

88 Pohl, "Report to Honorable Mayor and Board of Health," 1907; Pohl, "Report to Honorable Mayor and Board of Health," 1908; Esther C. Pohl,

"Portland's Health Record," (Portland) *Chamber of Commerce Bulletin* 8, no. 4 (April 1908): 15.

89 "Dr. Pohl Assails Her Predecessor," *Oregonian* January 22, 1909, 12.

90 Ibid.

91 "Portland Has a Quarter Million," *Oregon Journal*, January 24, 1909, 10.

92 "Proves Her Case by Dr. Wheeler," *Oregon Journal*, January 26, 1909, 8.

93 "Doctors Tilt in Police Court," *Oregon Journal*, March 30, 1906, 2.

94 "Criticises Dr. Pohl," *Oregonian*, January 25, 1909, 8.

95 "Esther C. Pohl, M.D., Health Officer, to Honorable Mayor and Board of Health, City Hall," April 30, 1909, box 1, folder 3, EPL 2001–004.

96 "Dr. E. C. Pohl Resigns," *Oregonian*, May 2, 1909, 9; "Dr. Pohl Is Eager to Resign," *Oregon Journal*, May 1, 1909, 1.

97 Lansing, *Portland*, 273–74.

98 "Name Dr. Wheeler," *Oregonian*, June 21, 1909, 14.

99 Esther Pohl Lovejoy to Anna Howard Shaw, May 3, 1914, 1, Khedouri Materials.

100 "A.M.A. Committee for Public Health Education among Women," *Woman's Medical Journal* 21, no. 9 (September 1911): 206–8.

5. WOMEN, POLITICS, AND POWER

Material from this chapter was originally published in a slightly different form in Kimberly Jensen, "'Neither Head nor Tail to the Campaign': Esther Pohl Lovejoy and the Oregon Woman Suffrage Victory of 1912," *Oregon Historical Quarterly* 108, no. 3 (Fall 2007): 350–83. Reprinted by permission of the author and the publisher.

1 Esther Pohl Lovejoy to Mrs. Medill McCormick, [ca. 1916], Amy Khedouri Materials, Scottsdale, Arizona; Kristie Miller, *Ruth Hanna McCormick: A Life in Politics, 1880–1944* (Albuquerque: University of New Mexico Press, 1992).

2 G. Thomas Edwards, *Sowing Good Seeds: The Northwest Suffrage Campaigns of Susan B. Anthony* (Portland: Oregon Historical Society Press, 1990); Rebecca J. Mead, *How the Vote Was Won: Woman Suffrage in the Western United States, 1868–1914* (New York: New York University Press, 2004); Kimberly Jensen, "'Neither Head nor Tail to the Campaign': Esther Pohl Lovejoy and the Oregon Woman Suffrage Victory of 1912," *Oregon Historical Quarterly* 108, no. 3 (Fall 2007): 350–83; Kimberly Jensen, "Woman Suffrage in Oregon," Oregon Encyclopedia, http://oregonencyclopedia.org/entry/view/woman_suffrage_in_oregon, accessed September 16, 2011.

3 Sara Hunter Graham, *Woman Suffrage and the New Democracy* (New Haven: Yale University Press, 1996).

4 Deborah M. Olsen, "Fair Connections: Women's Separatism and the Lewis and Clark Exposition of 1905," *Oregon Historical Quarterly* 109, no. 2 (Summer 2008): 174–203; Carl Abbott, *The Great Extravaganza: Portland and the Lewis and Clark Exposition* (Portland: Oregon Historical Society, 1981).

5 *HWS* 5:117–50; "The Portland Session," *Journal of the American Medical Association* 44, no. 25 (June 24, 1905), 1998; "The Portland A.M.A. Meeting," *Northwest Medicine* (Old Series) 3, no. 8 (August 1905): 243–46.

6 National American Woman Suffrage Association, *Thirty-Seventh Annual Convention of the National American Woman Suffrage Association: June 28 to July 5, 1905* (Portland, OR: Gotshall Printing, 1905), 4; "Ladies Committee for the AMA Convention," *Medical Sentinel* 13, no. 7 (July 1905), 146; *HWS* 5:134; "Woman Suffragists to Be Entertained," *Oregon Journal*, July 7, 1905, 5.

7 Lovejoy to McCormick, [ca. 1916].

8 *Thirty-Seventh Annual Convention*; *HWS* 5:117–50; "N.A.W.S.A. Convention," *Woman's Tribune*, July 8, 1905, 45; Edwards, *Sowing Good Seeds*, 216–44.

9 "Dr. Esther C. Pohl Addresses the A.N.E.S.A.," *Oregon Journal*, July 9, 1905, 15.

10 "Ladies Committee for the A.M.A. Convention," *Medical Sentinel* 13, no. 7 (July 1905): 146; AMA committee list, *Medical Sentinel* 13, no. 7 (July 1905): 231–33; "The Portland (Oregon) Woman's Medical Society and the Portland Medical Meeting," *Woman's Medical Journal* 15, no. 8 (August 1905): 181; "Entertained the Ladies," *Medical Sentinel* 13, no. 8 (August 1905): 289–90.

11 Born in England in 1847, Shaw immigrated with her family to Massachusetts and then to Michigan. She graduated from Boston University Divinity School in 1878, and from Boston University Medical School in 1888. Shaw was vice president of NAWSA from 1892 to 1904 under her suffrage mentor, Susan B. Anthony, and president of NAWSA from 1904 to 1915. See Anna Howard Shaw, *The Story of a Pioneer* (New York: Harper and Brothers, 1915); Trisha Franzen, "Singular Leadership: Anna Howard Shaw, Single Women, and the US Suffrage Movement," *Women's History Review* 17, no. 3 (September 2008): 419–34; and Franzen's forthcoming biography of Shaw.

12 "The National Convention," *Woman's Tribune*, July 8, 1905, 46; "Equal Suffrage Fight in Oregon," *Oregon Journal*, July 2, 1905, 10; "Women's Fight

for Ballot in Oregon," *Oregon Journal*, July 3, 1905, 9; Edwards, *Sowing Good Seeds*, 231–35.

13 Jensen, "Woman Suffrage in Oregon."

14 "Equal Suffrage Plans," *Oregonian*, August 1, 1905, 11; "Report Progress on Suffrage Petition," *Oregon Journal*, August 13, 1905, 17.

15 "Suffrage Petitions Are Popular," *Oregon Journal*, August 20, 1905, 17; "Suffrage Work in Oregon," *Woman's Tribune*, August 26, 1905, 58.

16 "Equal Suffrage Campaign Is On," *Oregonian*, November 9, 1905, 10; Sarah A. Evans wrote the section on Oregon for the sixth volume of the *History of Woman Suffrage*, Sarah A. Evans, "Oregon," *HWS* 6:541, note 2.

17 "Duniway, Coe, Cartwright, Evans, and Pohl to Dear Friend," May 16, 1906, series B, OSESA Records, 1872–1915, box 3, folder 5, "Correspondence and General Records, 1904–1912," Abigail Scott Duniway Papers, MSS 432, Oregon Historical Society Research Library, Portland, Oregon.

18 "Suffrage Petitions Filed with Secretary," *Oregon Journal*, December 14, 1905, 10.

19 "Conference on Suffrage," *Oregonian*, April 3, 1906, 14; "Equal Suffrage Conference," *Woman's Tribune*, April 14, 1906, 30–31, quote 31; "50 Attend First Session," *Oregon Journal*, April 4, 1906, 1.

20 Esther C. Pohl, "Letter to the Editor," *Oregon Journal*, May 4, 1906, 6; Esther C. Pohl, "Letter to the Editor," *Portland Evening Telegram*, May 29, 1906, 6.

21 Margaret Finnegan, *Selling Suffrage: Consumer Culture and Votes for Women* (New York: Columbia University Press, 1999), 12.

22 In addition to Finnegan, see Mead, *How the Vote Was Won*; Shanna Stevenson, *Women's Votes, Women's Voices: The Campaign for Equal Rights in Washington* (Tacoma: Washington State Historical Society, 2009); Jennifer M. Ross-Nazzal, *Winning the West for Women: The Life of Suffragist Emma Smith DeVoe* (Seattle: University of Washington Press, 2011); and Gayle Gullett, *Becoming Citizens: The Emergence and Development of the California Women's Movement, 1880–1911* (Urbana: University of Illinois Press, 2000).

23 "Notes from Oregon," *Progress*, March 2, 1906, n.p.; Anna Howard Shaw to Alice Stone Blackwell, April 18, 1906, Shaw, Anna Howard, 1888–1914, box 27, reel 18, "General Correspondence, 1839–1961," Records of the National American Woman Suffrage Association, Manuscript Division, Library of Congress, Washington, DC.

24 "Notes from Oregon."

25 *HWS* 6:542.

26 "The Oregon Campaign," *Woman's Journal*, May 19, 1906, 77.

27 *HWS* 6:542.

28 "Oregon Notes," *Woman's Journal*, May 26, 1906, 81; "The Oregon Suffrage Campaign," *Woman's Journal*, June 9, 1906, 89.

29 "Big Made-in-Oregon Parade Voted Success by Thousands," *Oregon Journal*, May 26, 1906, 3; "Parade Proves Big Attraction," *Oregonian*, May 26, 1906, 1, 10.

30 "The Oregon Suffrage Campaign," *Woman's Journal*, June 9, 1906, 89; "Parade Proves Big Attraction," 10; "Suffragists Win Friends and Cash Donations," *Oregon Journal*, May 27, 1906, 7; "Equal Suffrage Meeting," *Oregonian*, May 27, 1906, 18.

31 "Will Picket Polls," *Oregonian*, May 31, 1906, 9; Shaw, *Story of a Pioneer*, 292. In 1908, by initiative, petition voters passed the Corrupt Practices Act, which regulated campaign funds and put an end to campaigning and leafleting near the polls on election day. Jewel Lansing, *Portland: People, Politics, and Power, 1851–2001* (Corvallis: Oregon State University Press, 2003), 270–71.

32 "Will Picket Polls"; "The Oregon Election," *Woman's Journal*, June 16, 1906, 94.

33 Shaw, *Story of a Pioneer*, 292.

34 Anna Shaw to Esther Pohl, January 7, 1907, 4, Khedouri Materials; "Insults for None," *Oregonian*, June 5, 1906, 8; "Women Work at the Polls," *Oregon Journal*, June 4, 1906, 1, 2; "Oregon Women Active at Polls Today," *Portland Evening Telegram*, June 4, 1906, 1, 8.

35 "Insults for None," 5; "Oregon Women Active at Polls," 8; "Women Work at Polls," 2.

36 "Vote Promises to Be a Large One," *Portland Evening Telegram*, June 4, 1906, 2; "Oregon Women Active at Polls," 8.

37 Shaw to Pohl, January 7, 1907, 3.

38 Jensen, "'Neither Head nor Tail,'" 356–58; Mead, *How the Vote Was Won*, 102–6; Edwards, *Sowing Good Seeds*, 262–93.

39 Oregon Secretary of State, *A Pamphlet Containing a Copy of All Measures . . . at the General Election to Be Held on the Eighth Day of November, 1910, Together with the Arguments Filed* (Salem: Oregon State Printer, 1910), 3; *HWS* 6:544.

40 Ernestine Strandborg to Esther Lovejoy, March 1, 1946, box 2b, folder 19, "Lovejoy, Esther Pohl, Posthumous Papers and Biographical Information," AWH Records.

41 Anna Shaw to Esther Pohl, January 10, 1911, Khedouri Materials.

42 "Notable Meeting," *Oregon Journal*, February 5, 1912, 2; Esther Pohl, "Madame Chairman, Mr. Toastmaster, and Fellow-citizens," speech to

University of Oregon Alumnae Association, [February 1912], Khedouri Materials.

43 Lancaster Pollard, *A History of the State of Washington*, vol. 3 (New York: American Historical Society, 1937), 42–43; "Hofer to Talk to Business Men," *Oregonian*, January 18, 1912, 7; "Suffragists Get Married," *Oregonian*, August 9, 1912, 16.

44 George Albert Lovejoy and Esther Clayson Pohl, marriage registration 1912–09–022561, July 30, 1912, Victoria, British Columbia, Department of Vital Statistics, British Columbia Archives, microfilm B11370. See "Suffragists Get Married," 16.

45 "Suffragists Get Married," 16.

46 Jensen, "'Neither Head nor Tail,'" 350, 366–67.

47 See Mead, *How the Vote Was Won*; Ross-Nazzal, *Winning the West for Women*; Stevenson, *Women's Votes, Women's Voices;* and Gullett, *Becoming Citizens.*

48 John Milton Cooper, *Pivotal Decades: The United States, 1900–1920* (New York: W. W. Norton, 1990), 188.

49 Rebecca Edwards, "Pioneers at the Polls: Woman Suffrage in the West," in *Votes for Women: The Struggle for Suffrage Revisited*, ed. Jean Baker (New York: Oxford University Press, 2002), 99; Edwards, *Angels in the Machinery: Gender in American Party Politics from the Civil War to the Progressive Era* (New York: Oxford University Press, 1997).

50 Jensen, "'Neither Head nor Tail,'" 359–67.

51 "Laws Held Unfair: Pioneer Men and Women Discuss Equal Suffrage," *Oregonian*, April 7, 1912, 15.

52 Jensen, "'Neither Head nor Tail,'" 368; Regular meeting, Portland Woman's Club, January 12, 1912, 269, box 1, folder 8, "May 1905–Oct. 1912," PWC; "Report of the Woman's Club Suffrage Campaign Committee for the Period of Feb. 20 to Nov. 5, Inclusive," scrapbook, 1906–1914, box 13, folder 63, PWC. Anna Shaw to Esther Pohl, February 7, 1912, Khedouri Materials; Anna Shaw to Esther C. Pohl, February 29, 1912; Khedouri Materials.

53 "Novel League Forms: Everybody's Organization Is Popular in Oregon," *Oregonian*, October 23, 1912, 20; "Mrs. Belmont Sends Coin," *Oregonian*, October 28, 1912, 1.

54 "Suffrage League Is Gaining Rapidly," *Oregon Journal*, October 24, 1912, 13.

55 "Mrs. Belmont Sends Coin," 1; *HWS* 6:548.

56 "Suffragists Arrange Meetings," *Oregonian*, January 29, 1912, 7.

57 "Notable Meeting," *Oregon Journal*, February 5, 1912, 2; "Asks Transpor-

tation Club to Aid Suffrage," *Portland Evening Telegram*, July 25, 1912, 8; "Oregon Urged to Act," *Oregonian*, August 18, 1912, 7; "Colored Suffragists Meet Tonight," *Oregonian*, September 16, 1912, 9.

58 See, for example, "Oregon Urged to Act," *Oregonian*, August 18, 1912, 7.

59 For example, see "Asks Transportation Club to Aid Suffrage," 8.

60 Esther Pohl Lovejoy, "Mr. Chairman, Men, and Women of the Oregon Grange," [August 1912], Khedouri Materials.

61 Esther C. Pohl, "An Argument for Woman Suffrage," (Salem) *Capital Journal*, May 18, 1912, 6.

62 Ibid.

63 Ibid.

64 "Suffrage Literature Is Flooding Oregon," *Portland Evening Telegram*, March 13, 1912, 3; "Oregon Women Are in Race for Votes," *Woman's Journal*, April 6, 1912, 106–7; and "Report of the Woman's Club Campaign Committee."

65 "Women Appeal to Fans," *Oregonian*, April 14, 1912, 15.

66 "Women Urge Suffrage," *Oregonian*, February 24, 1912, 4.

67 "Suffrage Advertised on Theater Curtain," *Portland Evening Telegram*, February 27, 1912, 7; "What Suffragists Are Doing," *Oregon Journal*, October 21, 1912, 11.

68 "What Suffragists Are Doing," 11.

69 Graham, *Woman Suffrage*, 60–61.

70 "Women Workers on Tour," *Oregonian*, October 20, 1912, 13.

71 "Votes-for-Women Ballyho Wagon," *Portland Evening Telegram*, June 8, 1912, 2; "Suffrage Sandwiches Go Like Hotcakes," *Portland Evening Telegram*, June 12, 1912, 10; "Buns to Boost Suffrage," *Oregonian*, June 10, 1912, 10; "Suffragists to Send Out Lunch Truck," *Oregon Journal*, June 10, 1912, 9.

72 "Suffrage Sandwiches," 10.

73 "Votes for Women are Made by Sandwiches," *Portland Evening Telegram*, June 13, 1912, 3; "Orpheum Bills Big Star," *Oregonian*, June 9, 1912, 4:2.

74 "Suffragists in Parade," *Oregonian*, June 13, 1912, 13.

75 Shaw, *Story of a Pioneer*, 299–303.

76 "Anna Shaw No Admirer of T. R.," *Pendleton East Oregonian*, September 23, 1912, 1.

77 Shaw, *Story of a Pioneer*, 300–301; "Dr. Shaw Finds People Not Satisfied with President Taft," *Pendleton East Oregonian*, September 28, 1912, 2; "Big Show Pleases," *Oregonian*, September 29, 1912, 7.

78 "Woman of World Prominence Here," *Oregonian*, September 29, 1912, 16; "Suffrage Leader Sways Crowd in Stirring Address," *Oregon Journal*, September 29, 1912, 1, 9.

79 "Another Fine Tribute Paid Suffragist," *Oregon Journal*, September 30, 1912, 5; "Hundreds at Luncheon to Suffragist Leader," *Portland Evening Telegram*, September 30, 1912, 3; "Absolute Belief Inspires Leader," *Oregonian*, October 2, 1912, 9; "Anna Shaw Tells Why She Is Working for the Women," *Portland News*, October 2, 1912, 8.

80 "Report of the Woman's Club Suffrage Committee."

81 Lovejoy, "Handy Note Book," box 8, EPL 2001–011.

82 Oregon Secretary of State, *Biennial Report of the Secretary of State of the State of Oregon to the Twenty-Seventh Legislative Assembly, 1913* (Salem: Oregon State Printer, 1912), 73.

83 Esther Pohl-Lovejoy, "Oregon's Sudden Conversion," *Woman's Progressive Weekly*, February 15, 1913, 8–9.

84 Katherine H. Adams and Michael J. Keene, *Alice Paul and the American Suffrage Campaign* (Urbana: University of Illinois Press, 2008), 141–48; Christine Lunardini, *From Equal Suffrage to Equal Rights: Alice Paul and the National Woman's Party, 1910–1928* (New York: New York University Press, 1986), 60–70; "Suffragists Vote to Oppose New Bill," *New York Times*, August 30, 1914, 13; Alice Paul to George E. Chamberlain, October 1, 1914, series I, correspondence, reel 12, "National Woman's Party Papers: The Suffrage Years, 1913–1920," (NWP Papers), Library of Congress, Microfilm Division, Microfilming Corporation of America, 1981.

85 "Anna Howard Shaw Sends Out Letter Strongly Denouncing Action of Women," *Oregon Journal*, September 20, 1914, 6.

86 "An Appeal to the Women Voters," *Suffragist*, September 19, 1914, 3.

87 Stubbs was legislative secretary and treasurer for the Illinois Suffrage Association and a state organizer for the suffrage association of New York State. "Departure of the Campaigners," *Suffragist*, September 19, 1914, 4–5; Larry Anderson, *Benton MacKaye: Conservationist, Planner, and Creator of the Appalachian Trail* (Baltimore: Johns Hopkins University Press, 2002), 78–86; "Additional Organizers Leave for the West," *Suffragist*, September 26, 1914, 5; Jessie Hardy Stubbs to Alice Paul, September 24, 1914, 2, reel 12, NWP Papers. Biographical information on Arnold may be found with her photographic entry number MNWP 147008, at Photographs from the Records of the National Woman's Party, Library of Congress, Washington, DC, at http://hdl.loc.gov/loc.mss/mnwp.147008, accessed May 13, 2012.

88 Jessie Hardy Stubbs to Alice Paul, September 20, 1914, reel 12, NWP Papers.

89 Jessie Hardy Stubbs to Esther Pohl Lovejoy, September 22, 1914, Khedouri Materials.

90 Jessie Hardy Stubbs to Alice Paul, October 5, 1914, 1914, reel 12, NWP Papers.

91 Esther Pohl Lovejoy to Anna Howard Shaw, December 6, 1914, Khedouri Materials.

92 Nancy F. Cott, *The Grounding of Modern Feminism* (New Haven: Yale University Press, 1987), 112.

93 "Women Steadfast in Opposing Fight upon Geo. E. Chamberlain," *Oregon Journal*, September 24, 1914, 20.

94 "Chamberlain Given a Hearty Reception by Portland Women," *Oregon Journal*, October 20, 1914, 4; "Democratic Women Praise Chamberlain and Indorse Flegel," *Oregon Journal*, October 22, 1914, 15.

95 "Democratic Women Praise Chamberlain," 15.

96 Esther Pohl Lovejoy to Anna Howard Shaw, December 6, 1914, Khedouri Materials.

97 "Eastern Interlopers Scorned by Women Regardless of Party," *Oregon Journal*, October 9, 1914, 13.

98 Stubbs to Paul, September 20, 1914, NWP Papers. Stubbs wrote to organizer Doris Stevens, "I keep it *tight* here that the grand suite of rooms is given to me free." Jessie Hardy Stubbs to "Dearest Dodo" [Doris Stevens], September 21, 1914, NWP Papers.

99 Esther Pohl Lovejoy to Anna Howard Shaw, December 6, 1914, Khedouri Materials; Esther Pohl Lovejoy to Anna Howard Shaw, May 30, 1916, Khedouri Materials.

100 "Women's Fight on Democrats Opens," *Oregonian*, September 19, 1914, 13; "Oregon Women Will Oppose Democrats," *Portland Evening Telegram*, September 19, 1914, 18.

101 "Women Steadfast," 20.

102 Lovejoy to Shaw, May 30, 1916.

103 "Fund Source Is Given," *Oregonian*, October 30, 1914, 21.

104 Esther Pohl Lovejoy to Anna Howard Shaw, December 6, 1914, Khedouri Materials. Chamberlain won 111,748 votes; Republican R. A. Booth, 88,297; Progressive Party candidate William Hanley, 26,220; Socialist candidate B. F. Ramp, 10,666, and H. S. Stine, Prohibition Party candidate 8,649. Oregon Secretary of State, *Oregon Blue Book and Official Directory, 1915–1916* (Salem: State Printing Department, 1916), 136–37.

105 Jessie Hardy Stubbs to Alice Paul, October 27, 1914, NWP Papers.

106 Lunardini, *Equal Suffrage*, 67.

107 "Suffrage Union Spikes Enemy Guns," *Oregonian*, September 16, 1915, 4; "Behave Like Gentlemen, Suggestion to Women," *San Francisco Chronicle*,

September 16, 1915, 1; "Suffrage Plea, Three Miles Long, Off Tonight," *San Francisco Call*, September 16, 1915, 7. My sincere thanks to Michael Helquist for providing references about the conference from San Francisco newspapers.

108 "Women Voters in an Uproar," *San Francisco Examiner*, September 16, 1915, 6.

109 "Suffrage Union Spikes," 4.

110 Rosalyn Terborg-Penn, *African American Women in the Struggle for the Vote, 1850–1920* (Bloomington: Indiana University Press, 1998), 107–35, quote 132.

111 Graham, *Woman Suffrage*, 85–98; Maud Wood Park, *Front Door Lobby* (Boston: Beacon Press, 1960); "Congressional Chairmen," *National American Woman Suffrage Association Headquarters News Letter*, December 30, 1916, 8.

112 Esther Pohl Lovejoy to Carrie Chapman Catt, January 10, 1917, Khedouri Materials; Esther Pohl Lovejoy to Anna Howard Shaw, March 11, 1917, Khedouri Materials; "Suffrage Body Forms," *Oregonian*, December 14, 1916, 19; "Suffragists Plan Aid," *Oregonian*, January 10, 1917, 15.

113 Lovejoy to Catt, January 10, 1917.

114 "Women Voice Loyalty," *Oregonian*, March 1, 1917, 8; "Carrie Chapman Catt Here to Help Women Mobilize for Service," *Oregon Journal*, May 25, 1917, 3.

115 "Women's Clubs," *Oregonian*, April 4, 1917, 12; "Women to Organize Aid" and "Women, Will You Help?" *Oregonian*, April 10, 1917, 8.

116 Carrie Chapman Catt and Nettie Rogers Shuler, *Woman Suffrage and Politics: The Inner Story of the Suffrage Movement* (New York: Charles Scribner's, 1923; repr., Seattle: University of Washington Press, 1969), 343–488; Graham, *Woman Suffrage*, 128–46; Senate Gives Way for Mrs. Thompson," *Oregonian*, January 14, 1920, 6.

117 Catt and Shuler, *Woman Suffrage and Politics*, 400; "Speeding the Emergency Corps," *Woman Citizen*, May 1, 1920, 1195, 1200.

118 "Suffrage Victory Is Celebrated by Women at Lunch," *Oregon Journal*, August 29, 1920, 3; "Suffragists Here Celebrate Victory," *Oregonian*, August 29, 1920, 1:20; "Women of Portland Celebrate Saturday," *Oregonian*, August 26, 1920, 1.

6. THE FIRST WORLD WAR AND TRANSNATIONAL ACTIVISM

1 Kimberly Jensen, *Mobilizing Minerva: American Women in the First World War* (Urbana: University of Illinois Press, 2008).

2 Dennis E. Hoffman and Vincent J. Webb, "Police Response to Labor Radicalism in Portland and Seattle, 1913–19," *Oregon Historical Quarterly* 87, no. 4 (Winter 1986): 341–65.

3 Kathleen Kennedy, *Disloyal Mothers and Scurrilous Citizens: Women and Subversion During World War* I (Bloomington: Indiana University Press, 1999); Christopher Capozzola, *Uncle Sam Wants You: World War I and the Making of the Modern American Citizen* (New York: Oxford University Press, 2008); Jensen, *Mobilizing Minerva*; Adam J. Hodges, "At War Over the Espionage Act in Portland: Dueling Perspectives from Kathleen O'Brennan and Agent William Bryon," *Oregon Historical Quarterly* 108, no. 3 (Fall 2007): 474–86; Robert Johnston, *The Radical Middle Class: Populist Democracy and the Question of Capitalism in Progressive Era Portland, Oregon* (Princeton: Princeton University Press, 2003), 99–114.

4 Johnston, *Radical Middle Class*, 42–45.

5 "Lane Repudiated by Entire State," *Oregonian*, March 6, 1917, 1, 6, quote 6.

6 Dr. Marie D. Equi, San Quentin, to Mr. C. E. S. Wood, San Francisco, April 10, 1921; "Warner" to Marie D. Equi, June 23, 1921; both at United States Department of Justice, Mail, and Files Division, "Department of Justice File on Dr. Marie Equi," copy at Lewis and Clark College Special Collections, Portland, Oregon.

7 Alan Dawley, *Changing the World: American Progressives in War and Revolution* (Princeton: Princeton University Press, 2003); Daniel T. Rogers, *Atlantic Crossings: Social Politics in a Progressive Age* (Cambridge, MA: Harvard University Press, 1998).

8 Ellen S. More, *Restoring the Balance: Women Physicians and the Profession of Medicine, 1850–1995* (Cambridge, MA: Harvard University Press, 1999), 122–26; and see Bertha Van Hoosen, "Looking Backward," *Journal of the American Medical Women's Association* 5, no. 10 (October 1950): 406–8.

9 Jensen, *Mobilizing Minerva*, 77–97.

10 Esther Pohl Lovejoy, *Women Physicians and Surgeons: National and International Organizations* (Livingston, NY: Livingston Press, 1939), 29–33; "Medical Women's National Association, Report of the Second Annual Meeting, New York City, June 5th and 6th," *Woman's Medical Journal* 27, no. 6 (June 1917): 140–43.

11 "Dr. Lovejoy Learns Opportunity in War for Woman Is Large," *Oregon Journal*, June 27, 1917, 7.

12 Lovejoy, *Women Physicians*, 33–34; "Opportunity in War for Women Is Large"; Meeting of the War Service Committee, Medical Women's National Association, June 9, 1917, box 30, folder 2, "Minutes, General and Executive Committee Meetings, 1917–1919," AWH Records; "Dr. Lovejoy's

Report, Children's Bureau," box 847, "Commission to France, World War I, Children's Bureau," folder 942, 11/08, p. 1, Record Group 200, "Records of the American National Red Cross, 1917–1934," National Archives II, College Park, Maryland. This report was also reprinted in the *Woman's Medical Journal* as "Official Report of Dr. Esther Clayton [*sic*] Lovejoy, Council of National Defense Circular 113," *Woman's Medical Journal* 28, no. 5 (May 1918): 109–13.

13 "Bertha Van Hoosen, President Medical Women's National Association, War Service Committee of the Medical Women's National Association, Meeting of June 9, 1917, New York City," box 3, folder 13, EPL 2001–011.

14 Emily Newell Blair, *The Woman's Committee United States Council of National Defense: An Interpretive Report, April 21, 1917, to February 27, 1919* (Washington, DC: US Government Printing Office, 1920); Penelope Brownell, ""The Women's Committees of the First World War: Women in Government, 1917–1919" (PhD diss., Brown University, 2002).

15 Meeting of the Presidents of National Organizations of Women, Tuesday, June 19, 1917; minutes of meetings of the Committee on Women's Defense Work, May 2, 1917–February 12, 1919; and weekly and monthly reports of the Committee on Women's Defense Work, May 12, 1917–October 15, 1918, 51–54, 62, all three of above sources available in National Archives Microfilm Publication M1074, Records of the Council of National Defense, Record Group 62, National Archives and Records Service, Washington, DC. Eliza M. Mosher, "Important Conference of Representatives of Women's Organizations at Washington, DC, June 19th, Called Together by the Woman's National Council of Defense," *Woman's Medical Journal* 27, no. 6 (June 1917): 134–35, quote 135.

16 Mosher, "Important Conference," 135; "Meeting of Presidents of National Organizations," 72; Lovejoy, *Women Physicians*, 34.

17 Minutes of meeting of executive committee, August 1, 1917, 147; minutes of the meetings of the Committee on Women's Defense Work; Ida Clyde Clarke, *American Women and the World War* (New York: D. Appleton, 1918), 38.

18 Kenneth A. J. McKenzie, "To Whom It May Concern," June 7, 1917, box 1, folder 3, AWH Records; and George E. Chamberlain to J. J. Jusserand, June 13, 1917, Amy Khedouri Materials, Scottsdale, Arizona.

19 Eliot Wadsworth to J. J. Jusserand, June 15, 1917, Khedouri Materials; Esther Lovejoy to J. J. Jusserand, June 16, 1917, Khedouri Materials.

20 J. J. Jusserand to Esther Lovejoy, June 18, 1917, Khedouri Materials; Esther Lovejoy to J. J. Jusserand, June 21, 1917, Khedouri Materials; Esther Lovejoy to Eliot Wadsworth, June 21, 1917, Khedouri Materials;

Eliot Wadsworth to Anna Howard Shaw, June 23, 1917, Khedouri Materials.

21 Esther Lovejoy to Edward Filene, n.d. box 1, folder 2A, EPL 2001–011.

22 "Mr. Folkes, Director of Department of Civil Affairs to Dr. Lucas, Chief of Children's Bureau, Employment of Dr. Esther Lovejoy, September 14, 1917," box 1, folder 2B, EPL 2001–011; "Mr. W. D. Smith, Secretarial Department, to Dr. Esther Lovejoy," October 1, 1917, box 1, folder 2B, EPL 2001–011.

23 The *Oregonian* reprinted portions of Lovejoy's letters. "Dr. Esther Lovejoy Given Commission," *Oregonian*, October 17, 1917, 10.

24 "The Fête at the Résidence Sociale in Honour of Docteur Esther Lovejoy," *American Women's Club of Paris Bulletin* 1, no. 21 (September 1924): 693.

25 Evelyne Diebolt, "Women and Philanthropy in France from the Sixteenth to the Twentieth Centuries," in *Women, Philanthropy, and Civil Society,* ed. Kathleen D. McCarthy (Bloomington: Indiana University Press, 2001), 45, 49.

26 Esther Pohl Lovejoy, *The House of the Good Neighbor* (New York: MacMillan, 1919), 3–29.

27 Jane Addams, "The Subjective Value of a Social Settlement" and "The Objective Value of a Social Settlement," in *Philanthropy and Social Progress: Seven Essays Delivered before the School of Applied Ethics, at Plymouth, Mass., during the Session of 1892,* ed. Bernard Bosanquet, Jane Addams, and Franklin Henry Giddings (New York: Thomas Y. Crowell, 1893): 1–26, 27–56.

28 Lovejoy, *Good Neighbor,* 5.

29 "Regular Session of the Portland Woman's Club, March 14, 1919," 105, bound volume, "Club 1917–1920," box 1, folder 10, PWC.

30 Jensen, *Mobilizing Minerva,* 113–14.

31 "Esther Lovejoy Report to Executives of the American Women's Hospitals," July 1, 1920, box 3, folder 20, "Lovejoy, E. P. Reports, 1920," AWH Records; Esther Lovejoy to Mathilda Wallin, February 9, 1923, box 1, folder 1:2, AWH Records; Lovejoy, *Women Physicians,* 66–67.

32 Lovejoy, *Good Neighbor,* 142.

33 Ibid., 151, 143.

34 Susan R. Grayzel, *Women's Identities at War: Gender, Motherhood, and Politics in Britain and France during the First World War* (Chapel Hill: University of North Carolina Press, 1999), 86–120, quote 103.

35 Gail Bederman, *Manliness and Civilization: A Cultural History of Gender and Race in the United States, 1880–1917* (Chicago: University of Chicago Press, 1995), 192–215.

36 Fred Lyman Adair, notes on "Birth Rate: France," taken from a 1917 article by G. LePage, "Note Sur le Relèvement de la Natalité Francaise," in *Le Revue Philanthropique* and *Transactions, Academy of Medicine*, April 17, 1917, copies in box 1, "SF Adair, Fred L. Birth and Death Rates in France (1912–1918)"; and Fred Lyman Adair, "Abortion," box 1, "SF Adair, Fred L., Abortion, Adair"; both in Fred Lyman Adair Papers, Herbert Hoover Presidential Library, West Branch, Iowa (Adair Papers).

37 Fred L. Adair, "The Development of Prenatal Care and Maternal Welfare Work in Paris under the Children's Bureau of the American Red Cross," 7, box 1, "Adair, Fred L. Prenatal Care," Adair Papers.

38 Adair, "Development of Prenatal Care," 10–11, 12.

39 Lovejoy, *Good Neighbor*, 77.

40 Ibid., 68–69.

41 Ibid., 70.

42 "Official Report of Dr. Lovejoy," 109–10.

43 Ibid., 110.

44 "Dr. Esther Lovejoy Will Return to This Country in February," *Oregon Journal*, January 20, 1918, 6; Homer Folks, "Dr. Lovejoy's Visit to America," letter to Dr. W. P. Lucas, January 3, 1918, box 1, folder 2B, EPL 2001–011; Homer Folks to Dr. Esther Lovejoy, January 3, 1918, box 1, folder 2B, EPL 2001–011.

45 "Minutes of the General Meeting of the American Women's Hospitals," February 7, 1918, box 30, folder 293, "Minutes, General and Executive Committee Meetings, 1917–1919," AWH Records. "Dr. Lovejoy's Report," minutes of the meeting of the Woman's Committee Council of National Defense, February 27, 1918, 381.

46 Kimberly Jensen, "Esther Pohl Lovejoy, M.D., the First World War, and a Feminist Critique of Wartime Violence," in *The Women's Movement in Wartime: International Perspectives, 1914–19*, ed. Alison Fell and Ingrid Sharp (London: Palgrave Macmillan, 2007), 175–93.

47 "Dr. Lovejoy to Ride in Air," *Oregonian*, April 29, 1919, 13; "She's Real 'Champ' at Bond Selling," *Washington Times*, April 30, 1919, 2:1.

48 Esther Lovejoy, "The Most Interesting Spot in the World," *Ladies' Home Journal* 35, no. 5 (May 1918): 75–76.

49 Esther Lovejoy to Marie-Jeanne Bassot, April 26, 1919, box 3, folder 17, EPL 2001–011; "Dr. Lovejoy Helps Sale," *Oregonian*, April 25, 1919, 15. Esther Lovejoy, "Democracy and Health," *Woman's Medical Journal* 29, no. 6 (June 1919): 116–24.

50 Jensen, "Lovejoy and a Feminist Critique of Wartime Violence," 184–89.

51 Lovejoy, *Good Neighbor*, 146; "Liberty Loan Meetings Held in Benton County," (Corvallis) *Gazette-Times*, September 16, 1918, 1.

52 Lovejoy, *Good Neighbor*, 145, 147.

53 "Official Report of Dr. Lovejoy," 112.

54 This was from Lovejoy's speech on May 8 to the General Federation of Women's Clubs in Arkansas. Esther Lovejoy, "Red Cross Abroad," typescript of speech, May 8, box 3, folder 20, "Lovejoy, Esther Pohl, Papers," 1920, AWH Records. Also see Esther Lovejoy, "The Red Cross Abroad," General Federation of Women's Clubs, *General Federation of Women's Clubs Fourteenth Biennial Convention, Official Report* (1918): 430–44.

55 Lovejoy, *Good Neighbor*, 6–7.

56 Ibid., 17.

57 Ibid., 172.

58 Ibid., 173.

59 "Official Report of Dr. Lovejoy," 110.

60 "Liberty Loan Meetings," 1.

61 Lovejoy, *Good Neighbor*, 180.

62 Ibid., 179.

63 Ibid., 180.

64 Lovejoy, "Red Cross Abroad," 5.

65 "Dr. Lovejoy's Speech Thrills," *Rogue River Courier*, September 10, 1918, 1.

66 Lovejoy, *Good Neighbor*, 148.

67 Ibid., 215.

68 "Decorated in France," *Northwest Medicine* (New Series) 18, no. 10 (October 1919): 214.

69 Mary Merritt Crawford to Esther Lovejoy, January 2, 1919, box 1, folder 1, AWH Records.

70 Lovejoy to Bassot, April 26, 1919, 4–5.

71 David M. Kennedy, *Over Here: The First World War and American Society* (New York: Oxford University Press, 1980), 150, 166–67. Voluntary organizations, including the Red Cross, appealed the policy. In August 1918, general John Pershing relented on part of the policy and agreed that a sister of a man in the American Expeditionary Force could serve in the Red Cross, Salvation Army, Knights of Columbus, and the Young Men's Christian Association "only if she is specially qualified by training for the post she is to fill." "Sisters Can Come as Relief Workers," *Stars and Stripes*, August 9, 1918, 2.

72 Esther Lovejoy to Mr. Lester, September 3, 1918, box 3, folder 17, EPL 2001–011.

73 Esther Pohl Lovejoy, "From the Beginning of the War," speech, n.d., box 3,

folder 17, EPL 2001–011.

74 "Third Annual Meeting, Medical Women's National Association, Chicago, Ill., June 10–11, 1918," *Woman's Medical Journal* 28, no. 6 (June 1918): 135–38.

75 "The Tragic Line of Rapatriés," *Woman's Medical Journal* 28, no. 6 (June 1918): 128–32.

76 "Third Annual Meeting, MWNA," 136; "Report of the Fourth Annual Meeting of the Medical Women's National Association Held in Atlantic City, June 9–10, 1919," *Woman's Medical Journal* 29, no. 7 (July 1919): 140.

77 "Dr. Esther Lovejoy: New Chairman of the American Women's Hospitals," *Woman's Medical Journal*, 29, no. 8 (August 1919): 163; Lovejoy, *Women Physicians*, 9.

78 Etta Gray to Esther Lovejoy, August 3, 1919, box 1, folder 1, AWH Records.

79 Esther Lovejoy to Mathilda Wallin, February 26, 1920, box 1, folder 1, AWH Records.

80 Jensen, *Mobilizing Minerva*, 77–115; More, *Restoring the Balance*, 122–47; Leah Leneman, "Medical Women at War, 1914–1918," *Medical History* 38, no. 2 (April 1994): 160–77; Jennian F. Geddes, "Deeds *and* Words in the Suffrage Military Hospital in Endell Street," *Medical History* 51, no. 1 (January 2007): 79–98; Esther Pohl Lovejoy, *Women Doctors of the World* (New York: Macmillan, 1957), 163, 277–307; Clelia Lollini, "The Italian Medical Women's Association," *Medical Woman's Journal* 29, no. 5 (May 1922): 82–84.

81 Esther P. Lovejoy, Martha Whelpton, and Kate Campbell Hurd-Mead, "The Medical Women's International Association," (n.d.), p. 1, box 27, folder "Minutes and Other Records, 1919–1924," Medical Women's International Association Collection, accession 271, Legacy Center, Drexel University College of Medicine, Philadelphia, Pennsylvania; International Conference of Women Physicians, *Proceedings of the International Conference of Women Physicians*, 6 vols. (New York: The Womans Press, 1920); Lovejoy, *Women Physicians*, 15–24; "Women Physicians and Women's Health: The Y.W.C.A. Conference," *Survey*, November 15, 1919, 110–11. The conference was organized by members of the War Work Council of the Young Women's Christian Association of the United States.

82 "A Memorable Occasion: Meeting of the East and the West—A Fraternal Renaissance," *Woman's Medical Journal* 29, no. 11 (November 1919): 225–26.

83 Lovejoy, Whelpton, and Hurd-Mead, "Medical Women's International Association," 3.

84 Jensen, *Mobilizing Minerva*, 80–84; More, *Restoring the Balance*; Leneman, "Medical Women at War," and Leneman, "Medical Women in the First

World War—Ranking Nowhere," *British Medical Journal* (December 18, 1993): 1592–94.

85 "Memorable Occasion," 226.

86 Marie Chard, MD, to "Dear Doctor," circular letter, [ca. 1920], box 96, folder "International Organisation Subcommittee, 1920–1924," Medical Women's Federation/Medical Women's International Association, accession SA MWF K1, The Wellcome Library, London, England.

87 Lovejoy et al., "Medical Women's International Association," 5–6; Lovejoy, *Women Physicians*, 15–24. The executive board included Lovejoy (United States), Christine Murrell (England), Lucie Thuillier-Landry (France), Kristine Munch (Norway), Marie Feyler (Switzerland), Martha Whelpton (United States), Ellen Potter (United States), Radmila Lazarevitch (Serbia), Alicia Moreau (Argentina), Daisy Robinson (United States), and Tomo Inouye (Japan). National Representatives included Alicia Moreau (Argentina), Grace Ritchie England (Canada), Ida Kahn (China), Christine Murrell (England), Lucie Thuillier-Landry (France), Ada Potter (Holland), Clelia Lollini (Italy), Tomo Inouye (Japan), Kristine Munch (Norway), Frances S. Johnston (Scotland), Radmila Lazarevitch (Serbia), Alma Sundquist (Sweden), Marie Feyler (Switzerland), Esther Lovejoy (United States), and Alice Armand Ugon (Uruguay).

88 "Jane Walker," *Lancet* 235 (November 26, 1938): 1259–61; *Oxford Dictionary of National Biography*, ed. H. C. G. Matthew and Brian Harrison, vol. 56 (London: Oxford University Press, 2004), s.v. "Walker, Jane Harriett."

89 Louisa Martindale, *A Woman Surgeon* (London: Victor Gollancz, 1951); "L. Martindale," *Medical Woman's Journal* 31 no. 6 (June 1921): 177–78; "Louisa Martindale," *British Medical Journal* (26 February 1966): 547–49; *Oxford Dictionary of National Biography*, vol. 37, s.v. "Martindale, Louisa." The Louisa Martindale Collection, MSS.3470–3487, housed at the Wellcome Library, London, details much of Martindale's life and work with the Medical Women's Federation and the Medical Women's International Association.

90 Christopher St. John, *Christine Murrell, M.D.: Her Life and Her Work* (London: Williams & Norgate, 1935); *Oxford Dictionary of National Biography*, vol. 40, s.v. "Murrell, Christine Mary"; Lucy Noakes, *Women in the British Army: War and the Gentle Sex, 1907–1948* (London: Routledge, 2006), 50–52.

91 Lovejoy, *Women Physicians*, 15–23; Christine Bard, *Les Filles de Marianne: Histoire des Féminismes, 1914–1940* (Paris: Fayard, 1995), 30, 180.

92 Mary Louise Roberts, *Civilization without Sexes: Reconstructing Gender in Postwar France, 1917–1927* (Chicago; University of Chicago Press, 1994), 184–87, 196–205.

93 Lovejoy, *Women Doctors*, 177–78.

94 Carlotta Hacker, *The Indomitable Lady Doctors* (Toronto: Clarke, Irwin & Company, 1974), 167; Lovejoy, *Women Physicians*, 15–17; "Dr. Grace Ritchie England," *Canadian Medical Association Journal* 58, no. 3 (March 1948): 305.

95 Asunción Lavrin, *Women, Feminism, and Social Change in Argentina, Chile, and Uruguay, 1890–1940* (Lincoln: University of Nebraska Press, 1995), 140–44, 321–52; Lovejoy, *Women Doctors*, 269.

96 Lovejoy, *Women Doctors*, 267; "Dr. Alicia Moreau," *International Woman Suffrage News* 14, no. 5 (February 1920): 70; Marifran Carlson, *¡Feminismo! The Woman's Movement in Argentina from Its Beginnings to Eva Perón* (Chicago: Academy Chicago Publishers, 1988), 133–35; Lavrin, *Women, Feminism, and Social Change*, 34–35, 44, 263–78.

97 "Delegates to the First International Conference of Women Physicians Held in New York City," *Outlook* 123 (October 1, 1919): 187; "Women Physicians Here from Abroad," *New York Times*, September 16, 1919, 28; Tomo Inouye to Esther Lovejoy, August 17, 1920, box 6, folder 20, EPL 2001–011; Lovejoy, *Women Doctors*, 236; and Nicholas S. Steneck, "Early Diversity in the Health Sciences at the University of Michigan," *Retrospectives: Health Care and the Health Sciences in Michigan*, newsletter 1:2.

98 Leila Rupp, *Worlds of Women: The Making of an International Women's Movement* (Princeton: Princeton University Press, 1997), 44.

7. CANDIDATE LOVEJOY AND A SHOPGIRL'S RISE

1 Sheila Tobias discusses the importance of war service in twentieth-century politics in "Shifting Heroisms: The Uses of Military Service in Politics," in *Women, Militarism, and War: Essays in History, Politics, and Social Theory*, ed. Jean Bethke Elshtain and Sheila Tobias (Savage, MD: Rowman & Littlefield, 1990), 163–85.

2 Fred Lockley, "Observations and Impressions of the Journal Man," *Oregon Journal*, September 25, 1920, 6.

3 These figures do not include the numbers of women who ran for local offices. Oregon Secretary of State, *Biennial Report of the Secretary of State of the State of Oregon to the Twenty-Eighth Legislative Assembly, Regular Session, 1915, for the Biennial Period Beginning October 1, 1912, Ending September 30, 1914* (Salem: Oregon State Printer, 1915), 89–102; Oregon Secretary of State, *Biennial Report of the Secretary of State of the State of Oregon to the Twenty-Ninth Legislative Assembly, Regular Session, 1917, for the Biennial Period Beginning October 1, 1914, Ending September 30, 1916* (Salem: Oregon State Printer, 1917), 107–26; Oregon Secretary of State, *Biennial Report*

of the Secretary of State of the State of Oregon to the Thirtieth Legislative
Assembly, Regular Session, 1919, for the Biennial Period Beginning October 1,
1916, Ending September 30, 1918 (Salem: Oregon State Printer, 1919), 68–79;
Oregon Secretary of State, Biennial Report of the Secretary of State of the
State of Oregon to the Thirty-First Legislative Assembly, Regular Session, 1921,
for the Biennial Period Beginning October 1, 1918, Ending September 30, 1920
(Salem: Oregon State Printer, 1921), 82–98.

4   Kimberly Jensen, "Revolutions in the Machinery: Oregon Women and
    Citizenship in Sesquicentennial Perspective," Oregon Historical Quarterly
    110, no. 3 (Fall 2009): 346–49.

5   Jensen, "Revolutions," 345–46.

6   Sophonisba P. Breckinridge, Women in the Twentieth Century: A Study of
    Their Political, Social, and Economic Activities (1933; New York: Arno Press,
    1972), 295–342; Jo Freeman, A Room at a Time: How Women Entered Party
    Politics (New York: Rowman and Littlefield, 2000).

7   E. D. Dover, "Parties and Elections," in Oregon Politics and Government: Pro-
    gressives Versus Conservative Populists, ed. Richard A. Clucas, Mark Henkels,
    and Brent S. Steel (Lincoln: University of Nebraska Press, 2005), 49–50.

8   "Dr. Lovejoy May Run for Congress," Oregon Journal, March 10, 1920, 1.

9   National American Woman Suffrage Association, Convention of the
    National American Suffrage Association and Congress of the League of Women
    Voters, 1920 (New York: National American Woman Suffrage Association,
    1920); "Teach Women How to Think Is Aim of New Organization," Oregon
    Journal, February 29, 1920, 12; "Women Voters' League to be Launched,"
    Oregon Journal, March 4, 1920, 13.

10 "Dr. Lovejoy Is Out for Congress: Pledges Herself to Child Welfare,"
    Oregon Journal, March 11, 1920, 1.

11 "Fifth Annual Meeting, Medical Women's National Association, New
    Orleans, La.," Medical Woman's Journal, 27, no 5 (May 1920): 131–41.

12 "Dr. Lovejoy Is Out for Congress," Oregon Journal, March 11, 1920, 1.

13 "Woman's Democratic Club Adopts New Constitution," Oregon Journal,
    April 26, 1920, 2; "Research Club at Political Pow-Wow," Oregon Journal,
    April 27, 1920, 10.

14 "Woman's Lovejoy-for-Congress Club Will be Organized," Oregon Journal,
    March 25, 1920, 3.

15 "Mrs. Thompson's Bonnet Is in Ring," Oregon Journal, April 14, 1920, 2.

16 Ibid.

17 "Mrs. Alexander Thompson," Oregon Voter, January 4, 1919, 64; "Our
    Woman Legislator," Oregon Voter, November 27, 1920, 16–21; "Death Takes
    Suffragist," Oregonian, February 25, 1950, 7.

18   Oregon Secretary of State, Oregon Legislators and Staff Guide, 1917
     Regular Session, 1919 Regular Session, 1920 Special Session, Oregon State
     Archives, http://arcweb.sos.state.or.us/legislative/histleg/statehood/
     statehood.htm, accessed September 30, 2011.

19   Oregon Legislative Assembly, Senate, Oregon, Legislative Assembly,
     House of Representatives, Journals of the Senate and House of the Thirtieth
     Legislative Assembly, 1920 (Salem: Oregon State Printer, 1920), 28; "Senate
     Gives Way for Mrs. Thompson," Oregonian, January 14, 1920, 6.

20   "Senate Gives Way for Mrs. Thompson," 6; "Live Meet Ahead for Demo-
     crats," Oregon Journal, April 29, 1920, 2; "Myers, Fired, Sore, Attacks
     Chamberlain," Oregon Journal, May 14, 1920, 1, 2.

21   "Brisk Voting is Feature of Primary," Oregon Journal, May 21, 1920, 1, 2.

22   Oregon State Archives, "Abstract of Votes Cast at the Primary Nomi-
     nating Election for the Democratic Party Held in Multnomah County,
     Oregon, on the Twenty-First Day of May, A.D. 1920," filed June 18, 1920,
     box 118, folder 1, accession 92A-24, Multnomah County, folder "Election
     Voting Abstracts, 1920, May, Democratic—US Senate, Representative and
     State," Oregon. Lovejoy contributed $839.88, former governor Oswald
     West, $50, and the Lovejoy for Congress Club, $245. Thompson was the
     sole donor to her campaign. Oregon Secretary of State, Biennial Report
     of the Secretary of State of the State of Oregon to the Thirty-First Legislative
     Assembly, Regular Session, 1921, for the Biennial Period Beginning October 1,
     1918, Ending September 30, 1920 (Salem: Oregon State Printer, 1921), 84.

23   "Dr. Lovejoy Is Confident She Will Win Seat," Oregon Journal, May 29,
     1920, 5.

24   Montagu Colmer, comp., History of the Bench and Bar of Oregon (Portland,
     OR: Historical Publishing Company, 1910), 175–76; "Hon. Clifton Nesmith
     McArthur," in Charles Henry Carey, History of Oregon, vol. 3 (Portland,
     OR: Pioneer Historical Publishing, 1922): 267–68; "C. N. M'Arthur
     Dies Suddenly," Oregonian, December 10, 1923, 1,4; "'Pat' Prominent in
     Sport," Oregonian, December 10, 1923, 4; "McArthur, Clifton Nesmith,
     (1879–1923)," in United States Congress, Biographical Directory of the
     United States Congress, http://bioguide.congress.gov/scripts/biodisplay.
     pl?index=M000298, accessed September 30, 2011.

25   "Hon. Clifton Nesmith McArthur," 267. For more on the league, see
     Christopher Capozzola, Uncle Sam Wants You: World War I and the Making
     of the Modern American Citizen (New York: Oxford University Press, 2008),
     117–43; Robert D. Ward, "The Origin and Activities of the National Secu-
     rity League, 1914–1919," Mississippi Valley Historical Review 47, no. 1 (June
     1960): 51–65.

26 "Dr. Lovejoy to Be Honor Guest at Lawn Fete," *Oregon Journal*, August 15, 1920, 4:4.

27 "Oregon Women Joyous Because Suffrage Wins in Tennessee," *Oregon Journal*, August 18, 1920, 1, 2.

28 "Roosevelt Has No Doubt Whatever," *Oregon Journal*, August 22, 1920, 1, 16.

29 "Lovejoy Campaign Gathers Momentum," *Oregon Labor Press*, October 30, 1920, 1.

30 "Dry Party Confirms Naming Dr. Lovejoy," *Oregonian*, September 9, 1920, 11; "Labor Notes," *Oregon Journal*, September 5, 1920, 2:5.

31 "Candidacy of Dr. Lovejoy Makes a Stir," *Oregon Labor Press*, September 25, 1920, 1; "Non-Partisans Formed to Advance Dr. Lovejoy Cause," *Oregon Journal*, September 26, 1920, 13.

32 "Non-Partisans Formed," 13.

33 "Candidacy of Dr. Lovejoy Makes a Stir," 1; "Non-Partisans Formed," 13.

34 "Labor Notes," *Oregon Journal*, September 26, 1920, 4:6.

35 "Democrats to Meet," *Oregon Journal*, September 27, 1920, 3; "M'Arthur Faces Strenuous Fight, Friends Realize," *Oregon Journal*, September 29, 1920, 4.

36 "Dr. Lovejoy Carries Her Campaign All Over County," *Oregon Journal*, October 10, 1920, 4.

37 They were among those that signed the general election letter to voters from the Lovejoy for Congress Club; Lovejoy for Congress Club letter, n.d., box 1, folder 2A, EPL 2001–011.

38 These figures are from a close reading of the *Oregon Journal*, the *Oregon Labor Press*, the *Portland News*, the *Oregonian*, and the *Spectator*.

39 "Meat Cutters Loudly Cheer for Dr. Lovejoy," *Portland News*, October 14, 1920, 13.

40 "Catholic Women's League," *Oregon Journal*, October 24, 1920, 4:6; "Dr. Lovejoy to Speak at Albina Library," *Portland News*, October 18, 1920, 7.

41 "Dr. Lovejoy Pledges Strong Support to the Prohibition Cause," *Oregon Journal*, September 29, 1920, 3.

42 "A Shopgirl's Rise," *Oregon Journal*, October 12, 1920, 10.

43 Lovejoy for Congress Club letter.

44 Fred Lockley, "Observations and Impressions of the Journal Man," *Oregon Journal*, August 8, 1920, 2:2; Lockley, "Observations and Impressions," September 19, 1920, 4:4; Lockley, "Observations and Impressions," September 22, 1920, 6; Lockley, "Observations and Impressions," September 25, 1920, 6; Lockley, "Observations and Impressions," September 27, 1920, 6.

45 "Building Laborers Hear Dr. Lovejoy Outline Aims," *Oregon Journal*, October 20. 1920, 3.

46 "Dr. Lovejoy Stirs Labor with Speech," *Oregon Labor Press*, September 11, 1920, 1.

47 "Lovejoy Campaign Gathers Momentum," *Oregon Labor Press*, October 30, 1920, 1.

48 "Meeting for Lovejoy Like Holy Crusade," *Portland News*, October 27, 1920, 14.

49 "Dr. Lovejoy Would Turn Light on Lower House," *Oregon Journal*, October 16, 1920, 3.

50 "Dr. Lovejoy Gives Political Views," *Oregon Journal*, August 16, 1920, 1, 2.

51 "Persons Who Cry Loudest Called Worst," *Portland News*, October 14, 1920, 3.

52 "Meat Cutters Loudly Cheer Dr. Lovejoy," *Portland News*, October 14, 1920, 13.

53 "Dr. Lovejoy Files for Nomination to Congress," *Oregon Journal*, April 8, 1920, 2.

54 "Bonus for Ex-Service Men Is Favored by Dr. Lovejoy," *Oregon Journal*, October 19, 1920, 17.

55 "Lovejoy for Congress" card, box 1, folder 2A, EPL 2011–011.

56 "Dr. Lovejoy Raps Her Opponents," *Oregon Journal*, August 17, 1920, 3.

57 "Dr. Lovejoy Stirs Labor with Speech," *Oregon Labor Press*, September 11, 1920, 1.

58 "Lovejoy for Congress" card.

59 "Social Justice Is Need of the Nation, Says Dr. Lovejoy," *Oregon Journal*, October 14, 1920, 3.

60 For more on prohibition and the WCTU in Oregon, see Carli Crozier Schiffner, "Continuing to 'Do Everything' in Oregon: The Woman's Christian Temperance Union, 1900–1945 and Beyond," (PhD diss., Washington State University, 2004); Dale E. Soden, "The Woman's Christian Temperance Union in the Pacific Northwest: A Different Side of the Social Gospel," in *Gender and the Social Gospel,* ed. Wendy J. Deichmann Edwards and Carolyn De Swarte Gifford (Urbana: University of Illinois Press, 2003): 103–15.

61 Esther Lovejoy, "Democracy and Health," in *Democracy in Reconstruction*, ed. Frederick A. Cleveland and Joseph Schafer (New York: Houghton Mifflin, 1919): 165–92, quote 186.

62 "Candidates Argue Campaign Issues," *Oregonian*, October 26, 1920, 1, 3.

63 "Persons Who Cry Loudest," 3.

64 "Fighting for Lovejoy," *Oregon Journal*, October 22, 1920, 10.

65 "M'Arthur Is Given Flaying by Minister," *Portland News*, October 9, 1920, 1.

66 "A Statement by Mr. McArthur," *Oregon Journal*, October 8, 1920, 10; "Mr. M'Arthur Challenged," *Oregon Journal*, October 9, 1920, 6.

67 Lulu M. Horning, "Replies to Charges of Pat McArthur," *Portland News*, October 20, 1920, 4.

68 "Meeting for Lovejoy Like Crusade," 14.

69 "Dr. Lovejoy Will Address Labor Unions Friday Eve," *Oregon Journal*, October 7, 1920, 3.

70 W. Thomas White, "Railroad Labor Relations in the Great War and After, 1917–1921," *Journal of the West* 25, no. 2 (April 1986): 36–43; Philip S. Foner, *History of the Labor Movement in the United States,* vol. 7, *Labor and World War I, 1914–1918* (New York: International Publishers, 1987), 149–50, 159.

71 White, "Railroad Labor Relations," 39; Philip S. Foner, *History of the Labor Movement in the United States,* vol. 8, *Power Struggles, 1918–1920* (New York: International Publishers, 1988), 16–19.

72 White, "Railroad Labor Relations," 39–40.

73 Ibid., 40.

74 "M'Arthur Mixes with Plumb League in Fiery Exchange," *Oregon Journal*, May 9, 1920, 6.

75 Horning, "Replies to Charges of Pat McArthur," 4.

76 "Take Him Out," *Portland News*, October 28, 1920, 4.

77 "Lovejoy Campaign Gathers Momentum," *Oregon Labor Press*, October 30, 1912, 1.

78 "M'Arthur Served with Talk Only; Declares Veteran," *Oregon Journal*, October 26, 1920, 3.

79 "M'Arthur Replies to Hannan Attack," *Oregon Journal*, October 27, 1920, 3.

80 "M'Arthur Is Called Falsifier," *Portland News*, October 13, 1920, 1.

81 "Dr. Lovejoy's Book Forced Off Display," *Oregon Labor Press*, October 23, 1920, 1.

82 Ibid., "Dr. Lovejoy to Be for Oregon First of All," *Portland News*, October 26, 1920, 11; "Parade Plans Finished," *Oregonian*, October 31, 1920, 19.

83 "Esther Pohl Lovejoy: Candidato Democratico e Proibizioni," *La Tribuna Italiana*, 29 Ottobre, 1920, 6.

84 "Mawsh Members," *Searchlight on Congress* 1, no. 9 (October 1916): 1.

85 "As Individuals," *Searchlight on Congress* 1, no. 9 (October 1916): 7–9.

86 "'The Third District in Congress' Five Reel Comedy Featuring MAWSH McArthur," "Reel 1: Mawsh on 'Public Welfare'"" *Oregon Journal*, October 22, 1920, 3; "Reel 2: Mawsh on 'Labor,'" *Oregon Journal*, October 23, 3; "Reel

3: Mawsh on 'Labor Some More,'" *Oregon Journal*, October 25, 9; "Reel 4: Mawsh, the Prohi and Suffragette," *Oregon Journal*, October 26, 12; "Reel 5: Climax: 'The Real Mawsh,'" *Oregon Journal*, October 27, 4.

87 "Oregonian Kills Ad in Behalf of Dr. Lovejoy," *Oregon Journal*, October 23, 1920, 2.

88 "Our Candidate and Her Work," "Article No. 1: A Business Program," *Oregon Journal*, October 27, 1920, 6; "Article No. 2: To the Women of Multnomah County," *Oregon Journal*, October 28, 15; "Article No. 3: To the Mothers and Fathers," *Oregon Journal*, October 29, 19; "Article No. 4: To the Moral Forces of Multnomah County," *Oregon Journal*, October 30, 8; "Article No. 5: To the Believers in True Democracy," *Oregon Journal*, October 31, 2:2; and the final installment, "Your Candidate and Her Work," *Oregon Journal*, November 1, 6.

89 Oregon Secretary of State, *Biennial Report, 1921*, 92.

90 "Dr. Lovejoy," *Portland News*, October 25, 1920, 4.

91 "She Deserves Election," *Oregon Journal*, October 29, 1920, 12.

92 "Oregon Needs Her in Congress; Give Your Vote to Dr. Lovejoy," *Portland News*, October 30, 1920, 14.

93 "Dr. Lovejoy Gets Dry Nomination," *Oregon Journal*, August 15, 1920, 1.

94 "A Woman for Congress," *Portland News*, October 27, 1920, 1.

95 "Take Him Out," 4.

96 "Mr. M'Arthur Is Asked for a Correction," *Oregon Journal*, October 14, 1920, 10.

97 "Dr. Lovejoy to Be for Oregon First," 11.

98 "Location of Polling Places in Multnomah," *Oregon Journal*, October 31, 1920, 2:2; "Dr. Lovejoy Exercising Franchise," *Oregon Journal*, November 2, 1920, 1.

99 John Milton Cooper, *Pivotal Decades: The United States, 1900–1920* (New York: W. W. Norton, 1990), 371–72.

100 Oregon Secretary of State, *Oregon Blue Book and Official Directory, 1921–1922* (Salem: Oregon State Printer, 1921), 173.

101 The secretary of state reprinted the approximate numbers of registrants by sex in the *Oregon Blue Book* from 1917 to 1924. The *Blue Book* figures do not include the 1920 primary or general elections, and so I have used the figures published by the *Oregon Journal* in October 1920 as a more close approximation of the totals. They may be found in "Registration Total 110, 632; Increase Over 1918 is 11,194," *Oregon Journal*, October 15, 1920, 9.

102 *Oregon Blue Book 1921–22*, 173.

103 "Tho Defeated, Dr. Lovejoy Is Still Smiling," *Portland News*, November 5, 1920, 16.

104 "Dr. Lovejoy Is the Best Little Loser," *Oregon Labor Press*, November 6, 1920, 1.

105 Esther Pohl Lovejoy union card from the Pacific Coast Metal Trades District Council, and Otto Hartwig, "To All Labor Organizations, Greeting," December 5, 1920, both in box 1, folder 2A, EPL 2001–011.

106 "Oregon Democrats Start to Rebuild," *Oregonian*, November 9, 1920, 7.

107 "Dr. Lovejoy Will Continue Fight Upon Sanitarium," *Oregon Journal*, November 20, 1920, 2.

108 The Winchester Dam was constructed in 1890 and enlarged in 1907. It supplied water and electricity for the area until 1923 and now contains a fish ladder and fish-counting station. Oregon Department of Fish and Wildlife, "Winchester Dam," http://www.dfw.state.or.us/fish/fish_counts/winchester_dam.asp, accessed September 30, 2011.

109 "Lovejoy Will Continue Fight," 2; "Sanitarium Is in the Limelight," *Roseburg News-Review*, November 18, 1920, 1; "Fight Is Started on Sanitarium," *Roseburg News-Review*, November 12, 1920, 1.

110 "Sanitarium Fight in Roseburg Gains Marked Intensity," *Oregon Journal*, November 14, 1920, 10; "Patent 1,337,798: Therapeutic Device for Treatment of the Lower Portion of the Body, Vern Linn Ruiter, Roseburg, Oregon," filed May 28, 1919, renewed March 15, 1920, date of Issue April 20, 1920, in United States Patent Office, *Official Gazette of the United States Patent Office*, vol. 273 (April 1920), 531.

111 "Sanitarium Plans May Be Defeated," *Oregonian*, November 17, 1920, 6.

112 Ibid.

113 "Sanitarium Fight to Finish Promised," *Oregonian*, November 1, 1920, 9.

114 "Dr. Lovejoy Makes New Move in Legal Spat with Hubby," *Oregon Journal*, November 21, 1920, 2.

115 "Sanitarium Is in the Limelight," 1; Olof Larsell, *The Doctor in Oregon: A Medical History* (Portland, OR: Binfords & Mort for the Oregon Historical Society, 1947), 468; Regular session, Common Council, City of Roseburg, July 19, 1920, 475–76, book 4, Roseburg City Council Records, Roseburg City Council Archives, Roseburg, Oregon; "Board Is Opposed to Plan for Sanitarium," *Oregon Journal*, September 19, 1920, 9; "Sanitarium Site on Power Dam Is Refused by State," *Oregon Journal*, October 12, 1920, 15.

116 Special session, Common Council, City of Roseburg, November 10, 1920, 4, book 5, Roseburg City Council Records; "Fight Is Started on Sanitarium," 1; "Sanitarium Fight Gains Marked Intensity," 10.

117 Regular session, Common Council, City of Roseburg, November 15, 1920, 5, book 5, Roseburg City Council Records.

118 "Other Side Hospital Controversy," *Roseburg News-Review*, November 15,

1920, 1; "Sanitarium Plans May Be Defeated," 6.

119 "Dr. Lovejoy Admits Hope to Sell Land," *Oregonian*, November 20, 1920, 6.

120 "Injuction Granted to Halt Building of Proposed Sanitarium," *Oregon Journal*, November 30, 1920, 9; "Action Against Hospital Begun," *Oregon Journal*, December 14, 1920, 4.

121 *Oregon State Board of Health* v. *Winchester Hospital for the Cure of Tuberculosis*, Suit for Injunction, December 15, 1920, Case No. 3261 in the Circuit Court, Douglas County, Oregon. See also "Injunction Action To Bar Sanitarium Erection is Filed, *Oregon Journal*, December 16, 1920, 11.

122 *Oregon State Board of Health* v. *Winchester Hospital for the Cure of Tuberculosis*, Order of Default, and *Oregon State Board of Health* v. *Winchester Hospital for the Cure of Tuberculosis*, Decree, February 2, 1921, case no. 3261, Circuit Court, Douglas County, Oregon.

123 *Winchester Hospital for the Cure of Tuberculosis and George Lovejoy*, case no. 45121, Douglas County, Oregon Deeds, vol. 82, 11, Douglas County Clerk's Office, Roseburg, Oregon.

124 *Esther Pohl and George Lovejoy to Annie Mary Clayson*, Trust Agreement, case no. 45520, Douglas County, Oregon Deeds, vol. 82, 125–28, Douglas County Clerk's Office, Roseburg, Oregon.

125 Because the dissolution of marriage was part of property agreements in Douglas County, the full complaint is entered in the record there. *Esther Pohl Lovejoy v. George A. Lovejoy*, Complaint, case no. 45521, Douglas County, Oregon Deeds, vol. 82, 128–29, Douglas County Clerk's Office, Roseburg, Oregon.

126 "Cruelty Alleged by Dr. Lovejoy," *Oregon Journal*, July 29, 1921, 6.

127 Other women candidates took similar steps, including Adelina Otero-Warren, a 1922 Republican candidate for the legislature in New Mexico. See Elizabeth Salas, "Ethnicity, Gender, and Divorce: Issues in the 1922 Campaign by Adelina Otero-Warren for the U.S. House of Representatives," *New Mexico Historical Review* 70, no. 4 (October 1995): 367–82.

128 *Esther Pohl Lovejoy v. George A. Lovejoy*, Decree of Divorce, Oregon Eighth Judicial District, Circuit Court Journal, November Term, Friday, December 10, 1920, Baker, Oregon; Findings of Fact and Decree reprinted in case no. 45521, Douglas County, Oregon Deeds, vol. 82, 129–13, Douglas County Clerk's Office, Roseburg, Oregon.

129 Anderson also wrote of his appreciation for Esther's congratulations on his recent marriage, invited Esther Lovejoy to their home when in the area, and spoke of reading material that they had discussed. Gustav Anderson to Doctor Lovejoy, December 10, 1929, box 1, folder 2B, EPL 2001–011.

130 "Cruelty Alleged," 6; "George Albert Lovejoy," in *A History of the State of Washington*, vol. 3, ed. Lancaster Pollard (New York: American Historical Society: 1937): 42–43.

131 George Lovejoy did have a history of litigation. "Sues for His Skin," *Oregonian*, October 15, 1905, 4; *George A. Lovejoy* v. *City of Portland* (1918), Oregon Supreme Court Records, no. 9803, file No. 3880, Oregon State Archives, Salem, Oregon.

132 "George Albert Lovejoy," 43; "George Lovejoy, Ex-Senator, Dies," *Seattle Times*, March 2, 1944, 22; "Mrs. G. A. Lovejoy," *Oregon Journal*, August 20, 1966, 3.

8. THE QUAY AT SMYRNA AND BEYOND

1 Esther Lovejoy, *Women Physicians and Surgeons: National and International Organizations* (New York: Livingston Press, 1939), 121. The name of the city Smyrna changed to Ismir in 1930.

2 Lovejoy, *Women Physicians*, 121.

3 Giles Milton, *Paradise Lost, Smyrna 1922: The Destruction of a Christian City in the Islamic World* (New York: Basic Books, 2008), 321; Marjorie Housepian Dobkin, *Smyrna 1922: The Destruction of a City* (New York: Newmark Press, 1971).

4 Esther Lovejoy, *Certain Samaritans* (New York: Macmillan, 1933), 136–37.

5 Lovejoy, *Certain Samaritans*, 196–296; Lovejoy, *Women Physicians*, 117–84.

6 Lovejoy, *Certain Samaritans*, 145–46.

7 Ibid., 154, 147.

8 Ibid., 146.

9 Ibid., 162.

10 Milton, *Paradise Lost*, 3.

11 Peter Balakian, *The Burning Tigris: The Armenian Genocide and America's Response* (New York: Harpers, 2003), 363–72, quote 366.

12 Milton, *Paradise Lost*, 235, 279. Many US civilians, including Lovejoy, did provide aid.

13 Lovejoy, *Certain Samaritans*, 150. Emphasis in original.

14 Milton, *Paradise Lost*, 352–71.

15 Lovejoy, *Certain Samaritans*, 150.

16 Ibid., 157–58.

17 Ibid., 162–63.

18 "Woman Pictures Smyrna Horrors," *New York Times*, October 9, 1922, 3; Lovejoy, *Certain Samaritans*, 158–60.

19 "Statement of Dr. Esther Lovejoy, Chairman of the Executive Board of

American Women's Hospitals," United States House of Representatives, Committee on Immigration and Naturalization, *Admission of Near East Refugees, Hearings Before the Committee on Immigration and Naturalization, House of Representatives, Sixty-Seventh Congress, Fourth Session, on HR 13269, December 15, 16, and 19, 1922, Serial 1-C* (Washington, D.C.: Government Printing Office, 1923), 73.

20 "Smyrna Refugees Lashed by Turks," *Oregonian*, October 3, 1922, 2.

21 Esther Lovejoy, "Smyrna," *Woman Citizen*, November 4, 1922, 8–9, 29; "Statement of Dr. Esther Lovejoy," 74; Lovejoy, *Certain Samaritans*, 164–66; "Woman Pictures Smyrna Horrors," 3.

22 "Smyrna Refugees Lashed," 2.

23 Lovejoy, *Certain Samaritans*, 184.

24 "Dr. Esther Pohl Lovejoy Declares Blame of Crime of Smyrna Lies in Christians," *Oregonian*, June 17, 1923, 11.

25 "U.S. Position Rebuked," *Oregonian*, July 13, 1923, 4.

26 Virginia A. Metaxas, "Ruth A. Parmalee, Esther P. Lovejoy, and the Discourse of Motherhood in Asia Minor and Greece in the Early Twentieth Century," in *Women Physicians and the Cultures of Medicine*, ed. Ellen S. More, Elizabeth Fee, and Manon Perry (Baltimore: Johns Hopkins University Press, 2009), 274–93, quotes 278, 290.

27 Lovejoy, *Certain Samaritans*, 174, 154.

28 Ibid., 235–36.

29 Esther Pohl Lovejoy, "Report of Chairman of Medical Service, A.W.H.," *Bulletin of the Medical Women's National Association* 4 (July 1923): 30–34.

30 Lovejoy, *Women Physicians*, 127–31.

31 Esther Pohl Lovejoy, "Report of the Chairman of the American Women's Hospitals," *Medical Woman's Journal* 34, no. 6 (June 1927): 175–78.

32 These requests may be found in the minutes of executive board meetings throughout this period. See box 31, folder 296, "Minutes, Executive Board Meetings, 1919–1926," AWH Records.

33 Lovejoy, *Women Physicians* and *Certain Samaritans*.

34 Lovejoy, *Women Physicians*, 187.

35 Alan M. Kraut, *Goldberger's War: The Life and Work of a Public Crusader* (New York: Hill and Wang, 2003).

36 Esther P. Lovejoy, "Report of American Women's Hospitals," *Bulletin of the Medical Women's National Association* 34 (October 1931): 11–12; Esther P. Lovejoy, "Report of Medical Service Committee—American Women's Hospital," *Bulletin of the Medical Women's National Association* 37 (July 1932): 19; Lovejoy, *Women Physicians*, 187–217.

37 Estelle Fraade and Alma Dei Morani, "The American Women's Hospitals:

A Half Century of Service," *Journal of the American Medical Women's Association* 22, no. 8 (August 1967): 548–71.

38 Esther Lovejoy, "Handy Notebook," box 8, EPL 2001–011.

39 Rosalie Slaughter Morton, *A Woman Surgeon: The Life and Work of Rosalie Slaughter Morton* (New York: Frederick A. Stokes, 1937); Regina Morantz-Sanchez, *Sympathy and Science: Women Physicians in American Medicine* (Chapel Hill: University of North Carolina Press, 2000), 146–47, 284–86; Ellen S. More, *Restoring the Balance Women Physicians and the Profession of Medicine, 1850–1995* (Cambridge, MA: Harvard University Press, 1999), 128–31, quote 129.

40 "Medical Women's National Association Report of the Second Annual Meeting," *Woman's Medical Journal* 27, no. 6 (June 1917): 141; Morton, *Woman Surgeon*, 270–74.

41 More, *Restoring the Balance*, 137. Morton represented women physicians on the General Medical Board of the Council of National Defense, and she continued her medical practice and teaching while taking on the War Service Committee duties.

42 Bertha Van Hoosen to Rosalie Slaughter Morton, July 28, 1917; Belle Thomas to Bertha Van Hoosen, August 4, 1917; Bertha Van Hoosen to Rosalie Slaughter Morton, September 10, 1917; all in box 2, folder 14, "Medical Women's National Association, War Service Committee, 1917–1922,"AWH Records; minutes, general meeting, American Women's Hospitals, September 6, 1917; and minutes, executive committee, American Women's Hospitals, December 19, 1917; both in box 30, folder 293, "Minutes, General and Executive Committee Meetings, 1917–1919," AWH Records.

43 "Medical Women's National Association Report of the Second Annual Meeting," *Woman's Medical Journal* 28, no. 6 (June 1918): 136.

44 Bertha Van Hoosen, "Looking Backward," *Journal of the American Medical Women's Association* 5, no. 5 (May 1950): 408.

45 The editorial, "The American Women's Hospitals," reprinted Morton's June 19, 1918, resignation letter and discussed the new leadership. "The American Women's Hospitals," *Woman's Medical Journal* 28, no. 8 (August 1918): 187–88. There is also a copy in box 22, folder 216, "Morton, Rosalie Slaughter, 1918–1937," AWH Records.

46 Van Hoosen, "Looking Backward," 408.

47 Lovejoy, "Handy Notebook."

48 "Dr. Lovejoy New Chairman of the American Women's Hospitals," *Woman's Medical Journal* 29, no. 8 (August 1919): 163; Van Hoosen, "Looking Backward," 408; Etta Gray to Rosalie S. Morton, June 27, 1919, box 22, folder 216, "Morton, Rosalie Slaughter, 1918–1973," AWH Records.

49　"American Women's Hospitals Organized by War Service Committee of the Medical Women's National Association, Bertha Van Hoosen, MD, President (June, 1917)," box 1, folder 1, "American Women's Hospitals Historical Records, 1917–1937," AWH Records; "Origin of the American Women's Hospitals: Report of Committee," *Bulletin of the Medical Women's National Association* 4 (July 1923): 44–46.

50　Grace N. Kimball to Frances Eastman Rose, February 5, 1924, box 22, folder 216, "Morton, Rosalie Slaughter, 1918–1937," AWH Records.

51　Rosalie Slaughter Morton to Marion Potter, November 25, 1932, box 3 "General Correspondence," folder 7, Rosalie Slaughter Morton Papers, Herbert Hoover Presidential Library, West Branch, Iowa.

52　Rosalie Slaughter Morton to Inez Hayes Irwin, December 17, 1955, box 3 "General Correspondence," folder 7, Morton Papers. Morton sent a copy of the letter to Kate Campbell Mead, box 1, "Subject File American Women's Hospital 1917–1934," Morton Papers. See also Inez Hayes Irwin, *Angels and Amazons: A Hundred Years of American Women* (Doubleday, Doran: 1933), 284–90.

53　Mead published the first volume of her *History of Women in Medicine* in 1938. She was completing the manuscript of the second volume in 1941 when she died in an accidental fire. See the finding aid for her collection at the Arthur and Elizabeth Schlesinger Library on the History of Women in America, Radcliff College, online at http://oasis.lib.harvard.edu/oasis/deliver/~sch00733. Rosalie Slaughter Morton revisions to Kate Campbell Mead, draft, box 1, "Subject File AWH 1917–1934," Morton Papers.

54　Rosalie Slaughter Morton to Kate Campbell Mead, April 12, 1934, box 1, "Subject File AWH 1917, 1934," Morton Papers.

55　C. A. Duniway to Rosalie Slaughter Morton, October 26, 1924, box 3, folder 5, Morton Papers; Rosalie Slaughter Morton to C. A. Duniway, box 5, "Subject File: Memberships: League of Nations—Nonpartisan Association," Morton Papers.

56　Correspondence and numerous drafts of the resolutions may be found across several files in her papers. Correspondents included Mead, Potter, Ruth Parmalee, Emily Dunning Barringer, Sara E. Foulks (formerly of the AWH), and Michigan physician Mary McKibben Harper. See box 1, "Subject File: American Women's Hospital, 1917–1934," Morton Papers; box 1, "Subject File: American Women's Hospital, 1935–1939," Morton Papers; box 1, "Subject File: American Women's Hospital, 1940," Morton Papers; and box 3, "Folder, General Correspondence," folder 7, Morton Papers.

57　"Banquet in Honor of Dr. Rosalie Slaughter Morton," *Medical Woman's Journal* 41, no. 8 (August 1934): 224–25.

58 "American Women's Hospitals Organized by War Service Committee of the Medical Women's National Association." The thirty-page report appears throughout the AWH Records, and a copy is attached to the minutes of the executive committee, March 10, 1937, AWH Records. See also Morton, *A Woman Surgeon*, 269–93.

59 The audits of the AWH from 1918 to 1970 are filed in box 32C, "William B. Johnson, Certified Public Accountant," AWH Records; box 32C, "Johnson, Wood & Co., Certified Public Accountant," AWH Records; and box 32D, "Johnson, Wood & Co., Certified Public Accountant," AWH Records.

60 This is true in her yearly reports to the MWNA, held in the AWH files and published in medical women's journals throughout her tenure and in her popular works *Certain Samaritans* and *Women Physicians and Surgeons*.

61 Estelle Fraade to Ms. Elizabeth H. Thompson, October 4, 1978, box 3, folder 19, EPL 2001–0011.

62 Esther Lovejoy to Carrie Chapman Catt, November 6, 1940, box 5, folder 33, EPL 2001–011.

63 Esther Lovejoy to Mary M. Crawford, March 19, 1958, box 17F, folder 142, "Miscellaneous Correspondence 'C,'" AWH Records.

64 Esther Pohl Lovejoy, *Women Doctors of the World* (New York: Macmillan, 1957), vii; Esther P. Lovejoy, "American Women's Hospitals (Medical Service Committee)," *Women in Medicine* 46 (October 1934): 19.

65 Amy Khedouri, e-mail message to author, October 22, 2004.

66 Esther P. Lovejoy, "The Possibilities of the Medical Women's International Association," *Medical Woman's Journal* 30, no.1 (January 1923): 17–18.

67 Lovejoy, *Women Physicians*, 117–125; Eliza M. Mosher, MD, "The Smyrna Disaster and the Part Taken by the A.W.H. in the Relief of Appalling Conditions," *Woman's Medical Journal* 30, no. 1 (January 1923): 22–25; Esther P. Lovejoy to the Medical Women's National Association, April 1, 1926, "Report of Year 1925–1926", 7, box 3, folder 24, "Lovejoy, Esther Pohl, Reports, 1926–1930," AWH Records.

68 Lovejoy, *Women Physicians*, 114–15; "Modern Medical Women in China," box 1, folder 6 "American Women's Hospitals, Articles, Reports, etc., 1917–1948," AWH Records; minutes, AWH Executive Board, September 21, 1945, p. 2, box 31, folder 298 "Minutes, Executive Board Meetings, 1938–1948," AWH Records.

69 Esther Lovejoy to Louisa Martindale, January 10, 1940; Janet Campbell to Esther Lovejoy, August 10, 1940; both in GC/25 Folder B4, "LM's Correspondence 1940," Martindale, Louisa Correspondence, Wellcome Library, London, England.

70 Lovejoy, *Women Physicians*, 87.

71 There are examples throughout the minutes of the executive board meetings. See box 31, folder 296, "Minutes, Executive Board Meetings, 1919–1926," AWH Records.

72 "Esther Lovejoy to Murray S. Kenworthy, Acting Executive Secretary, American Friends Service Committee," April 21,1924, box 15, folder 123, "Russia, 1923–1925," AWH Records.

73 Mabel Rew to Lousia Martindale, August 13, 1940, copy of letter from Janet Campbell enclosed, GC/25 Folder B4, "LM's Correspondence 1940," Martindale Correspondence.

74 "Esther Lovejoy Report to Executives of the American Women's Hospitals," July 1, 1920, 5, box 3, folder 20, "Lovejoy, E. P., Reports, 1920," AWH Records.

75 Lovejoy, *Women Physicians,* 30; Lovejoy, *Certain Samaritans,* 236.

76 "Woman Relief Worker Sails in Steerage to Save Funds," *New York Times,* August 8, 1923, 1.

77 "Esther Lovejoy Report to Executives," 5.

78 "Motion Picture Exhibit," *Bulletin of the Medical Women's National Association 4,* (July 1923): 6.

79 "An Interesting Book and a Contribution to the A.W.H.," *Woman's Medical Journal* 29, no. 12 (December 1919): 256.

80 William B. Johnson, "The American Women's Hospital Report from May 15, 1922 to June 15, 1923," box 32C, AWH Records; "The American Women's Hospital Report from May 31, 1921 to May 15, 1922," box 32C, AWH Records; "The American Women's Hospital Report from April 30, 1927 to December 31, 1928, box 32C, AWH Records.

81 Executive board meeting, AWH, February 19, 1952, box 31, folder 298, "Minutes, Executive Board Meetings, 1938–1948," AWH Records.

82 Executive board meeting, AWH, January 23, 1935, 1, box 31, folder 297, "Minutes, Executive Board Meetings, 1927–1937," AWH Records; "Minutes of the Annual Meeting of the Medical Women's National Association, June 12, 1933," and "Meeting of Board of Directors, Tuesday, June 13," *Bulletin of the Medical Women's National Association* 41 (July 1933): 8–10.

83 Johnson, Wood & Co., "The American Women's Hospital Report of Cash Receipts and Disbursements from the Beginning to May 31, 1967," box 32D, AWH Records.

84 William Holtz, *The Ghost in the Little House: A Life of Rose Wilder Lane* (Columbia: University of Missouri Press, 1993).

85 Entries for February 5 and 10, 1923, Rose Wilder Lane Diary, box 20, "Diaries and Notes Series Item #17: 1923 Diary, Lane," Rose Wilder Papers, Herbert Hoover Presidential Library, West Branch, Iowa.

86 Rose Wilder Lane diary, July 30, 1923.

87 Esther Pohl Lovejoy to Mabel Akin, September 12, 1932, box 62, folder 33, "AMWA Presidents Papers, 1932–1933 (part 1)," American Medical Women's Association Records, accession 37, Legacy Center, Drexel University College of Medicine, Philadelphia, Pennsylvania.

88 Esther Pohl Lovejoy, "President's Address," *Bulletin of the Medical Women's National Association* 37 (July 1932): 8–9.

89 Notes in Esther Lovejoy's handwriting on the back of photograph: "Esther Lovejoy, Woman Street Cleaner, Marian Cruikshank in front of Italian Military Headquarters in Constantinople, n.d.," box 11, folder 41, EPL 2001–011.

90 Alan Dawley, *Changing the World: American Progressives in War and Revolution* (Princeton: Princeton University Press, 2003), 297–99.

91 Esther Lovejoy, "Women's [sic] Big Job Is Man—His Creation, Care, and Preservation," 1–2, typescript of speech, [1928], box 1, folder 5, EPL 2001–011.

92 Ibid., 3–4.

93 Ibid., 5–8.

94 Ibid., 14–16.

95 Lovejoy, *Women Doctors*, vii.

96 Alma Dei Morani, MD, "Reflections," *Journal of the American Medical Women's Association* 22, no. 8 (August 1967): 571.

9. FEMINIST TRANSNATIONAL ACTIVISM AND INTERNATIONAL HEALTH

Material from this chapter was originally published in a slightly different form in Kimberly Jensen, "Feminist Transnational Activism and International Health: The Medical Women's International Association and the American Women's Hospitals, 1919–1948," in *Women and Transnational Activism in Historical Perspective*, ed. Kimberly Jensen and Erika Kuhlman (Dordrecht, The Netherlands: Republic of Letters, 2010): 143–72. Reprinted by permission of the author and the publisher.

1 Esther P. Lovejoy, MD, "The Possibilities of the Medical Women's International Association," *Medical Woman's Journal* 30, no. 1 (January 1923): 14–18.

2 Renée Fox, "Medical Humanitarianism and Human Rights: Reflections on Doctors Without Borders and Doctors of the World," in *Health and Human Rights*, ed. Jonathan Mann et al. (New York: Routledge, 1999): 417–35, quotes 417, 420, 421.

3 "American Medical Women's Overseas Service," *Medical Woman's Journal* 51, no. 10 (October 1944): 20; Esther Pohl Lovejoy, "Historical Sketch of

the Medical Women's International Association," *Journal of the American Medical Women's Association* 1, no. 8 (November 1946): 245–51.

4 "American Women's Hospitals Report," *Medical Woman's Journal* 28, no. 12 (December 1921): 315.

5 Elaine Israel, "Service Sage Dubbed Loner," *Long Island Star-Journal*, February 28, 1967, copy in folder "Lovejoy, Esther, M.D.," American Medical Women's Association Collection, Legacy Center, Drexel University College of Medicine, Philadelphia, Pennsylvania.

6 "Minutes of the MWIA Meeting," Waldorf Astoria Hotel, New York City, October 25, 1919, box A-27, "Minutes and Other Records, 1919–1924," Medical Women's International Association Collection, Legacy Center, Drexel University College of Medicine, Philadelphia, Pennsylvania (MWIA Collection); "Medical Women's International Association Constitution" in *Medical Women's International Association, Report of 1924 Meeting, July 15th to 19th, London, England*, copy at the National Library of Medicine, Washington, DC; "The Value of Organization to Medical Women," *Medical Woman's Journal* 29, no. 5 (May 1922): 92–93.

7 Nitza Berkovitch, *From Motherhood to Citizenship: Women's Rights and International Organizations* (Baltimore: Johns Hopkins University Press, 1999), 69.

8 See J. Ann Tickner, *Gender in International Relations: Feminist Perspectives on Achieving Global Security* (New York: Columbia University Press, 1992), 18; and Tickner, *Gendering World Politics: Issues and Approaches in the Post–Cold War Era* (New York: Columbia University Press, 2001).

9 "Banquet of the Medical Women's International Association, Geneva, Switzerland, September 7, 1922," *Medical Woman's Journal* 29, no. 10 (October 1922): 236–39; "Convention of Medical Women's International Association/Association Internationale De Femmes Medecins," *Medical Woman's Journal* 29, no. 10 (October 1922): 234–35.

10 Lovejoy, "Possibilities,"14–18.

11 Ibid., 14.

12 Ibid., 17.

13 "Self-Pity Is Despicable, Says Dr. Esther Lovejoy," *Oregonian*, July 15, 1923, 12.

14 Berkovitch, *Motherhood to Citizenship*; Alan Dawley, *Changing the World: American Progressives in War and Revolution* (Princeton, NJ: Princeton University Press, 2003); Leila Rupp, *Worlds of Women: The Making of an International Women's Movement* (Princeton, NJ: Princeton University Press, 1997); Erika Kuhlman, *Reconstructing Patriarchy: Women, Gender, and Postwar Reconciliation between Nations* (New York: Palgrave Macmillan, 2008); and Kimberly Jensen and Erika K. Kuhlman, eds. *Women and*

Transnational Activism in Historical Perspective (Dortrecht, The Nether-lands: Republic of Letters, 2010).

15   Rupp, *Worlds of Women*, 212–22, quote 212.

16   Lady Berry [Dr. Dickinson Berry], "International Health Work and the Medical Women's International Association," *Medical Women's International Journal* 1, no. 2 (November 1925): 61–66.

17   Esther Pohl Lovejoy, *Women Doctors of the World* (New York: MacMillan, 1957), 178, 181.

18   Berry, "International Health Work"; "Report of the Second Quinquennial Congress, Paris, 10th–15th April 1929," *Bulletin Association Internationale des Femmes Médicins/Medical Women's International Association* (hereafter *BAIFM/MWIA*) 1 (December 1929): 15–24, quote 20; and "Report of the Fifth Council Meeting, Vienna, September 15–20, 1931," *BAIFM/MWIA* 5 (December 1931): 15.

19   "Secretary's Report, Council Meeting, Paris, April 10, 1929," *BAIFM/MWIA* 1 (December 1929): 25; Esther Pohl Lovejoy and Ada Chree Reid, "The Medical Women's International Association: An Historical Sketch, 1919–1950," *Journal of the American Medical Women's Association* 6, no. 1 (January 1951): 29–38.

20   Esther Pohl Lovejoy, *Women Physicians and Surgeons: National and International Organizations* (Livingston, New York: Livingston Press, 1939), 97.

21   Marilyn Ogilvie and Joy Harvey, eds., *Biographical Dictionary of Women in Science: Pioneering Lives from Ancient Times to the Mid-Twentieth Century*, vol. 2 (New York: Routledge, 2000), s.v. "Lebdeva, Vera Pavlovna"; Jeanette E. Tuve, *The First Russian Women Physicians* (Newtonville, MA: Oriental Research Partners, 1984), 60–68, 111, 113–16.

22   Alexandra Kollontai, "The Labour of Women in the Revolution of the Economy," in *Selected Writings of Alexandra Kollontai,* trans. and ed. Alix Holt (London: Allison & Busby, 1977), 143; Kollontai quotes Lebedeva.

23   Telegram from Vera Lebedeva to Esther Lovejoy, January 1923, box 15, folder 122, "Russia, 1921–1923," AWH Records; Esther Lovejoy to Vera Lebedeva, April 23, 1923, box 15, folder 122, "Russia, 1921–1923," AWH Records.

24   "Greetings from Countries Represented: Dr. Lebedeva," *Medical Women's International Association, Report of Third General Conference, July 15th to 19th, 1924,* 11.

25   The text of Lebedeva's speech is reprinted in V. Lebedev (*sic*), MD, "Mothers' and Children's Welfare in Soviet Russia," *Medical Woman's Journal* 31, no. 11 (November 1924): 307–9. A typescript copy by the same title is located in box 15, folder 123, "Russia, 1923–25," AWH Records.

26   Lebedeva, "Mothers' and Children's Welfare," 309.

27 Wendy Z. Goldman, *Women, the State, and Revolution: Soviet Family Policy and Social Life, 1917–1936* (New York: Cambridge University Press, 1993), 337.

28 Ibid., 122–23.

29 Ibid., 118.

30 Esther Pohl Lovejoy to Vera Lebedeva, April 19, 1925, box 15, folder 123, "Russia, 1923–1925," AWH Records; Effie Graff to Esther Lovejoy, April 21, 1925, box 15, folder 123, "Russia, 1923–1925," AWH Records; Anna J. Haines, *Health Work in Soviet Russia* (New York: Vanguard Press, 1928).

31 Esther Lovejoy to Dr. E. Eremin, January 8, 1943, box 15, folder 124, "Russia, 1925–1947," AWH Records. Lebedeva was deputy of the People's Commissariat of Social Security until 1934. From 1934 to 1938 she served as inspector of public health, and finished her career as director of the Central Institute of Advanced Training for Physicians in Moscow. She died in 1968. Tuve, *Russian Women Physicians*, 116–17.

32 Alice Hamilton to Jane Addams, January 24, 1925, in *Alice Hamilton: A Life in Letters*, ed. Barbara Sicherman (Cambridge, MA: Harvard University Press, 1984), 279–80.

33 "In re Accounts of Ernst Brücke and Dora Brücke-Teleky," September 21, 2005, 7, "In re Holocaust Victim Assets Litigation Case No. CV96–4849," United States District Court for the Eastern District of New York, Chief Judge Edward R. Korman, Presiding, Claims Resolution Tribunal of the Holocaust Victim Assets Litigation against Swiss Banks and other Swiss Entities, www.crt-ii.org/_awards/_apdfs/Brucke_Ernst.pdf; "Necrology: Dr. Dora V. Brücke-Teleky," *Pirquet Bulletin of Clinical Medicine* 10 (1963): 116; Ernst-August Seyfarth, "Ernst Theodor Von Brücke (1880–1941) and Alexander Forbes (1882–1965): Chronicle of a Transatlantic Friendship in Difficult Times," *Perspectives in Biology and Medicine* 40, no. 1 (Autumn 1996): 49, n. 2; Lisa Appignanesi and John Forrester, *Freud's Women* (New York: Basic Books, 2001), 140.

34 "Medical Women of Today—Dora Brücke-Teleky, M.D.," *Medical Woman's Journal* 40, no. 1 (January 1933): 18; Esther Pohl Lovejoy to Dr. Effie Graff, September 22, 1922, box 15, folder 122, "Russia, 1921–1923,"AWH Records.

35 "Dora Brücke-Teleky, M.D.," 18.

36 "Banquet of the Medical Women's International Association," 236–37.

37 "Dr. Lovejoy," *Bulletin of the Medical Women's National Association* 4 (July 1923): 16–17.

38 *Medical Women's International Association, Report of 1924 Meeting*, 5, 10; *Medical Women's International Journal* 1, no. 1 (May 1925): 1; "Dora Brücke-Teleky, M.D.," 18; editorial board list, *Medical Woman's Journal* 49, no. 6 (June 1942): ii.

39 "Meetings of the Council," *Association Internationale des Femmes-Medecins* 5 (December 1931): 43; "Summary of the Discussion on Birth Control," *Medical Women's International Journal* 9 (December 1934): 44–52.

40 "Austria," *Medical Women's International Journal* 13 (December 1938): 13; Germaine Montreuil-Straus to Louisa Martindale, October 25, 1938, box 20, folder "Martindale, Louisa, President, and Montreuil-Straus, G., Secretary, 1937–1940," MWIA Collection.

41 "Transatlantic Friendship," 50–51.

42 Louisa Martindale, "Review of International Events, January 26, 1940," typescript, box B, folder B.13, "MWIA President's Reports, 1940–1946," box B, GC 25, "Louisa Martindale Correspondence," Wellcome Library, London (hereafter Martindale Correspondence); Lovejoy, *Women Doctors,* 196, "Transatlantic Friendship," 50.

43 "In re Accounts of Ernst Brücke and Dora Brücke-Teleky," 2; "Necrology: Dr. Dora v. Brücke-Teleky"; Martindale, "Review of International Events"; Louisa Martindale to Esther Pohl Lovejoy, November 3, 1939, box B, folder B3, "L. M.'s Correspondence, 1939," GC 25, Martindale Correspondence; Esther Pohl Lovejoy to Louisa Martindale, November 20, 1939, box B, folder B3, "L. M.'s Correspondence, 1939," GC 25, Martindale Correspondence; "Transatlantic Friendship," 51; Dora Brücke-Teleky to Louisa Martindale, December 4, 1942, box B, folder B.6, "L. M.'s Correspondence, 1942–43," box B, GC 25, Martindale Correspondence; "Prof. E. T. Von Brücke," *New York Times* (June 13, 1941), 19.

44 Lovejoy and Reid, "Medical Women's International Association," 34; "Resolutions and Recommendations Adopted," *Bulletin of the International Federation of University Women* 20 (1938): 18.

45 Kate C. Hurd-Mead, "News from France," *Women in Medicine* 69 (July 1940): 20.

46 "Report of the Honorary Secretary, Dr. Montreuil-Straus," *Bulletin of the Medical Women's International Association* (December 1946): 9, [typescript], copy in Medical Women's Federation/Medical Women's International Association Collection, SA/MWF, Wellcome Library, London.

47 "Report of the Refugee Committee of the American Medical Women's Association," *Women in Medicine* 62 (October 1938): 19; "Relief of Distressed Women Physicians: June 1940," *Women in Medicine* 70 (October 1940): 17–18; "Address of Retiring President Elizabeth Mason-Hohl, [AMWA] Annual Meeting, June 2, 1941," *Women in Medicine* 73 (July 1941): 25. In addition to Finkler, members of the committee included Lydia B. Hauck, Elizabeth Mason-Hohl, Louise Tayler-Jones, Nadina Kavinoky, Kate C. Mead, Ellen C. Potter, Frances Eastman Rose, and Bertha Van Hoosen.

48 "Report of the Honorary Secretary Dr. Montreuil-Straus," 10. Rita Finkler reported the arrival of the following refugee women physicians in the States by December 1939: from Austria, Drs. Marianne Baker-Jokl, Dora Brücke-Teleky, Gertrude Oberlander, and Pauline Feldman "expected to arrive any day"; from Germany, Anita DeLomone, Toni Engel, and Hedwig Fischer; from Italy, Gina Castalnova; and from Turkey, Ericka Bruck. Rita Finkler to Louisa Martindale, December 23, 1939, box B, folder B3, "L. M.'s Correspondence, 1939," GC 25, Martindale Correspondence.

49 "Report of Honorary Secretary Dr. Montreuil-Straus," 10.

50 Atina Grossmann, "New Women in Exile: German Women Doctors and the Emigration," in *Between Sorrow and Strength: Women Refugees of the Nazi Period*, ed. Sybylle Quack (Washington, DC: German Historical Institute / New York: Cambridge University Press, 1995), 215.

51 Grossmann, "German Women Doctors," 232. Grossmann does not include a discussion of the support from the Medical Women's International Association, the American Women's Hospitals, and other women physicians for their colleagues.

52 David H. Popper, "International Aid to German Refugees," *Foreign Policy Reports* 14, no. 16 (November 1, 1938): 186; David S. Wyman, *Paper Walls: America and the Refugee Crisis, 1938–1941* (Amherst: University of Massachusetts Press, 1968); David S. Wyman, *The Abandonment of the Jews: America and the Holocaust, 1941–1945* (New York: New Press, 1984); Roger Daniels, *Guarding the Golden Door: American Immigration Policy and Immigrants Since 1882* (New York: Hill and Wang, 2004), 71–80.

53 "Report of Honorary Secretary Dr. Montreuil-Straus," 9.

54 Erika Mann and Eric Estorick, "Private and Governmental Aid of Refugees," *Annals of the American Academy of Political and Social Science* 203 (May 1939): 153.

55 David L. Edsall, MD, "The Emigré Physician in American Medicine," *Journal of the American Medical Association* 114, no. 12 (March 23, 1940): 1071. Only Arizona, California, the District of Columbia, and Indiana required neither citizenship nor first papers. "Refugees and the Professions," *Harvard Law Review* 53, no. 1 (November 1939): 112–22; Maurice R. Davie et al., *Refugees in America: Report of the Committee for the Study of Recent Immigration from Europe* (New York: Harper & Brothers, 1947), 257–86.

56 "Report of Honorary Secretary Dr. Montreuil-Straus," 10; "Report of the Refugee Committee," 20.

57 Tomo Inouye to Esther Lovejoy, August 17, 1920, box 6, folder 20, EPL 2011–011; Lovejoy, *Women Physicians*, 112–13.

58 Executive board meeting, American Women's Hospitals, March 12, 1925,

box 31, folder 296 "Minutes, Executive Board Meetings, 1919–1926," AWH Records.

59 Janet Campbell to Esther Lovejoy, August 10, 1940, box B, folder B4, "L. M.'s Correspondence, 1940," GC/25, Martindale Correspondence; Esther Lovejoy to Louisa Martindale, January 10, 1940, box B, folder B4, "L. M.'s Correspondence, 1940," GC/25, Martindale Correspondence; minutes, AWH Executive Board, January 22, 1946, 2, box 31, folder 298, "Minutes, Executive Board Meetings, 1938–1948," AWH Records; letter to the editor from Janet Campbell, President, Medical Women's Federation, "Help from Women Doctors," *Lancet*, June 30, 1945, 834–35, copy in SA/MWF box 97 K.8/5, MWIA London Meeting 1946, Medical Women's Federation/Medical Women's International Association Collection; Janet Campbell, "Medical Women in the Bombing of Britain," *Journal of the American Medical Women's Association* 1, no. 9 (December 1946): 309–18.

60 "Round Robin," *Medical Woman's Journal* 51, no. 10 (October 1944): 21.

61 Minutes, AWH executive board, January 22, 1946, 2, box 31, folder 298, "Minutes, Executive Board Meetings, 1938–1948," AWH Records; G. Montreuil-Straus, "Comité Feminin de Service Médical," *Journal of the American Medical Women's Association* 1, no. 8 (November 1946): 277.

62 Esther P. Lovejoy, "The American Women's Hospitals in Norway," *Journal of the American Medical Women's Association* 1, no. 1 (April 1946): 18–19.

63 Estelle Fraade and Alma Dei Morani, "The American Women's Hospitals: A Half Century of Service," *Journal of the American Medical Women's Association* 22, no. 8 (August 1967): 548–71.

64 Ibid., 566; Estelle Fraade to Mr. L. Robert Oaks, February 24, 1966, box 20, folder 199, "Lovejoy, Dr. Esther Pohl, 1959–1967," AWH Records.

65 Esther Lovejoy to Carrie Chapman Catt, November 6, 1940, box 5, folder 33, EPL 2011–011.

66 Fraade to Oaks, February 24, 1966.

CONCLUSION

1 Esther Pohl Lovejoy, *Women Physicians and Surgeons: National and International Organizations* (Livingston, New York: Livingston Press, 1939), 225.

2 Eva Hansl consulted with Lovejoy and with Kate Campbell Mead, MD, Martha Tracy, MD, and Emily Dunning Barringer, MD. Eva Hansl to Kate Cambell Hurd-Mead, March 6, 1940, box 4, folder 7, "Hansl, Eva Papers, 1930–1975," MS 72, Sophia Smith Collection, Smith College, Northampton, Massachusetts; *Gallant American Women*: "Women in Medicine," 16, March 12, 1940, US Office of Education, Federal Security Agency, Washington," box 2, folder 34, "No. 32., 'Women in Medicine,'" Hansl, Eva Elise

von Baur Papers, 1939–1954, MS A-118, Arthur and Elizabeth Schlesinger Library on the History of Women in America, Radcliffe Institute, Harvard University, Cambridge, Massachusetts.

3 "Call to the Congress," *Woman's Centennial Congress, Woman's Century, 1840–1940, November 25, 26, 27, 1940, Hotel Commodore, New York City*, box 5, folder 33, EPL 2011–011.

4 Correspondence between Carrie Chapman Catt and Esther Lovejoy, October and November 1940, all in box 5, folder 33, EPL 2011–011.

5 Esther Pohl Lovejoy, "Women Wanted Women Physicians in 1840," in *Woman's Centennial Congress*, 104–5.

6 Esther Pohl Lovejoy, *Women Doctors of the World* (New York: Macmillan, 1957).

7 Ibid., viii.

8 Ibid., 121, 258, 270.

9 Ibid., 254.

10 Ibid., vii–viii.

11 Linda K. Kerber, Jane Sherron De Hart, and Cornelia Hughes Dayton, eds., *Women's America: Refocusing the Past*, 7th ed. (New York: Oxford University Press, 2011), 2–3.

12 "MWIA Golden Jubilee Souvenir, Esther Pohl Lovejoy, M.D.: Founder and First President, Medical Women's International Association," 1970, copy in box 5, folder 38, EPL 2011–011.

13 The correspondence in EPL 2011–011 and EPL 2011–004 attests to Fraade's important work.

14 Mabel Akin to Esther Lovejoy, October 5, 1932, box 62, folder 33, "A.M.W.A. Presidents Papers 1932–1933," American Medical Women's Association Records, Legacy Center, Drexel University College of Medicine, Philadelphia, Pennsylvania.

15 Minutes, regular board meeting, December 14, 1936, 160, Oregon State Board of Higher Education Records, Oregon University System Archives, Oregon State University, Corvallis, Oregon; "Pohl Memorial Scholarship," box 1, folder 1, EPL 2001–011. The scholarship continues to be awarded.

16 "Ex-Official, Now 93, Visits," *Oregon Journal*, August 6, 1963, 4.

17 Esther Pohl Lovejoy to "Margaret," October 12, 1957, box 2b, folder 19 "Lovejoy, Esther Pohl, Posthumous Papers and Biographical Information," AWH Records.

18 Esther Lovejoy to Dr. Elizabeth Mason Hohl, March 19, 1958, box 27, folder 264 "Pan American Medical Women's Assoc., 1958–1964," AWH Records.

19 Jessie Laird Brodie, *"Dr. Jessie": The Odyssey of a Woman Physician* (Portland, OR: Caroline Pacific Publishing, 1991), 263.

20 Esther Lovejoy to American Women's Hospitals Executive Board, May 1, 1967, box 32, folder 300, "Minutes, Board of Directors, 1960–1975," AWH Records.

21 See http://www.friendsoflonefircemetery.org, accessed September 30, 2011.

22 Cynthia Enloe, *The Curious Feminist: Searching for Women in a New Age of Empire* (Berkeley: University of California Press, 2004).

23 David M. Hardy, Section Chief, Record/Information Dissemination Section, Records Management Division, Federal Bureau of Investigation, to Author, Subject: Lovejoy, Esther Clayson Pohl, August 27, 2004," copy in possession of author.

24 Esther Pohl Lovejoy, *Certain Samaritans*, rev. ed. (New York: Macmillan, 1933), 243.

25 Nancy Cott, *The Grounding of Modern Feminism* (New Haven, CT: Yale University Press, 1987), 242, 249–50.

26 "Self-Pity Is Despicable, Says Dr. Esther Lovejoy," *Oregonian*, July 15, 1923, 12.

27 Nancy Snook Frankovic, discussion with author, June 2009, Spokane, Washington.

28 Women of Woodcraft, *Ritual of the Women of Woodcraft* (Portland, OR: Portland Printing House, 1912), 12–13.

29 Esther Lovejoy, autobiographical fragments, box 1, folder 7, EPL 2001–011.

30 Esther C. Pohl, "An Argument for Woman Suffrage," (Salem) *Capital Journal*, May 18, 1912, 6.

31 Linda K. Kerber traces these continuing views in *No Constitutional Right to Be Ladies: Women and the Obligations of Citizenship* (New York: Hill and Wang, 1998).

32 Esther Lovejoy to "Dear Relations," September 1, 1922, box 1, folder 2B, EPL 2001–011.

33 Esther P. Lovejoy, "What Is the American Women's Hospital Service?" May 25, 1962, box 3, folder 15, EPL 2011–011.

34 Lovejoy, *Women Physicians and Surgeons*, 220–21.

35 The American Women's Hospitals Service, www.amwa-doc.org/page3–9/AMWAHospitalService, accessed September 30, 2011.

36 The Medical Women's International Association, www.mwia.net, accessed September 30, 2011.

37 United Nations Fourth World Conference on Women, Beijing, China, September 1995, Platform for Action C.89, Action for Equality, Development and Peace, UN Women: United Nations Entity for Gender Equality and the Empowerment of Women, http://www.un.org/womenwatch/daw/beijing/platform/health.htm, accessed September 30, 2011.

BIBLIOGRAPHY

ARCHIVAL COLLECTIONS

Adair, Fred Lyman. Papers. Herbert Hoover Presidential Library, West Branch, Iowa.

American Medical Women's Association Records, Legacy Center, Archives and Special Collections on Women in Medicine and Homeopathy, Drexel University College of Medicine, Philadelphia, Pennsylvania.

American National Red Cross Records, 1917–1934. Record Group 200. National Archives II, College Park, Maryland.

American Women's Hospitals. Historical Materials, 1917–1982. Legacy Center, Archives and Special Collections on Women in Medicine and Homeopathy, Drexel University College of Medicine, Philadelphia, Pennsylvania.

British Columbia. Department of Vital Statistics, British Columbia, Canada.

City of Portland Board of Health Annual Reports, 1905–12, 1918. City of Portland Archives and Records Center, Portland, Oregon.

City of Portland Board of Health Minutes, 1903–1909. City of Portland Archives and Records Center, Portland, Oregon.

City of Portland City Council Documents. City of Portland Archives and Records Center, Portland, Oregon.

Records of the Council of National Defense. Record Group 62. Committee on Women's Defense Work. "Meeting of the Presidents of National Organizations of Women and Weekly and Monthly Reports of the Committee on Women's Defense Work." National Archives Microfilm Publication M1074. National Archives and Records Service, Washington, D.C.

Davis Phillips, Lucy I. Collection on Oregon Women Medical School Graduates. Accession 2004–030. Historical Collections & Archives, Oregon Health & Science University, Portland, Oregon.

Death Certificates. Health Division. Accession 91A17. Oregon State Archives, Salem, Oregon.

Duniway, Abigail Scott. Papers. MS 432. Oregon Historical Society Research Library, Portland, Oregon.

Faubion, Nina Lane. Papers. Accession Ax 185. University of Oregon Special
Collections and Archives, Eugene, Oregon.

Florence Crittenton Refuge Home, Portland, Oregon. Minutes, Board of Managers, 1903–1906. Accession B 90. University of Oregon Special Collections
and Archives, Eugene, Oregon.

Hansl, Eva Elise von Baur. Papers, 1939–1954. MS A-118. Arthur and Elizabeth
Schlesinger Library on the History of Women in America, Radcliffe Institute, Harvard University, Cambridge, Massachusetts.

Hansl, Eva. Papers, 1930–1975. MS 72. Sophia Smith Collection, Smith College,
Northampton, Massachusetts.

Hauptly, Jacob. Diary, 1872–1899. Typewritten transcript. Kitsap County Historical Society Archives, Bremerton, Washington.

Jefferson County, Washington, Naturalization Records. Washington State
Archives, Olympia, Washington.

Khedouri, Amy. Materials. Private Collection of Esther Lovejoy Materials,
Scottsdale, Arizona.

Lane, Harry. Subject File. City of Portland Archives and Records Center, Portland, Oregon.

Lane, Rose Wilder. Papers. Herbert Hoover Presidential Library, West Branch,
Iowa.

Lovejoy, Esther Pohl. Collection. Accession 2001–004. Historical Collections &
Archives, Oregon Health & Science University, Portland, Oregon.

Lovejoy, Esther Pohl. Collection. Accession 2001–011. Historical Collections &
Archives, Oregon Health & Science University, Portland, Oregon.

Loveridge, Emily. "As I Remember." Typescript. Item 16. Box 1. Linfield-Good
Samaritan School of Nursing Archives, Linfield College, McMinnville,
Oregon.

Martindale, Louisa. Correspondence. MSS 3470–3487. Wellcome Library, London.

Mead, Kate Campbell. "Collection Finding Aid." Arthur and Elizabeth
Schlesinger Library on the History of Women in America, Radcliff College,
Cambridge, Massachusetts. Available at http://oasis.lib.harvard.edu/oasis/
deliver/~scho0733. Accessed September 30, 2011.

Medical Women's Federation/Medical Women's International Association Collection. SA/MWF. Wellcome Library, London.

Medical Women's International Association Collection. Legacy Center,
Archives and Collections on Women in Medicine and Homeopathy, Drexel
University College of Medicine, Philadelphia, Pennsylvania.

Medical Women's International Association, Report of 1924 Meeting, July 15th
to 19th, 1924, London, England. Copy at the National Library of Medicine,
Washington, DC.

Morton, Rosalie Slaughter. Papers. Herbert Hoover Presidential Library, West Branch, Iowa.

Motor Vehicle Registration Record, 1905–1910. Record of Statements and Certificates Issued to Owners of Automobiles. Index of Automobile and Motorcycle Licenses Issued. Office of Secretary of State. Oregon State Archives, Salem, Oregon.

Multnomah County, Election Voting Abstracts. Accession 92A-24. Oregon State Archives, Salem, Oregon.

Records of the National American Woman Suffrage Association, Manuscript Division, Library of Congress, Washington, DC.

National Woman's Party Papers. "The Suffrage Years, 1913–1920." Library of Congress. Microfilm Division, Microfilming Corporation of America, 1981.

Oregon Marriage License Index and Record. Oregon State Archives, Salem, Oregon.

Oregon State Board of Health. Records. Accession 91A. Oregon State Archives, Salem, Oregon.

Oregon State Board of Higher Education. Records. Oregon University System Archives, Oregon State University, Corvallis, Oregon.

People's Institute and Free Dispensary. Records. Accession 2008–010. Historical Collections & Archives, Oregon Health & Science University, Portland, Oregon.

Photographs from the Records of the National Woman's Party. American Memory Project. Library of Congress, Washington, DC. Available at http://memory.loc.gov/ammem/collections/suffrage/nwp/index.html. Accessed September 17, 2011.

Portland Birth Index. Oregon State Archives, Salem, Oregon.

Portland Woman's Club (Oregon). Records, 1895–1995. MS 1084. Oregon Historical Society Research Library, Portland, Oregon.

Probate Case Files. Clackamas County and Multnomah County. Oregon State Archives, Salem, Oregon.

Proceedings of County Commissioners, Kitsap County, also Record of Liquor Licenses Bonds, Etc. Kitsap County Auditor's Office, Port Orchard, Washington.

Roseburg City Council. Records. Roseburg City Council Archives, Roseburg, Oregon.

United States Department of Justice. Mail and Files Division. "Department of Justice File on Dr. Marie Equi." Copy at Lewis and Clark College Special Collections, Portland, Oregon.

Willamette University Medical Department. Records. Accession 1999–01. Historical Collections & Archives, Oregon Health & Science University, Portland, Oregon.

NEWSPAPERS, CONTEMPORARY MAGAZINES,
JOURNALS AND CATALOGUES

American Women's Club of Paris Bulletin
Annals of the American Academy of Political and Social Science
Annual Announcement of the Medical Department of the University of Oregon
Association Internationale des Femmes-Médecins
British Medical Journal
Bulletin Association Internationale des Femmes Médicins/Medical Women's International Association
Bulletin of the International Federation of University Women
Bulletin of the Medical Women's National Association
Canadian Medical Association Journal
[Portland] *Chamber of Commerce Bulletin*
Eclectic Medical Journal
Fairbanks News-Miner
Foreign Policy Reports
[Corvallis] *Gazette-Times*
Good Housekeeping
Harvard Law Review
International Woman Suffrage News
Journal of the American Medical Association
Journal of the American Medical Women's Association
[Portland] *La Tribuna Italiana*
Ladies' Home Journal
Lancet
Medical Sentinel
Medical Woman's Journal
Medical Women's International Journal
National American Woman Suffrage Association Headquarters News Letter
New York Times
Nome Gold Digger
Nome News
Northwest Medicine
Old Oregon
Oregon Journal
Oregon Labor Press
Oregon Voter
Oregonian
Outlook
Pacific Coast Journal of Homeopathy

Patriarch
Pendleton East Oregonian
Pirquet Bulletin of Clinical Medicine
Portland City Directory
Portland Evening Telegram
Portland News
Progress
Rebel Battery
Rogue River Courier
Roseburg News-Review
[Salem] *Capital Journal*
[Salmon, Idaho] *Recorder-Herald*
San Francisco Call
San Francisco Chronicle
San Francisco Examiner
Searchlight on Congress
Seattle City Directory
Seattle Post-Intelligencer
Seattle Republican
Seattle Times
Stars and Stripes
Suffragist
Survey
Transactions of the Annual Meeting of the Oregon State Medical Association
Washington Times
Willamette University Bulletin
Woman Citizen
Woman's Journal
Woman's Medical Journal
Woman's Progressive Weekly
Woman's Tribune
Women in Medicine

SOURCES

Abbott, Carl. *The Great Extravaganza: Portland and the Lewis and Clark Exposition*. Portland: Oregon Historical Society, 1981.

Adams, Katherine H., and Michael J. Keene. *Alice Paul and the American Suffrage Campaign*. Urbana: University of Illinois Press, 2008.

Addams, Jane. "The Subjective Value of a Social Settlement" and "The Objective Value of a Social Settlement." In *Philanthropy and Social Progress: Seven Essays Delivered before the School of Applied Ethics, at Plymouth, Mass., during the Session of 1892*, by Bernard Bosanquet, Jane Addams, and Franklin Henry Giddings, 1–26, 27–56. New York: Thomas Y. Crowell, 1893.

Additon, Lucia H. Faxton. *Twenty Eventful Years of the Oregon Woman's Christian Temperance Union, 1880–1900*. Portland, OR: Gotshall Printing, 1904.

Aiken, Katherine G. *Harnessing the Power of Motherhood: The National Florence Crittenton Mission, 1883–1925*. Knoxville: University of Tennessee Press, 1998.

Alumni Association of the University of Oregon Medical School. *Twenty-Fifth Annual Meeting and Directory of the Alumni Association of the University of Oregon Medical School*. Portland, OR: Alumni Association of the University of Oregon Medical School, 1937.

American Medical Women's Association. American Women's Hospitals Service. Available at http://www.amwa-doc.org/awhs. Accessed May 20, 2012.

"An Act Preventing the Manufacture and Sale of Adulterated or Misbranded or Poisonous or Deleterious Foods." 1907 Or. Laws 318–22. February 25, 1907.

Anderson, Larry. *Benton MacKaye: Conservationist, Planner, and Creator of the Appalachian Trail*. Baltimore: Johns Hopkins University Press, 2002.

Antler, Joyce. "Feminism as Life-Process: The Life and Career of Lucy Sprague Mitchell." *Feminist Studies* 7, no. 1 (Spring 1981): 134–57.

Appignanesi, Lisa, and John Forrester. *Freud's Women*. New York: Basic Books, 2001.

Baker, S. Josephine. *Fighting for Life*. New York: MacMillan, 1939.

Balakian, Peter. *The Burning Tigris: The Armenian Genocide and America's Response*. New York: Harpers, 2003.

Bard, Christine. *Les filles de Marianne: Histoire des féminismes, 1914–1940*. Paris: Fayard, 1995.

Barringer, Emily Dunning. *Bowery to Bellevue: The Story of New York's First Woman Ambulance Surgeon*. New York: Norton, 1950.

Bederman, Gail. *Manliness and Civilization: A Cultural History of Gender and Race in the United States, 1880–1917*. Chicago: University of Chicago Press, 1995.

Benson, Susan Porter. *Counter Cultures: Saleswomen, Managers, and Customers in American Department Stores, 1890–1940*. Urbana: University of Illinois Press, 1986.

Berkovitch, Nitza. *From Motherhood to Citizenship: Women's Rights and International Organizations*. Baltimore: Johns Hopkins University Press, 1999.

Bittel, Carla. *Mary Putnam Jacobi and the Politics of Medicine in Nineteenth-Century America*. Chapel Hill: University of North Carolina Press, 2009.

Blair, Emily Newell. *The Woman's Committee United States Council of National Defense: An Interpretive Report, April 21, 1917, to February 27, 1919*. Washington, DC: US Government Printing Office, 1920.

Bonner, Thomas Neville. *American Doctors and German Universities: A Chapter in International Intellectual Relations*. Lincoln: University of Nebraska Press, 1963.

———. *To the Ends of the Earth: Women's Search for Education in Medicine*. Cambridge, MA: Harvard University Press, 1992.

Borst, Charlotte G. *Catching Babies: The Professionalization of Childbirth, 1870–1920*. Cambridge, MA: Harvard University Press, 1995.

Bowen, Angie Burt. *Early Schools of Washington Territory*. Seattle, WA: Lowman and Hanford, 1935.

Bowen, William M. "The Five Eras of Chinese Medicine in California." In *The Chinese in America: A History from Gold Mountain to the New Millennium*, ed. Susie Lan Cassel, 174–92. New York: Rowman & Littlefield, 2002.

Breckinridge, Sophonisba P. *Marriage and Civic Rights of Women: Separate Domicil and Independent Citizenship*. Chicago: University of Chicago Press, 1931.

———. "Separate Domicil for Married Women." *Social Science Review* 4, no. 1 (March 1930): 37–52.

———. *Women in the Twentieth Century: A Study of Their Political, Social, and Economic Activities*. 1933. Reprint, New York: Arno Press, 1972.

Bredbenner, Candice Lewis. *A Nationality of Her Own: Women, Marriage, and the Law of Citizenship*. Berkeley: University of California Press, 1998.

Brodie, Janet Farrell. *Contraception and Abortion in Nineteenth-Century America*. Ithaca, NY: Cornell University Press, 1994.

Brodie, Jessie Laird. *"Dr. Jessie": The Odyssey of a Woman Physician*. Portland, OR: Caroline Pacific Publishing, 1991.

Brooks, Alfred H. et al. *Mineral Resources of Alaska: Report on Progress of Investigations in 1914*. United States Geological Survey Bulletin 622. Washington, DC: US Government Printing Office, 1915.

Brown, Adelaide. "The History of the Children's Hospital in Relation to Medical Women." In *Who's Who Among the Women of California*, ed. Louis S. Lyons and Josephine Wilson, 171–72. San Francisco: Security Publishing, 1922.

Brownell, Penelope. "The Women's Committees of the First World War: Women in Government, 1917–1919." PhD diss., Brown University, 2002.

"In re Accounts of Ernst Brücke and Dora Brücke-Teleky," September 21, 2005, 7. "In re Holocaust Victim Assets Litigation." Case no. CV96–4849. United States District Court for the Eastern District of New York, Chief Judge Edward R. Korman, Presiding. Claims Resolution Tribunal of the Holocaust Victim Assets Litigation against Swiss Banks and other Swiss Entities.

Available at www.crt-ii.org/_awards/_apdfs/Brucke_Ernst.pdf. Accessed
September 30, 2011.

Capozzola, Christopher. *Uncle Sam Wants You: World War I and the Making of the
Modern American Citizen*. New York: Oxford University Press, 2008.

Carey, Charles Henry. *History of Oregon*. 3 Vols. Portland, OR: Pioneer Historical Publishing, 1922.

Carlson, Marifran. *¡Feminismo! The Woman's Movement in Argentina from Its
Beginnings to Eva Perón*. Chicago: Academy Chicago Publishers, 1988.

Catt, Carrie Chapman, and Nettie Rogers Shuler. *Woman Suffrage and Politics:
The Inner Story of the Suffrage Movement*. New York: Charles Scribner's, 1923.
Reprint, Seattle: University of Washington Press, 1969. Page references are
to the 1969 edition.

Center for Volga German Studies. "The Volga Germans in Portland." Concordia
University, Portland, Oregon. Available at http://www.volgagermans.net/
portland. Accessed September 15, 2011.

Chase, Marilyn. *The Barbary Plague: The Black Death in Victorian San Francisco*.
New York: Random House, 2004.

Chin, Art. *Golden Tassels: A History of the Chinese in Washington, 1857–1992*.
Seattle, WA: Chin, 1992.

Clarke, Ida Clyde. *American Women and the World War*. New York: D. Appleton, 1918.

In RE Clayson's Will, 24 Or., 1893, 542–49.

Clayson, Edward, Sr. *Historical Narratives of Puget Sound, Hoods Canal, 1865–
1885: The Experience of an Only Free Man in a Penal Colony*. Seattle: R. L.
Davis, 1911. Reprint ed. Fairfield, WA: Ye Galleon Press, 1969. Page references are to the 1969 edition.

Clayson v. Clayson, 66 Pacific Reporter, 1902, 410–11.

Clifford, Howard. *The Skagway Story*. Anchorage: Alaska Northwest Publishing
Company, 1975.

Cole, Terrence Michael. "A History of the Nome Gold Rush: The Poor Man's
Paradise." PhD diss., University of Washington, 1983.

Colmer, Montagu, comp. *History of the Bench and Bar of Oregon*. Portland, OR:
Historical Publishing Company, 1910.

Conway, Jill Kerr. *When Memory Speaks: Reflections on Autobiography*. New York:
Alfred A. Knopf, 1998.

Cooper, John Milton. *Pivotal Decades: The United States, 1900–1920*. New York:
W. W. Norton, 1990.

Cott, Nancy. *The Grounding of Modern Feminism*. New Haven, CT: Yale University Press, 1987.

———. *Public Vows: A History of Marriage and the Nation*. Cambridge, MA: Harvard University Press, 2000.

Cox, Thomas R. *Mills and Markets: A History of the Pacific Coast Lumber Industry to 1900.* Seattle: University of Washington Press, 1974.

Curtis, Allan. "Christmas Day Murders." *Canadian West* 13 (Fall 1988): 81–85, and *Canadian West* 14 (Winter 1988): 126–33.

Dana, Marshall N. *Newspaper Story: The First Fifty Years of the Oregon Journal, 1902–1952.* Portland, OR: Binfords & Mort, 1951.

Daniels, Roger. *Guarding the Golden Door: American Immigration Policy and Immigrants since 1882.* New York: Hill and Wang, 2004.

Davie, Maurice R., et al. *Refugees in America: Report of the Committee for the Study of Recent Immigration from Europe.* New York: Harper & Brothers, 1947.

Davis, Lucy I. "History of Women Graduates of Oregon Medical School." *Twenty-Fifth Annual Meeting and Directory of the Alumni Association, University of Oregon Medical School,* 17–20. Portland: Alumni Association of the University of Oregon Medical School, 1937.

Dawley, Alan. *Changing the World: American Progressives in War and Revolution.* Princeton: Princeton University Press, 2003.

Derickson, Alan. *Workers' Health, Workers' Democracy: The Western Miners' Struggle, 1891–1925.* Ithaca: Cornell University Press, 1988.

Diebolt, Evelyne. "Women and Philanthropy in France from the Sixteenth to the Twentieth Centuries." In *Women, Philanthropy, and Civil Society,* ed. Kathleen D. McCarthy, 29–63. Bloomington: Indiana University Press, 2001.

Dobkin, Marjorie Housepian. *Smyrna 1922: The Destruction of a City.* New York: Newmark Press, 1971.

Dover, E. D. "Parties and Elections." In *Oregon Politics and Government: Progressives Versus Conservative Populists,* ed. Richard A. Clucas, Mark Henkels, and Brent S. Steel, 47–62. Lincoln: University of Nebraska Press, 2005.

Edwards, G. Thomas. *Sowing Good Seeds: The Northwest Suffrage Campaigns of Susan B. Anthony.* Portland: Oregon Historical Society Press, 1990.

Edwards, Rebecca. *Angels in the Machinery: Gender in American Party Politics from the Civil War to the Progressive Era.* New York: Oxford University Press, 1997.

———. "Pioneers at the Polls: Woman Suffrage in the West." In *Votes for Women: The Struggle for Suffrage Revisited,* ed. Jean Baker, 90–101. New York: Oxford University Press, 2002.

Enloe, Cynthia. *The Curious Feminist: Searching for Women in a New Age of Empire.* Berkeley: University of California Press, 2004.

Esther Pohl and George Lovejoy to Annie Mary Clayson. Trust Agreement. Case no. 45520. Douglas County, Oregon, Deeds. Vol. 82, 125–28. Douglas County Clerk's Office, Roseburg, Oregon.

Esther Pohl Lovejoy v. *George A. Lovejoy.* Complaint. Findings of Fact and Decree. Case no. 45521. Douglas County, Oregon, Deeds. Vol. 82, 128–31. Douglas County Clerk's Office, Roseburg, Oregon.

Esther Pohl Lovejoy v. *George A. Lovejoy.* Decree of Divorce. Oregon Eighth Judicial District, Circuit Court Journal, November Term, Friday, December 10, 1920, Baker, Oregon.

Ferrell, Ed. *Frontier Justice: Alaska 1898: The Last American Frontier.* Westminster, MD: Heritage Books, 2007.

Ficken, Robert E. *The Forested Land: A History of Lumbering in Western Washington.* Durham, NC: Forest History Society / Seattle: University of Washington Press, 1987.

———. *Washington Territory.* Pullman: Washington State University Press, 2002.

Fine, Eve. "Women Physicians and Medical Sects in Nineteenth-Century Chicago." In *Women Physicians and the Cultures of Medicine,* ed. Ellen S. More, Elizabeth Fee, and Manon Perry, 245–73. Baltimore: Johns Hopkins University Press, 2009.

Finnegan, Margaret. *Selling Suffrage: Consumer Culture and Votes for Women.* New York: Columbia University Press, 1999.

Flanagan, Maureen A. *Seeing with Their Hearts: Chicago Women and the Vision of the Good City, 1871–1933.* Princeton: Princeton University Press, 2002.

Foner, Philip S. *History of the Labor Movement in the United States.* Vol. 7, *Labor and World War I, 1914–1918.* New York: International Publishers, 1987.

———. *History of the Labor Movement in the United States.* Vol. 8, *Power Struggles, 1918–1920.* New York: International Publishers, 1988.

Fox, Renée. "Medical Humanitarianism and Human Rights: Reflections on Doctors Without Borders and Doctors of the World." In *Health and Human Rights,* ed. Jonathan Mann et al., 417–35. New York: Routledge, 1999.

Frankel, Noralee, and Nancy S. Dye, eds. *Gender, Class, Race, and Reform in the Progressive Era.* Lexington: University Press of Kentucky, 1991.

Frankovic, Nancy Snook. Discussion with author. June 2009. Spokane, Washington.

Franzen, Trisha. "Singular Leadership: Anna Howard Shaw, Single Women, and the US Suffrage Movement." *Women's History Review* 17, no. 3 (September 2008): 419–34.

Freedman, Estelle B. *Feminism, Sexuality, and Politics: Essays by Estelle B. Freedman.* Chapel Hill: University of North Carolina Press, 2006.

———. "Separatism as Strategy: Female Institution Building and American Feminism, 1870–1930." *Feminist Studies* 5, no. 3 (Fall 1979): 512–29.

Freeman, Jo. *A Room at a Time: How Women Entered Party Politics.* New York: Rowman and Littlefield, 2000.

French, Hiram T. *History of Idaho: A Narrative Account of Its Historical Progress, Its People, and Its Principal Interests*. Vol. 2. Chicago: Lewis Publishing, 1914.

Fricks, L. D. *Review of Plague in Seattle (1907) and Subsequent Rat and Flea Surveys*. Washington: US Government Printing Office, 1936.

Friends of Lone Fir Cemetery. Available at http://www.friendsoflonefircemetery.org. Accessed September 30, 2011.

Gatke, Robert Moulton. *Chronicles of Willamette: The Pioneer University of the West*. Portland, OR: Binfords & Mort, 1943.

Geddes, Jennian F. "Deeds *and* Words in the Suffrage Military Hospital in Endell Street." *Medical History* 51, no. 1 (January 2007): 79–98.

Gedosch, Thomas Frederick. "Seabeck, 1857–1886: The History of a Company Town." Master's thesis, University of Washington, 1967.

General Federation of Women's Clubs. *General Federation of Women's Clubs Fourteenth Biennial Convention, Official Report* (1918).

George A. Lovejoy v. *City of Portland* (1918). Oregon Supreme Court Records. No. 9803. File no. 3880. Oregon State Archives, Salem, Oregon.

Goldman, Wendy Z. *Women, the State, and Revolution: Soviet Family Policy and Social Life, 1917–1936*. New York: Cambridge University Press, 1993.

Graham, Sara Hunter. *Woman Suffrage and the New Democracy*. New Haven, CT: Yale University Press, 1996.

Grayzel, Susan R. *Women's Identities at War: Gender, Motherhood, and Politics in Britain and France during the First World War*. Chapel Hill: University of North Carolina Press, 1999.

Grossmann, Atina. "New Women in Exile: German Women Doctors and the Emigration." In *Between Sorrow and Strength: Women Refugees of the Nazi Period,* ed. Sybylle Quack, 215–38. Washington, DC: German Historical Institute / New York: Cambridge University Press, 1995.

Gullett, Gayle. *Becoming Citizens: The Emergence and Development of the California Women's Movement, 1880–1911*. Urbana: University of Illinois Press, 2000.

Haarsager, Sandra. *Organized Womanhood: Cultural Politics in the Pacific Northwest, 1840–1920*. Norman: University of Oklahoma Press, 1997.

Hacker, Carlotta. *The Indomitable Lady Doctors*. Toronto: Clarke, Irwin & Company, 1974.

Haines, Anna J. *Health Work in Soviet Russia*. New York: Vanguard Press, 1928.

Haller, John S. *The History of American Homeopathy: The Academic Years, 1820–1935*. New York: Pharmaceutical Products Press, 2005.

———. *Medical Protestants: The Eclectics in American Medicine, 1825–1939*. Carbondale: Southern Illinois University Press, 1994.

Hamilton, Alice. "Alice Hamilton to Jane Addams, January 24, 1925." In *Alice*

Hamilton: A Life in Letters, ed. Barbara Sicherman, 279–80. Cambridge, MA: Harvard University Press, 1984.

Harmon, Alexandra. *Indians in the Making: Ethnic Relations and Indian Identities around Puget Sound*. Berkeley: University of California Press, 2000.

Hendricks, Rickey. "Feminism and Maternalism in Early Hospitals for Children: San Francisco and Denver, 1875–1915." *Journal of the West* 32, no. 3 (July 1993): 61–69.

Hines, H. K. *An Illustrated History of the State of Oregon*. Chicago: Lewis Publishing, 1893.

Hodges, Adam J. "At War Over the Espionage Act in Portland: Dueling Perspectives from Kathleen O'Brennan and Agent William Bryon." *Oregon Historical Quarterly* 108, no. 3 (Fall 2007): 474–86.

Hoffman, Dennis E., and Vincent J. Webb. "Police Response to Labor Radicalism in Portland and Seattle, 1913–19." *Oregon Historical Quarterly* 87, no. 4 (Winter 1986): 341–65.

Holbo, Paul S. "Senator Harry Lane: Independent Democrat in Peace and War." In *Experiences in a Promised Land: Essays in Pacific Northwest History*, ed. G. Thomas Edwards and Carlos A. Schwantes, 242–59. Seattle: University of Washington Press, 1986.

Holtz, William. *The Ghost in the Little House: A Life of Rose Wilder Lane*. Columbia: University of Missouri Press, 1993.

Hoy, Suellen. *Chasing Dirt: The American Pursuit of Cleanliness*. New York: Oxford University Press, 1995.

International Conference of Women Physicians. *Proceedings of the International Conference of Women Physicians*. 6 Vols. New York: The Womans Press, 1920.

Irwin, Inez Hayes. *Angels and Amazons: A Hundred Years of American Women*. Doubleday, Doran: 1933.

Jacobi, Mary Putnam. "Woman in Medicine." In *Woman's Work in America*, ed. Annie Nathan Meyer, 139–205. New York: Henry Holt & Co., 1891.

Jellett, J. H. *Pacific Coast Collection Laws*. San Francisco: Bacon and Company, 1876.

Jensen, Kimberly. "Esther Pohl Lovejoy, M.D., the First World War, and a Feminist Critique of Wartime Violence." In *The Women's Movement in Wartime: International Perspectives, 1914–19*, ed. Alison Fell and Ingrid Sharp, 175–93. London: Palgrave Macmillan, 2007.

———. *Mobilizing Minerva: American Women in the First World War*. Urbana: University of Illinois Press, 2008.

———. "'Neither Head nor Tail to the Campaign': Esther Pohl Lovejoy and the Oregon Woman Suffrage Victory of 1912." *Oregon Historical Quarterly* 108, no. 3 (Fall 2007): 350–83.

———. "Revolutions in the Machinery: Oregon Women and Citizenship in Sesquicentennial Perspective." *Oregon Historical Quarterly* 110, no. 3 (Fall 2009): 336–61.

———. "Woman Suffrage in Oregon." Oregon Encyclopedia. http://oregonency clopedia.org/entry/view/woman_suffrage_in_oregon. Accessed September 16, 2011.

Jensen, Kimberly, and Erika K. Kuhlman, eds. *Women and Transnational Activism in Historical Perspective*. Dordrecht, The Netherlands: Republic of Letters, 2010.

Johnston, Robert D. *The Radical Middle Class: Populist Democracy and the Question of Capitalism in Progressive Era Portland*, Oregon. Princeton, NJ: Princeton University Press, 2003.

Keir, Allissa Franc. "A Daughter of Pioneers." *Everybody's Magazine* 54, no. 3 (March 1926): 34–35, 168–72.

Kennedy, David M. *Over Here: The First World War and American Society*. New York: Oxford University Press, 1980.

Kennedy, Kathleen. *Disloyal Mothers and Scurrilous Citizens: Women and Subversion during World War* I. Bloomington: Indiana University Press, 1999.

Kerber, Linda K. *No Constitutional Right to Be Ladies: Women and the Obligations of Citizenship*. New York: Hill and Wang, 1998.

———. *Toward an Intellectual History of Women: Essays by Linda K. Kerber*. Chapel Hill: University of North Carolina Press, 1997.

Kerber, Linda K., Jane Sherron De Hart, and Cornelia Hughes Dayton, eds. *Women's America: Refocusing the Past*, 7th ed. New York: Oxford University Press, 2011.

Kessler-Harris, Alice. *In Pursuit of Equity: Women, Men, and the Quest for Economic Citizenship in Twentieth-Century America*. New York: Oxford University Press, 2001.

Kimmel, Michael S. *Manhood in America: A Cultural History*. New York: Free Press, 1996.

King, William Harvey. *History of Homeopathy and Its Institutions in America*. Vol. 1. Chicago: Lewis Publishing Company, 1905.

Kirschmann, Anne Taylor. *A Vital Force: Women in American Homeopathy*. New Brunswick, NJ: Rutgers University Press, 2004.

Kollontai, Alexandra. "The Labour of Women in the Revolution of the Economy." In *Selected Writings of Alexandra Kollontai,* trans. and ed. Alix Holt, 142–49. London: Allison & Busby, 1977.

Kraut, Alan M. *Goldberger's War: The Life and Work of a Public Crusader*. New York: Hill and Wang, 2003.

———. *Silent Travelers: Germs, Genes, and the "Immigrant Menace."* Baltimore: Johns Hopkins University Press, 1994.

Kuhlman, Erika K. *Of Little Comfort: War Widows, Fallen Soldiers, and the Remaking of the Nation after the Great War.* New York: New York University Press, 2012.

———. *Reconstructing Patriarchy after the Great War: Women, Gender, and Post-war Reconciliation between Nations.* New York: Palgrave Macmillan, 2008.

Lansing, Jewel. *Portland: People, Politics, and Power, 1851–2001.* Corvallis: Oregon State University Press, 2003.

Larsell, Olof. *The Doctor in Oregon: A Medical History.* Portland: Bindfords & Mort for the Oregon Historical Society, 1947.

Lavrin, Asunción. *Women, Feminism, and Social Change in Argentina, Chile, and Uruguay, 1890–1940.* Lincoln: University of Nebraska Press, 1995.

Laws of the Territory of Washington Enacted by the Legislative Assembly in the Year 1873, Together with Joint Resolutions and Memorials. Olympia, WA: C. B. Bagley, Public Printer, 1873.

Laws of the Territory of Washington Enacted by the Legislative Assembly in the Year 1877. Olympia, WA: C. B. Bagley, Public Printer, 1877.

Leavitt, Judith Walzer. *Brought to Bed: Childbearing in America, 1750–1950.* New York: Oxford University Press, 1986.

———. *Typhoid Mary: Captive to the Public's Health.* Boston: Beacon Press, 1996.

Leneman, Leah. "Medical Women at War, 1914–1918." *Medical History* 38, no. 2 (April 1994): 160–77.

———. "Medical Women in the First World War—Ranking Nowhere." *British Medical Journal* (December 18, 1993): 1592–94.

Lovejoy, Esther C. P., with introduction by Bertha Hallam. "My Medical School, 1890–1894." *Oregon Historical Quarterly* 75, no. 1 (March 1974): 7–35.

Lovejoy, Esther Pohl. *Certain Samaritans.* New York: Macmillan, 1927.

———. *Certain Samaritans.* Rev. ed. New York: Macmillan, 1933.

———. "Democracy and Health." In *Democracy in Reconstruction,* ed. Frederick A. Cleveland and Joseph Schafer, 165–92. New York: Houghton Mifflin, 1919.

———. *The House of the Good Neighbor.* New York: Macmillan, 1919.

———. *Women Doctors of the World.* New York: Macmillan, 1957.

———. *Women Physicians and Surgeons: National and International Organizations.* Livingston, NY: Livingston Press, 1939.

Ludmerer, Kenneth. *Learning to Heal: The Development of American Medical Education.* Baltimore: Johns Hopkins University Press, 1996.

Lunardini, Christine. *From Equal Suffrage to Equal Rights: Alice Paul and the National Woman's Party, 1910–1928.* New York: New York University Press, 1986.

Lusk, William Thompson. *The Science and Art of Midwifery.* 4th ed. New York: D. Appleton and Company, 1892.

MacColl, E. Kimbark, with Harry H. Stein. *Merchants, Money, and Power: The Portland Establishment, 1843–1913*. Portland, OR: Georgian Press, 1988.

MacMurchy, Helen. "Hospital Appointments: Are They Open to Women?" *New York Medical Journal* (April 27, 1901): 712–16.

Marrett, Cora Bagley. "Nineteenth-Century Associations of Medical Women: The Beginning of a Movement." *Journal of the American Medical Women's Association* 32, no. 12 (December 1977): 469–74.

———. "On the Evolution of Women's Medical Societies." *Bulletin of the History of Medicine* 53, no. 3 (Fall 1979): 434–48.

Martindale, Louisa. *A Woman Surgeon*. London: Victor Gollancz, 1951.

"McArthur, Clifton Nesmith (1879–1923.)" Biographical Directory of the United States Congress. Available athttp://bioguide.congress.gov/scripts/biodisplay.pl?index=M000298. Accessed September 30, 2011.

McNeill, William H. *Plagues and Peoples*. New York; Anchor Books, 1976.

Mead, Rebecca J. *How the Vote Was Won: Woman Suffrage in the Western United States, 1868–1914*. New York: New York University Press, 2004.

Meany, Edmond S., Jr. "The History of the Lumber Industry in the Pacific Northwest to 1917." PhD diss., Harvard University, 1935.

Medical Society of the State of California. *Official Register and Directory of Physicians and Surgeons in the State of California, to Which is Added a Directory of Physicians and Surgeons in Oregon and Washington and a Directory of California State Nurses' Association*. San Francisco: Medical Society of the State of California, 1905.

Medical Women's International Association. Available at http://www.mwia. net. Accessed September 30, 2011.

Metaxas, Virginia A. "Ruth A. Parmalee, Esther P. Lovejoy, and the Discourse of Motherhood in Asia Minor and Greece in the Early Twentieth Century." In *Women Physicians and the Cultures of Medicine*, ed. Ellen S. More, Elizabeth Fee, and Manon Perry, 274–93. Baltimore: Johns Hopkins University Press, 2009.

Miller, Kristie. *Ruth Hanna McCormick: A Life in Politics, 1880–1944*. Albuquerque: University of New Mexico Press, 1992.

Milton, Giles. *Paradise Lost, Smyrna 1922: The Destruction of a Christian City in the Islamic World*. New York: Basic Books, 2008.

Mintz, Steven. *Huck's Raft: A History of American Childhood*. Cambridge, MA: The Belknap Press of Harvard University Press, 2004.

Mohr, James C. *Plague and Fire: Battling Black Death and the 1900 Burning of Honolulu's Chinatown*. New York: Oxford University Press, 2005.

Moldow, Gloria. *Women Doctors in Gilded-Age Washington: Race, Gender, and Professionalization*. Urbana: University of Illinois Press, 1987.

Morantz-Sanchez, Regina Markell. *Conduct Unbecoming a Woman: Medicine on Trial in Turn-of-the-Century Brooklyn*. New York: Oxford University Press, 1999.

———. "Female Patient Agency and the 1892 Trial of Dr. Mary Dixon Jones in Late-Nineteenth-Century Brooklyn." In *Women Physicians and the Cultures of Medicine*, ed. Ellen S. More, Elizabeth Fee, and Manon Perry, 69–88. Baltimore: Johns Hopkins University Press, 2009.

———. *Sympathy and Science: Women Physicians in American Medicine*. Chapel Hill: University of North Carolina Press, 2000.

More, Ellen S. *Restoring the Balance: Women Physicians and the Profession of Medicine, 1850–1995*. Cambridge, MA: Harvard University Press, 1999.

Moreland, Kimberly S. *History of Portland's African American Community, 1805 to the Present*. Portland, OR: Bureau of Planning, 1993.

Morse, Kathryn. *The Nature of Gold: An Environmental History of the Klondike Gold Rush*. Seattle: University of Washington Press, 2003.

Morton, Rosalie Slaughter. *A Woman Surgeon: The Life and Work of Rosalie Slaughter Morton*. New York: Frederick A. Stokes, 1937.

Mullan, Fitzhugh. *Plagues and Politics: The Story of the United States Public Health Service*. New York: Basic Books, 1989.

Myers, Gloria E. *A Municipal Mother: Portland's Lola Greene Baldwin, America's First Policewoman*. Corvallis: Oregon State University Press, 1995.

Nathan, Maud. *The Story of an Epoch-Making Movement*. New York: Doubleday, 1926.

National American Woman Suffrage Association. *Convention of the National American Suffrage Association and Congress of the League of Women Voters, 1920*. New York: National American Woman Suffrage Association, 1920.

———. *Thirty-Seventh Annual Convention of the National American Woman Suffrage Association: June 28 to July 5, 1905*. Portland, OR: Gotshall Printing, 1905.

Neergard, Christine A. "Dr. George V. Calhoun." *Washington Historical Quarterly* 25, no. 4 (October 1934): 286–93.

Noakes, Lucy. *Women in the British Army: War and the Gentle Sex, 1907–1948*. London: Routledge, 2006.

Northwest Women's Law Center Legal Voice. "Brief *Amici Curiae* of History Scholars, 12–14, *Andersen et al. v. King County, Washington*, and *Castle et al. v. State of Washington*, The Supreme Court of the State of Washington, nos. 75934–1 and 75956–1." Available at http://nwwlc.org/pdf/Historians_Brief.pdf. Accessed September 10, 2011.

Nye, Robert A. "The Legacy of Masculine Codes of Honor and the Admission of Women to the Medical Profession in the Nineteenth Century." In *Women*

Physicians and the Cultures of Medicine, ed. Ellen S. More, Elizabeth Fee, and Manon Perry, 141–59. Baltimore: Johns Hopkins University Press, 2009.

Oldham, Kit. "Dr. Thomas T. Minor, Former Mayor of Port Townsend and Seattle, Drowns on a Duck-Hunting Expedition to Whidbey Island in December 1889." August 13, 2004. HistoryLink.org, "The Free Online Encyclopedia of Washington State History." Available at http://www.historylink.org/index.cfm?DisplayPage=output.cfm&file_id=5730. Accessed September 10, 2011.

Olsen, Deborah M. "Fair Connections: Women's Separatism and the Lewis and Clark Exposition of 1905." *Oregon Historical Quarterly* 109, no. 2 (Summer 2008): 174–203.

Oregon Department of Fish and Wildlife. "Fish Counts: Winchester Dam." Available at http://www.dfw.state.or.us/fish/fish_counts/winchester_dam.asp. Accessed September 30, 2011.

Oregon, Legislative Assembly, Senate. Oregon, Legislative Assembly, House of Representatives. *Journals of the Senate and House of the Thirtieth Legislative Assembly, 1920.* Salem: Oregon State Printer, 1920.

Oregon Secretary of State. *A Pamphlet Containing a Copy of All Measures . . . at the General Election to be Held on the Eighth Day of November, 1910, Together with the Arguments Filed.* Salem: Oregon State Printer, 1910.

———. *Biennial Report of the Secretary of State of the State of Oregon to the Twenty-Seventh Legislative Assembly, 1913.* Salem: Oregon State Printer, 1912.

———. *Biennial Report of the Secretary of State of the State of Oregon to the Twenty-Eighth Legislative Assembly, Regular Session, 1915, for the Biennial Period Beginning October 1, 1912, Ending September 30, 1914.* Salem: Oregon State Printer, 1915.

———. *Biennial Report of the Secretary of State of the State of Oregon to the Twenty-Ninth Legislative Assembly, Regular Session, 1917, for the Biennial Period Beginning October 1, 1914, Ending September 30, 1916.* Salem: Oregon State Printer, 1917.

———. *Biennial Report of the Secretary of State of the State of Oregon to the Thirtieth Legislative Assembly, Regular Session, 1919, for the Biennial Period Beginning October 1, 1916, Ending September 30, 1918.* Salem: Oregon State Printer, 1919.

———. *Biennial Report of the Secretary of State of the State of Oregon to the Thirty-First Legislative Assembly, Regular Session, 1921, for the Biennial Period Beginning October 1, 1918, Ending September 30, 1920.* Salem: Oregon State Printer, 1921.

———. *Oregon Blue Book and Official Directory, 1915–1916.* Salem: Oregon State Printer, 1916.

———. *Oregon Blue Book and Official Directory, 1921–1922.* Salem: Oregon State Printer, 1921.

———. Oregon Legislators and Staff Guide, 1917 Regular Session, 1919 Regular Session, 1920 Special Session, Oregon State Archives. Available at http://arcweb.sos.state.or.us/legislative/histleg/statehood/statehood.htm. Accessed September 30, 2011.

Oregon State Board of Health. *First Biennial Report of the Oregon State Board of Health, 1905*. Salem: Oregon State Printer, 1905.

Oregon State Board of Health v. Winchester Hospital for the Cure of Tuberculosis. Suit for Injunction, December 15, 1920. Order of Default and Decree. February 2, 1921. Case no. 3261. Circuit Court, Douglas County, Oregon.

Oregon State Board of Medical Examiners. *Medical Register of Oregon*. Salem: State Medical Board and Oregon State Printer, 1898.

Painter, Nell Irvin. *Standing at Armageddon: The United States, 1877–1919*. New York: Norton, 1987.

Park, Maud Wood. *Front Door Lobby*. Boston: Beacon Press, 1960.

Pascoe, Peggy. *What Comes Naturally: Miscegenation Law and the Making of Race in America*. New York: Oxford University Press, 2009.

Peitzman, Steven J. *A New and Untried Course: Woman's Medical College and Medical College of Pennsylvania, 1850–1998*. New Brunswick, NJ: Rutgers University Press, 2000.

Peterson del Mar, David. *Beaten Down: A History of Interpersonal Violence in the West*. Seattle: University of Washington Press, 2002.

Pollard, Lancaster. *A History of the State of Washington*. Vol. 3. New York: American Historical Society, 1937.

Portland Historical Timeline. Portland City Auditor's Office. Portland Archives and Records Center. Available at http://www.portlandonline.com/auditor/index.cfm?a=284518&c=51811. Accessed September 15, 2011.

Putman, John C. *Class and Gender Politics in Progressive-Era Seattle*. Reno: University of Nevada Press, 2008.

Reed, Meribeth Meixner. "Describing the Life Cycle of U.S Marine Hospital #17, Port Townsend, Washington, 1855–1933." *Military Medicine* 170, no. 4 (April 2005): 259–67.

Ridley, Glenn Arthur. "The Causal Factors in the Development of Olds, Wortman, and King into a Modern Department Store." Master's thesis, University of Oregon, 1937.

Robbins, William. *Colony and Empire: The Capitalist Transformation of the American West*. Lawrence: University Press of Kansas, 1994.

Roberts, Mary Louise. *Civilization without Sexes: Reconstructing Gender in Postwar France, 1917–1927*. Chicago: University of Chicago Press, 1994.

Rockafellar, Nancy, and James Havland, eds. *Saddlebags to Scanners: The First One Hundred Years of Medicine in Washington State*. Seattle: Washington

State Medical Association, 1989.

Rogers, Daniel T. *Atlantic Crossings: Social Politics in a Progressive Age*. Cambridge, MA: Harvard University Press, 1998.

Rossiter, Margaret. *Women Scientists in America: Struggles and Strategies to 1940*. Baltimore: Johns Hopkins University Press, 1982.

Ross-Nazzal, Jennifer M. *Winning the West for Women: The Life of Suffragist Emma Smith DeVoe*. Seattle: University of Washington Press, 2011.

Rupp, Leila. *Worlds of Women: The Making of an International Women's Movement*. Princeton: Princeton University Press, 1997.

Salas, Elizabeth. "Ethnicity, Gender, and Divorce: Issues in the 1922 Campaign by Adelina Otero-Warren for the U.S. House of Representatives." *New Mexico Historical Review* 70, no. 4 (October 1995): 367–82.

Sappol, Michael. *A Traffic of Dead Bodies: Anatomy and Embodied Social Identity in Nineteenth-Century America*. Princeton: Princeton University Press, 2002.

Scheppke, Jim. "The Origins of the Oregon State Library." *Oregon Historical Quarterly* 107, no. 1 (Spring 2006): 130–40.

Scheuerman, Richard D., and Clifford E. Trafzer. *The Volga Germans: Pioneers of the Northwest*. Moscow: University Press of Idaho, 1980.

Schiffner, Carli Crozier. "Continuing to 'Do Everything' in Oregon: The Woman's Christian Temperance Union, 1900–1945 and Beyond." PhD diss., Washington State University, 2004.

Seyfarth, Ernst-August. "Ernst Theodor Von Brücke (1880–1941) and Alexander Forbes (1882–1965): Chronicle of a Transatlantic Friendship in Difficult Times." *Perspectives in Biology and Medicine* 40, no. 1 (Autumn 1996): 45–54.

Sharp, Ingrid, and Matthew Stibbe, eds. *Aftermaths of War: Women's Movements and Female Activists*. Leiden: Brill, 2011.

Shaw, Anna Howard. *The Story of a Pioneer*. New York: Harper and Brothers, 1915.

Soden, Dale E. "The Woman's Christian Temperance Union in the Pacific Northwest: A Different Side of the Social Gospel." In *Gender and the Social Gospel*, ed. Wendy J. Deichmann Edwards and Carolyn De Swarte Gifford, 103–15. Urbana: University of Illinois Press, 2003.

Spain, Daphne. *How Women Saved the City*. Minneapolis: University of Minnesota Press, 2001.

Spude, Catherine Holder. "Bachelor Miners and Barbers' Wives: The Common People of Skagway in 1900." *Alaska History* 6, no. 2 (Fall 1991): 17–29.

Standard Medical Directory of North America, 1902. Chicago: G. P. Englehard, 1901.

Stanton, Elizabeth Cady, Susan B. Anthony, Matilda Joslyn Gage, and Ida Husted Harper, eds. *History of Woman Suffrage*. 6 Vols. Reprint of the 1881–1922 ed. New York: Arno Press, 1969.

Starr, Paul. *The Social Transformation of American Medicine.* New York: Basic Books, 1982.

Steneck, Nicholas S. "Early Diversity in the Health Sciences at the University of Michigan." *Retrospectives: Health Care and the Health Sciences in Michigan Newsletter* 1, no. 2 (Fall 1992): 1–2.

Stevenson, Shanna. *Women's Votes, Women's Voices: The Campaign for Equal Rights in Washington.* Tacoma: Washington State Historical Society, 2009.

St. John, Christopher. *Christine Murrell, M.D.: Her Life and Her Work.* London: Williams & Norgate, 1935.

Stone, Wilbur Fiske. *History of Colorado.* Vol. 2. Chicago: S. J. Clarke, 1918.

Straus, Robert. *Medical Care for Seamen: The Origin of Public Medical Service in the United States.* New Haven, CT: Yale University Press, 1950.

Stuckman, Emily. "More Than a Sign of the Times: Progressive-Era Educational Efforts of the Portland Section, National Council of Jewish Women." Paper presented at Game Changers and History Makers: Women in Pacific Northwest History conference, November 2010, Spokane, Washington.

Terborg-Penn, Rosalyn. *African American Women in the Struggle for the Vote, 1850–1920.* Bloomington: Indiana University Press, 1998.

Tickner, J. Ann. *Gendering World Politics: Issues and Approaches in the Post–Cold War Era.* New York: Columbia University Press, 2001.

———. *Gender in International Relations: Feminist Perspectives on Achieving Global Security.* New York: Columbia University Press, 1992.

Title Guarantee Company v. Wrenn. 35 Or. 1899, 62–75.

Tobias, Sheila. "Shifting Heroisms: The Uses of Military Service in Politics." In *Women, Militarism, and War: Essays in History, Politics, and Social Theory,* ed. Jean Bethke Elshtain and Sheila Tobias, 163–85. Savage, MD: Rowman & Littlefield, 1990.

Todd, Frank Morton. *Eradicating Plague from San Francisco: Report of the Citizens' Health Committee and an Account of Its Work.* San Francisco: C. A. Murdock, 1909.

Tomes, Nancy. *The Gospel of Germs: Men, Women, and the Microbe in American Life.* Cambridge, MA: Harvard University Press, 1998.

Tone, Andrea. *Devices and Desires: A History of Contraceptives in America.* New York: Hill and Wang, 2001.

Turnbull, George S. *History of Oregon Newspapers.* Portland, OR: Binfords & Mort, 1939.

Tuve, Jeanette E. *The First Russian Women Physicians.* Newtonville, MA: Oriental Research Partners, 1984.

United Nations Fourth World Conference on Women. Beijing, China, September 1995. "Platform for Action C.89: Women and Health." Available

at http://www.un.org/womenwatch/daw/beijing/platform/health.htm.
Accessed September 30, 2011.

United States Department of Commerce, Bureau of the Census. *Historical Statistics of the United States: Colonial Times to 1970*. Washington, DC: US Government Printing Office, 1975.

———. *Tenth Census of the United States, 1880*. Washington, DC: United States Bureau of the Census, 1880.

———. *Twelfth Census of the United States, 1900*. Washington, DC: United States Bureau of the Census, 1900.

———. *Fourteenth Census of the United States, 1920*. Washington, DC: United States Bureau of the Census, 1920.

United States Department of the Interior. *Report of the Territorial Mine Inspector to the Governor of Alaska for the Year 1915*. Washington, DC: Government Printing Office, 1916.

United States House of Representatives, 41st Congress. 2nd Session. Executive Document 314. *Report of the Postmaster General*, no. 4. Washington, DC: Government Printing Office, 1870.

United States House of Representatives, Committee on Immigration and Naturalization. *Admission of Near East Refugees, Hearings Before the Committee on Immigration and Naturalization, House of Representatives, Sixty-Seventh Congress, Fourth Session, on H.R. 13269, December 15, 16, and 19, 1922, Serial 1-C*. Washington, DC: Government Printing Office, 1923.

United States Office of Education. "Statistics of Schools of Medicine for 1893–94." *Report of the Commissioner of Education for the Year 1893–94*. Vol. 2, parts 2 and 3. Washington: Government Printing Office, 1896.

United States Patent Office. *Official Gazette of the United States Patent Office*. Vol. 273. April 1920, 531.

United States Senate. *Executive Documents, First and Second Sessions of the Forty-Fifth Congress, 1877 and '78*. Vol. 1, no. 9, document 306D. Washington, DC: Government Printing Office, 1877.

Van Hoosen, Bertha. *Petticoat Surgeon*. Chicago: Pellegrini & Cudahy, 1947.

Walsh, Mary Roth. *Doctors Wanted: No Women Need Apply: Sexual Barriers in the Medical Profession, 1835–1975*. New Haven, CT: Yale University Press, 1977.

Ward, Jean M., and Elaine A. Maveety, eds. *Pacific Northwest Women, 1815–1925: Lives, Memories, and Writings*. Corvallis: Oregon State University Press, 1995.

Ward, Robert D. "The Origin and Activities of the National Security League, 1914–1919." *Mississippi Valley Historical Review* 47, no. 1 (June 1960): 51–65.

Warner, John Harley, and James M. Edmonson. *Dissection: Photographs of a Rite of Passage in American Medicine, 1880–1930*. New York: Blast Books, 2009.

West, Elliott. *Growing Up with the Country: Childhood on the Far Western Frontier.* Albuquerque: University of New Mexico Press, 1989.

White, W. Thomas. "Railroad Labor Relations in the Great War and After, 1917–1921." *Journal of the West* 25, no. 2 (April 1986): 36–43.

Winchester Hospital for the Cure of Tuberculosis and George Lovejoy. Case no. 45121. Douglas County, Oregon Deeds Volume 82, 11. Douglas County Clerk's Office, Roseburg, Oregon.

Winter, Jay, *Remembering War: The Great War between Memory and History in the Twentieth Century.* New Haven, CT: Yale University Press, 2006.

Women of Woodcraft. *Ritual of the Women of Woodcraft.* Portland, OR: Portland Printing House, 1912.

Wong, Marie Rose. *Sweet Cakes, Long Journey: The Chinatowns of Portland, Oregon.* Seattle: University of Washington Press, 2004.

Woodside, Henry. "The Great Yukon Murder Case" *Wide World Magazine* 8, no. 44 (December 1901): 154–62.

Wright, E. W., ed. *Lewis and Dryden's Marine History of the Pacific Northwest.* New York: Antiquarian Press, 1961.

Wyman, David S. *Paper Walls: America and the Refugee Crisis, 1938–1941.* Amherst: University of Massachusetts Press, 1968.

———. *The Abandonment of the Jews: America and the Holocaust, 1941–1945.* New York: New Press, 1984.

Zenk, Henry, with Tony A. Johnson. "A Northwest Language of Contact, Diplomacy, and Identity: Chinuk Wawa/Chinook Jargon." *Oregon Historical Quarterly* 111, no. 4 (Winter 2010): 444–61.

INDEX

feminism: 1920 election and, 149; American Women's Hospitals and, 169–92; birthrate in France, 130–33; international health and, 5, 9, 193–207, 208; without borders, 193–94, 197, 207

feminist curiosity: defined, 8, 215; EPL and, 8, 50, 172, 188, 192

Feyler, Marie, 278n87

Filene, Edward, 126

finances and fundraising: 1912 election and, 160; American Women's Hospitals and, 179–81, 182, 184, 185–86, 209; Congressional Union and, 118–19; refugee women physicians and, 204; woman suffrage in Oregon and, 107, 114

Finkler, Rita S., 204

Finland, 177, 210

First World War, 40, 122–44, 212; aftermath of, 141–44, 149–50, 160–78; demobilization, 149; Harry Lane opposes US entrance, 123; Marie Equi opposes, 123–24; transnationalism and, 122; violence against women, 122, 135, 136–38; woman suffrage and, 120–21; women's contributions to, 135–36

Florida, 177

Flower Mission and Day Nursery, 53

Forbes, Alexander, 202–3

Ford, Angela, 36

Ford, Ella J., 36

Fraade, Estelle, 4, 181–82, 183–84, 207, 213, 215

France, 126–33, 171, 174, 184, 204–5, 210, 278n87

fraternal organizations, 53, 64, 70, 105. *See also* Arctic Brotherhood

French Association of University Women, 204

French, Gertrude, 103

French Medical Women's Association, 143, 204, 206

fundraising. *See* finances and fundraising

G

Gallant American Women radio series, 209

Gee, Lizzie, 151

gender: analysis, 212; and EPL congressional campaign, 146, 160–61; discrimination and medical internships, 48–49; discrimination and Red Cross, 126; medical education and, 46–49; refugee women physicians and, 204–5. *See also* feminism; feminist curiosity; Oregon woman suffrage; women physicians; working women

General Federation of Women's Clubs 133, 137–38, 201

Geneva, Switzerland, 193–96, 198, 202, 204, 220

George, Henry, 15

George W. Elder, 61

Germany, 177, 202, 204–5

Giesy, A. J., 77–78

Gilman, Charlotte Perkins, 100

gold rush. *See* Klondike Gold Rush

Golden Rule Hotel, 32

Good Samaritan Hospital, 42, 43, 48

Gordon, Kate, 103

Graff, Effie, 198, 199

Gray, Etta, 140–41, 170

Gray, Katherine, 103

Gray's Anatomy, 38, 39

Great Britain, 142, 171, 177, 184, 204, 205–6, 278n87. *See also* England; London; Medical Women's Federation of Great Britain

Great Depression. *See* Depression of 1930s

Greco-Turkish Civil War, 169–77, 184, 186–87
Greece, 169–77, 184, 186, 210
Greeley, Helen Hoy, 123
Green, B. A., 157, 159, 161, 166

women physicians (con't.)
cation, 35–36, 40–49, 194, 210–11;
Progressive Era social medicine,
52–54; in public health office, 78; as
sympathetic practitioners, 49–51,
54; transnational identity, 141–44,
194–207; "Women in Medicine" segment for *Gallant American Women*
radio series, 209. *See also* American Women's Hospitals; Medical
Women's International Association;
Medical Women's National Association; Oregon women physicians;
individual women physicians
*Women Physicians and Surgeons: National
and International Organizations*
(EPL), 186, 208–9, 211–12
Women's Democratic Club, 148
Women's International League for
Peace and Freedom, 193, 196, 201
Women's Medical Institute, St. Petersburg, 197
women's rights, 6, 80, 170. *See also* citizenship; Oregon woman suffrage;
woman suffrage
women's separate institutions, 54–55,
89–90, 124, 184–85, 187–88, 220–21
Women's Social and Political Union
(Great Britain), 143
Women's Union, Portland, 53
women's voluntary associations and
clubs, 89–90, 92–93, 190, 220
Women Voters Conference, 119–20
Wood, C. E. S., 123
Woodruff, Polly (maternal grandmother of EPL), 10
working class, 5–6, 17–18, 40–42, 104,
215–16. *See also* working women
working women, 53, 101, 143; in First
World War France, 129–30,131–32,
135–36; Medical Women's International Association and, 197; in

Soviet Union, 198–200; and woman
suffrage, 104, 107, 109–10, 136
Workingmen's Party, 15

Y

Yarros, Rachelle, 179
Young Men's Christian Association
(YMCA), 133, 171
Young Women's Christian Association
(YWCA), 90
Yukon, Canada, 62, 65

Z

Zaik, Aaron, 84, 85
Ziegler, Amelia, 64, 73, 103